Strategies for growth in SMEs

The role of information and information systems

ELSEVIER BUTTERWORTH-HEINEMANN INFORMATION
SYSTEMS SERIES

Series Editors

Professor David Avison, BA, MSc, Phd, FBCS
Department SID
ESSEC Business School
Avenue Bernard Hirsch
BP 105
95021 Cergy-Pontoise
FRANCE

E-mail: avison@essec.fr

Professor Guy Fitzgerald, BA, MSc, MBCS
Department of Information Systems and Computing
Brunel University
Uxbridge Middlesex UB8 3PH
UK

E-mail: Guy.Fitzgerald@brunel.ac.uk

This is a new series under the Elsevier Butterworth-Heinemann imprint
which will provide medium for quality publications in the information
systems field. It will also provide continuity with the McGraw-Hill
information systems series, which has been discontinued. The new series
of texts is aimed at first degree and postgraduate students, and the global
research community in information systems, computer science and
business management. Information systems is multi-disciplinary. Where
formerly emphasis was placed on the technological aspects which remain
significant, it now stresses the importance of, and the links to, the
business environment particularly, in regard to the social and
organizational aspects.

If you have a book proposal for this series, please contact either of the
Series Editors.

Strategies for growth in SMEs

The role of information and information systems

Margi Levy

and

Philip Powell

ELSEVIER
BUTTERWORTH
HEINEMANN

AMSTERDAM • BOSTON • HEIDELBERG • LONDON • NEW YORK • OXFORD
PARIS • SAN DIEGO • SAN FRANCISCO • SINGAPORE • SYDNEY • TOKYO

Elsevier Butterworth-Heinemann
Linacre House, Jordan Hill, Oxford OX2 8DP
30 Corporate Drive, Burlington, MA 01803

First published 2005

British Library Cataloguing in Publication Data
Strategis for growth in SMEs: the role of information systems
1. Small business – Data processing
I. Levy, Margi   II. Powell, Philip
658'.022'0285467

ISBN 0 7506 6351 0

Typeset by Charon Tec Pvt. Ltd, Chennai, India
www.charontec.com
Printed and bound in United Kingdom

Contents

Dedication   vi
Foreword   vii

1   Introduction   1

Part 1   Concept of the SME   17

2   Background to SMEs   19

3   Information and IS in SMEs   35

4   Flexibility in IS   51

5   Evaluating IS in SMEs   69

Part 2   Issues of IS strategy planning   87

6   Understanding IS strategy in SMEs   89

7   An organizational approach to IS strategy   109

8   Case example of ISS: Heath Springs   137

Part 3   Strategic resource: attitudes to information   157

9   Strategic context of IS investment   159

10   Strategic IS dynamics   177

11   Exploring business transformation through IS   201

12   Strategic alignment   217

Part 4   Knowledge and development of IS   235

13   IS role in co-opetition and knowledge sharing   237

14   Role of core competencies in developing ISS in knowledge-based SMEs   265

15   Exploring business process re-engineering in SMEs   293

Part 5   Future: Internet adoption and strategy   315

16   Exploring e-business in SMEs   317

17   Strategic intent and e-business   339

18   E-business influencers   355

19   Managing IS: the future   373

Dedication

To Michael, Nick and Aithne
To Paula and Sara

Foreword

It is beyond question that a key influence upon the competitiveness of enterprises of all types in a modern economy is their ability to utilize information systems (IS). But, as in many other respects, the exemplars of what is viewed as "good practice" is seen to be derived exclusively from amongst large firms. Such firms are held up as illustrating the benefits of developing a long-term approach to competitiveness through appropriate use of IS. They have separate information technology (IT) departments with a wide range of skills; they implement systems often with substantial over-capacity in order to accommodate the expansion that subsequently takes place. Their foresight is therefore rewarded.

The contrast with the "typical" small- and medium-sized enterprise (SME) is stark. Setting aside the difficulty of identifying a "typical" SME, the smaller organizations are viewed as, at best, reluctant users of IT. Perhaps even more seriously they are accused of being misguided, even stupid, in not recognizing the benefits IS can bring to their businesses. In this respect there is a strong parallel with SMEs supposed reluctance to invest in training of employees, as in both cases the SMEs are seen to "under-spend", compared with larger firms.

But such criticism of SMEs, in their decisions over IS is as misguided as it is in the area of staff training, and for very similar reasons. As Levy and Powell point out, small firms are not scaled-down versions of large firms. Their owners have a diversity of objectives, almost none of which correspond to enhancing shareholder value, which is supposed to "drive" larger firms. Instead some owners have much shorter-term objectives. They seek to run their business "flexibly" by which we mean minimizing that part of their cost-base which cannot be adjusted quickly to unexpected changes in circumstances. Hence the SME is very unlikely to invest any excess capacity in IS, not necessarily because of a lack of appreciation of the potential contribution of the long-term development of the firm, but rather because the costs of being locked-in are potentially fatal to the survival of the firm. In no sense, therefore, it is a stupid or ill-informed reason from the perspective of the SME, but to the outside observer it does appear very different from the strategy adopted by large firms. What is clear is that, even size-adjusted expenditure on items likely to yield primarily long-term returns, is lower amongst small than large firms.

Superimposed upon this determination to avoid being financially locked-in are other special characteristics of SMEs. In particular, the unique role played by the owner — "the ego on legs" also requiring emphasis, since the diversity amongst SMEs reflects the diversity of human beings, making generalizations hazardous at the best. As the authors emphasize some SME owners are "teckies" and their firms reflect this, whilst to others computer systems are a last resort.

This book avoids the key pitfall of being judgemental on SMEs. Instead, with its extensive use of case studies, it accurately reflects the diversity of the SME sector. Its value is to recognize that the economic and social environment in which SMEs find themselves, is different from that of large firms, but it also illustrates the situations in which SMEs' investment in IS has yielded substantial economic benefits. These case-based illustrations are much more persuasive to an SME owners than the hectoring frequently meted out by those with responsibility for enhancing productivity.

Professor David Storey
Director, CSME
Warwick Business School
University of Warwick
Coventry CV4 7AL
UK

1 Introduction

■ Why research strategic information systems in SMEs

Information is transnational: like money, information has no "fatherland". Because information knows no national boundaries, it will also form new transnational communities of people ... who are in communion because they are in communication (Drucker, 1989).

Over the last decade, the rise in the importance of information and knowledge for business activity has been phenomenal. Globalization has become a reality and competition is more dynamic (Porter, 1998) as firms source materials and manufacture goods in many locations, while innovation is vital for future business growth. Information is now critical for the management and growth of business value. Knowledge about competitors and customers is essential to understand the future direction of business development. Harnessing this resource is important, and yet, difficult. One means of tackling it is through the development of organizational information systems that enable the collection and dissemination of data, information and knowledge. Organizations are increasingly using information technology to deliver outputs from such systems. Data, information and knowledge can all enhance competitiveness.

Information is a primary management resource. Like finance, operations and marketing, its management cannot be left to chance. In an increasingly competitive market there are three major reasons why effective management of IS is essential for competitiveness. First, the intensity of market competitiveness means that firms are under pressure to work smarter and innovate faster than the competition. As the retail banks have demonstrated, effective use of IS and IT can shorten cycle times, while transforming the basis of competitiveness. Second, no firm is an island. The value-adding process is one of transforming inputs into profitable outputs. This means that the producers are dependent upon the co-operation of suppliers, distribution networks and customers. Third, information is an enabler of globalism. Changes in international trading agreements and the monopoly power of local suppliers is driving firms to use global sourcing in order to remain competitive. But a precondition for accessing global resources is planned IS.

These issues have been researched extensively in large organizations, and there is a vast literature on the values of IS and IT to improve competitiveness. However, there is little literature that explores these issues in small- and medium-sized enterprises (SMEs). The strategic role of information is not necessarily a prerogative of large firms. This is particularly true in the Internet age where "pureplays", firms set up solely through and because of the Internet, abound. While many have succumbed to the dot.com demise, some have gone on to develop and grow. However, it is not only these firms that are of interest. Many large corporations only continue in business due to their suppliers. These suppliers range from small specialist firms to medium-sized ones producing commodities. The rise of the small business sector is phenomenal. The drivers for this rise vary from a decline in agriculture in the developing world to a focus on core business leading to outsourcing of services by large corporations. However, there are not only macro-economic reasons driving the growth of small firms; the desire for independence or an innovative idea leads many people to start their own firms.

Business drivers are no different for small firms than for large. There is still a need to manage the operational activities, identify suppliers, market goods and services, determine customer requirements and consider the impact of competitor actions. Thus information and knowledge is as important to small firms as their larger counterparts. Information systems can assist small organizations work more effectively. Many SMEs already invest heavily in production technologies to produce their goods or services. However, their use of IS and IT to manage business more effectively is often problematic.

The problems may be due to the operational focus of many small businesses where the owner's knowledge is directed to the delivery of orders to customers. However, as larger firms have found, it is possible to use IS to manage more efficiently and effectively. Others reasons may include difficulties in finding systems and technologies appropriate to the size of business, limited skills and knowledge about IS within the smaller business. A key reason is the financial investment involved in IS, with many smaller businesses preferring to spend their limited capital on production and operational technologies rather than management support.

However, the advent of personal computers and local area networks has made investment in IS and IT more accessible. Information technology suppliers are recognizing that small businesses have a requirement for business systems. Even large IT suppliers such as Microsoft, IBM and SAP are seeking opportunities in the smaller business market. There is often a natural scepticism in small business owners that makes them want to ensure that they obtain value for money from any investment. Hence, they tend to be cautious and drive relatively hard bargains when it comes to IT.

The danger for many SMEs is that they defer investment in IS until their businesses have outgrown existing systems. These crises of growth require urgent action by the smaller business if it is to develop. This book examines the reasons for the limited investment in IS and IT. It proposes approaches that the smaller business can take in planning and developing strategies to manage investment in IS and IT. By understanding the business drivers and approaches to business growth, the smaller business can make manageable investments in IS and IT that will enable it to have effective management IS.

This book considers the role of IS in supporting the strategic management of smaller firms. It considers the relevance of the role of current IS management theory to smaller businesses. The extant theory is adapted, where necessary, to provide insights that are relevant to SMEs. The knowledge generated provides a way for small businesses to consider the strategic role of IS when planning their future investments. From the IS theory perspective, the outcomes of this research invite questions about the validity of the theory as to its generic applicability. This is not to say that IS management theory should always be generic, but that it should specify the nature of the organizations to which it refers.

The research that underpins this book is developed from multiple case studies of firms undertaken since 1994. The cases have been researched primarily by the authors and some by associates. The research process is ongoing, and many of the case firms have been researched longitudinally. The cases focus on the way the small firm uses information to manage their business within the strategic context. An outcome of the case analysis is the development of theories that suggest how small businesses might consider investment in IS to manage the business. These theories focus on IS strategy and information as a strategic resource.

The book, therefore, provides support and knowledge of the strategic use of information to two main audiences. It will be of benefit to both academics and business advisers. The book provides IS academics with knowledge of the relevance and appropriateness of strategic IS concepts to smaller businesses. It provides the entrepreneur, innovation academic and small business advisers with models and frameworks that are directly relevant to information strategy in small, fast-growing firms. Where relevant, chapters demonstrate implications for theory and for management practice.

■ Researching SMEs

SMEs are interesting phenomena to study, particularly as they are not a homogeneous group and come in many sizes, shapes and structures. This makes researching SMEs an exciting opportunity. Yet such research is fraught with difficulties due to the fluidity of structure and management that applies to growing firms. This is an issue for this book as management

IS theory suggests a steady growth and development path towards the use of more complex systems to achieve business value. This implies some conflict between the aims of SMEs and that of IS theory. The book seeks understanding of the role of IS in managing SMEs. The research underpinning this book contributes to that understanding.

The background to the research undertaken over the last 10 years is discussed to outline the rationale for the approach taken. The role of case studies in research is then discussed. It presents some of the theoretical reasons for the validity of this approach.

The next part of this chapter presents the background to the case studies that are used as the basis for the research in this book. The book is primarily based on 68 different SME cases in the West Midlands of the UK. However, from the literature the similarities between these cases and others cited are strong. The literature on IS adoption and Management IS issues presented in Chapter 3 is international and also generally supports the research in this book.

■ Background to the research

The authors' interest in IS and SMEs has developed over the last 10 years. The big question posed is what makes SMEs different in their adoption of IS. The authors' background was IS, so our main objective was to understand the drivers for SMEs. We wanted to understand their approach to strategic decision-making and how this affected their approach to IS strategy.

The early part of our research was exploratory, we wanted to know whether and in what way SMEs' IS adoption approaches were similar to those of large corporations. At this stage we decided to reduce variables and to concentrate initially on manufacturing firms. What we found was an exciting and vibrant business community that was starting to use IS to manage the business. However, there was less than clear understanding of its value to the business. We also found that integration of IS with business processes was less advanced. Chapters 4–6 are developed from the findings of this early research revisited with hindsight.

From the understanding that we gained from our early case studies further issues emerged that form the basis of our later research. We needed to build a larger base of knowledge of SMEs to review and develop our understanding. Using the knowledge gained from the exploratory research we developed a case study approach that allowed us to gather data on more SMEs by refining our questions. It became clear as we did the exploratory research that it was important to talk to as many people as possible in the SMEs to gain a good understanding of the relationships. What makes this research different is its consideration of the importance of the SME owner in understanding the firm and, in particular, the reasons that they were in business. Since 1995 we have developed a detailed set of 68 different cases in different industries and with different strategic objectives. As we are investigating the strategic role of information in SMEs we wanted to see whether there were any industry differences. What we found, as is discussed in Chapter 7, is that industry is not a dominant factor in use of strategic information.

We have followed 15 of the case firms over the years assessing their development, growth and, in one or two cases, their demise. This enables us to develop longitudinal research on the firms and helps in theory development on IS adoption and growth. Chapters 9–12 demonstrate our use of the range of cases employed to develop and test theory and to identify growth paths.

We have been helped in access to these firms by being located in a university that runs a Business Growth Programme for SME owners. This programme is designed to offer management skills and knowledge in marketing, finance and human resource management to owners. The participants on this programme are supportive of our research. Interestingly, although the programme is about business growth, there are a number of firms for which this is not an objective: some family firms joined to develop their skills base.

More recent research has focused on Internet adoption and the development of e-business in SMEs. The approach taken here is to develop questions that help in our understanding of attitudes of owners, as the key decision-maker, towards the Internet. A separate study of 50 cases over a 3-year period was undertaken to find out who influences SMEs' IS decisions towards Internet adoption. This is discussed in Chapter 18. Additionally, we had the opportunity to be part of a larger data gathering exercise through a telephone survey. The data is used to gain an understanding of strategic intent and the enablers and inhibitors of Internet adoption. Chapter 17 discusses the outcomes of this research.

■ Case studies: primary research approach

The early research looked at whether IS models and theories are applicable to SMEs. There is little evidence of this in the academic literature. The early research discussed in this book is, therefore, largely exploratory. Case studies are a useful approach to exploratory research such as this as it is possible to pose reflective questions. Additionally, case research is effective when theory is relatively underdeveloped (Eisenhardt, 1989). In particular, when the boundaries of the research are not clear, there is a need to investigate the issue within a real life context, drawing on the views of a number of sources (Yin, 1994).

The focus of the research developed to consider the role of IS strategy and, as discussed in Chapter 6, the focus is on the strategic role of information from an organizational perspective. Hence, the objective of the research is understanding the organizational dynamics and the inter-relationships that enable and inhibit the use of IS. Case studies are useful here as they provide a rich medium for gaining understanding both of the "soft" organizational issues and the flows of information in the organization (Walsham, 1993; Eisenhardt, 1989).

The importance of an organizational perspective when studying IS is highlighted by Walsham (1993). As many surveys on important issues in IS show, the main concerns all have organizational implications: strategic planning, IS alignment and competitive advantage. He argues that it is difficult to understand the relationships involved in an organization by taking a "rational-economic" perspective that is "based on the view that the world exhibits objective cause–effect relationships".

Information systems research needs to look at the context and the processes influenced by IS. The context needs to be recognized as dynamic process, as argued by Mintzberg (1991). Therefore, there is a need to study the relationships between the actors and their effect on the resources and competences in the organization. In other words, it is the interaction between context and process that provides the basis for understanding the IS situation.

The study of social phenomena may be seen as a hermeneutic process (Klein and Myers, 1999; Nandhakumar and Jones, 1997). Learning develops as researchers' understanding increases. Thus, further issues were identified that needed exploration as a result of the early research. One of the key issues to emerge was the need to discover whether the role of information as a strategic resource in SMEs was dependent upon strategy, market or firm. It was also important to increase the research base. However, the authors believe that they are still seeking understanding and, therefore, case studies are the most appropriate method.

Case studies provide a rich dataset that can be used to identify issues within a research objective (Mingers, 2001). Multiple cases ensure that common patterns are identified rather than generalized from what might be the chance of occurrences (Eisenhardt, 1989). Evidence from multiple cases is "often considered more compelling, and the overall study is therefore regarded as being more robust" (Yin, 1994: p. 45). This is so with the research in this book. Multiple case studies have been useful in developing the theoretical framework that is central to the contribution of IS adoption theory discussed in Chapter 8, the focus-dominance model. This model is derived from knowledge of the similarities and differences generated from multiple cases.

Data collection

Undertaking case studies requires gaining access to SMEs. Here, access was facilitated by the university connection and general support of the firms for research. Interviews are a key feature of successful cases. In case study research it is important to have open questions to enable the interviewee to explain their view of the situation (Yin, 1994). One of the most striking aspects for the authors as interviewers was the openness with which SME owners shared their views on the business and its success and concerns. Interviews are held with other management and staff in the SMEs to provide additional and collaborative evidence for the validity of the data. Documentation, when available, is also used to support the interviews.

The approach taken in data collection is to focus on the interviewees' role in the firm. Listening is a key skill for data collection. The use and value of IS to the interviewee was explored through their role. Interviews were summarized and accuracy confirmed with interviewees. The overall understanding of the SMEs' approach to use of management IS was confirmed with the SME owner.

Problems of case research

There are a number of issues that can make case study research problematic. The first is generalisability. Multiple cases that are used to consider research questions provide a valid basis for understanding (Yin, 1994). The second issue is one of the data collection. Interviews need to be carefully constructed to avoid bias in response. The accuracy of interview data needs to be confirmed, as it is possible for the interviewer to misunderstand or misconstrue what has been said (Yin, 1994). These issues have been voided as far as possible in this research by confirming understanding with the SMEs.

■ Case background

The cases used in this book are outlined in Table 1.1. This provides information about the business and ownership of the firm. All names are anonymized unless the firm's permission to use their name has been given. The year the first intervention in each case was undertaken is also given. Where the firm has been revisited for longitudinal analysis the dates and staff numbers are provided.

The industry breakdown is summarized in Table 1.2.

The firms are not selected for size, although many of the cases are small firms. However, for completeness the firm size breakdown is included here (Table 1.3). Where longitudinal cases are involved, the first intervention is used. For these longitudinal case firms, a number have grown. There is movement from micro to small (Mobile Phone Surveyors) and from small to medium (Soil Analysis Co. and Holiday Coach Co.). Clutch Assembly Co. has grown beyond an SME. Decline is also evident in one or two firms (e.g. Systems Design and Employment Co. and Landfill Gas Co.).

Table 1.1: Background to case firms

Name	Business	Ownership	Staff	Year
Business services				
Public Sector Advocates	Community and public sector legal work	Partnership	108	1999
			150	2000
Electrical Accreditation Agency	Electrical accreditation	Electrical industry	22	1997
Soil Analysis Co.	Chemical analysis of soil	CEO	63	1999
			100	2001
			130	2002
		Group	130	2004
Energy Saving Co.	Environmental consultancy, energy maximization	CEO	17	1996
Family Attorneys	Legal affairs	Partnership	20	1994
			25	1995
Specialist Fuel Distributor	Distributor of specialist fuels	Family	100	2000
Chemical Analysis Co.	Geotechnical and environmental consultancy	Family	38	1996
Accountancy Firm	Chartered accountants	Three partners	23	1998
Patent Attorneys	Patent Attorneys	Partnership	21	2001
Design and Marketing Co.	Marketing communications consultancy	Family	16	1998
Events Management Co.	Conference Organization	Three partners	20	1995
Mobile Phone Surveyors	Identification of land sites for erection of radio communication masts	CEO	6	1995
			36	1997
			28	1999
Energy Management Consultancy	Environmental consulting services	CEO	11	2000
Training Brokerage Co.	Management Training Agency	CEO	9	1996
Seven Stars Printers	Printers of high quality colour work	Family, general manager introduced	10	1994
Queensway Photographic	Development of window display photos	CEO	25	1998
Conference and Marketing Co.	Events management	CEO	80	1999
Specialist Insurance Broker	Specialist insurance brokers	Two partners	27	1997
Information technology				
Biotechnology Software Developers	Development of software for scientific imaging analysis	Three directors	20	1998
Systems Design and Employment Co.	IT employment and systems development agency	Two owners	29	1999
			13	2001
IT Systems Development Co.	Software development	Three directors	120	2002
Manufacturing				
Light Assembly Co.	Assembly of light fittings	Family, General manager introduced	24	1994

Table 1.1: (Continued)

Name	Business	Ownership	Staff	Year
Epoxy Resin Co.	Development and Manufacture of epoxy resins	Family	15	1997
			22	1999
			22	2000
			26	2002
			21	2004
Photo Lamps Co.	Specialist lamp manufacturer	Family	35	1997
Enamel Box Co.	Manufacture of enamel gift boxes	Family and CEO	60	1997
Kitchen Furniture Manufacturer	Kitchen furniture manufacturer	Family	127	2001
Oil Flow Co.	Manufacture of oil flow systems	CEO	13	2001
Car Paint Co.	Manufacture of car paints	Family, general manager introduced	36	1994
			40	1996
Corporate Gift Co.	Design and manufacture of corporate gifts	Family	27	1997
			36	2002
Heath Springs	Coil spring manufacturer	Group	112	1994
			130	2001
Marine Cable Co.	Marine cable design and manufacture	Group autonomous division within multi-national	20	1998
Burring Engineers	Manufacture of deburring machines	Family	24	1996
Clutch Assembly Co.	Manufacture of automotive sub-assemblies	Family	285	1994
			400	1998
Copper Tube Manufacturer	Manufacture of copper piping	Family	37	1999
Tractor Attachment Co.	Manufacture of compact tractor attachments	Family	30	2004
Precision Tool Co.	Precision tooling manufacturer	Group	24	1994
Car Sign Design Co.	Graphic design liveries for the automotive industry	CEO	15	1997
Landfill Equipment Co.	Design and manufacture of landfill gas extraction equipment	CEO	10	1999
Perforated Products Manufacturer	Manufacture of perforated products for the filtration industry	CEO	50	1996
Metal Finishing Co.	Metal plating products	CEO	50	2000
Metal Fabrication Manufacturer	Manufacture of metal fabrication and land fill gas stacks	Two directors	20	2000
Specialist Car Parts Manufacturer	Design and manufacture of specialist automotive products	Family	35	2004

(continued)

Table 1.1: (Continued)

Name	Business	Ownership	Staff	Year
Wood Pallet Manufacturer	Wood pallet manufacturer	Family	44	1998
Reduced Power Co.	Development and manufacture of energy saving devices	CEO	14	2001
Optical Lens Manufacturer	Manufacture of optical lenses	CEO and company secretary	10	1997
Landfill Gas Co.	Production of equipment to extract methane from landfill sites	Family	40 20	1994 1995

Social services, education and not-for-profit firms

Name	Business	Ownership	Staff	Year
Urban Health Practice	Fund-holding GP surgery	Partnership	23	1995
Rural Health Practice	Fund-holding General Practice	Senior Partner and four partners	22	1995
Horticultural Charity	Horticultural Charity	Board of Trustees	30	2002
Recycling Training Co.	Training for people with disabilities using recycling	Owned by two partners	5 5	1995 1996
Skills Training Co.	Training provider	Family, not for profit organization	23	1996
Tree House Health	Private high dependency care nursing home	Partnership	108 108	1995 1999
Newtown Surgery	Fund-holding GP surgery	Partnership	22	1995
IT Education Charity	IT educational charity	Trustees	150	1997
Garden Health Care	Private nursing home and sheltered accommodation	CEO	30	1995
University Arts Centre	Theatre, concert and conference complex	Non-profit organization	20	1999

Wholesale and retail trade

Name	Business	Ownership	Staff	Year
Curtain Material Wholesale Co.	Wholesale retailer of curtain fabrics	Family	7	2001
Regional Travel Co.	Independent travel agent	Family	25	1995
Holiday Coach Co.	Coach holiday and bus service providers	Family	48 120	1997 2004
Agricultural Machinery Co.	Sale and repair of agricultural machinery	CEO and FD	36	2001
Model Toy Co.	Supply and distribution of model car collectables	Two owner-managers	5 4	1996 1999
Equipment Hire Centre	Product hire to building trade	CEO	7	2001
Savoury Pie Manufacturer	Manufacture of pies	CEO	75	2001
Landrover Repair Co.	Renovation and repair of Landrovers	CEO	16	1996
Garden Pottery Co.	Manufacture of garden pottery	CEO	30	2001
Wholesale Garden Nursery	Garden nursery wholesaler	Family	26	2000
Heating Maintenance Co.	Heating systems maintenance	Family	14	1997
Bird Designs	Design and manufacture of paper and wood goods	Family	16 16	1995 2002

Table 1.2: Industry groups of case firms

Industry groups	Number of firms
Business Services	18
Information Technology	3
Manufacturing	25
Social Services and Public Administration	10
Wholesale and Retail Trade	12

Table 1.3: Size breakdown of case firms

Firm size (employees)	Number of firms
0–9	5
10–99	55
100–250	8

Throughout the book case study are interspersed to provide examples of some of the theoretical points made. Explanatory case studies are used to support the theory that is developed in the book.

■ Structure of the book

The book is structured in five parts.

■ *Part 1* introduces the concept of the SME. It then presents an outline of IS issues before considering SMEs' approach to IS. An introduction to the problematic nature of management IS in SMEs is provided by considering issues of flexibility and evaluation.

■ *Part 2* addresses the issues of IS strategy and planning in SMEs. First, existing IS strategy literature and its validity in the SME context is considered. Second, an approach to information systems strategy (ISS) is developed. Third a substantial, worked case study that describes use of the ISS approach is provided.

■ *Part 3* considers attitudes to information as a strategic resource in SMEs, and a model is developed that shows that SMEs cannot be considered as a homogeneous group. This model is used to assess the way that SMEs can transform themselves, over time, through use of IS. The part also considers the appropriateness of IS strategic transformation models and their potential for SMEs.

■ *Part 4* considers managing knowledge and the development of information strategies to achieve this. The relevance of core competence theory to the development of IS strategies for SMEs is discussed. The issue of managing knowledge in SMEs in general, and the need for business process change to do this, is addressed.

■ *Part 5* moves towards the future with an analysis of Internet adoption amongst SMEs. The rationale and policy drivers for SMEs are discussed and a model of Internet adoption is developed. The relationship between Internet adoption and strategy is discussed.

Chapters

In the first part, chapter 2 sets the context for the research undertaken here. The basic premise is that SMEs are not small versions of large corporations, but have a business dynamic that means that they act differently and have different drivers for success.

The different definitions of an SME are reviewed and a view taken on which is the most appropriate in the context of the research. Key issues that impact on SME growth are discussed. In particular, the role of the owner is highlighted. Additionally, the reasons for SMEs existence vary, leading to different business strategies that impact on investment decisions. The chapter briefly considers the SME in different cultural contexts.

Chapter 3 discusses the role of IS as a management tool to improve internal efficiency and effectiveness, and external competitiveness. Thus, it assesses the use of such systems rather than the detail of the systems themselves. The chapter outlines the changes in technology over the last 20 years and the impact of these changes on SMEs. The strengths and limitations in the use of IS to manage SMEs are explored. The chapter shows that SMEs tend to use simple systems to manage their businesses and, where complex systems are adopted, they are often not used effectively. This book contends that this is often because of a limited link with business strategy and also little or no IS strategy in most SMEs.

Chapter 4 considers the issue of flexibility, as SMEs are generally considered to be flexible, adaptive organizations. Although lagging behind their larger counterparts, SMEs are beginning to invest more in IS. This chapter investigates whether SMEs really do exhibit flexibility and if their use of IS enhances or inhibits such flexibility.

Chapter 5 investigates the issues associated with evaluation of IS in SMEs. While evaluation has long been considered important to large organizations so that they can monitor value from IS, little work has examined evaluation in SMEs. The chapter discusses IS evaluation in the context of SMEs by identifying issues particularly relevant to such firms. The chapter identifies a lack of business and IS/IT strategy, limited access to capital resources, an emphasis on automating, the influence of major customers and limited information skills as contributing to limited evaluation practice.

Part 2 focuses on ISS. Chapter 6 reviews the nature of ISS and the reasons why it is thought necessary for ISS to be undertaken. The development of ISS is often performed in an *ad hoc* manner, though it may be undertaken with the support of frameworks. Some of these frameworks are the codification of existing practice, while others are the result of theory development. Some are tried and trusted, while others languish unused. This chapter evaluates the usefulness of ISS frameworks in the context of SMEs and assesses the applicability of the frameworks.

Chapter 7 presents an organizational approach to ISS in SMEs. The chapter reviews existing approaches to ISS for SMEs, finding them largely out-dated and technology-focused. It develops a new approach that reflects on the role of information as a strategic resource. It argues that ISS recommendations in small firms need to take account of organizational change issues as much as IS implementation.

Chapter 8 provides a detailed case study of the use of the organizational ISS approach. The case discusses the strategic and organizational issues that impact upon the development of information strategies for a manufacturing firm.

Part 3 moves on to consider the IS adoption strategies in SMEs. Chapter 9 recognizes that obtaining benefits from IS depends upon business focus and owner requirements. This chapter develops a model to understand and plan IS strategy in SMEs. The model reflects the relative dominance of SME customers on one hand and the strategic focus of the firm on the other.

Chapter 10 takes the ideas presented in the previous chapter and considers the role of IS strategy in relation to business growth. The process by which small firms invest in IS as they grow is little understood. The chapter discusses the concept of stages of growth as applied to SMEs and identifies key criteria for growth firms. Variances can be explained primarily by three factors, entrepreneurs' desire to grow, understanding of the need for a strategy for growth and knowledge of the potential of IS. This implies that growth firms follow a "stages" model, while others use IS to reinforce the existing competitive positioning.

Chapter 11 reviews business transformation opportunities in SMEs, which may use IS for efficiency, co-ordination, collaboration or innovation but there is little investigation of how SMEs progress from one use to another. This chapter uses the Venkatraman (1990) model of business transformation to investigate progression in IS in SMEs and the consequences for them. The Venkatraman model is based upon research into large firms, and this is the first research into its applicability in the small firm sector. The chapter demonstrates why some SMEs ossify at certain stages of transformation and others may not achieve the benefits they hope.

Chapter 12 recognizes that little is understood about the process of alignment of IS in SMEs. Alignment considers the relationship between business strategy, organizational structures, management processes, IT and roles and skills of people in the organization. Research into alignment in large firms has identified a number of alignment paths. This chapter investigates alignment in SMEs through understanding how different groups of SMEs use IS. Four new paths to alignment are identified for SMEs. Three of these offer only partial alignment. This may help explain why many SMEs fail to gain the benefits that might be expected from their IS investments.

Part 4 focuses on resource-based strategy and managing knowledge in SMEs. Resource-based strategy argues that competitive advantage arises from the ability to accumulate resources and capabilities that are rare, valuable, non-substitutable and difficult to imitate.

Chapter 13 discusses the role of IS as firm resources and the role of such resources in small firms. The use of core competencies or capabilities, a key aspect of resources, is proposed as a basis for the development of an information strategy. This is contrasted with the use of a structural approach exemplified here by the value chain. Chapter 14 extends the debate about the development of an information strategy by developing a more detailed resource-based framework as an integral part of the organizational ISS framework introduced in Chapter 7. The argument in this part moves on to consider the role of knowledge management in SMEs. Chapter 14 considers the strategic issues for SMEs in sharing knowledge with customers. Co-opetition, simultaneous co-operation and competition, is a recent phenomenon. Co-opetition entails sharing knowledge that may be a key source of competitive advantage. Thus, the knowledge gained by co-operation may also be used for competition. This chapter empirically investigates the issues in the context of SMEs. SMEs provide an interesting setting as they are innovators (hence knowledge generators), but are poor at knowledge exploitation.

The final chapter in this part, Chapter 15, focuses on how to bring change about in SMEs. Business process re-engineering identifies relevant business processes that add business value and attempts to re-engineer the firm so that it focuses on these processes only. The issues that SMEs need to consider to achieve this strategic change are discussed.

Part 5 looks at the role of the Internet for SMEs. Emerging technologies, such as the Internet, are viewed as enabling firms to alter radically their competitive positioning. The Internet provides the opportunity to trade globally and there are, potentially, few limits to growth. What is less clear is how SMEs can take advantage of these opportunities.

Chapter 16 considers how SMEs Internet investments are decided. The influence of business strategy and the value to the business of the Internet are explored. It demonstrates that those SMEs that do exploit the Internet mainly use it for research rather than trading. In order to give impetus to Internet use, the chapter argues that the Internet can only be of value to SMEs if they take a radical collaborative approach to its implementation. The future may lie with the development of enterprise networks rather than individual competitive gain. An information strategy helps SMEs to focus better on the potential added value from emerging technologies.

Chapter 17 investigates how strategic intent influences small firms adoption of e-business. The chapter considers the effect of issues such as market position, product innovation and industry sector. The impact of drivers and inhibitors that influence adoption are reviewed. The research demonstrates that strategic intent influences decisions to invest in e-business. Those SMEs remaining in their existing markets are the least likely to invest, primarily due to the Internet not being seen as necessary for growth. Product innovation rather than market penetration that drives e-business, and e-business drivers and inhibitors to provide insights into this.

Chapter 18 considers the role of government in supporting Internet adoption amongst SMEs. This chapter looks at the roles governments take to support Internet adoption by SMEs in a number of countries including the UK, Canada, Malaysia and Singapore. It considers, in detail, the drivers for adoption amongst UK SMEs and the influence of the role of government.

Chapter 18 also reviews the current attitudes to investment in information and communication technologies, particularly the Internet, by SME. It reflects on the need for change in today's information economy, focusing on innovation, speed and predatory behaviour by large firms. The proposition is made that Internet adoption in SMEs is limited by attitudes to growth. In an earlier chapter it is suggested that a stages of growth model is not appropriate for SMEs. This chapter suggests that this does not allow for the flexibility required by businesses to compete in the 21st century. A network enterprise model is proposed that enables SMEs to compete more effectively, while acknowledging their reluctance to invest in IS. The role of the network as information broker is proposed through enabling SMEs to exchange information through interfaces with the network hub.

The final chapter (Chapter 19) summarizes the ideas raised in this book and lays out lessons that SMEs can address to manage information as a strategic resource.

Part 1   Concept of the SME

The first part sets the scene for the research on information systems and small- and medium-sized enterprises that is presented in this book. The text is designed for a variety of audiences with different interests, experiences and types of knowledge. While some readers will have extensive knowledge of the issues, others will find the introductions to SMEs and IS useful.

Chapter 2 introduces SMEs. It discusses their nature and the various influences on them such as the market, people, flexibility and innovation. The focus then moves on to SME growth and shows that growth is determined by a combination of the entrepreneur, strategy and the firm organization. Changes in organizational structure as SMEs grow are discussed. Models of stages of growth are explored to explain the different management emphases at different phases. The role of systems in SMEs is outlined.

Chapter 3 first discusses the role of information as a strategic resource. Gaining the value from this resource requires planning and management of IS. The value of IS strategy and the importance of alignment are outlined. The various management IS that are commonly used by firms are defined here. The focus of the chapter then moves to discussing the use of IS in SMEs. The limited development of IS strategy is highlighted as an issue that affects SMEs gaining benefits from IS. The owner is as important to IS investment decisions as to other decisions. Limited knowledge and IS skills mean that SMEs tend to outsource development. However, as the chapter demonstrates, this may cause difficulties as cost always looms over decisions. IS adoption is dependent upon a number of factors, not least of which is the information technology knowledge and skills in the organization. Management IS in SMEs often focus on simplicity, but this limits their capacity to provide strategic information.

Flexibility is highlighted as one of the important strengths of SMEs in Chapter 2. Thus, it is important to review flexibility from an IS perspective. Chapter 4 defines flexibility using a model that suggests four forms of flexibility: pre-emptive, exploitive, protective and corrective. The first two are likely to lead to competitive advantage, while the last two are essential for survival. The chapter discusses flexibility issues and their relationship with IS investment in general and for SMEs in particular. Information systems flexibility in SMEs is largely unexplored. The chapter presents the results of an exploratory study of four of the case firms shown in Chapter 1. The study reviews flexibility through the case firms' use, organization and development of IS, which tends to be limited to production and efficiency systems. The customer is shown to be highly influential. The chapter reviews opportunities for IS flexibility in SMEs and demonstrates that there is little evidence. Any response is in terms of survival, leading to protective and corrective measures of flexibility.

Limited resources in SMEs means that decisions on large capital investments, such as are often required for IS, may be difficult. Customer pressures, as well as the need to improve efficiency, are highlighted as issues that affect IS investment decisions. Thus, evaluation of these decisions is problematic. The final chapter in this part reviews the evaluation process using the four cases introduced in Chapter 4. This part highlights the main issues that affect SMEs' use of IS as a strategic resource.

2   Background to SMEs

■ Introduction

Small- and medium-sized enterprises are a vibrant and growing sector in most economies round the world. Global economic conditions have spurred the rise in SMEs over the last 10–15 years. This is seen not only in the UK, USA, Australasia and Europe, but also in Africa, Latin America, Korea and Indonesia. Within the Organisation for Economic Co-operation and Development (OECD), 95% of firms are SMEs employing between 60% and 70% of workers. These firms are exciting as many are highly entrepreneurial and are often involved in exploiting new innovations. While such innovation is a motivator for many SME owners, there are also those for whom independence is the prime objective.

SMEs are often considered as a single group by researchers and policy makers, but they are heterogeneous with diverse needs and objectives. For many owners of small businesses, lifestyle choice is the reason that they set them up. For others, the entrepreneurs, it is the excitement and risk of growing an empire. Between these extremes there are a range of reasons for people wanting their own business, not least of which is to provide a pension plan or something to pass on to the children. The characteristics of small firms vary; once they employ more than 10 people there is a need to consider management issues and to set up a formal structure to organize the activities. The focus of this book is on the role that IS and technology can play in the management of small businesses.

In considering the role of management IS in SMEs it is useful to understand their characteristics and driver of growth. This chapter first defines the SME and considers the influences on them. Success, which is primarily seen in terms of growth, is defined through interaction between the role of the entrepreneur, strategy and the firm. Many owners start their firms with the intention of growing them. This chapter reviews paths for growth and identifies some of the problems for SMEs in managing that growth. This organizational issues that impact on management of small business are introduced.

By understanding these issues it is possible to consider the different ways that SMEs work and, thus, appreciate the background for the discussion in Chapter 3 on the role of IS in SMEs.

■ Defining SMEs

The SMEs, tend to be thought of as a homogeneous group, especially by governments. However, this hides the great differences in size, structure

Table 2.1: EU definitions for micro-, small- and medium-sized enterprises

Criterion	Micro	Small	Medium
Maximum number of employees	9	49	250
Maximum annual turnover	n/a	7 million euros	40 million euros
Maximum annual balance sheet total	n/a	5 million euros	27 million euros
Maximum % owned by one, or several enterprises not satisfying the same	n/a	25%	25%

Source: SBS 2003.

n/a: not available.

and purpose that pertain in the sector. Defining the SME sector, and particularly small businesses, is fairly difficult, as there are differences in what is appropriate to describe as "small" in different industries (Burns, 2001; Storey, 1994). The main criteria that predominate to define the SMEs sector are the number of employees, turnover and the balance sheet total (Burns, 2001). The European Union (EU) definition for micro-, small- and medium-sized enterprises is shown in Table 2.1.

Other definitions include the OECD, which uses employee numbers with slightly different criteria: micro-firms having fewer than 20 employees, small 20–99 and medium 100–299 employees. Meanwhile, the US definition considers all firms employing fewer than 500 employees as SMEs. The US definition is too large for most countries, where the vast majority of firms employ fewer than 250 people. Additionally, the organizational characteristics of firms with 500 employees tend to be similar to large firms with formal structures for this to be a useful definition for research into SMEs.

Employee size is the most useful discriminator in the context of management research (Burns, 2001; Storey, 1994). In particular, it is the move towards more formal management structures that occurs in small firms, but is not seen in micro-enterprises (firms with fewer than 10 employees) (Burns, 2001; Storey, 1994). The move towards formality is seen in larger small firms and is usually well defined in larger medium-sized ones. The EU definition provides a good basis for addressing management issues in general as it allows for the maximum diversity in SME type. It is also useful for this book as it allows differentiation of management IS issues between different groups of SMEs.

■ Influences on SMEs

There are five key influences on small business: market, independence, personal influences, flexibility and innovation.

Market

The competitive environment in which the SME operates affects the chance of survival (Storey and Cressy, 1995). Market uncertainty is high in most SMEs as they tend to have a smaller share of the market, to have one or two major customers and are hence less able to influence price. SMEs tend to be price-takers. The high market share of large firms means that they usually determine prices. An additional danger for SMEs is from those large firms that enter a market and can compete on price. Thus, many SMEs operate in classic perfect competition (Storey and Sykes, 1996). There are a few SMEs that compete in slim market niches where there is little or no competition. These firms may influence price and quantity sold (Burns, 2001).

For many SMEs the problem to selling to a single large customer causes difficulties as the customer sets both the price and quantity of goods. There are high risks here for the SME, particularly when the large customer is faced with downturns in the market. One reason for this is the lower margins that SMEs have when selling to a single customer. SMEs may find it difficult to build up sufficient funds to build new resources (Storey and Sykes, 1996) and may reduce their ability to take strategic initiatives (Roper, 1999).

These issues are relevant for managing the business and demonstrate a need to understand the market and customer requirements. As discussed in Chapter 9, customer pressure is a deciding factor in attitudes to investment in management IS. But for many SMEs the lack of such information increases the risk to the business.

Independence

Independence means that SMEs are not beholden to a larger firm for financing or decision-making. This is thought to be somewhat controversial by Burns (2001) who argues that the attitude of the owner or general manager may have considerable influence over the behaviour of the firm. Thus small firms that are owned by larger groups should be included in the definition. The first four firms discussed in this book are in this category. They are all family firms that have been bought by larger groups to further their aims of moving into European markets. However, in all cases the chief executive officers (CEOs) are able to make decisions and take action independently of the parent group. Their behaviours and actions are the same as independently owned SMEs. In particular, investment decisions are made by the CEO. The difference for these firms is that the parent group provides an additional source of funds to develop and grow the business. They are not as reliant on sources such as banks and venture capitalists. However, a good business case for investment is still required.

Personal

The management of the small firm is personified by the owner and their attitude to business. The owner is likely to be involved in all aspects of managing a business and, as is discussed below, this can sometime lead to problems when the firm has grown such that there is a need to delegate decision-making. Burns (2001) describes a "real small firm" as one that has *"two arms, two legs and a giant ego"*. The personality of the owner-manager totally influences all aspects of the business. Attitudes to risk and uncertainty that are the main influences are discussed below.

Flexibility and innovation

SMEs are thought to be flexible and innovative organizations that are able to respond quickly to customer and market demands. Flexibility, the ability to adapt to changing circumstances, is a key characteristic of SMEs. Flexibility is desirable, but dependent upon other factors in the organization (Hansen *et al.*, 1994; Naylor and Williams, 1993; Lefebvre and Lefebvre, 1992). However, the desire for flexibility is not often justified. The production technologies of many manufacturing SMEs may inhibit flexibility (Gupta and Cawthorn, 1996), while Carrie *et al.* (1994) believe that it is people rather than technology that provide flexibility. This is explored in more detail in Chapter 4.

Innovation is also regarded as a key characteristic of SMEs, mainly due to the attitude of the owner/manager (Hay and Kamshad, 1994; Lefebvre and Lefebvre, 1992). Innovation is largely about being able to respond within the bounds of the knowledge about existing products or services to changes required by customers within their niche market (Storey, 1994). While SMEs tend not to undertake extensive research and development, they can be more innovative than larger firms (Storey, 1994).

SMEs tend to have small product runs that make it easier to be both innovative and flexible. However, while innovation may be a characteristic of start-up firms, limited resources make continuing innovation unlikely in SMEs (Keasey and Watson, 1993). These are positive characteristics that lead to SME success. Conversely, SMEs are found to often be resource poor not only financially, but also in skills (Carrie *et al.*, 1994; Hansen *et al.*, 1994). This often leads to SMEs using external consultants to provide the skills that they lack. This resource poverty implies an unwillingness to "introduce new technology and work practices" and thus reduces the capacity for change (Keasey and Watson, 1993).

■ Birth, death and growth

The SME sector is dynamic. There has been an increase in the rate at which new businesses start up over the last 30 years. This has become more evident as economic change, particularly changes in technology, subcontracting by large firms, rising unemployment in some economies and government policies towards welfare and a desire to support the enterprise culture have occurred (Storey, 1994). SME owners enjoy the challenge of being their own boss, offering potential job security for themselves and their family (Analoui and Karami, 2003).

While many new firms start up each year, survival is more difficult. The first 3 years of a business are the most critical, with up to 50% ceasing to trade during that time (Burns, 2001). For example, small firms in the UK are six times more likely to fail than their larger counterparts (Storey, 1994) and 80% of US businesses fail before the third generation (Bianchi, 2002). Failure is often caused by SMEs looking inward and not focusing on customer and market requirements, limited management skills and the owner's belief that they can do it all (Analoui and Karami, 2003). Poor financing, under-capitalization and poor product quality may also contribute to their demise (Bianchi, 2002; Storey, 1994). The dot.com boom and bust provide evidence of the ease with which firms can be set up, but also the speed at which they can fold. The main reasons for this are an over-reliance on a new technology (the Internet) combined with limited market and customer analysis of new business opportunities.

Case study 2.1

Online Computing started business in 1999 to develop and sell e-learning content to universities. It was started by two university graduates and was supported by a university enterprise scheme. The firm employed six people all of whom were highly knowledgeable about IT. By 2001 the firm had gone into liquidation. This was due to over-reliance on one customer that cancelled work. Additionally, there is evidence that the market was not ready for online training.

While there is a considerable element of risk in starting an SME, most owners intend to grow and develop their firms. It is usually assumed that all SMEs desire growth. However, only 40% of firms survive after 10 years and 4% of those firms create 50% of new employment (Storey, 1994). The attitude of the owner to their business determines much of its future development. Business growth is regarded as important by two main groups of owners, those who plan to sell off their business once it has effectively maximized profits for them and the second group who are planning to expand to an enlarged empire (Hay and Kamshad, 1994).

The majority of firms do not grow, with many focusing on survival, what Storey calls the "trundlers" (p. 117). Trundlers may be in business for lifestyle advantages or they may have owners who want to control every aspect of the business. In many cases these lifestyle firms are in business to provide owners with an adequate income from an activity that they enjoy. Management activity is carried out in a routine way at an operational level to ensure that the day-to-day issues are addressed. The owners of these firms do not think about long-term business strategy. Change is only brought about when the business begins to fail, most likely because the market has, unbeknownst to the owner, changed (Burns, 2001). These firms rarely use management IS to provide them with knowledge and information about the state of the business or industry. As is discussed later, SMEs have as much need for business intelligence as large firms.

Case study 2.2

Bird Designs started in 1989 and is owned by a husband and wife team. The firm manufactures and sells gift products with design based around bird themes. The husband is the designer with the wife managing the business. There are eight full time employees with an additional pool of 10–20 outworkers. The firm is run as a family firm and the ethos is one of caring. Employees are well looked after. Care of the environment is particularly important to the firm and this is reflected in their customer base. The turnover of the firm has grown slightly over the years, but the aim is "to run a successful family business based on ethical values and provide a commercial vehicle for my husband's designs".

However, a number of SMEs do set up with the intention of growth. Many of the owners are entrepreneurs. The ability to take risks and to respond rapidly to changing circumstances are essential for growth firms. Success depends upon the owner focusing on achieving the strategic objectives and not being diverted. Thus, it is important to have good strategic management tools in place to monitor all aspects of the business (Burns, 2001). One of the issues that often arise for growth firms is that they may set up monitoring systems at start-up, but they do not continue to invest in them. As with lifestyle firms, investment in new systems may be a response to crisis.

Case study 2.3

Soil Analysis Co. was started by the owner in 1986 to provide a service to the building trade by analysing soil samples. The firm grew rapidly in the 1990s with 23 employees in 1996 to 63 in 1999. The current management structure was introduced in 1996 with the objective to improve customer services, quality control and sales. By 2001, the firm had moved to new premises as it had grown to over 100 employees. The market was beginning to consolidate with the number of significant competitors reduced from 15 to 9. The owner was less involved with the day-to-day operation, having employed a general manager. The owner turned his attention more to the opportunities from IT. By the beginning of 2002 the firm had been bought by a much larger water analysis firm although it was working as a separate entity.

Thus, growing firms need a combination of: the entrepreneur's resources, the firm and strategy to be successful (Storey, 1994). Figure 2.1 demonstrates the connection between the three elements and the main criteria that are in each.

Entrepreneur

The age, educational experience, managerial knowledge of the entrepreneur are essential to manage growth. Older and more mature owners are more successful. Having a higher level of education is also instrumental in growth-focused SMEs (Roper, 1999; Storey, 1994). Management experience provides the ability not only to manage the business but also the work of others, which ensures that the business is organized effectively (Storey, 1994; Churchill and Lewis, 1983). Alongside this are the identification of market opportunity and willingness to work in partnership with others (Liedholm, 2002; Storey, 1994). These characteristics are often looked for by venture capitalists when they are considered supporting a new venture (Burns, 2001).

Alongside these characteristics are more personal ones. Owner-managers have a need to be independent and want to be their own managers. They

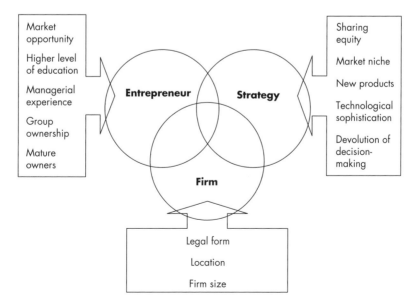

Figure 2.1: Characteristics of growth firms. (*Source*: adapted from Storey, 1994.)

believe that they can control and change the environment within which they work, to their benefit. They often are high-achievers and are looking for recognition of their success (Burns, 2001). The difficulty for many successful owner-managers is that they do not know how to delegate once the firm has grown to a size where more formal management structures are required. This manifests itself in loss of strategic direction as there is only an implicit strategy in the owner's head. Managers may not always be privy to the direction the owner wants to pursue. Management IS may provide one approach that owner-managers can use to share organizational knowledge in the firm.

The ability to manage uncertainty and risk is important for owner-managers (Knight, 2000). The fear associated with lack of income, of missing a business opportunity often leads owners to work a 24/7 lifestyle. The macro-economic uncertainties of the market also have to be overcome. The previous section highlighted some of the difficulties SMEs face when competing against large firms as they often cannot match prices. SMEs may have to borrow money to stay in business, but have no influence on borrowing rates (Burns, 2001). This often leads to under-capitalization as SMEs are nervous about borrowing from banks and other financial institutions. This may be one of the reasons why SMEs are reluctant to invest in management IS as they do not see their direct benefit to the firm, whereas production technologies are recognized as essential.

Strategy

Focusing the firm's strategy on sharing equity, identifying a particular market niche, identifying new products, technological sophistication and devolution of decision-making are key to growth (Feindt *et al.*, 2002; Storey, 1994). Fast growth businesses tend to be those that extend ownership of the firm to others in exchange for equity. In a number of countries the scarcity of capital resources inhibits growth, so it is not surprising that access to finance makes growth easier (Berry *et al.*, 2002; Bianchi, 2002; Storey, 1994). Market niches allow fast growth firms to exploit the quality of their product, as they tend to compete on quality rather than price (Storey, 1994). Innovation, particularly amongst small high technology firms is likely to lead to growth (Chaston *et al.*, 2001; Knight, 2000; Storey, 1994). In other words, these firms develop high value innovative products that are held in high esteem.

A danger for many SMEs is that attitudes to managing uncertainty and risk may lead to short-term decision-making and the strategic objectives are ignored. Day-to-day survival is often behind many decisions taken as SMEs balance the needs of customers with the demands of suppliers and financiers. However, successful owners do try to keep options open because of future uncertainty in the market.

Management devolution is essential for growth as it becomes impossible for the entrepreneur to manage on their own. Those firms that recruit experienced managers from larger firms are likely to be more successful (Storey, 1994). A management team that is too small is likely to be too busy to manage growth effectively. More non-owner-managers regard business growth as important than owners and are prepared to take greater risks to bring about this growth than owner-managers (Hay and Kamshad, 1994).

SMEs' strategy tends to be emergent and informal. SMEs primarily adopt a differentiation strategy, where the product or service delivered is different from those already in the market. This is often further refined to a particular market niche (Burns and Harrison, 1996). This may enable the SME to grow more successfully as it exploits a gap in the market. Investment in product innovation is usually the main strategy for growth (Hay and Kamshad, 1994). It also allows the SME to focus on quality, innovation and flexibility in delivering the product or service (Burns and Harrison, 1996).

Strategy is usually focused on the medium term rather than long term (Hadjimanoulis, 2000). SMEs tend to focus on operational planning with limited strategic planning, the main objective being one of providing the product or service efficiently and effectively (Hagmann and McCahon, 1993). However, where firms monitor and develop external relationships it is likely to bring competitive advantage (Goldberg et al., 2003; Savios and Blum, 2002). Those SMEs that use strategic planning effectively usually perform better than those who merely react to circumstance (Smith, 1998). In Scotland, for example, more successful SMEs do plan ahead and this has positive influences on survival (Reid and Smith, 2000).

Determining strategy is often tied in with the firms' innovativeness. In knowledge-based firms, a resource-based view of strategy (Chapter 12) may support innovation (Savioz and Blum, 2002). As demonstrated below, this is a key characteristic of SMEs and one that may demand flexible strategies for success. Hence, SMEs are reluctant to commit to long-term strategies. Strategy in SMEs is better seen as creating new visions of the future as a result of decisions taken: that is, a learning process (Bianchi, 2002). There are few formal systems and relatively little strategic planning done by SMEs until they are nearly at maturity. Therefore, it is not surprising that formal strategic planning provides few performance benefits to the SME (McKiernan and Morris, 1994), particularly given the need to satisfy customers and respond to competitive pressures. The owner's knowledge of the market is critical to successful achievement of business strategies (Feindt et al., 2002).

Firm

Legal form, size and location are indicators of successful SMEs. Limited companies tend to have faster growth than firms in sole ownership (Storey, 1994). Sole traders find it difficult to borrow money as financial institutions prefer to lend money to limited companies as they can have greater control over what is done with the funds. However, many firms start as sole traders and become limited companies once their growth demands it. The sole trader may also be risk averse as they are liable for all the firm's debts. This may also impact upon speed of growth.

Smaller firms tend to grow faster than larger ones, which is not surprising as they are establishing themselves and are developing their markets.

The importance of location seems to vary between countries. In the UK, accessible rural firms grow faster than urban ones, although less accessible rural firms do not grow as rapidly. This contrasts with the US where urban firms grow faster (Storey, 1994). A similar finding emerges from Kenya where urban firms also grow more rapidly than rural (Liedholm, 2002). This may be due to access to resources in developing countries because of poor infrastructure (Mambula, 2003), although it does not account for the US findings. Location is an issue for the use of IS and technology. While the developed world has ready access to telephony, for much of the developing world the supply of resources such as electricity and data communications are erratic and sometimes non-existent. Even in the US, rural firms rely more on the use of telephone and fax than on the Internet for communication with customers (Premkumar and Roberts, 1999). In Canada, Internet connections through broadband have been instigated by rural communities with government support. The impact on these communities is that business is now relocating to more rural areas. However, in the UK, investment in broadband has been directed at business. Many small firms have yet to be convinced of the business benefits. This is particularly true of those firms in rural locations.

Case study 2.4

Garden Pottery is located in delightful countryside. They design and make large pots for the garden industry. They sell to garden centers and also individuals directly. The owner wanted to live and work in the same location. The business has grown over the years, but the owner has no plans to relocate. One of the employees has developed a simple brochureware web site for the firm and has e-mails sent to his home. The firm does not see the web site as contributing to their marketing and sales in any way. They believe their customers prefer brochures and also their exhibits at flower shows.

■ Growing the business

As discussed, new firms grow faster than well-established ones. Key to this growth is the ability to evolve and develop. Managerial skills become more important to the firm as there needs to be greater attention paid to finance, marketing and management staff (Burns, 2001). The organizational structure will need to be more formal, although most owners attempt to try to keep it from becoming bureaucratic. The ability to respond to changing circumstances to manage growth becomes an important role for the owner.

SME growth can be modelled through stages of development (Scott and Bruce, 1987; Churchill and Lewis, 1983). Change may be in response to a crisis, after which the SME moves or folds (Scott and Bruce, 1987). However, Churchill and Lewis do acknowledge that some SMEs will decide not to grow and remain at their current stage. This is often because the owner-manager does not wish to relinquish control, which is necessary for growth, as is discussed later.

The hypothesis of stages of growth models is that SMEs grow from small entities that are managed closely by the owner-manager to larger ones where professional managers take over the running. The owner is still key to planning and strategy but the danger is that their management style is still informal and directive, which does not fit with managerialist organizations. Each stage may be precipitated by a management crisis (Table 2.2).

Existence or inception is about staying alive. The firm is working hard to find customers and to deliver orders. The owner is closely involved in each stage of the operation. The organization is relatively simple with staff usually reporting directly to the owner. Strategic direction is lost in short-term management and there is no strategic planning. There will be minimal investment in IS. As the business continues owners find they have to spend more time on administration. They have to focus on profitability to keep the business viable. This leads owners towards the next stage.

Survival focuses more on establishing the customer base and the main products or services. Effort needs to be put into managing cash flow and

Table 2.2: Reasons for changes in stages of growth

Churchill and Lewis stage	Scott and Bruce stage	Precipitating crises
Existence	Inception	Administrative demands; increased demands on time; focus on profitability
Survival	Survival	Managing an expanding customer base; increasing need for better information
Success	Growth	Owner and management roles may diverge; competitive pressure from large firms; more formal systems required
Take-off	Expansion	Owner and management roles separate; finance may be an issue; managing customer requirements may be an issue
Maturity	Maturity	Lack of innovation; owner displaced

increasing revenues. The organization still has the same structure as at start-up, with the owner heavily involved in all decisions. The only monitoring that is done is of cash-flow forecasts; otherwise there is no strategic planning. Information systems are simple; spreadsheets may be used by the owner to monitor costs. The success of the firm at this stage precipitates the move to the next stage as the firm has to invest to manage its expanding customer base. The owner finds it more difficult to manage the growing number of staff. There is a need for better management information to ensure that the firm can monitor the market.

Success or growth is where the firm is well established, with a reasonable customer base. Managers are appointed to support activities such as finance, marketing and operations. Plans are medium term, but focus on operational issues and budgets. At this stage the paths that SMEs take diverge depending upon the owner's attitude to growth. Some firms decide to continue to work within their market niche, maintaining service to their existing customers. Firms in this position need to be able to adapt to maintain their market position; otherwise there is a danger that they fall back to the survival stage. Other firms are set upon the growth path and at this stage strategic planning becomes essential. Owners need to have a vision for future growth which is shared with staff throughout the organization. There is a need for greater control and management to ensure profitability while managing the growth. Information systems are more important to firms to manage the expanding customer base. Databases, spreadsheets accounting systems are common. The growth of the firm precipitates the move to expansion, as the firm requires more formal systems to be in place to manage increasing complexity of business processes and relations with the market. Competitors are likely to be an issue for the growing firm.

Take-off or expansion is a difficult time for many SMEs. The owner is about to try to move the firm to become a larger player in the market. This requires great skills of planning and leadership as well as sufficient financial resources to provide the step change required for expansion. Owners need to be the visionary providing the strategic direction; they need to have a good, reliable management team in place to ensure success. The owner often recognizes the need for IS to improve communication and access to data within the firm. The growth of the firm means that the owner will become more remote from management making it likely that managerial power may well precipitate the move to maturity. Competitive pressures mean that there is a need for a greater external focus on industry requirements that may require a different management style to that of the owner.

Maturity occurs when the firm has grown to sufficient size to be directed by the management team. There is no clear role for the owner in the management of the business. Strategic planning is likely to be well established as a formal, managerial activity. Formal IS to support managerial decision-making are in place. The owner is no longer involved in the business and the danger for the firm is that it may ossify around the existing products and services unless the innovative style of management has been maintained.

Stages of growth models for SMEs have been argued to be problematic, as many SMEs do not pass through "stages". Many SMEs are locked into one stage and never develop (Burns and Harrison, 1996). Other firms may reach a stage and then cease to trade, often precipitated by the crises identified by Scott and Bruce. Additionally, there may be different models of growth such as growth by acquisition that are not catered for by stages models (Storey and Sykes, 1996; Storey, 1994).

The value for this book in looking at stages of growth models for SMEs is not in assuming that all SMEs follow any particular path, it is clear that many prefer to stay small, but in seeking to address the changes that are needed in the organization and its structure if it is to grow. This has considerable relevance where the role of management IS and their relevance to SMEs is being considered. As indicated, it is likely that there will be different requirements for management information at different stages of growth and understanding the underlying rationale of growth is helpful.

▪ Organizing and managing SMEs

As the previous section demonstrated, SMEs have different management and organizational requirements at different stages of their growth. SMEs move from relatively unstructured organizations at start-up led by an owner-manager to more formal structures as the firm grows. Initially all staff report to the owner in what Burns (2001) describers as a "spider's web". As the firm grows and moves into survival mode more staff are employed. The organizational structure of SMEs still tends to be fairly flat. There may be a small management team but only as the SME grows. While a management or supervisory structure is in place, staff often circumvent it and refer decisions directly to the owner. The owner is still dominant in the hierarchy. This causes some difficulties and resentment as the owner cannot delegate. Given that the owner knows what they are trying to do and may have difficulty in expressing it to staff, there is a tendency for the management style to be fairly autocratic. Decisions styles tend to be reactive, as owners often do not have the relevant information (Bianchi, 2002).

Once the firm grows to about 12 employees there is a need to change the structure to become more formal. The structure chosen depends upon the nature of the business. Hierarchical structures tend to suit firms that deliver standard products or services. The value of a hierarchy is that it gives managers the assurance that they have the authority to manage. Consultancy firms often take a more project-based approach to organization, with teams reforming to undertake different activities based on individuals' expertise. The structure also varies according to the industry. For example, in hi-tech SMEs the organizational structure is usually organic to take advantage of staff skills and projects (Warren and Hutchinson, 2000). There may still be a hierarchy, but it is likely to be flatter and sufficient to manage the project teams.

Case study 2.5

Electrical Accreditation Agency provides manufacturers with safety approval for appliances. The accreditation services are organized by individual engineers who develop relationships with their customer base. A key part of their activity is co-ordinating with testing laboratories. There is a small management team that co-ordinates finance, marketing, sales and management reporting. Engineers manage their own time and activities. While the structure works well, the firm has now realized that there is a need to co-ordinate information to enable marketing, in particular, to be more effective.

As SMEs grow, owners have to delegate activities to professional managers. The more successful SMEs are those where owners allow managers to take decisions without interference, preferring to consider the overall business strategy. The size and knowledge of the management team is a determining factor in preventing failure. First, a larger team is likely to be less dependent upon the knowledge of one individual and second, there will be a better mix of skills, which is important for business growth. Formal information flows are of limited value to the SME primarily because of the lack of middle management prevalent in large organizations. Hence, there are few barriers to the flow of information in SMEs. However, information flows may not work effectively, particularly in the early stages of a business where the hierarchy is circumvented (Storey and Cressy, 1995).

At start-up the only management skills reside in the owner. The owner may be either technically strong, which occurs when owners want the opportunity to develop a product or service where they are the innovator. Alternatively, they may be managerially strong, which occurs when owners have started a business based on their belief they can provide a service better than the firm for which they originally worked (Hadjimanoulis, 2000; Burns and Harrison, 1996).

As the business grows it becomes necessary for managers to be employed. Usually the first manager is likely to be in finance, with production and sales following on closely. As the SME grows the management skills required increase. There is a need to be able to respond to the increasing divisionalization of the firm and the increasing distance between the owner and the firm. Good managerial skills are able to influence performance (Barth, 2003).

Owners may not however have strong IT skills unless it is their particular area of expertise, which may account for the reluctance to use IS to support the business. Staff in SMEs tend to be generalists rather than specialists. This is often because at start-up it is expected that everyone will contribute to ensuring business survival. The SME cannot readily bear the cost of specialist staff. Staff skills are usually related closely to the job they do, and many do not have IT skills.

Management training is not often undertaken by SMEs. Management skills are usually weak, although the best SMEs recognize the value of workforce training (Liedholm, 2002; Mambula, 2002).

Systems implications in managing SMEs

Different organizational structures demand different management IS. Hierarchies tend to focus on control and thus IS tend to reflect this with exception reporting and analysis being the norm. Matrix-based organizations are often knowledge-based. Knowledge is the main currency of the firm. It is important to store the knowledge in such a way that it is accessible to all that need it in the organization. Information systems need to be accessible, open and to promote analysis of formal and informal information.

Business systems in SMEs tend to be simple. Complexity does not arise until SMEs start to become larger and there is a need to organize into business units. As shown in Chapter 3, the IS are usually simple, with mainly operational systems. As SMEs grow there is investment in operational management systems such as production, sales and some financial monitoring (Roper, 1999; Scott and Bruce, 1987; Churchill and Lewis, 1983). Small firms are dependent upon external information for their on-going development. Much of this information is acquired informally through the development of personal relationships and involvement in professional associations. This reflects the informal nature of management within the SME and may make the acquisition of formal IS less valued (Roper, 1999).

■ Conclusions

This chapter defines SMEs and the characteristics of growth firms that require a combination of the entrepreneur, strategy and the firm. The influences of the market, location, the personal characteristics of the owner, independence, flexibility and innovation are highlighted as important for the successful SME.

Growth is shown to be the objective of many SMEs, although it may not always be planned. A number of precipitating cries are identified that make the SME change its business practices. As SMEs grow the owner's role changes from being at the center of a spider's web where they make all the decisions to one of guiding the strategic direction of the firm. As the firm grows functional managers are appointed and systems become more formal. While recognizing the limitations of stages models in analysing SME growth, the chapter demonstrates their value in helping to understand the changes in management and administrative styles that lead to different systems requirements. The competitive position of many SMEs is outlined which demonstrates the precariousness of their position. However, the flexibility and innovativeness of the sector may go some way to mitigate this.

Chapter 3 investigates the role of IS in managing the SME in more detail. It considers issues of IS strategy, adoption and the value of management IS.

3 Information and IS in SMEs

■ Introduction

Information is a strategic resource that both measures business success and also provides opportunities for diversification. Small- and medium-sized enterprises are part of the information society and need to access and use information strategically if they are going to compete effectively. Information systems provide the means to collect, sort, analyse and query data to support this process. This chapter presents the main ideas on the role of management IS and their role in supporting business. The chapter does not consider production technologies as these are likely to be industry specific. Indeed, given the operational focus of most SMEs it is likely that investment in production technologies will be managed effectively.

The concern in this chapter is that while SMEs invest wisely in production technologies, they often only invest in a limited way in IS to manage the business. While this is not an issue when SMEs start up, as they grow it becomes more difficult to manage the business to ensure profitability. As demonstrated in Chapter 2, it is clear that the relationship with customers is critical to growing SMEs. Not understanding the strengths and weaknesses of the relationship can potentially be critical for SMEs, hence the need for better management IS.

The key difficulty for SMEs is that their strategic horizon tends to be short. This means that they have little interest in information that provides the input for longer-term strategic thinking. However, the majority are being pulled into the information age by their customers. Given that SMEs' customers are focusing more on the value and use of information it is vital that SMEs take an interest in their investment in IS. Hence, IS strategy and planning are important for all SMEs, but particularly those that are growth minded. This issue is discussed briefly here and expanded in Part 2.

The chapter first considers the role and nature of information as it is used within this book. It then defines management IS and the role of strategy. The benefits of strategic alignment in gaining value from IS are outlined. The next part of the chapter moves on to specifically address management IS issues for SMEs. IS strategy, sourcing and the introduction of management IS are discussed.

■ Nature, role and value of information

Data, information, knowledge, are all terms that are bandied about with little clarity. There have been many attempts to define these terms. For example, data are the building blocks: the quanta of the information world. Examples are names, addresses, order quantities, employee details, etc. Data is a way of codifying basic facts about a situation or person. Data tends to be formal. SMEs vary considerably in their approach to collecting data. All SMEs have some requirement to keep accounts. This may range from basic book-keeping to cash-flow analysis. Some will hold the data on computer systems, yet others will have it in written form. As SMEs grow and systems become more formal data requirements become greater. Customers begin to demand evidence of order progress, for example. It is likely that data becomes more complex and demanding as an SME grows, not only to satisfy external demands but also to ensure the smooth running of the firm. As functional managers are appointed they will require data to manage and control the various business activities.

Information requires data to be put into a situational context for it to become meaningful (Galliers, 1987). There needs to be some purpose in the use of data for it to be categorized as information. The quality of data is critical to ensure that the derived information is accurate as it is only with accurate information that effective decisions can be made. SMEs use of information varies. As discussed later in this chapter, the use of management IS is variable. However, the value of having information about the financial health of the firm is immense. Knowing which customers are contributing to profitability provides a basis for targeting sales effort. Managing inventory so that production is not held up is another use of management information that can help the SME. However, few SMEs have such systems tending to rely on spreadsheets. Information is useful in managing the operation of the firm to ensure that it is working efficiently. However, there are other benefits to be had as it is possible to use more complex IS to analyse data and provide answers to queries about the firm. Senior managers might want to review the product profile to determine issues, such as location, quantity and type of goods sold. The capacity to use data to monitor the current business strategy should not be underestimated; this is discussed in more detail in Chapter 7.

So, what is knowledge? If information is data plus context, knowledge is information plus experience. Human experience is essential if use is to be made of information. Knowledge management systems, such as "Lotus Notes", have been developed to capture unstructured information. For example, this can include a note about a customer's requirement for delivery that may be outside the norm. For consultants, knowledge management systems allow them to record details of discussions with clients that might be useful in the future. The system is accessible to other staff in the firm who will be the future contacts for the customer or client.

The information on the system provides a way for them to utilize the knowledge already acquired. Knowledge management systems are not only the prerequisite of large firms, as shown later, but knowledge-based SMEs can also benefit.

Case study 3.1

Mobile Phone Surveyors is a small firm of six surveyors started by the owner in 1986. He introduced a knowledge management system, Lotus Notes, to capture the knowledge that the surveyors gained about the different sites for mobile phone masts. This included information about environmental, local and political issues that affected the decision-making process. The objective was to reduce the time spent in redoing work as well as providing a Knowledge Base of potential sites.

To use knowledge, the strategic role of information needs to be understood. It is always useful to ask owners: how do you know you are successful? This question can be broken down through looking at critical success factors, those aspects of the business that must be achieved for the business to be considered to be achieving its goals. For many SMEs, as discussed later, this is translated into financial goals. However, wider objectives – particularly to do with customer satisfaction – the effectiveness of business processes, and innovation all contribute to the financial goals (Heskett *et al.*, 1994). Critical success factors can be broken down into performance measures that provide detailed targets. Chapter 8 demonstrates the use of critical success measures in determining IS. The basic building block that is required to measure performance is information. Deciding what data needs to be collected to measure business success is an important role for owners. Figure 3.1 demonstrates the connection between these components.

For information to be useful it needs to be grouped together in a meaningful way. The next section discusses the role of management IS.

■ Importance of management IS

Today, most firms cannot survive without using IS. Information systems are the programs that provide the basis for the capture and dissemination of data throughout an organization. They are enabled by IT. In some instances IT provides new opportunities to develop innovative support systems as with the Internet and World Wide Web. As IS and technology becomes more complex it is important for organizations to manage and control their effectiveness through policies on standards, privacy and data protection. All of these aspects are inter-related. This is demonstrated usefully by Earl (1989) (Figure 3.2).

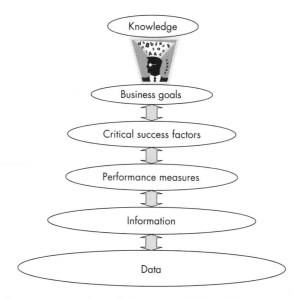

Figure 3.1: The relationship between data, information, knowledge and business goals.

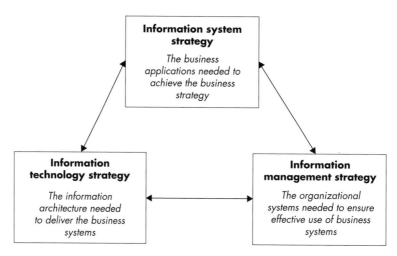

Figure 3.2: Inter-relationship of systems, technology and information management. (*Source*: adapted from Earl, 1989.)

Growth-minded SMEs need to reflect upon their management IS use to consider whether it is adequate to support their growth. As Chapter 1 indicated, many SMEs do not plan their systems to match their growth, with formal systems only appearing once managerial organizational structures are in place.

However, the IS literature stresses the value to organizations of IS that enable the business to be managed effectively. Several stages of development of management information have occurred since the 1970s. First, the focus was on efficiency, primarily through the introduction of accounting systems. Second, management IS provided managers with information to monitor and control the business; latterly, information for competitiveness is seen as imperative to gain competitive advantage. While competitiveness is not achieved through technology alone as it is relatively easy to copy systems and technology, the alignment of technology with business strategy and its use may allow competitive advantage to be achieved. Though the focus today is more on the opportunity for strategic advantage, it is essential that the core systems, those that contribute to efficiency and effectiveness, provide quality data as all other systems build on from these.

Case study 3.2

Wooden Pallet Manufacturer is a family-owned firm that makes wooden pallets primarily for the automotive industry. Planning to retire, the owners set up a new management team headed up by the son of one of the founders. Recognizing that this is a highly competitive market the new CEO started to develop a business strategy that focused on high value-adding products to the top end of the market, relying on superior service to remain competitive. To achieve this, the firm became more formal and employed more managers; a matrix management structure was employed. It also recognized that staff would need to be more highly skilled. At the same time the new CEO recognized the need to have a computerized management IS to manage the operation. The firm appointed a consultant to oversee the analysis and development of the system. The decision was taken to use Microsoft packages as they were not too expensive and also systems support was readily available.

There are many different IS from the simplest accounting systems to complex executive IS. Table 3.1 provides a taxonomy of systems.

There is often debate over whether systems provide tactical or strategic advantage. This depends upon their use and impact within individual organizations (Ward and Peppard, 2002). Figure 3.3 provides a perspective on systems as they might be used in an organization.

Support systems are those that improve efficiency, such as e-mail and word processing. They do not generally contribute to business competitiveness. Key operational systems are those that are essential for the effective production of the goods or service that the organization makes. Examples here include enterprise resource planning (ERP), materials requirements planning (MRP) and Extranets. Strategic applications contribute to competitiveness, for example customer relationship management (CRM), while high potential systems are often employed experimentally to identify whether or what part they can play in future competitiveness; for example, e-business and knowledge management systems.

Table 3.1: IS in organizations

Goal	Type of systems	Use of systems
Operational (efficiency)	Accounting	Basic financial information: general ledger, sales, purchases
	Management IS	Exception reporting to management
	E-mail	Internal and external communication
	Word processing	Production of documents
	Order processing	Management of customer orders
	Stock control	Systems to manage inventory
	Intranets	Internal knowledge and communication management using Internet technology
Tactical (effectiveness)	Electronic data interchange (EDI)	EDI is a computerized system that enables electronic transmission of orders and invoices between customers and suppliers
	Decision support systems	Systems that allow the opportunity to interrogate data and ask "what if" questions
	Executive IS	Graphical interface systems that enable senior managers to analyse the achievement of the firm's strategic objectives and undertake trend analysis by using summary data derived from the firm's operational systems
	Financial analysis systems	Cash flow; profit and loss; balance sheet; ability to analyse the firm's operating performance
	Materials requirements planning (MRP)	Identifies inventory requirements for the development of products from an analysis of forecasts and orders
	Materials resource planning (MRP II)	An integrated system for production resource planning that also allows for analysis of all aspects of the business including forecasting, sales, marketing, financial analysis. Has been superceded by ERP systems
	Enterprise planning systems	An integrated system that extends MRP II by incorporating all system and organizational functions required to plan and support manufacturing, finance, distribution/logistics and additional areas, such as engineering and maintenance
Strategic (competitiveness)	Extranets	Closed Internet-based system between trading partners for exchange of data and knowledge
	E-business	An integrated service enabled by web-based technologies to conduct business online along the whole supply chain
	Customer relationship management	System to collate information about customers' requirements and approaches to work from all employees who work with them. The objective is to build a rich and coherent view of the customer that can be used in developing the individual customer relationship
	Knowledge management systems	Captures tacit and explicit information; enables formal and informal knowledge to be shared and analysed

Strategic	**High potential**
Applications that are critical to the achievement of business strategic objectives both now and in the future	Applications that may be important to the firm in achieving its future business strategy
Applications that the firm requires to manage its day-to-day business operation	Applications essential for efficiency and to ensure the effective working of the firm
Key operational	**Support**

Figure 3.3: Applications portfolio analysis. (*Source*: adapted from Ward and Peppard, 2004.)

The introduction of IS is not itself enough to change or develop organizations. There needs to be alignment between the business strategy, technology, organizational structure, management processes and the roles and skills of people in the organization. These relationships are described by Scott Morton (1991) (Figure 3.4). The traditional approach that firms take is to determine their business strategy. They then design the organizational structure to support the business strategy. Management processes, IS and the appropriate people are brought together to support the strategy. The traditional view is that strategy drives structure which drives management processes (Yetton, 1997). In Chapter 11 strategic alignment paths for SMEs are explored to determine whether they follow this traditional route.

The model in Figure 3.4 provides the basis for considering the issues that a firm needs to address when planning its IS investments. The business strategy sets the overall direction for the firm. IS can play two roles here. First, IS can provide the information so that the business knows it is successful. Second, IS may provide an alternative route for

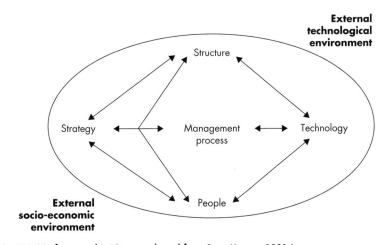

Figure 3.4: MIT '90s framework'. (*Source*: adapted from Scott Morton, 1991.)

Table 3.2: Description of MIT '90s issues

Strategic alignment issue	Questions to be answered
People	Do individuals have the skills to take advantage of IS? Is management investing in staff development?
Management processes	Do management processes support organizational learning, or is the focus on control?
Technology	How versatile is the existing technology and what opportunities are there to introduce new technologies? Is the impact of new technology on work *designed* or *discovered*?
Organizational structure	Do the organizational structures enable or inhibit the introduction of IS?
Strategy	What is the business trying to achieve and what part can IS play?

the delivery of the product or service. Different organizational structures may require different IS set-ups. A new strategy may require different access to information for managers. The management processes need to be considered in deciding on appropriate IS. For example, in a production environment there is likely to be an emphasis on control to monitor inventory and work in progress to ensure best use of resources. Technology and systems change rapidly. The firm needs to review the existing technologies to ensure that they are able to achieve the new targets set by the business strategy. Finally, there is a need to ensure that all staff have the skills to succeed in the new strategic environment. Table 3.2 outlines questions that firms can usefully ask if they are to successfully align their business strategy.

Acknowledgement of the relationships between strategy, structure, management, systems and people enables an organizational perspective on the role of IS to be taken. This ultimately leads to competitive advantage as firms will both introduce and react to IS differently.

Case study 3.3

Flower and Samios is a firm of Australian architects. In the 1980s, they were reasonably successful but lost a major contract which they expected to win. The successful firm used computer-aided design (CAD) processes in their winning bid.

Flower and Samios could see the writing on the wall. They bought the latest software and hardware for architecture design and embarked on a steep learning curve, influenced by their assessment of a need to review their strategic direction to accommodate the emerging role of IS and IT in their industry. All their architects were required to become proficient in the use of IS. All new employees had to be able to use the systems from day one.

Business value from IS dramatically increased as architects could reuse components from other designs. An electronic library was gradually built up which improved efficiency. Designs were shared through a local area network.

Flower and Samios has been successful in integrating IS into its business strategy and has achieved recognition as one of the leaders in its field.

(Adapted from Yetton *et al.*, 1994).

Introducing IS requires planning. The development of an IS strategy that recognizes the strategic objectives of the business, and both reacts and suggests innovative solutions, is recognized in the literature as essential to ensuring competitiveness (Earl, 1996a; Galliers, 1991).

The next section reviews IS issues as they affect SMEs. Strategic IS planning and the problems for SMEs are discussed first. The role of the owner in the SME is as critical to IS adoption as other decisions, this is discussed next. The issues of IS sourcing and adoption are then introduced. This is followed by discussion on the value of management IS to SMEs.

■ IS strategy and planning in SMEs

Few SMEs plan for the systems they purchase and most planning is done for operational systems (Hagmann and McCahon, 1993). That management and strategic IS are purchased, but not planned, is a concern. The main focus of IS planning is to improve the efficiency of operations (particularly management support, office automation and forecasting) and there is little concern with competitiveness. However, there is evidence that SMEs lose market share if they do not use IT (Igbaria *et al.*, 1998). The short-term perspective of many SMEs due to external pressures may limit their IS planning (Riemenschneider *et al.*, 2003).

Information systems planning (ISP) provides the enabling mechanism for strategic alignment by identifying the IS and information architecture required to support the business strategy. Thus, ISP can directly affect the competitiveness of an organization. ISP and strategy is not something that is commonly carried out by SMEs, even though competitiveness may be a concern (Hagmann and McCahon, 1993). The speed of technology innovation makes it essential for SMEs to plan their IS to maintain competitiveness (Blili and Raymond, 1993). There is little evidence that ISP is carried out at all, even when decisions to purchase new technologies are made (Hagmann and McCahon, 1993). Where planning is carried out the focus is on systems to improve productivity. Far less planning is undertaken for systems that help manage the business (Hagmann and McCahon, 1993). Any planning tends to take a short-term perspective and is based on identifying a particular system (Thong, 2001). However, where IS planning is undertaken there are fewer systems problems and greater satisfaction with IS (Proudlock *et al.*, 1998). Competitiveness is not seen as a criterion for ISP. This may be a function of the limited knowledge of owners and the lack of IS departments and expertise that is common in SMEs. However, owners in SMEs do need to plan as technology becomes more integrated with the business processes. In particular, there is a need to plan to manage business growth. There is also, frequently, no link between levels of computerization and IS planning. In other words, systems are adopted in an *ad hoc* fashion as determined by the SME owner (Hagmann and McCahon, 1993; Cragg and King, 1992a).

While, as Chapter 2 shows, there is some debate over the usefulness of a "stages of growth" theory for SMEs, the contention that successful growth needs to be planned for is incontrovertible. Indeed, successful small businesses will have systems in place in advance of their next stage of growth (Churchill and Lewis, 1983). As SMEs become more mature, planning is increasingly important as more formal business systems are likely to be required (Reid, 1999). User satisfaction with IS is greater when ISP is carried out (Thong, 2001). The process that SMEs use needs to be "more simple, robust and flexible" (Blili and Raymond, 1993) than those used by large corporations. Part 2 discusses IS planning and strategy in more detail and develops an organizational approach that satisfies these criteria.

Case study 3.4

Holiday Coach Co is a regional coach holiday supplier. It is a family-owned business. As business improved it outgrew the high street premises that it occupied. The CEO decided it was time to build a new office building that would integrate the whole firm. Previously, all support, scheduling and maintenance of coaches had been carried out on another site where the offices were in temporary buildings. The sales office and all administration were in a converted house, where the family had once lived. The CEO recognized that IS were playing an increasing role in the business. Further growth was planned. Hence, the firm invested in a computer network that was installed as part of the new built. The network has sufficient capacity to support the future plans to expand into providing a more comprehensive travel service.

■ Owner's role in introducing IS

Typically, the interest, knowledge and enthusiasm of owners drive IS adoption (Thong, 2001; Premkumar and Roberts, 1999; Cragg and King, 1993). The SME owner is the prime information user and the key decision-maker, thus they are in the best position to drive IS adoption (Thong, 2001; Thong *et al.*, 1997). Among the reasons for this is that they are more likely to use computers than their staff (Igbaria *et al.*, 1998). The SME owner is the only person with the authority and knowledge to identify IS opportunities (Blili and Raymond, 1993). The greater the involvement of the owner with IT adoption decisions, the more successful they will be (Palvia and Palvia, 1999; Fink, 1998; Cragg and King, 1993). Similarly, the more closely SME owners are involved with IS development, the more likely it will be successful (Caldeira and Ward, 2002; Martin, 1989).

For most SMEs, their failure to plan the introduction and exploitation of new technology is due to management limitations. These include management having insufficient time to spend on future business developments and management teams having little experience, skill or interest in exploiting technology (Rothwell and Beesley, 1989). The age and experience of the owner is frequently the most important factor in decisions in IS-based success, with younger owners tending to value technology-based systems more than older ones. More highly educated users are more likely to use IT and also to develop the skills of the workforce (Palvia and Palvia, 1999). Conversely, lack of knowledge among owners about the value of IT limits the development of it within the SME (Cragg and King, 1992b). Due to their limited financial resources, small businesses spend proportionally less than large businesses on IS (Thong, 2001; Foong, 1999; Premkumar and Roberts, 1999). Given these limitations it is unsurprising that few SMEs have an in-house IS resource, preferring to outsource their IS provision.

■ Sourcing IT

Most SMEs do not have an IS department. They tend to employ generalists rather than specialists (Thong, 2001). Thus, they often look outside the firm for IS development. This brings them into contact with vendors and consultants. Many SME owners are unsure about the quality of advice they receive (Igbaria *et al.*, 1998). The role of consultants is not always understood by SMEs and owners do not often know how to select a good one (Yap *et al.*, 1992). However, where external consultants and vendors are experienced with particular products and services relevant to SMEs there is a higher rate of success with IS adoption as they "lower the knowledge barriers" (Thong, 2001) and the SME owner's involvement is less important (Thong *et al.*, 1997). Additionally, where the owner works closely with a consultant there is likely to be greater success (Thong, 2001; Fink, 1998).

This nervousness about consultants and vendors, combined with the lack of IS strategy, leads many SME owners to look closer to home in developing their systems. It is not uncommon for SMEs to use relatives or friends to develop systems (it is sometimes commented that the average age of SMEs' IS experts is 13!). In some cases, systems are developed by sole-owner IT firms. This is often done to reduce costs, but may also be seen as an investment opportunity by the SME (Caldeira and Ward, 2002; Fuller, 1996). Outsourcing IS development to another SME that has the same types of problems is an unlikely way to reduce risk.

The owner or finance director are the two people in SMEs who usually identify IS sources. There are a number of factors that influence the decision to invest in IS. One of the primary aspects is the need for systems support. Local support is preferred, hence the importance of local IT firms to the SME sector. An additional issue for many SMEs is that software is often designed with larger firms in mind. This is certainly the case with ERP systems, for example. Even when ERP providers develop a reduced-scale system it is often too expensive and complex for smaller SMEs. Thus, SMEs often prefer to commission bespoke software from a local supplier.

◼ IS adoption issues

It is likely that the greatest success in IS adoption arises through a combination of planning and owner involvement (Fuller, 1996). Where IS projects are led by a senior manager other than the owner, most often the finance director, then IS adoption tends to be less successful (Caldeira and Ward, 2002). However, when communication breaks down or planning is not undertaken, then there is less likelihood of success (Fuller, 1996). One of the problems for SMEs is that they often underestimate the effort and time required to implement IT (Riemenschneider et al., 2003). IS adoption is often driven by perceived benefits to the SME, particularly competitor pressure, and this leads to minimal consideration of issues, such as security, time and maintenance, when making adoption decisions (Riemenschneider et al., 2003). The greater the knowledge of IT amongst users and management, the more likely IS adoption will be successful. Conversely, the lack of IT knowledge severely limits successful IS adoption (Thong, 2001).

Information systems adoption in SME is less likely to be successful when there is limited IT knowledge (particularly on the part of the owner), problems with prior systems developments and limited finance (Proudlock et al., 1998; Cragg and King, 1992a). The lower spend on IS by SMEs makes it difficult to meet objectives; for example, SMEs are less likely to appoint quality IS consultants (Thong, 2001).

Time is a further constraint on SMEs as managers and owners do not spend sufficient time on either IS planning or implementation. If users are involved in implementation this may compensate for the

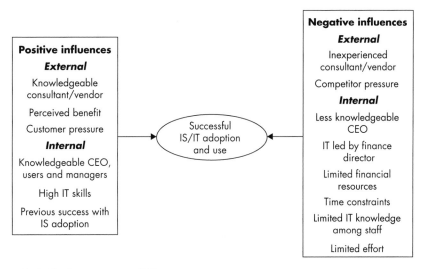

Figure 3.5: IS adoption issues in SMEs.

lower involvement of owners (Thong, 2001). Figure 3.5 summarizes IS adoption issues.

Thus, the SME can successfully implement IS providing the owner appreciates the value of IS, staff have good quality IT skills, and the SME uses a consultant who understands the issues. Customer pressure and previous success with adoption are also positive influences. In general, the obverse of these issues can mean that IS adoption is less successful.

■ Introduction of management IS in SMEs

The introduction of IS into SMEs, like its early introduction into large organizations, tends to be fragmented, based round operational support and transaction processing (Foong, 1999; Blili and Raymond 1993; Martin, 1989). Most SMEs use IS to manage the day-to-day operations; competitor and environmental information is only used when the SME is not doing well (Lybaert, 1998). In contrast, IS for supporting management decisions are less common, most SMEs have word processing and accounting systems, but few, if any have decision support systems (Lybaert, 1998; Martin, 1989). The most valued systems in SMEs are accounting, sales order entry and billing and cash management (Igabria *et al.*, 1998). SMEs tend not to use financial analysis, forecasting or project management tools, instead relying on intuition for decision-making (Thong, 2001). However, in a study of New Zealand SMEs, Igbaria *et al.* (1998) find that financial analysis systems are valued. As other studies find only the use of simple systems, Igbaria *et al.*'s sample may be unusual.

However, management IS appear to impact negatively on performance. Further, firms with more sophisticated IS tend to perform worse than those with more limited systems. This is primarily due to SMEs' limited IS knowledge and skills which precludes them from taking advantage of strategic information (Roper, 1999; Julien and Raymond, 1994).

However, while planned efficiency benefits do not materialize, unplanned benefits from analysis of information do arise. Simple decision support systems, such as spreadsheets, used by SMEs to provide strategic, financial information, leads Naylor and Williams (1994) to suggest that IS is used for "more complex procedures than has previously been reported". Their research highlights that once managers use available information to consider strategic issues, benefits accrue and SMEs are more inclined to invest further in IS. However, SMEs tend not to upgrade their systems often, preferring to repair existing systems (Cragg, 1992).

A number of recent start-up SMEs owe their existence to IS and technology. These firms are innovative and invest in IS to provide products and services that are only possible because of technological advances. IS investment for these firms is a priority, reflected in higher initial capital investments. However, there is evidence that investment in IS declines over time for these SMEs, as resources become scarce once the business is up and running (Rothwell and Beesley, 1989).

Investment by SMEs in Internet technologies appears to follow a similar path to their other IS investments. Many SMEs use e-mail to contact some customers (Premkumar and Roberts, 1999). However, limited customer use still inhibits wholesale e-mail adoption for customer communication (Sillence et al., 1998). While some SMEs are developing web sites, few have them linked to their transaction processing systems (Poon and Swatman, 1999). There are limited direct benefits from Internet use for SMEs, although indirect benefits, such as improving communications efficiency, presenting a modern image, access to web-based information and identifying new business opportunities, are reasons given for developing such systems (Poon and Swatman, 2000). Not surprisingly, SMEs generally are as yet unwilling to develop e-commerce systems or to change current business models (Keindl, 2000).

IT-based competitive advantage is typically accidental, not planned. SMEs' propensity to invest in IS incrementally, rather than in a planned fashion, is a problem (Hashmi and Cuddy, 1990). While this is typically an inhibitor to the effective use of IS, where incremental investment is tied in with organizational learning, it can be a means of increasing competitiveness (Yetton et al., 1994).

■ Conclusions on IS investment in SMEs

Overall, the evidence depicts limited use of management IS in SMEs (Premkumar and Roberts, 1999). Consistent with this, IS provide few benefits to SMEs in terms of performance (Cragg and King, 1992b).

Indeed, firms with more sophisticated IS tend to perform worse than those with more limited systems. This is primarily due to an SMEs' limited IS knowledge and skills, precluding them from taking advantage of the strategic information available from the more sophisticated systems in which they have invested. In manufacturing and trading firms, SMEs that make strategic IS investments do not obtain strategic benefits unless IS is seen as integral to business strategy (Lesjak and Lynn, 2000; King *et al.*, 2000). Finally, firms that adopt a low-cost strategy are less likely to use IS strategically (Lesjak and Lynn, 2000).

Thus, current research into IS use in SMEs gives mixed messages. On one hand, many SMEs have transaction processing systems used in quite sophisticated ways that are oriented towards strategic management information. On the other, investment in management IS does not bring the anticipated benefits, although unplanned benefits may be realized. This is similar to findings of Farbey *et al.*'s (1992) for large organizations.

The introduction of IS into SMEs, like the early introduction into large firms, has tended to be fragmented, based around operational support and transaction processing (Foong, 1999; Blili and Raymond, 1993). Typically, the interest and enthusiasm of owners drive IS adoption (Premkumar and Roberts, 1999). Not surprisingly, adoption is often not planned strategically. For example, small manufacturing businesses invest in systems to improve production processing without integrating the order processing system or developing stock control systems. Also, while some SMEs are developing web sites, few have them linked to their transaction processing systems (Poon and Swatman, 1999).

In such businesses, IT-based competitive advantage is typically accidental, not planned. SMEs' propensity to invest in IS incrementally, rather than in a planned fashion, is a problem (Hashmi and Cuddy, 1990). While this is typically an inhibitor to the effective use of IS, where incremental investment is tied in with organizational learning, it can be a means of increasing competitiveness (Yetton *et al.*, 1994).

Considering the above findings, IS investment in SMEs is successful when it takes one of two forms. It is either a low-cost investment to provide efficiency savings or the enabling of a value-added strategy. The former is taken by those SMEs for which IS are not central to their business and where the owners' experience of IS is limited. In this case, IS are likely to be focused on transaction processing systems. The latter is either driven by necessity, as in the case of manufacturing, or due to innovative owners who are looking for business growth. IS investment is then likely to be more innovative with a greater emphasis on management information.

4 Flexibility in IS

Introduction

"Information technology offers exciting opportunities to revitalize customer service by moving a firm and its product offerings closer to the customer, thereby recapturing the conditions of intimacy and flexibility that characterized earlier eras" (Ives and Mason, 1990: p. 67). As discussed in Chapter 2, the small- and medium-sized enterprises are often depicted as flexible enterprises, while IS and IT are held to be keys to the future, flexible organization. Since both SMEs and IS are providers of flexibility, the expectation might be that IS would enhance the flexibility of SMEs; particularly as they invest more in technology as computing costs decline. Indeed, SMEs' *"speed of adoption of new technology (e.g. new software system) is often greater ... [than that] ... required in large firms"* (Storey and Cressy, 1995).

This chapter investigates whether SMEs are, in fact, the flexible beasts as portrayed, whether IS are universal providers of flexibility and if the development of IS capabilities in SMEs inhibit or enhance flexibility. This discussion is illustrated by the experiences of four case firms.

Flexibility issues

Flexibility is a much-discussed issue (Genus and Dickson, 1995). Flexibility is the ability to change direction rapidly or deviate from a predetermined course of action (Eardley *et al.*, 1997) – or the *"ability to do something other than that which was originally intended"* (Evans, 1991). Indeed, as Evans states, strategic flexibility is a critical success factor when most elements of an organization's environment and systems are in a state of continuous flux. Flexibility may be characterized as a strategic response to the unseen (Eppink, 1978). There is an inherent paradox in the concept of flexibility – it must be combined with stability (Volberda, 1996). On one hand, organizations need to be able to adapt quickly, while on the other, they can only obtain efficiency from stable processes.

Under the "hypercompetition" that characterizes the present environment, firms will thrive only if they have adaptive capabilities (Volberda, 1996). More specifically, organizations desire flexibility since it offers three major advantages (Avison *et al.*, 1995). First, if the environment is turbulent, the ability to respond flexibly to forced change may be necessary for basic survival. Second, flexibility may allow the organization to achieve superior levels of internal efficiency through such activities as business process re-engineering (Hammer, 1990), though the truly flexible organization would not seem to require process re-engineering. Third, flexibility of response may give competitive advantage through its ability to develop new performance-enhancing features and to exploit first-mover advantages (Van de Ven, 1986; Porter and Millar, 1985). To these can be added the issue of slack resources that are a key issue in promoting innovation. In small firms with little slack, innovation may be stifled. There is lack of clarity as to the meaning of flexibility (Genus, 1995), though its essence can be derived from synonyms such as robustness, which refers to a system's ability to absorb or withstand the impacts of unpredicted events (Rosenhead et al., 1986) and versatility, the capability to respond to a range of future events or to modify behaviour quickly (Bonder, 1976).

The concern in this chapter is the process of flexibility attainment, especially via IS. The above discussion suggests that there are two aspects to strategic flexibility: temporal and intentional. The temporal aspect may be *ex ante* – preparing in advance for an unpredictable future change – or *ex post* – making adjustments after an event has occurred. Likewise, the intentional aspect may be offensive or defensive. Evans uses these to develop a framework of four manoeuvres, termed as pre-emptive, protective, corrective and exploitive (Figure 4.1).

A pre-emptive manoeuvre allows a firm to take advantage of possible future events and is most useful where the future is unpredictable and where the exploitation of innovation is a tool of competition (Eardley et al.,

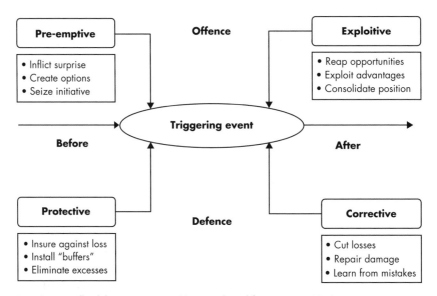

Figure 4.1: Strategic flexibility manouevres. (*Source*: adapted from Evans, 1991.)

1997). The actions of firms which create a domain into which new products, distribution channels or business methods can be introduced as "enframing" (Heidegger, 1977), implying that an options' framework is set up, from which a future choice can be made. A robust strategy is one that creates and leaves open options, that is, it has the maximum number of reachable outcomes and will absorb changing circumstances and cater for objectives not being fully formulated. Pre-emptive manoeuvres imply some future tactical actions (Eardley *et al.*, 1997). Conversely, whereas pre-emptive tactics are put into effect before an unforeseen trigger, exploitive tactics are deployed after the event. Exploitive manoeuvres capitalize on the opportunities created by chance or pre-emptive tactics. A firm's ability to use IS or IT to exploit these depends on its ability to identify situations appropriate to its IT skills and to develop the right IS quickly.

Protective manoeuvres applied before unpredictable events are contingencies that attempt to limit the damage caused by an unknown future. Insurance against an unsuccessful strategy is obtained by having a choice of options available. Evans includes the installation of buffers, such as large inventories, in this category. It is significant that applications of IT, such as just-in-time (JIT) systems aim to supplant these by improved use of information. A further protection is barriers to entry. There are numerous, mostly unsuccessful, examples of the use of IT and IS as a barrier to deter potential rivals from entering a market (for instance, ASAP from American Hospital Supply and CMA from Merrill Lynch). Due to the nature of technology, these barriers are usually temporary: the major problem with using IT for competitive advantage is that it is easily transferable (Cragg and Finlay, 1991). Lastly, corrective manoeuvres, such as survival manoeuvres to prevent more damage, are used when other tactics fail.

Flexibility advantages (survival, internal process alignment and competitive advantage) can be modelled against the four manoeuvres of flexibility (pre-emptive, exploitive, protective and corrective) (Figure 4.2).

This suggests that organizations take pre-emptive action to gain competitive advantage or use business process redesign for internal process alignment, which makes them more flexible and able to respond to opportunities in the market. Exploitive actions are linked to competitive advantage since they are about seizing opportunities as they are identified. Protective actions are taken to survive in a changing market and may also be used as a means of improving effectiveness within the organization. Corrective actions are associated with survival. The contention is that IS can be used to give flexibility in large firms using the four manoeuvres but their applicability in SMEs remain unexplored. This chapter begins that exploration, based on analysis of four of the case SMEs.

	Advantages of flexibility		
Manoeuvres for flexibility	Survival	Internal process alignment	Competitive advantage
Pre-emptive		◆	◆
Exploitive			◆
Protective	◆	◆	
Corrective	◆		

Figure 4.2: Manoeuvres to gain advantage from flexibility.

■ SMEs and flexibility

As identified in Chapter 2, one of the main characteristics attributed to SMEs is flexibility. Indeed, their survival is often ascribed to their adaptability and speed of response to environmental change, though environmental change is multi-faceted and responses to some aspects may be easier than to others. Small firms *"are perceived of as being significantly more 'flexible' than large firms"* (Storey and Cressy, 1995). "Dynamism" is used to describe SMEs' approaches to increasing productivity and market differentiation to compete globally. Product differentiation is more critical than IS in competitiveness (Julien *et al.*, 1994).

SMEs have the reputation of being able to respond readily to customers' changing needs. Several reasons are cited for this form of flexibility. First, owners of SMEs have considerable knowledge about their firms' capabilities. The CEO's personal characteristics, personality and decision styles are positively correlated with innovativeness in small firms. The attitude of the CEO influences the effort put into the research and development that is essential for innovation (Lefebvre and Lefebvre, 1992).

Second, SME management structures tend to be flat and there is an absence of bureaucracy since management teams are small and most SMEs' managers work together closely on a day-to-day basis. Flexible manufacturing provides a means of enabling SMEs to provide customers with new and innovative products, that is, to respond flexibly to market demands. Critically, it is the organizational culture which is important for an SME to be seen as flexible, particularly a culture which encourages learning rather than control (Gupta and Cawthorn, 1996). This is supported by Carrie *et al.* (1994) who identify 13 types of industrial situation in which SMEs operate. In a key example of the flexible firm, they indicate that it is people who provide flexibility rather than complex, advanced manufacturing systems. Third, due to close management involvement there is tight control over production processes. Tight control, though, is a double-edged sword. It might lead to rigidity when coupled with repetitive procedures in a command and control environment (Gupta and Cawthorn, 1996). Finally, SMEs can respond quickly to changes in demand as their production runs tend to be small.

■ Planning for flexibility through IS

Response to rapid change in the environment and in technology requires flexibility in strategic processes supported by flexible infrastructures (Evans, 1991). However, SMEs seldom have formal corporate plans or strategies and are even less likely to have IS or IT strategies (McKiernan and Morris, 1994; Hagmann and McCahon, 1993). "Top executives preferred flexibility. Written plans are more difficult to change". Lederer and Mendelow (1986) demonstrates the disparity between the desire for flexibility on the part of top management in large firms when implementing strategy and the requirement for a precise definition of future plans to be given to IS developers. This poses a problem for the IS planners as they are trying to develop systems to support manoeuvres and structures which may not even exist in any planned way (Eardley et al., 1997). Hence, something of a paradox exists – top management develops strategies that are purposively undefined which change rapidly and unpredictably, while traditional IS developers require stability and predictability.

There is no doubt that the major organizations that are the dominant customers of most SMEs have felt the impact of IT on their business environment. Parsons (1985) concludes that, "*industries using IT in the competitive domain will continue to experience even more strategic consequences*". He continues "*although it may seem obvious that IT applications should be consistent with the business strategy, in too many firms there is a monumental lack of attention given to understanding how IT will influence the firm's competitive position in the industry, or how IT might support a business strategy*". This is especially true of SMEs where there is a lack of strategic planning, limited investment in IT and hence little regard for the interaction between them (Hagman and McCahon, 1993).

Although flexibility is nearly always seen as beneficial, its costs are not well identified (Eardley *et al.*, 1997). Tangible costs involve hardware, software, training, reorganization and on-going costs, while opportunity costs include the trade-off between the attributes necessary to support flexibility and other system characteristics – such as political realities, system complexity, effectiveness and the need for standardisation (Avison *et al.*, 1995). "*This implies that strategic flexibility is a compromise; that optimal achievement of short-term goals should be sacrificed in order to keep open an optimally robust option set. While this makes empirical and pragmatic sense, a really flexible strategy would allow the optimal achievement of both short-term and long-term goals"* (Eardley *et al.*, 1997).

One further route to flexibility might be via outsourcing. This is a popular route for large organizations, though SMEs have always relied on outside sources for much of their IS needs, and while there is evidence that some large organizations do gain from outsourcing, it is not necessarily the route to flexibility (Robertson and Powell, 1997).

■ IS and IT

SMEs can be more innovative than large organizations because they are less bound by bureaucracy and cumbersome organizational systems (Lefebvre and Lefebvre, 1992). Innovation is often driven by information, particularly about the external environment. Use of IT makes small production run easier and, hence, SMEs will be able to be more competitive as they can introduce new manufacturing technologies quickly. These new technologies, it is argued, enable SMEs to be more flexible and better able to respond to customer needs. Quality and variety of products is also seen as being improved by the introduction of new production technologies.

The work of Lefebvre and Lefebvre echoes that of Tofler (1987). Past examples of IS built by large organizations were based on strategies in which the potential for manoeuvre was fixed in the long term and in which economies of scale were important (Eardley *et al.*, 1997). Yet, the trend is towards what Tofler terms demassification. This is a reversal of the trend which large-scale inter-organizational systems (IOS) helped to create. As production runs are getting shorter, the work units that produce them are getting smaller, and firms are becoming more geographically disbursed. This, argues Tofler, is a return to pre-industrial revolution customization. This view encompasses the *"adaptive corporation" – a firm form which is able to "restructure itself into more fluid and flexible forms"* implying flexibility in strategy, infrastructure and vision (Eardley *et al.*, 1997). This view is also valid for SMEs particularly reflecting that the organization structure (Gupta and Cawthorn, 1996) and the style of the owner (Carrie *et al.*, 1994) is paramount in determining flexibility.

Information technology is the key to flexibility in SMEs. Information is an important resource in enabling SMEs to compete more effectively by integrating operational and management IS (Abdullah and Chatwin, 1994). Reductions in the costs of technology and the increasing user-friendliness of software obviate the need for computing expertise that may allow SMEs to be more advanced in their use of IS rather than merely for transaction processing (Naylor and Williams, 1994). However, few SMEs consider the ability of their IS to adapt or evolve to changing circumstances (Hagmann and McCahon, 1993).

One reason for this might be that investment in both management IS and advanced manufacturing techniques in SMEs is characterized by incrementalism. SMEs move to automation by investing in a single area and then later expanding into another. This usually leads to the SME having a number of incompatible systems that are difficult to network. However, because of the high cost of investment already made, the SMEs are unlikely to redevelop their systems (Hashmi and Cuddy, 1990). Generally, SMEs view investments in IS/IT in the same way as they view their production systems – they expect them to last for a considerable time. This supports the contention that SMEs are not particularly flexible as they see themselves continuing in their chosen market. An alternative view of lack of investment in IT might be that SMEs attempt to remain flexible by holding cash rather than becoming committed to a particular system.

The literature on SMEs, IS and flexibility indicates that not all SMEs can have or require a flexible response to their environment. Flexibility in SMEs is enhanced by an organic organization structure and a learning environment, managed by a visionary CEO with knowledge of IT. The opportunities for a flexible response may be more dependent upon these factors than those indicated earlier for large firms. Information systems have far less influence on flexibility. Additionally, SMEs may not have the internal resources to develop flexible IS.

■ Understanding flexibility in SMEs: the cases

This exploratory study addresses the contention that IS in SMEs do not influence flexibility. Four cases are used here to explore these issues. Three are described in detail, while Heath Springs is briefly outlined as this case is discussed at length in Chapter 8.

Case study 4.1

Light Assembly Co. is a family-owned firm that assembles light fittings for sale to major retailers. The firm employs 130 people and has a turnover of £5 million. The firm has a relatively flat management structure with an operations director who runs most of the day-to-day business. Light Assembly has invested in an AS400 minicomputer with networked terminals. The firm has a bespoke MRP system developed by a small computer supplier.

Until recently, a national chain of department stores bought almost the firm's entire output. Apart from the commercial advantage of assured sales into a prestigious segment of the market, Light Assembly also enjoyed the advantage of planning information. Every quarter, the major customer would share its predicted sales data with Light Assembly enabling effective production planning. However, following a major strategic review, the national retailer informed Light Assembly that they intend to foster greater competition among their suppliers and that the firm would, in future, receive a smaller proportion of their business. Thus, Light Assembly has not only been faced with finding new outlets for its products, but also to review its production planning systems. Despite its success in obtaining orders from three other major retail chains, Light Assembly is aware of the need for better inventory control.

In meeting the challenge, Light Assembly adopted two prime strategies. First, it embarked on an internal cultural change process to ensure that the workforce was involved in modifications to work practices. In particular, this included the increased importance of internal information recording and communication systems; these are partially effected through a bespoke MRP system. Second, they sought to develop IT links with all its major customers and now receives order forecasts through three separate EDI systems. The EDI system for their original customer is integrated with the MRP system. However, data from other customers has to be entered manually into an operational database to enable the firm to plan its supplies and production systems. Actual customer orders are received weekly.

However, they still face problems. There is little management information that compares orders with forecasts and with subsequent sales by the customer. This information would help Lighting Manufacturer reduce its inventory exposure.

Case study 4.2

Precision Tool Co. manufactures precision tools for the automotive industry; these are considered to be durable items. Motor manufacturers are their major customers but they also have many small customers. The firm is privately-owned and part of a large group that is regarded as a world leader. It sells as much as 30% of its production to the parent company, although there is no guarantee that this level will continue. Precision Tool Co. sells its products worldwide. Its turnover exceeds £1.6 million.

The firm went through lean times in the 1980s with its workforce being reduced from 60 to 16 in 1984: there are currently 24 employees. The organization is hierarchical and reactive to customer requirements. Its main concern is to manage capacity to fill orders. Production planning is performed manually each week. Precision Tool is concerned about rising stock levels both of inventory and finished goods. Its approach is that once a machine is set up to manufacture a particular precision tool, an optimum batch should be made, regardless of orders.

Precision Tool Co. has an AS400 IBM minicomputer with networked terminals. They purchased an MRP system to manage inventory, order processing, financial systems and, in the future, production planning. The choice of MRP system was determined by the need for a stable system tailored to the SME market. Additionally, local service and support of the system was a key determining factor. The system is modular and the firm is gradually introducing different components. There is some concern about the cost and requirement to upgrade regularly. The MRP system complements existing IS. It is working at full capacity and operatives have to work overtime to complete orders. While formal monthly management meetings are held, most organizational systems are based on face-to-face meetings between managers. Additionally, the finance director and marketing department have standalone PCs. This means that data from the MRP system has to be input manually for both departments to analyse. Analysis is mainly through Excel spreadsheets.

Case study 4.3

Clutch Assembly Co. has grown from a Victorian, family-run business in tube and wire bending. It is now a first-tier supplier to two major automotive manufacturers (i.e. they deal directly with them) and a second-tier firm to five others, through wholesalers. There are 285 employees and turnover is £12 million.

In the late 1980s the firm realized that it was losing competitiveness through creeping inefficiencies and poor management. They were located in several city centre sites, which made it difficult to run the firm efficiently. At this point the firm made two major decisions as a result of an audit report. First, it brought in a finance director and production director; where previously the owner had held these positions. Second, the firm moved to the city outskirts in order to operate at a single site.

The audit report also highlighted the need for better management information, in particular, accounting information, which had previously only been available months after the event. Clutch Assembly Co. also lacked an effective inventory control system. Not only there were pressures to improve internal management IS, but the major automotive manufacturers insisted on a quality IS to provide performance measures that allowed them to assess production and process quality.

The technology used in the firm is an AS400 with dumb terminals. They also have purchased an MRP system. The firm has introduced both accounting and production IS. It has EDI links with one major manufacturer for orders and CAD. However, the firm has introduced these systems in a reactive manner to address individual situations. There was no attempt to develop an ISS to look at the internal integration of systems. The quality

IS is managed by the finance director on a standalone PC. It is spreadsheet-based and is not integrated with production systems.

Case study 4.4

Heath Springs was founded in 1904 to manufacture shirt bands; it later expanded into the manufacture of springs of all kinds. The firm is owned by US-based interests and is now a major supplier of coil springs to the automotive industry. It has three major customers and has an "open book" partnership with one of them: the firms share information pertinent to the contract to ensure the twin objectives of competitive pricing and reasonable profit margins.

It produces springs to order. The customer usually designs the products and the firm provides an estimate of material cost and time requirements. The firm has purchased a number of its rivals and this has led to the introduction of computers to manage the accounts of the larger firm. The CEO has recently purchased an MRP system to help manage a high level of inventory and finished stock. However, production planning is carried out manually with information subsequently being fed into the system. Orders are filled on the basis of machine optimisation (i.e. making the best use of a particular set-up) rather than order priority. There is no integration of the MRP and business processes.

The main focus of the four SMEs is survival in a competitive environment. This manifests itself as "fire-fighting" to deal with operational matters. For all the four case firms, IS were purchased in order to improve the quality of transaction processing, which reflects a deep concern with high levels of inventory. However, a low priority is accorded by them all to the use of IS or IT for management information. While the four firms adopted IT to aid day-to-day production and stock management, none has realized the potential of connecting this data to overall strategic and competitive analysis. For example, the firms are concerned to keep their existing customers but their response is at an operational level by fulfilling orders quickly, rather than assessing the strategic value of their customers. Further, each firm is aware that they will only stay in business through being seen by their customers to have both quality products and processes. However, the link between management information and measurement of quality is not well recognized.

The firms are all closely involved in design of new items for their customers. Yet, they see this as an operational matter rather than being of strategic significance. For example, Precision Tool Co. was in close collaboration with an international car manufacturer to develop a new precision tool. This involved a high degree of innovation and understanding of the customer needs, yet this knowledge is only just beginning to be integrated within the wider strategic perspective of the firm. This typifies a general issue among SMEs: a preoccupation with day-to-day viability partly limits the time available to consider the strategic advantage inherent in production and customer interaction.

IS in the SMEs

All four SMEs have data processing systems that provided them with information about day-to-day operations. The systems were developed incrementally with MRP systems, a recent purchase in all cases: investment being made in automated production systems before considering IS. As is common, the four SMEs have invested in basic systems such as word processing, accounting and stock control but these systems are not integrated. Standalone systems provide an emphasis on efficiency and tangible benefits. However, the impact of the systems is likely to be local, with minimal organizational-wide impact. The risk involved in implementing these systems is slight. In contrast, integrated systems emphasize effectiveness across the whole system, providing considerable organizational impact (Meredith and Hill, 1987). None of the case firms have integrated their systems and are therefore unlikely to achieve the full benefits of those systems.

Material requirements planning systems are seen as the primary approach to better management of operations by all the four SMEs. The key reason given for purchasing an MRP system is to reduce production costs. The process of purchasing these systems has generally taken some months with considerable research being done by a senior manager as the purchase is regarded as a major investment for the long term. In Precision Tool Co., the Finance Director visited a number of exhibitions and conferences to identify suitable MRP systems. Most of his criteria were satisfied (local maintenance, established product) but he found few systems particularly directed at the SME market. He also wanted to purchase established hardware and therefore selected an IBM AS400. The approach the firm took was then to purchase core modules and grow the system, incrementally their knowledge increased. The software provider continues to provide the firm with information on the system's development, but Precision Tool are cautious about changing. They do not generally purchase new versions of software until the previous version is no longer supported.

None of the SMEs used IS to provide management information. When managers required summary data, they tend to extract it from operational reports and re-enter it onto a spreadsheet. The CEO of Heath Springs has developed his own spreadsheet applications to satisfy the quality conditions imposed by major customers. In the same firm the MRP system is not being used to plan production, merely to manage stock. The operations director of Light Assembly Co. estimates that he spends 3 days a month manually extracting data about stock problems from a detailed operational report. Clutch Assembly Co. has also developed a spreadsheet system to report on performance to their major customers. The use of spreadsheets by SMEs to provide strategic financial information suggests that IS are used for *"more complex procedures than has previously been reported"* (Naylor and Williams, 1994). Their research suggests that once managers use the information available to consider strategic issues, benefits accrue and SMEs are more inclined to invest further in IS.

The major interest for the SMEs is to manage their operations more effectively, to minimize wastage and improve stock control. In all the four cases this was the reason given for the purchase of the MRP system. Planning for IS focuses on improving the existing operation with which the senior management are familiar. In firms where IS planning occurs, the main focus is on tactical planning to meet operational requirements; competitiveness is not an issue considered by many SMEs (Hagmann and McCahon, 1993). None of the four case SMEs cite competitiveness as a reason for investing in IS.

Organization of IS in the SMEs

The IS function in SMEs usually reports to the accounting function, in line with the experience of many large firms and those of public sector organizations (Blili and Raymond, 1993). However, there are only limited IS management skills available to plan and organize IS in the case SMEs: none of the SMEs studied have specialist managers with the skills to manage IS. The Finance Director of Precision Tool Co. has responsibility for selecting computer systems, but his major computer skills are in using spreadsheets, the IS skills are provided by the software firm from which they purchased their system. In Heath Springs, the CEO passed the responsibility for IS to the operations manager who had no experience of IS but worked closely with an external consultant to develop appropriate skills.

This is the case where SMEs recognize that they do not have the skills to plan and manage IS. All use external firms to develop or purchase systems with support provided by the software firm as required. In Light Assembly Co. and Heath Springs support is provided by part-time independent consultants. The Heath Springs operations manager has developed an interest in IS and is developing programs to interface with their MRP system. Unfortunately, his lack of formal training is evident in the information management area as there are no security measures against loss of data. Light Assembly Co. has considerable dependency upon the bespoke system they use that was developed by a sole trader.

They recognize the risk, but cannot afford to change their system. The lack of IS expertise in small business managers and the lack of small business expertise in most external software/hardware consultants contribute to IS failure in SMEs (Yap *et al.*, 1992).

IS development in the SMEs

Information systems in the four case SMEs are typically developed by the technical methods that tend to be those of the structured school of systems analysis or the *ad hoc* approach of the self-taught. These systems are either produced for them by small software suppliers (Light Assembly Co.), bought off-the-shelf (the other three firms' MRP systems) or are do-it-yourself systems developed within the firm (Heath Springs' job costing system). Structured methods are inadequate for modelling future requirements of a business system, and the models and specifications produced by such systems may be rendered obsolete by minor changes in business process (Eardley *et al.*, 1997; Fitzgerald, 1990). The methods are therefore likely to produce systems lacking in flexibility to cope with future change. Requirement changes tend to be at the detailed operational level rather than aimed at meeting strategic objectives. Indeed, in the case of Precision Tool Co., the computer software supplier regularly recommended changes in functionality. Because of the time for development due to the traditional methods used it is clear that the SMEs are reluctant to change the original system specification. There is little evidence of IS being linked to strategy and investment being made to support strategy.

The technical infrastructure in SMEs is third generation. In particular, the software was designed using traditional methods that are weak at coping with changes to the application, and there are often difficulties in changing or adding functionality. This is typified by the prevalence of corrective maintenance that tries to modify software to cope with unforeseen changes in the business processes (Eardley *et al.*, 1997). For example, Clutch Assembly Co. employed a part-time programmer to make these changes. Further, SME IS have the characteristic of being embedded in the inflexible technology of the 1970s and 1980s. The IT infrastructure which was available then is not well suited to producing systems which can cope with changes in business process and with IT innovation.

Influence of customers on IS

There are three key areas in which customers influence IS in SMEs. First, customers seek evidence of quality in both product and production process (Light Assembly, Heath Springs and Clutch Assembly). Second, order processing is done automatically (Light Assembly, Heath Springs and Clutch Assembly) and third, there is integration in design of new products (Precision Tools, Heath Springs and Clutch Assembly).

All the firms have only one or two major customers who place substantial emphasis on the need to show evidence of both quality processes and products. This evidence is expected to be provided from production data that has been analysed by the SME to show, for example, wastage rates, productivity and machine down time. The carrot held out to the SME for introducing these systems is one of more open book management and a mitigation of the price reductions demanded by the customer (Heath Springs and Clutch Assembly). The purpose is to maintain the SMEs' preferred supplier status. Therefore, transactions processing systems are insufficient; management information is critical to the survival of the SME.

Customers also expect SMEs to introduce EDI systems, primarily for receipt of orders. However, in the case of Light Assembly Co., it is also used to support production forecasting as their major customer provides a schedule of estimated orders 3 months in advance. Problems can arise, with Light Assembly's EDI as every customer has a different system. While their major customer's EDI system is interfaced with their production planning system, those of two other large customers are not and data has to be re-entered manually into the production planning system. Electronic data interchange initiators, generally larger organizations, are known to gain at the expense of followers (Golden and Powell, 1996; O'Callaghan et al., 1992). Despite pressure from a major motor manufacturer Precision Tool does not think it worthwhile investing in EDI. This may be a reflection of the type of business. Orders tend to be large (e.g. tooling up a new production line) and do not occur regularly. The life of a precision tool is about 10 years, unless damaged. Precision Tool Co.'s preferred supplier status has not yet been threatened by their resistance.

The final area where IS in SMEs is influenced by the customer is in the area of CAD. Large motor manufacturers now include SMEs in the design process for new vehicles. For example, engineers from Clutch Assembly Co. work with the motor manufacturer to design new parts that enhance the overall design. Designs for new clutch assembly parts are sent via communications links between their CAD system and the customer's. Light Assembly Co. is considering the possibility of electronic transmission of light-fitting designs to one of their major customers to improve the quality and speed of the design process.

SMEs are driven by the needs of their customers. The decision of customers to introduce the hollow factory concept has led them to outsource much of their production: SMEs have been the main beneficiaries of this. SMEs are the providers, in the main, of the components or sub-assemblies required by major manufacturers. Just-in-time manufacturing is becoming the norm for major manufacturers: SMEs find that they become warehouses for their customers. Light Assembly Co. has built new warehouses to hold finished light fittings until customers require them to be delivered to stores.

Collaborative advantage between firms is driven through "value chain partnerships" that depend upon openness, good communication and a willingness to share information (Kanter, 1994). Clutch Assembly Co. has certainly benefited from this arrangement. They managed to convince their customer to accept prices higher than the customer initially requested as a result of sharing information about the Clutch Assembly's efforts to reduce costs. While customers are driving the four case SMEs to produce quality goods at a minimal price, the decision to promote one or two SMEs as preferred suppliers has ensured that the relationship has to be two way. The number of SMEs in the automotive industry is declining either through acquisition or attrition. This limits suppliers for the major automotive manufacturers: it is in their interest to provide support for SMEs.

■ Flexibility: the SME response

The four cases indicate that SMEs do not readily conform to the received wisdom that they are particularly flexible or adaptable. First, flexibility is defined as the ability to change strategic direction relatively quickly. The evidence here is that all the four SMEs have a specific skill in one main product or variants of that product. They believe that their expertise lies in that product and they are only competing in one market. In general, as with most SMEs, the four cases have one or two major customers upon whom they are dependent, with all the concomitant dangers. Light Assembly Co.'s one major customer decided to reduce their orders for light fittings from about 80% of output to about 40%, despite having invested effort in developing the firm to manufacture light fittings to their standard. Light Assembly Co. has since been successful in acquiring other customers with similar product lines.

Automotive manufacturers have taken a policy decision to move towards the "hollow factory" concept where they buy in sub-assemblies. They put considerable pressure on SMEs to conform to standards that they have set, both in terms of quality and price. Ford, for example, has developed a Quality Operating System to evaluate its suppliers. Those SMEs who supply Ford have to offer evidence that products conform to the required quality standard. All the four case SMEs have achieved the UK quality standard, BS 5750, and are working to ISO 9000. One conclusion is that it is not in the interests of customers for SMEs to be flexible. Customers demand a quality product and it may be in their interests to ensure that the SME hones this narrow expertise.

Flexibility as a strategic response to the unseen has limited validity in the context of the four case SMEs. There is scant evidence of strategic thinking in any of the SMEs: survival is the key issue for all of them. They focus on developing efficient production processes rather than thinking about alternative strategies. Efficient production means that firms try to maximize production runs regardless of whether orders exist. Precision Tool Co. argues that the set-up time for each machine is so long, 16 hours, that they need to make enough stock to minimize production costs. The outcome is a considerable amount of finished product stored awaiting a customer order. No attempt is made to calculate the production costs of each unit and to decide whether this was the best use of machines, labour or cash. Heath Springs go further in maximizing production runs: management spend 4 hours each week planning them. This often leads to orders being brought forward in order to maximize machine usage, leaving other, earlier orders unfilled until they became critical.

A further reason for limited flexibility in SMEs is their reliance on outdated machinery and under-investment for the future. Heath Springs has many machines dating back to the Second World War and little intention or capital set aside for re-investment. SMEs *"favour 'flexible' over 'fixed' investment and those with short rather than long-term payoffs"* (Storey and Cressy, 1995) due to the need to ensure survival in the immediate future and the wish to avoid high fixed costs.

In all the four cases the CEO is not particularly knowledgeable about IS and their potential as a strategic response. The purchase of IS in all the four cases is to improve efficiency. The CEOs are also not focusing on innovation although they were aware of the market changes, for example, a move to ceramic components will impact drastically on Heath Springs. The main objective appears to be one of maintaining current expertise.

SMEs are driven by a small dedicated group, thoroughly knowledgeable about the product range and the production processes being deployed (Bolk and Van Manen, 1990). Management are intimately aware of the potential of the product and are able to use this knowledge in attracting customers. However, their knowledge of the operation is detailed and there is a tendency to become involved in the day-to-day operation to the detriment of forward planning (Lybereas *et al.*, 1993), as Heath Springs demonstrates. While all the four management teams take advantage of the ability to communicate easily, the organization structures are not particularly organic and responsive. This limitation may inhibit opportunities for flexibility, particularly for competitive advantage, which make it unlikely that SMEs will use pre-emptive or exploitive manoeuvres.

■ Discussion

Analysis using Evans' framework suggests that SMEs cannot, or do not, use most of the range of tactics that might give flexibility. The firms focus on managing their current expertise more effectively and give very little thought to long-term strategic planning. Certainly there is little evidence that their purchase of their MRP systems is any more than a tactical response. Only Light Assembly Co. has reviewed its organizational structure such that there is now a learning environment. However, even in this firm, management information is not available from the IS. Thus, the two more proactive advantages of flexibility, internal process redesign and competitive advantage, are not being sought by the firms. Hence, it makes it unlikely that the firms can take advantage of pre-emptive, exploitive or protective strategies for flexibility.

Survival is the prime strategy of all the SMEs, and it could be argued that they have all taken advantage of corrective manoeuvres to ensure their continuing existence. However, it is not clear that their response, with regard to their investment in IS, will enable them to respond flexibly to changing circumstances.

This, in turn, suggests that their global flexibility is low compared to organizations that can employ a variety of such tactics. Hence, it may be the SME sector rather than the individual firm that is flexible due to organizational birth and death. Alternatively, it is the industry value chain that has flexibility not any component part, or perhaps any value chain is more flexible at the top (customers) than at the bottom (sub-assemblers). Also, the evidence here is that IS does not provide flexibility for SMEs. The literature on computer-integrated manufacturing (CIM) promotes it as a means of increasing flexibility and improving quality control (Ayres, 1991). However, there is little evidence in the study of integration of design, production and management IS that constitute CIM. This is largely due to the incrementalism that is a key feature of IS in SMEs. This may all be encapsulated in the IT-flexibility paradox to which Lucas and Olson (1994) point – technology can contribute to organizational flexibility since IT is inherently more flexible than its predecessors, but since technology ages so rapidly and becomes hard to maintain flexibility is quickly lost.

Implications for managers

As customers' demands increase a strategic response is required. SME management can usefully reflect upon the relationship with customers to assess whether and in what way they are contributing to profitability. While dependency upon one major customer is unlikely to change, SME owners can usefully build relationships through information exchange about the delivery of the product or service. This implies not only the development of internal IS to support management processes, but also using technology to exchange information with customers. The rise of Extranets and supply chain networks is evidence that this is happening, SMEs need to be proactive partners to gain the benefits.

Implications for research

This research is exploratory and only uses four cases to explore manoeuvres for flexibility. These four cases demonstrate a limited perspective on flexibility. The firms' focus on survival means that the only manouevre undertaken is corrective. The variety of organizational form that characterizes SMEs may also be a factor that should be considered, from the organic structure of initiation to the more formal structures as they grow.

■ Conclusions

This chapter investigates the role of IS in promoting or inhibiting flexibility in SMEs: all the four cases exhibit relative inflexibility in their general approach. Information systems do not seem to provide increased flexibility, but reinforce existing thinking. The key reasons are that SMEs view themselves as having a narrow product range which is used for the benefit of one or two customers. This leads them to consider the purchase of IS to improve the efficiency and effectiveness of current processes rather than considering its capacity to increase flexibility and improve competitiveness.

One of the reasons for the limited approach to IS investment may be the lack of knowledge about the potential from IS and the processes that can be used to assess or evaluate its use in the firm. Chapter 5 considers how this process of evaluation might be addressed.

5 Evaluating IS in SMEs

■ Introduction

As identified in Chapter 2, the small- and medium-sized enterprise sector is characterized by high firm failure rates; six times higher for small than large businesses. It may be that difficulties of evaluation practice in such organizations contribute to this high failure rate, if inadequately appraised investments are frequently undertaken.

The problematic nature of information systems/information technology evaluation is well recognized. However, as with many of the issues dealt with in this text, most empirical work in IS evaluation has been carried out in large organizations. Indeed, many of the techniques of evaluation are predicated upon complex organizations with subunits competing for organizational funding. What is less researched is whether many of the problems of IS/IT evaluation are atypical of some organizational types (e.g. service and manufacturing) or organizations of varying sizes (e.g. small, medium and large firms). This chapter discusses the theme of organization size in the context of IS evaluation by identifying the issues surrounding evaluation in SMEs. In doing so, it considers whether contextual factors, such as management style and organizational culture, constrain or amplify the evaluation problem.

This chapter outlines approaches to evaluation recognizing the value of an organizational multi-stakeholder perspective and drawing on evaluation practice. This highlights the expectations for evaluation practices in SMEs. Evidence of the actual evaluation practices of the four case firms described in Chapter 4 are used as illustrations. In doing so, the chapter identifies a set of issues that have particular relevance for evaluation practices in SMEs.

■ Evaluation of IS and IT

Evaluation of IS and IT is a major organizational issue, with many studies highlighting concerns over IS effectiveness measurement, cost justification and cost containment (Niederman *et al.*, 1991; Dickson and Nechis, 1984). The issue has, to some extent, come to the forefront of management attention due to the level of capital expenditure involved: management expect value for money. Investment in IS/IT is currently estimated at approximately 8% of turnover, putting it on a par with spending on research and development and advertising combined.

Information systems and technology evaluation is problematic, principally as a result of the difficulties inherent in measuring the benefits and costs associated with such investments (Ballantine *et al.*, 1995a). Information systems and technology evaluation is difficult because of the multi-dimensionality of cause and effect and multiple, often divergent, evaluator perspectives. Evaluation should not simply be viewed as a set of tools and techniques, but a process that must be fully understood in order to be effective (Symons and Walsham, 1988). "Evaluation of an IS cannot be an objective deterministic process based on a positivist 'scientific' paradigm, such a 'hard' quantitative approach to social systems is misconceived" (Angell and Smithson, 1991). A number of evaluation techniques that attempt to take a broader perspective than traditional financially-oriented techniques have emerged. Despite these developments, there is widespread agreement that there is a lack of evaluation tools that effectively address the problems.

Approaches to evaluation

In an IS context, evaluation has been defined as the process of *"establishing by quantitative and/or qualitative means the worth of IT to the organization"* (Willcocks, 1992). However, multiple purposes of evaluation are recognized. Evaluation serves a number of objectives (Farbey *et al.*, 1992):

- as a means of justifying investments,

- to enable organizations to decide between competing projects, particularly if capital rationing is an issue,

- as a control mechanism, enabling authority to be exercised over expenditure, benefits, and the development and implementation of projects,

- as a learning device enabling improved evaluation and systems development to take place in the future.

Similar rationales are identified for IS evaluation (Ginzberg and Zmud, 1988; Dawes, 1987):

- to gain information for project planning,

- to determine the relative merits of alternative projects,

- to ensure that systems continue to perform well,

- to enable decisions concerning expansion, improvement or postponement of projects to be taken.

While a wealth of evaluation techniques, for example, utilization, benchmarking, simulation, aggregate scoring techniques and user attitude surveys, are to be found in the IS literature, many of these have focused historically on quantitative, as opposed to qualitative, approaches. The danger of such approaches can lead to a positivistic rather than an interpretivistic approach being taken (Hirschheim and Smithson, 1988). To counter this, more recent work attempts to widen the IS/IT evaluation debate. As a result a number of models that recognize the context of evaluation have been put forward. Information Economics (Parker *et al.*, 1989), for example, introduces the concepts of value, risk, and human and management factors. As information is a key strategic resource it is essential that evaluation of the IS and IT that deliver it is considered within an organizational context. Therefore, evaluation needs to take into account the alignment of business strategy, organizational requirements, human resources and management structures (Willcocks, 2003). Multi-objective, multi-criteria methods that start from the assumption that the worth of an IT project can be determined in a measure other than money are useful here (Farbey *et al.*, 1992). Their approach recognizes that the benefits of an IS need to be analysed from different organizational perspectives and by the different stakeholders in the firm, acknowledging alternative views.

Overall, these different approaches are classified as *objective* and *subjective*. Objective methods attempt to attach values to system inputs and outputs, while subjective methods consider wider aspects of evaluation such as user attitudes. Objective methods (cost benefit analysis, value analysis, multiple criteria approaches, simulation techniques, etc.) endeavour to categorize the costs associated with IS. On the other hand, subjective methods (user attitude surveys, event logging, delphi evidence, etc.) *"try to quantify in order to differentiate between systems, but the quantification is of feelings, attitudes and perceptions"* (Powell, 1992).

The importance of stakeholders in IT evaluation is stressed, recognizing that there may be various stakeholders involved (Farbey *et al.*, 1992). The potential disagreements or conflicts among stakeholders may also usefully play a part in the assessment process by highlighting relevant issues (Walsham, 1993). Thus, a holistic approach is required to understand the benefits. This is achieved through use of a framework (Figure 5.1), derived from Mintzberg's (1983) model of organizational structure (Farbey *et al.*, 1993). This framework is used later to discuss evaluation in the case firms investigated in this chapter.

Evaluation practice

The evaluation of IS/IT investments in practice is well documented (Blackler and Brown, 1988). However, the majority of studies tend to concentrate on the extent to which financial techniques, such as payback, net present value and internal rate of return, are used to justify

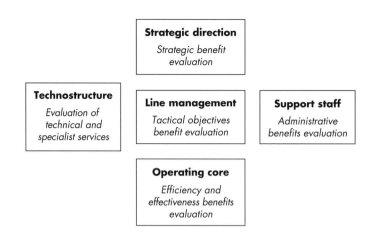

Figure 5.1: Evaluation framework. (*Source*: adapted from Farbey *et al.*, 1993.)

investments. There is a limited use of evaluation techniques in practice, suggesting that there is a lack of available tools which aid management with the task of evaluating, prioritizing, monitoring and controlling IS/IT investments (Farbey *et al.*, 1992; Hochstrasser, 1992).

The practice of evaluation is problematic for many organizations (Willcocks, 1992) as:

- budgeting practices tend to conceal full costs;

- there is a failure to understand and budget for human and organizational costs;

- knock-on costs are frequently overstated;

- costs are overstated in order to ensure that projects are developed within time and budget;

- there are various problems associated with using traditional-based evaluation techniques;

- organizations often neglect intangible benefits in the evaluation process;

- risk is not fully investigated.

Some of these problems are confirmed by empirical studies (Ballantine *et al.*, 1995a; Tam, 1992). The danger for IS evaluation is that it may become ritualistic. Evaluators may use the process to massage costs to present the required result. Hence, it is useful to consider the purpose of undertaking evaluation and the factors that are included in the process (Walsham, 1993). However, few of the issues are addressed in the context of small firms. These are investigated in the next section.

Table 5.1: Case firms and systems under evaluation

Firm	IS	Decision-maker	Stage of implementation
Light Assembly Co.	AS400 with MRP system, networked terminals Three EDI systems, one linked to MRP system	Operations manager	Fully implemented
Precision Tool Co.	AS400 with MRP system Finance director has stand-alone PC with spreadsheet Marketing department have stand-alone PC Stand-alone CAD/CAM system	Finance director	Partially implemented
Heath Springs	AS400 with MRP system CEO has PC-based performance measurement system	CEO	Partially implemented
Clutch Assembly Co.	AS400 with MRP system EDI link with major customer also used of CAD transfer Not linked to MRP Finance director has stand-alone PC-based performance measurement system	Finance director	Partially implemented

▦ SMEs and evaluation: the issues

This section examines how the four case SMEs described in Chapter 4 make decisions on the development and implementation of IS investments. Table 5.1 indicates the IS investments that were the subject of evaluation, who made the decision to invest and the stage of development.

All the IS have been purchased within the last five years. In three cases the purchase occurred more recently and implementation is only partially complete. As it is important to understand the organizational issues that drive IS/IT adoption, in particular the relationships that support alignment, it is useful to model the different elements that may affect the operation and management of the firm. The model that is used is the "Seven-S" model (Waterman *et al.*, 1991) as proposed by Galliers and Sutherland (1991) (Table 5.2).

A Seven-S analysis is carried out for each SME from the perspective of the role of IS in the organization (Table 5.3).

The overall ethos underpinning these firms is the urge for survival through cost reduction. Improving efficiency in the operation is vital to their survival. All the firms recognize the value of IS to support the drive

Table 5.2: Seven-S model

Element	Description
Strategy	The plan to achieve the business goals
Structure	The organizational structure (e.g. functional, matrix, project)
Systems	The operational processes: paper based and technological
Staff	The roles that are important to the firm
Style	The management style of the firm: controlling; facilitating; directive
Skills	The core skills that are vital to the firm
Shared values	The over-arching ethos of the firm

Source: adapted from Waterman *et al.*, 1991.

for efficiency. However, they have limited in-house IT skills. Most rely on external contractors to provide the main support and implementation of systems.

The following sections identify evaluation issues which, when compared to the extant literature, are seen to be specific to SMEs. These include: the lack of both a business and IS/IT strategy; limited access to capital resources; a focus on using IS/IT for efficiency rather than to support business goals; a lack of planning effort; the nature of the relationship between the organization and its principal customers; limited information skills; and finally, a lack of focus on integration of IS/IT.

Business and IS/IT strategy

As discussed, evaluation of IS/IT investments should be integrated within the strategic business context of the firm. The case SMEs do not have a clearly defined IS/IT or business strategy. However, while no explicit strategy exists, an implicit one often does. For all firms the strategy is one of survival (Table 5.3) leading to a focus on efficiency and cost reduction. Despite these implicit strategies, problems still exist as the strategy itself is neither written, nor indeed, and in one case, imparted to senior management. This is known to be a problem for IS/IT developers in larger organizations where corporate strategy may neither be fully formed nor communicated (Lederer and Mendelow, 1986). For example, in Precision Tool Co. the finance director was unaware that the parent firm was considering relocating production to the developing world, leaving the UK to focus on product design. Light Assembly Co.'s decision to purchase IS was a reaction to the need for more information about production in an increasingly growing and complicated business, as opposed to strategic considerations. This concurs with Hagmann and McCahon (1993) who report that fewer than 30% of the 300 SMEs they studied undertook any strategic planning. Additionally, fewer than 50% of the SMEs that owned or planned to purchase a specific IS devoted any significant planning effort to it.

Table 5.3: Attitudes to IS

Element	Heath springs	Lighting	Precision tools	Automotive tubes
Strategy	Production and performance oriented	Production oriented	Production oriented	Production and performance oriented
Structure	Managing director responsible for purchasing Operations manager responsible for ongoing systems development	Senior manager responsible for purchasing No internal IS organization	Senior manager responsible for purchasing No internal IS organization	Senior manager responsible for purchasing Part-time programmer for additional systems development
Systems	MRP package purchased; only partially implemented Interface being eveloped with estimating system	MRP package purchased and developed with small software supplier	MRP package purchased; only partially implemented Spreadsheet software available but not integrated	MRP package purchased; only partially implemented Spreadsheet software available but not integrated
Staff	Independent consultant and self-taught operations manager, additional support from software supplier	External contractors from software supplier provide systems support	External contractors from software supplier provide systems support	
Style	Senior management are concerned to have the right operational support to improve efficiency	Senior management are concerned to have the right operational support to improve efficiency	Senior management are concerned to have the right operational support to improve efficiency	
Skills	The operations manager has developed programming skills Otherwise, senior management have spreadsheet skills	There are no IT skills in the organization	There are no IT skills in the organization	Programming skills are held by the part-time programmer Otherwise, senior management have spreadsheet skills
Shared values	Cost reduction and efficiency improvement: survival	Cost reduction and efficiency improvement: survival	Cost reduction and efficiency improvement: survival	Cost reduction and efficiency improvement: survival

Information systems planning encapsulates not just the purchase of IS, but concomitant issues such as management of the systems, organizational changes and integration with current technology architectures (Galliers, 1991). The purchase of a MRP system formed the main recent effort of the four case SMEs. In Heath Springs, the CEO used a consultant to assist him in identifying efficiency improvements. However, organizational change, training and human resource issues were not considered and the MRP system merely provides partial information about inventory levels. Systems integration, flexibility or growth were not considered.

The lack of strategic planning, both business and IS/IT, which takes place in SMEs, has implications for IS/IT evaluation. One major implication is the lack of a clear yardstick or objective against which to measure the feasibility of potential IS and guide the decision process. The investment decisions of the four SMEs were made using purely financial criteria: mainly whether there would be an improvement in turnover as a result of adopting the IT system. However, the use of crude financial criteria and subsequent financial techniques of evaluation are likely to preclude the incorporation of other factors critical to success, including, quality and flexibility. However, as financial measures such as turnover might, indeed, reflect SMEs' critical success factors, the problems of solely using financial techniques may be somewhat less than for larger organizations.

Limited access to capital

Access to capital by SMEs is often limited due to restricted sources of financing in terms of borrowing or equity. Blili and Raymond (1993) recognize that this subsequently leads to weakness in "financing, planning, control of IS and training". Heath Springs and Precision Tool Co. are owned by larger groups that provide capital without the need for borrowing. They both have to make business cases for IS investment, justifying the cost in terms of efficiency improvement. Light Assembly Co., however, is constrained by limited funds while needing to satisfy quality demands of its single customer at that time. The firm worked with a local software supplier to develop an MRP system and effectively acted as a test site for the developer who hoped to sell the system to others. Therefore, less capital was employed than might otherwise have been required. Clutch Assembly Co. was able to take advantage of the availability of grants from local and central government to relocate their factory on the basis of creating employment in a deprived area. This capital injection enabled the firm to purchase its MRP system.

Consideration of limited capital resources leads to a number of implications for evaluation practice. First, there is a limit to the number of investments which likely to be evaluated at any time. In all the four cases, only MRP systems were being considered. As a result there is less need to use an evaluation technique that facilitates prioritization of projects. Thus, techniques of evaluation that consider a single investment in isolation may suffice.

The associated weaknesses in planning and control of IS of SMEs additionally results in a lack of feedback on IS/IT investments such that they are unlikely to be able to identify whether anticipated benefits have been realized. The advantage of evaluation in terms of providing feedback for control purposes, in addition to feedforward for planning, is unlikely to be achieved by SMEs. A further implication is the resulting emphasis placed on the development of incremental systems. This is confirmed by Hashmi and Cuddy (1990) who find that developments in SMEs are largely incremental for management IS and advanced manufacturing systems.

Emphasis on efficiency

In the SMEs researched here there is a greater emphasis on using IS/IT to improve efficiency than to provide managers with information on achievement of business goals. This is particularly evident in the type of IS invested in. The predominant systems are MRP, generally used in productivity strategy (Hashmi and Cuddy, 1990), their primary function being to improve efficiency through automation of transaction processing systems. Hence, their focus is on achieving existing productivity levels for a lower labour cost.

The role of IS in the four case SMEs is primarily directed at supporting operations as opposed to providing management information. For example, Heath Springs obtains management reports from the production support system, but they tend to be very detailed, necessitating the re-entry of data to a spreadsheet to provide summary reports. The MRP system is only used to identify stock and raw material availability; it is not used to plan production. A similar situation occurs in Light Assembly Co. where detailed reports from the production support system require considerable manual analysis by a manager to derive any useful information. Precision Tool Co., having purchased an MRP system has not yet fully implemented it. The MRP system is designed to manage the accounts, customer and suppliers details as well as stock control. Implementation is being undertaken gradually; meanwhile they are working with a batch stock control system and paper files. Clutch Assembly Co. is in a similar position to Heath Springs, with re-entry of data required to provide quality measurement information about the product and process required to satisfy customers and improve the business.

To summarize, the SMEs recognize the need for good operational systems to ensure that they can ensure timely product delivery. While data is generally used to manage the operational process effectively, there is little attempt to gain any added value except for the need to produce information on quality demanded by the customers. Evaluation of IS, therefore, is only based on whether efficiency improvements will be achieved. The potential of IS for learning and SME growth is unlikely to be evaluated.

Influence of major customers

The important influence of customers was discussed in Chapter 2. The problems that arise for IS flexibility was raised in Chapter 4, particularly when customers demand investment in IT. This is particularly marked, for example, where a condition of being a supplier to a major firm is that EDI is implemented: the choice of system is determined by the customer. Thus, the SME is "forced" to make an investment decision over which they have little or no control: evaluation is not seen as relevant. For example, Clutch Assembly Co. is required by one of its major customers to introduce EDI to enable automatic order processing and design transmission through CAD. The requirement to evaluate the costs of developing an interface to their major customer was not considered; rather, it is deemed a necessity. They are also unable to consider alternative interfaces that might give them future flexibility to add other customers. As a result they are locked into the software supplier who developed the interface. Lack of flexibility has also affected Light Assembly Co. that have had to purchase separate EDI systems each time they gained a new customer. Precision Tool Co. works more informally with its customers although it is being put under considerable pressure by a major customer to purchase EDI. They are reluctant to make the investment on cost grounds as they are only turning round the firm after recession and cannot readily see benefits from the introduction of EDI.

The experiences of the SMEs here reinforces the influence of major customers on SMEs, which has implications for IS evaluation. For example, it may be more appropriate in these circumstances to carry out collaborative evaluations with the business partner concerned. Alternatively, if SMEs are required to adopt systems and are given little or no say over the investment decision, then evaluation is unlikely to be a worthwhile exercise beyond simply assessing its affordability.

Limited IS skills

A further difficulty SMEs face is limited IS skills; they are dependant on external consultants and software firms for IS selection. The senior management of the four case SMEs have a clear knowledge of the business, and, therefore, their information requirements. On the positive side they all have spreadsheet skills and recognize their value in providing detailed financial analyses as required. However, they are largely dependent on external sources for advice on appropriate hardware and software. Heath Springs for example, recognized that it required an automated accounts system after acquiring a number of smaller competitors. The CEO's knowledge of IS was limited, therefore he employed an independent consultant to undertake a systems analysis. As a result an accounting package was purchased on the consultant's recommendation. Evaluation of the system was, however, based purely on the extent to which it was capable of processing accounting information within the limited budget available.

Light Assembly Co. relies on a sole trader software supplier. There is some concern about future support as the supplier's health is in some doubt. Amending the system to provide management reports is regarded as difficult by the firm; cost as well as disruption to the system is seen as problematic. Precision Tool Co. is also reliant on their software supplier for support and advice. As implementation is not complete, staff from the software supplier are often on the premises installing modules. There is little exchange of skills between the two firms. Clutch Assembly Co. employs a part-time programmer to make systems changes.

Limited IS skills in SMEs have implications for evaluation. There is a reliance and dependence on external providers for both technical and systems advice and support. As discussed in Chapter 3, external providers, particularly if SMEs themselves, are unlikely to have a breadth of experience in system development, or if they do it is likely to be from the structured school of development methods. These methods do not consider a wide range of stakeholders and inevitably produce inflexible systems based on a limited understanding of the current and future business. Thus, the evaluation procedures they adopt are likely to be objective than subjective.

Effects on evaluation practice: SMEs and large firms

The analysis of the four cases shows that SME characteristics have implications for evaluation practice. It is clear that the focus of evaluation in SMEs differs from that found in larger organizations. For SMEs, the prime drivers for investment are pressure from customers and improved efficiency. Limited strategic planning means that IS are purchased as required, hence their evaluation may be assessed more by financial criteria than might be the case with larger firms. Evaluation decisions are also made in isolation, as the IS investment decision is not made in competition with other systems. There is no evidence of intangible costs being assessed, indeed financial consideration of the cost of the system is the main criterion by which it is judged.

■ Discussion

Limited capital resources are a critical issue for SMEs. The problem for them is that this may be in direct conflict with customer pressure to invest to maintain position as a preferred supplier. This is discussed below using an evaluation framework for capital investments. The lack of business strategy, focus on efficiency and limited IS skills all affect attitudes to evaluation in SMEs. Discussion of these issues may benefit from reflection through an organizational lens as proposed by Farbey *et al.* (1993) (Figure 5.1).

Capital resources

As discussed, limited access to capital resources is likely to limit SMEs' IS investments. It was suggested that SMEs may only need to use an evaluation technique that considers a single investment. This is now assessed through the use of a framework that recognizes the extent to which organizations consider the process of evaluation, and the subsequent use of standard or non-standard evaluation approaches for capital investments (Ballantine *et al.*, 1995b). While the framework (Table 5.4) considers the arguments for adopting standard versus non-standard approaches to evaluation for all capital investments, it is used here to understand further the particular evaluation practices evidenced adopted by SMEs.

The framework identifies four alternative approaches to evaluation, each characterized by either the use of a standard or non-standard evaluation method, and the degree to which the process of evaluation is considered. For example, organizations that give little consideration to the process of evaluation are likely to use standard evaluation methods, such as routine accounting models, for evaluating all capital investments.

The "blind" use of a standard approach to evaluation may be the result of a lack of knowledge of the process or tools of evaluation, or of the project itself. The former would be more likely to occur in SMEs or in firms that do not regularly carry out evaluation. A lack of data or knowledge about the project itself may reflect its novelty or the firm's lack of desire to commit resources to planning. Other reasons for using a standard approach might be that SMEs see themselves as followers of a particular technology, not leaders, hence evaluation has already been done for them by others and they can clearly see the results of implementing the technology elsewhere.

Organizations that give much consideration to the evaluation process, yet use standard evaluation approaches, might do so because they consider that it is appropriate to adopt a standard approach on the grounds of

Table 5.4: Approaches to evaluation

Method of evaluation	Little consideration of process of evaluation	Much consideration of process of evaluation
Standard	Routine accounting models (e.g. net present value; cost benefit analysis)	Sceptical use of accounting models
Non-standard	"Strategic", naive	Considered approach

equity. Alternatively they might recognize that whilst sceptical of using standard methods, either no alternative is available or there are no justifiable reasons for the adoption of non-standard evaluation practices.

Organizations that give little consideration to the evaluation process, yet use a non-standard approach might do so on the basis that IT/IS is almost always in some way strategic. Alternatively a rigid approach to evaluation might not fit with the organization's culture, or the evaluators do not consistently believe in the process, the methods, or the outcomes of using a standard approach. Finally, IT/IS budgets may be infrequent and *ad hoc* so that consistent evaluation practice is not feasible.

In the final quadrant are those organizations that give much consideration to the process yet use a non-standard approach to evaluation. The overwhelming reason why organizations might fall within this quadrant revolves around the argument that at any time the range of investments considered by an organization are so varied that a standard approach is unlikely to encapsulate all significant features which need to be considered in the evaluation process.

Extrapolating from the four cases, positions SMEs in the quadrant using a standard evaluation approach after little consideration of the process. This, however, is a function of a number of factors including a lack of business and IS/IT strategy; limited access to capital resources; and limited skills within the organizations. Further, the emphasis in the case SMEs is on the adoption of a homogeneous technology, which is primarily used for efficiency improvements, adds further to the argument for adopting a standard evaluation approach for all IS investments. It would be informative to see whether a standard evaluation approach is adopted for other capital investments, and the extent of its similarity to that used for IS.

Opportunities from an organizational approach to evaluation

It was suggested earlier that an organizational approach to evaluation that took account of the views of different stakeholders is thought to be more relevant for many organizations. Figure 5.1 presented the Farbey *et al.* (1993) organizational evaluation framework as one that enabled the various perspectives to be assessed. However, from the analysis of the four case firms, the lack of a clear view of their strategic direction results in a failure to use IS/IT as a competitive tool. Therefore, whilst not at odds with Farbey *et al.* (1993) on the importance of strategic benefits, the lack of strategic direction and emphasis on efficiency in SMEs means that little attention is given to strategic evaluation.

The technostructure is defined by Farbey *et al.* (1993) as those "*people whose function it is to influence the way people work*" and includes IS staff. However, the experiences of the four SMEs here suggest there is little reflection on the way work is carried out within the organization. Rather, there are more urgent pressures in SMEs that leave little time for

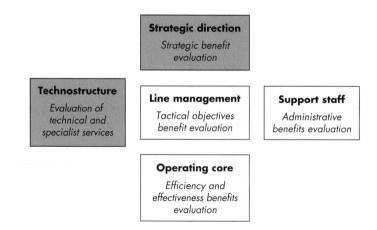

Figure 5.2: Adapted evaluation framework for SMEs.

reflective thought concerning the effectiveness of operations. Additionally, the limited IS and IT in SMEs as well as the approach taken to IS projects whereby they are carried out sequentially makes it unlikely that evaluation of the technostructure will be necessary. As shown in Chapter 4, the limited nature of flexibility in IS in SMEs means that they only replace technology when it becomes obsolete. Therefore evaluation of the technostructure in SMEs is unlikely to be an issue.

While these two issues may be less relevant for SMEs the model can be adapted (Figure 5.2).

The operational focus of IS in the four case SMEs suggests that an organizational perspective may still have some value. Evaluation is helpful from the perspective of the management team to understand the benefits of the system in providing them with better management reports. Staff will also benefit from an evaluation process that acknowledges potential business process changes. There are three further categories of IS benefits which are not encapsulated by Mintzberg's model of organizational structure: information benefits, communication benefits and learning benefits (Farbey *et al.*, 1993). However, the evidence here suggest that SMEs principally use information as a means of improving productivity and not as a means of enhancing communication and learning, which makes the three additional categories of benefits of less relevance. Further, the limited access to management information in SMEs makes it unlikely that the feedforward element of evaluation implied by the strategic and technostructure elements of the Farbey model would be considered by SMEs. Thus, the Farbey *et al.* (1993) model may be adapted for examining evaluation in SMEs by excluding the strategic and technostructure elements.

The findings of the cases suggest that the evaluation of tactical objectives, operational objectives and service provision are more appropriate to SME evaluation given the issues discussed earlier.

▓ Investment issues in SMEs

This chapter has identified five issues influencing the IS/IT evaluation processes in SMEs:

▓ a lack of business and IS/IT strategy,

▓ limited access to capital resources,

▓ emphasis on efficiency,

▓ influence of major customers,

▓ limited information skills.

The absence of an explicit business and IS/IT strategy within SMEs suggests that SMEs will adopt less formal capital investment decision processes than larger organizations. Since planning activities are minimal in SMEs, the resulting lack of clear objectives against which to evaluate potential investments is likely to lead to less consideration of the process of evaluation and the strategic benefits of IS than is evident in larger organizations. Similarly, SMEs are more likely to make investment decisions which are based on flawed decision processes since the evaluation approach adopted is unlikely to be documented, adding further to the adoption of *ad hoc*, inconsistent and informal approaches to evaluation. However, the lack of strategy further suggests that SMEs are poorer in their ability to identify when investments in IS/IT might be used to gain strategic advantage than large firms.

The absence of an explicit business strategy implies not only a lack of clearly defined business objectives, but also the absence of a clearly defined means of achieving objectives. Given this, SMEs are unlikely to recognize the strategic importance of potential IS/IT investments that might surface as a result of engaging in a strategic planning process. Additionally, lack of strategy will not facilitate an understanding, and realization, of the technostructure benefits (Mintzberg, 1983) of potential IS investments in SMEs. Therefore, the absence of a business and IS/IT strategy leads to greater emphasis on individual projects, as opposed to portfolio effects of IS/IT projects in SMEs. This approach to evaluation encourages organizations to consider IS/IT investments in isolation, largely ignoring the holistic nature of such systems, which implies an inability to reap the synergistic benefits of IS/IT investments that might otherwise accrue.

Limited access to capital resources within SMEs suggests that SMEs need not adopt evaluation processes that facilitate prioritization of IS/IT investments. However, the adoption of such an approach to evaluation might further encourage organizations to ignore the synergistic effects which a portfolio of investments might deliver, which, in turn, further emphasizes the development of incremental systems.

Given a lack of strategy in SMEs, they are unlikely to view the IS/IT evaluation process as a learning mechanism. The emphasis of evaluation in SMEs is more likely to be one of control rather than learning. As a result, the learning benefits of IS identified by Farbey *et al.* (1993) are unlikely to be considered in the evaluation process. However, the extent to which control mechanisms exist and are effective in SMEs requires more examination.

The emphasis in SMEs on information for efficiency rather than strategic advantage leads to the conclusion that financial techniques of evaluation are more appropriate for evaluating investments in IS/IT in SMEs than in large organizations, as these reflect the nature of projects invested in. Investment in automation projects is normally undertaken in order to achieve cost efficiencies. Thus, financial evaluation techniques that primarily focus on the identification of quantifiable costs and benefits are more likely to be appropriate methods of evaluation for such investments.

Financial evaluation techniques are more likely to be appropriate for evaluating investments in IS/IT in SMEs as these techniques reflect the factors critical to the success of SMEs themselves. The critical success factors reflecting SMEs survival, and ultimately success, include, for example, short-term liquidity, profitability and cash flow. Thus, financial techniques of evaluation which emphasis these aspects are more appropriate for the purposes of evaluation in SMEs. For example, the extensive usage of payback as a means of evaluating IS/IT investments is well documented in the literature. The use of payback recognizes the need to recoup the original investment within a period of time (on average two years for IS/IT investments in the UK). The payback approach, thus, emphasizes the importance of liquidity and so it is likely to be an appropriate technique of evaluation since it reflects one of the critical success factors of SMEs.

As discussed, many SMEs are heavily influenced by their major customers in terms of the systems they are required to adopt. This suggests that customer influences in SMEs are more likely to lead to decisions that are based on a "got-to-do" basis, rather than on a formal, rational decision process. Where major customers exert considerable influence over SMEs in terms of the systems they are required to adopt, decisions regarding the adoption of a particular technology are best taken on the basis of efficiency criteria or no evaluation where the customer has specified a particular system as a pre-requisite for trading. This reiterates the earlier arguments that financial techniques are possibly more appropriate techniques of evaluation in SMEs than other more qualitative techniques.

The lack of information skills within SMEs suggests that SMEs exhibit much greater reliance on the IS/IT decision processes of external bodies (e.g. consultants, software firms and external accountants) than large firms. Reliance is primarily due to a lack of internal IS skills and few IS personnel in SMEs. The outcome of this can manifest itself in two ways. First, as seen in Chapter 4, some SMEs choose to employ small software houses to develop bespoke system for them. This is a more risky approach with high dependence upon the software developer. Second, other SMEs will take a more cautious route and invest in industry standard hardware and software. For example, SMEs will invest in technologies that have been subjected to testing by others in the industry.

■ Conclusions

In conclusion, this chapter argues that organizational size is a factor which has largely been ignored in IS evaluation research to date. Further research is needed to examine the extent to which the size influences the adoption of particular evaluation practices. Five main pressures were identified as limiting IS evaluation in SMEs: lack of a business strategy, a focus on efficiency, customer pressure, lack of capital and limited IS skills. This chapter demonstrated that as these factors lead to SMEs investing serially in IS that financial evaluation techniques are probably sufficient. This chapter has highlighted the lack of strategic planning in SMEs, amongst other things, combined with the lack of flexibility in IS in evidence as indicated in Chapter 4 leads to the conclusion that IS planning needs to be more carefully considered by SMEs. This is the focus of Part 2 of this book.

Part 2 Issues of IS strategy planning

This part demonstrates the underlying theory that drives the analysis in this book. As discussed in Part 1, one of the main purposes of the research discussed here is to show the validity of current information systems strategy theory in the context of small business. Information system strategy has long been thought essential for large corporations that wish to add value to their businesses. However, there is little research on whether, or in what way, information systems are valuable to small- and medium-sized enterprises.

Information systems strategy theory in large firms emphasizes the link between IS and business strategy. Yet, as shown in Part 1, few SMEs have a clearly defined business strategy. There is a tendency for SMEs to grow haphazardly, making investments as the need arises, and IS investment often follows the same path. However, it is necessary to plan or have a strategy for systems ahead of their absolute necessity. Thus, it is likely that a strategy for IS will benefit SMEs. This part investigates this contention by reviewing the theory and practice of ISS within the context of small firms.

Chapter 6 investigates the validity of the models and frameworks that have been used in large corporations as analytical tools to understand the means by which the strategic use of IS can add value. This is important not only to validate existing theory, but also to provide researchers and practitioners with usable analytical tools to understand the SME context. Information systems are becoming more relevant to SMEs as markets become more complex and global. SMEs have to become more efficient in order to compete more effectively, and IS offer one means of achieving this efficiency.

However, it is not sufficient just to understand which analytical tools are valid for use in researching SMEs. Information systems strategy is known to provide large firms with an understanding of opportunities to use IS and IT competitively. Additionally, ISS enables efficiency and effectiveness opportunities to be developed. The shift in ISS theory from mechanistic contingent modelling to a more systemic organizational focus is discussed in Chapter 7. This shift is shown to be appropriate for researching SMEs, as such firms generally have an operational focus. An organizational approach to ISS recognizes the resource constraints that inhibit IS investment in SMEs. It focuses more on the strategic use of information and suggests that, in some cases, re-organization of business processes provides productivity improvements ahead of further investments technology. However, it is clear that technology investment often provides competitive benefits to growth-minded SMEs.

Chapter 8 demonstrates the use of the ISS framework through the development of an ISS for a manufacturing firm. The use of the models is demonstrated within the context of the business. The business processes are reviewed both through the contingent modelling of the value chain and the systemic perspective offered by soft systems methodology. The analysis demonstrates how the strategic content of IS for the future is developed. The value of the models and frameworks is reviewed as part of this demonstration.

This part provides the basic tools by which data is analysed for all the cases used in the book. The models found to be valid in the SME context are used to understand the use and application of IS. This provides a rich data set that can be used to demonstrate current and future potential from IS for SMEs. The strength of the ISS framework in Chapter 7 is that the models and tools within it are demonstrably generic. They have been validated both in large and small organizations. Thus, the framework is robust and can be used in most contexts.

6 Understanding IS strategy in SMEs

Introduction

There is a widely-held view (Galliers, 1987; King, 1987) that information systems strategy can play a critical part in helping organizations to increase efficiency, effectiveness and competitiveness (Sinclair, 1986). Further, ISS can provide the means to achieve truly innovative approaches to many management and competitive challenges.

Most research in ISS has been carried out in North America where the focus is on large corporations (Rackoff *et al.*, 1985) and on the development of methods. European contributions, in contrast, have tended to concentrate on developing frameworks that assist in identifying the position of strategic information systems planning within organizational environments (Walsham, 1993; Earl, 1989). To date, research interest in the role of ISS in small- to medium-sized enterprises in general, and manufacturing SMEs in particular, is surprisingly sparse and underdeveloped. SMEs in the US value ISS as a means of obtaining greater efficiencies in their internal organization, but that they are not used to increase competitiveness (Hagmann and McCahon, 1993). However, there are indications amongst UK manufacturing SMEs that changing market structures are forcing managers to think innovatively and ISS may be both a catalyst to, and guiding principle for, innovation. Given the paucity of SME-specific ISS frameworks, it is useful to consider whether it is possible to use those that are well established in large organizations. This chapter uses Earl's framework of frameworks to provide a means of exploring the applicability of ISS frameworks, identified as valuable in the corporate context, to SMEs.

Nature of ISS

An ISS defines the IS that an organization needs to be competitive (Galliers, 1991; Earl, 1989). This can range from systems to improve efficiency and effectiveness, which are internally focused or core, to those that lead directly to competitiveness, with an external, more strategic focus (Earl, 1989; Sinclair, 1986).

Information system strategy should be an integral part of business planning (Earl, 1996a; Galliers, 1991). Unless IS planning is integrated, it is likely that strategic systems will be developed in a piecemeal manner, neither contributing to strategic vision nor enhancing organizational flexibility to respond to market changes (Avison *et al.*, 1998). ISS also needs to change in response to the business environment (Earl, 1996a). Thus ISS needs to be dynamic, supporting the current business strategy, while responding to the changes in the market that influence strategic and technological change (Ward and Peppard, 2002). Figure 6.1 suggests the dynamic relationship between the role of IS to provide business information to enable firms to compete and learn from the market. This leads to the ability to recognize competitive change in the market and to review business strategy to take advantage of that change. Business processes are likely to change as a result of change in business strategy requiring a review of information requirements and hence new IS and information architectures.

Information system strategy need to encompass not only the systems that individual organizations require to compete in the market place, but also those that provide the means to improve competitiveness along the industry value chain (Porter and Millar, 1985). Relationships with suppliers and customers improve through the exchange of information. Additionally, organizations may look for collaborative advantage (Kanter, 1994). Sharing of information and systems is a key part of the openness that is necessary for the development of such collaborative relationships. However, rapid technology change often renders it infeasible for firms to attempt to gain competitive advantage through the introduction of information technology (Feeny and Ives, 1990). Indeed, Feeny and Ives argue that firms should not base their competitive strategy on IT unless they are confident it is not easily replicated.

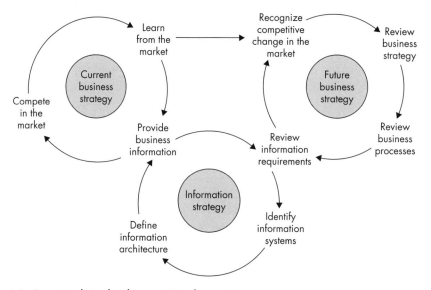

Figure 6.1: Dynamic relationships between ISS and competitiveness.

■ Strategic IS frameworks

Strategic IS encapsulate the notion that linking IS to business strategy may yield significant competitive advantage, may potentially transform the firm and perhaps the industry, and so should be an active concern of top management.

Frameworks are outline models of how IS can *potentially* fit with firms' objectives of gaining competitive advantage. Strategic IS frameworks were developed to assist analysis of an organization so that advantage could be taken of opportunities from IS (Doyle, 1991). Examples of these frameworks include Porter's five forces, the value chain and the information intensity matrix (Porter and Millar, 1985), discussed in more detail later in this chapter.

However, there are some important caveats to be borne in mind when using such frameworks, especially in the context of SMEs. First, strategic IS frameworks are predominantly based on models of strategic behaviour in the US business culture and their potential limitations in a non-US business context is under-researched. Second, the complex circumstances facing many SMEs may not be easily captured in the frameworks. For example, the role of the SME as a strategic partner to a larger manufacturing corporation greatly complicates the concept of appropriate competitive behaviour. Researchers offer little detailed guidance on how to benefit from IS or to avoid being marginalized by competitors' actions despite promises of strategic and competitive advantage.

Frameworks often codify common sense and could be argued to offer little of value to an organization that knows its own business. There is also an assumption that frameworks exist outside time, which may render some frameworks irrelevant, particularly when addressing the impact of new technologies (Doyle, 1991). For example, the Internet is radically changing the way firms do business and may make current frameworks seem parochial and dated.

This chapter reinforces the view, outlined in Part 1, that while SMEs are aware of the need to computerize, there is often little thought given to more than increasing operational efficiency. For the manager or SME owner, frameworks may also be viewed as an educational device to help increase sensitivity to IS and competitiveness, and as a planning tool. Frameworks provide a means of indicating to SMEs that strategic opportunities exist. These can be exploited using existing technologies but improved systems.

The range of frameworks on offer is bewildering to managers and some rationalization is required. Further, the value and limitations of frameworks is not always clear. Earl's framework of frameworks provides a useful means by which to consider the relative value of each. This chapter demonstrates which frameworks are useful in developing an ISS for SMEs. Earl developed the framework of frameworks to attempt to classify the plethora of frameworks that developed in the mid-1980s.

The reason for developing this is to enable the purpose of the different frameworks to be understood and to attempt to use frameworks in "the right purpose and in the right context" (Earl, 1989: p. 40). According to Earl, individual frameworks may be classified under one of three headings: awareness, opportunity or positioning. Table 6.1 summarizes the key characteristics of these categories of frameworks.

The frameworks Earl cites as exemplars are summarized in Table 6.2, some of these are explained in more detail later in the chapter.

Table 6.1: A framework of frameworks

Framework/attribute	Awareness	Opportunity	Positioning
Purpose	Vision	Ends	Means
Scope	Possibility	Probability	Capability
Use	Education	Analysis	Implementation

Source: adapted from Earl, 1989.

Table 6.2: Exemplar frameworks cited by Earl

Awareness	Opportunity	Positioning
Refocusing frameworks: identification of potential to use IS/IT in the organization **Exemplar**: Benjamin *et al.*, strategic opportunities framework	*Systems analysis frameworks*: identification of information flows within the business **Exemplar**: Porter, value chain	*Scaling frameworks*: identification of scale of importance of IT to an organization **Exemplar**: McFarlan and McKenney, strategic grid
Impact models: identification of impact which IS/IT could have on the organization's competitive position **Exemplar**: Porter, generic strategies	*Application search tools*: identification of specific application areas within the business which might benefit from IT **Exemplar**: Ives and Learmonth, customer resource life cycle	*Spatial frameworks*: identification of information management implications for an organization **Exemplar**: Earl, sector information management grid
Scoping models: identification of strategic scope of IT in industry sectors **Exemplar**: Porter and Millar, information intensity matrix	*Technology fitting frameworks*: identification of specific IT to achieve a business benefit to the organization **Exemplar**: industry dependent	*Temporal frameworks*: identification of IT suitable for the stage of IT development of organization **Exemplar**: stages of growth models
	Business strategy frameworks: identification of business strategy opportunities for IT **Exemplar**: Porter, five forces model	

Source: adapted from Earl, 1989.

The framework of frameworks is used in this chapter to determine the applicability of each of the exemplar models in the framework to ISS planning and practice in SMEs. The rationale for each framework is discussed and then its relevance and use within SMEs determined.

■ Background to the cases

The four cases introduced in Chapter 4 are used as the basis for this exploratory research. The value of the exemplar frameworks to SMEs in undertaking ISS is explored. As identified in Chapter 4 the main focus of the four case firms is survival in highly competitive environments. This manifests itself as "fire-fighting" to deal with day-to-day operational matters. As shown, in all cases IS have been purchased in order to improve the quality of transaction processing and this decision reflects a deep concern with high levels of inventory. However, a low priority is accorded to the use of IS or IT for management information. While the four case firms have adopted IT to aid day-to-day production and stock management, none has realized the potential of connecting this data to overall strategic and competitive analysis. For example, the firms wish to retain all their existing customers, but they operate by fulfilling orders quickly, rather than by asking themselves which customers they want and how they may deepen relationships with them.

Further, each firm is aware that they will only stay in business through being seen by their customers as having both quality products and processes. However, the link between management information and measurement of quality is not well recognized by the firms. They are all closely involved in design of new items for their customers. However, they see this as of operational rather than strategic significance. For example, Precision Tool Co. was involved in close collaboration with an international motor manufacturer to develop a new precision tool. This involved a high degree of innovation and understanding of customer needs, yet this knowledge and information is only beginning to be integrated within the wider strategic perspective of the firm. This typifies an issue for many SMEs: a preoccupation with day-to-day viability limits the time available to consider the strategic advantage inherent in production and customer interaction.

■ Framework analysis

This chapter now uses the four case firms: Precision Tool Co., Heath Springs, Clutch Assembly Co. and Light Assembly Co., as a basis upon which to explore the use of frameworks as defined through the framework of frameworks.

Awareness frameworks

Awareness frameworks indicate how IT can be used for strategic advantage. They provide insights at an industry level rather than at the firm level. They are intended to raise management awareness and show the value of changing the way the business works within the context of particular industries. The purpose, therefore, is to encourage creative thinking and questioning. Awareness frameworks are primarily educational tools. The application of these to SMEs may enable them to think more strategically and improve effectiveness through better use of management information. Thus, they may present opportunities for SMEs to compete through IS. Earl organizes awareness frameworks into three subsets: refocusing frameworks, impact and scoping models.

Refocusing frameworks raise awareness about the potential use of IT and IS in the organization. The example used in this category is adapted from the strategic opportunities framework developed by Benjamin *et al.* (1984) and extended by Earl (1989). The strategic opportunities framework invites senior managers to reflect on potential changes both internally and in the competitive market place. To achieve these changes the argument is that traditional systems as well as innovative technologies may provide strategic gains. Earl develops this framework by recognizing that internal processes require both back- and front-office support. The research discussed here has developed this further by considering IS/IT opportunities using established and new in three key business areas: production, management support and customer relations.

The refocusing framework is applied to Light Assembly Co. to identify potential opportunities for IT from the perspectives of production, management support and customer relations systems (Table 6.3). Potential systems for Light Assembly Co. are shown in italics in Table 6.3, while actual systems are presented in normal text. In production systems, Light Assembly Co. already has an effective MRP system. However, the competitive nature of a fast-moving industry suggests that the use of CAD to develop designs that could be sent electronically to customers could speed up analysis, design and production. Management support could be improved by modifying existing systems and providing exception reports. This would immediately free up management time. There is potential for the introduction of an executive IS to provide sales analysis by product line and to monitor forecasting. While the Light Assembly Co. already uses EDI to receive order information from customers, the provision of this could be extended to automate production planning for more of their customers. Apparently, management not only saw opportunities for new technologies, but they became aware that they could exploit existing technologies more effectively to improve operational management and provide strategic management information.

Table 6.3: Refocusing frameworks in Light Assembly Co.

	Production	Management support	Customer relations
Traditional support	Systems specifically designed to allocate stock to jobs and track work in progress. Essentially an MRP system	Transaction processing reports available from production support system No summary or exception reporting and considerable analysis is required for use	
New technologies and systems	*Potential for CAD being addressed; seen as particularly opportune as design becomes central to competitive advantage which involves getting products to market faster than competitors*	*EIS could be of value in showing the progress of different lines and the accuracy of forecasts by customers*	EDI enables forecasts and orders to be sent. Invoicing also through EDI. Where EDI unavailable, Fax is used

Impact models provide a means of considering whether IT can improve the competitive position of the organization, using Porter's generic strategies model to identify the target of a firm's strategy within the industry. This model considers whether the strategy is differentiation, cost or niche (Porter, 1980). Porter argues that competitive success results from following either providing the goods or service as lowest cost or by differentiating it in terms of value to the customer. Firms can either supply the whole market or focus on a particular market segment or niche.

The generic strategy of the case firms is not always clear. None are currently pursuing a *cost leadership* strategy. While they are being pushed by their customers to reduce prices, they all indicate that their main concern is to compete on quality and, thus, their strategy is one of differentiation. For example, Precision Tool Co. has a fine reputation in the precision tools business. It has invested in production machinery that enables efficient production. Design capability, while reactive, also assists in differentiation. Time has been spent building relations with major customers. Yet prices are not determined through a detailed analysis, and this makes a cost reduction strategy difficult. It is, however, recognized that efficiencies can be made and these are being addressed through the introduction of an activity-based costing system. Efforts are also being made to reduce inventory. While there is competition in the manufacture of precision tools, Precision Tool Manufacturer is convinced that it has the edge on quality.

At least one customer of Automotive Tube Manufacturer, a major automotive manufacturer, expects price reductions as a matter of course.

Information content of the product

		Low	High
High		Lighting Assembly Co.: assembly of lights	Lighting Assembly Co.: design of lights
		Precision Tool Co.: production of precision machine tools	Precision Tool Co.: design of precision machine tools
		Clutch Assembly Co.: production of clutch assemblies	Clutch Assembly Co.: design of clutch assemblies
		Heath Springs: spring production	Heath Springs: spring design
Low			

(Vertical axis label: Information intensity of the value chain)

Figure 6.2: Information intensity matrix for case firms.

This customer works closely with Automotive Tube Manufacturer to identify where savings can be made; recognizing that price reductions may take several years. Open book accounting provides a key tool for this collaborative approach. Information on the quality of process and production enable the firm to justify its proposals to customers.

Scoping models address the strategic potential for using information in an industry. The information intensity matrix (Porter and Millar, 1985) is the preferred model here (Figure 6.2). It provides a useful means of identifying whether IS/IT focuses on improving internal efficiencies and effectiveness (firm value chain) or competitiveness (industry value chain). The vertical axis considers the amount of information in the value chain. This means the quantity and quality of information that needs to be exchanged between the firm, its customers and suppliers in order for the product to be delivered to the market. The horizontal dimension represents the amount of information within the product itself for its development.

As Figure 6.2 shows, the value chain for a manufacturer requires a high level of information to manage the process from raw material to finished product. However, the information necessary for the development of the product or service itself varies. There is little information actually held in, what is essentially, an artefact. However, with a move into design the information intensity of the product is high. Therefore, there is much more scope here for the strategic use of IS/IT. Automotive Tube Manufacturer already exploits this with a major motor manufacturer through electronic transfer of engineering drawings.

Conclusions on use of awareness frameworks

While the firms here are relatively simple organizations, the models are useful in indicating the potential of IS/IT. It is clear that the use of technology at the production/operational level in the exemplars is relatively advanced and is essential for their survival in a highly competitive industry. In all cases, however, there is a paucity in the use of IS/IT for management information and, indeed, for strategic opportunity.

While Earl argues that awareness frameworks are more useful at an industry level they have highlighted issues specific to the firms. IS/IT is mainly being used to increase Light Assembly Co.'s operational efficiency and effectiveness, but there is potential for its use in increasing competitiveness, particularly linking design of lights to customer requirements. However, to make this effective the business strategy needs to be clear. Strategic direction has not been addressed: the firm is primarily driven by operational imperatives, typically survival.

In Precision Tool Co., IS/IT is also used to provide operational support, but is not integrated into the production and scheduling process. Management information is limited, although the firm expects this will change with the move to the flexibility of a client-server system. This is a networked computer system where each computer is either a client or a server. A server manages the overall system: disk drives, printers and the network itself. Clients are PCs or workstations that run applications. There may be considerable potential for IS/IT to be used to support the changing strategic direction of the whole group, and in this context, it will be essential to have an effective network. Design of precision machine tools seems to be the direction in which the firm is heading. CAD/CAM linked to major customers could provide a means of locking in customers by providing them with a quality, pro-active service. CAD/CAM is a computerized system that allows an engineer to both design a product and to control its manufacture directly.

Clutch Assembly Co. has started to recognize that IS/IT is important in running an effective and efficient business. However, systems have been developed to solve individual situations rather than to develop a coherent plan that enables the greater exploitation of existing information. While Clutch Assembly Co. has EDI links with its major customer, they have not taken the next step and integrated manufacturing processing and management information.

Opportunity frameworks

Opportunity frameworks enable individual organizations to identify suitable strategic opportunities from IS use. This involves analysing the immediate competitive environment, the information flows required to carry out the business activities, and technology opportunities available. Earl identifies four opportunity subsets: systems analysis frameworks, application search tools, technology fitting frameworks and business strategy frameworks.

Systems analysis frameworks consider the information flows within the business. A value chain analysis (Porter, 1980) may be used to identify information flows and gaps in value adding primary and secondary activities. The value chain provides an analysis of the value adding activities that contribute directly to profitability and support activities. The value chain (Figure 6.3) represents the different activities that are required by all firms to deliver a product or service to the market. Porter identifies two different types of business process. The primary value chain activities directly contribute to the development of the product or service and the secondary value chain activities are required to support the development. Porter identifies four primary value chain activities: inbound logistics (the raw materials required); operations (the process of making the product or service); outbound logistics (delivery to the customer); and marketing, sales and service (the aftercare that can lock in customers). The secondary value chain includes the firm infrastructure that is defined as the activities such as accounting, order processing and office support. Human resource management involves the development of workforce skills to enable product manufacture. Technology developments consider the role of all technologies in both production and support, for

Quality management	Quality standards (BS 5750, 60001); quality checks and goals important			
Firm infrastructure	Regular and detailed financial reports contribute to effective negotiation over terms with customers. MRP system in place			
Human resource management	Commitment to staff training; communication processes in place between staff and management; pay structures reviewed to enhance communication			
Technology development	Looking for new products; market testing with major customer; some design work; exploring use of design software			
Procurement	Personal contact with overseas suppliers; seeking new sources in Eastern Europe; reviewing processes with sub-assembly agents			
	Inbound logistics	**Operations**	**Outbound logistics**	**Marketing, sales and service**
	Quality checks on all deliveries through "traffic light" criteria (green accept, red reject, orange minor defect) Record and process deliveries Store materials	Send raw materials for processing (e.g. plating) Send raw materials for part assembly Assemble bins of raw materials and parts ready for transfer to final checks and packaging Forecasting problematic	Check product against template Check safety and operation of electrics Check glass fittings Final packaging Store finished goods	Maintain relations with major customers Obtain sales data form major customers EDI system tailored to customers needs Explore new markets

Figure 6.3: Value chain for Light Assembly Co.

example, the telephone network or the IT network. Finally, procurement involves the processes that ensure that raw materials are available for both primary and secondary activities.

Information flows and constraints are also indicated in the value chain. All the case SMEs emphasize the need to demonstrate quality processes and products to customers. Porter argues that quality is inherent within the firm infrastructure, however, that is not demonstrated by the SMEs here. It is seen as a necessary and important part of their business. Hence the value chain has been adapted to highlight quality.

The implication for SMEs is that better management IS are required to link to production systems and to provide reports to customers. Currently, this is a time-consuming process with transaction processing data re-entered into spreadsheets to provide reports on quality.

A key operational focus for SMEs is on improving management information to reduce inventory, finished stock, and work in progress. The value chain also shows that, while the manual process ensures that machines are working to maximum capacity, SMEs should improve the availability of management information.

Application search tools help in the identification of specific application areas within the business that might benefit from IT. The Ives and Learmonth customer resource life cycle demands an understanding of the relationship of IS with customer requirements. There are four phases to the customer resource life cycle: requirements establish and specify needs, acquisition (selection and purchasing), stewardship (managing the system) and retirement (managing obsolence). The intention is to understand how IS/IT can be used to strengthen the relationship with customers by providing added value, ultimately locking in customers (Earl, 1989).

Application search tools are not found to be useful for SMEs. This reflects the relatively simple nature of the organizations and the cautious approach taken to purchasing IS. Most SMEs have fairly informal relationships with their customers or have systems imposed. For example, MRP systems have been introduced to satisfy customers, however, their exploitation in increasing efficiency and effectiveness is limited. While Lighting Manufacturer worked with a customer to integrate EDI into their systems, it was only done in a limited fashion that made delivery of orders easier, there was little exchange of information that contributed competitive benefits.

Technology fitting frameworks are used to indicate whether IT supports a business need, has potential to add value and thus derives its organizational impact. Earl suggests the use of industry-specific frameworks. As all the cases used in this chapter are manufacturers, Meredith and Hill's (1987) AMT framework is deemed most appropriate, since it highlights differences in the attitude to automation in manufacturing (Figure 6.4).

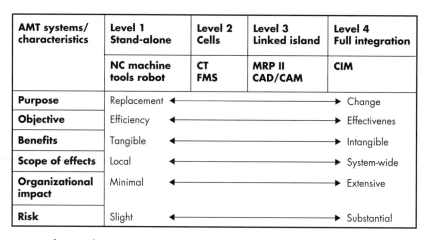

AMT systems/ characteristics	Level 1 Stand-alone	Level 2 Cells	Level 3 Linked island	Level 4 Full integration
	NC machine tools robot	CT FMS	MRP II CAD/CAM	CIM
Purpose	Replacement ◄		►	Change
Objective	Efficiency ◄		►	Effectivenes
Benefits	Tangible ◄		►	Intangible
Scope of effects	Local ◄		►	System-wide
Organizational impact	Minimal ◄		►	Extensive
Risk	Slight ◄		►	Substantial

Figure 6.4: AMT framework. CIM, computer integrated manufacturing; CT, cell technology; FMS, flexible manufacturing system; NC, numerically controlled. (*Source*: adapted from Earl, 1989.)

The AMT framework demonstrates the different levels of benefits that can be obtained by increasing levels of automation through the use of production technologies. These range from the simplest where an individual machine manufactures an artifact to full integration where design and manufacture are a seamless process. The benefits, risks organizational impacts are indicated for each level of automation.

The AMT framework enables managers to determine whether and in what way different technologies can resolve different problems or identify opportunities. The strength of the framework is in enabling managers to understand the effects of the introduction of AMT on the organization. The introduction of limited stand-alone technologies has a minimal impact on the organization while the introduction of fully integrated manufacturing is likely to have profound effects. The problem for SMEs is that customer pressure has forced the introduction of the new technologies, particularly MRP II and CAD/CAM. The SMEs themselves have not understood the changes that are required for successful integration. This framework again may well be overly-complex for an SME.

Business strategy frameworks consider strategic opportunities for the organization and the potential for competitive advantage from IT. Porter's five forces model (Figure 6.5) provides the exemplar as it is a well-established model for analysing strategic opportunities. The five forces model proposes that business success for a firm is achieved within the context of its industry. There are different competitive pressures for different industries. The firm needs to understand and develop relationships with customers and suppliers. However, it also has to compete in an existing market and needs to understand the role of its competitors. There will also be new firms attempting to break into the market and the dynamics of the industry need to be understood to ensure that they do not damage the firm. Meanwhile substitute products

Competitive force	How IS/IT can create competitive advantage	Explanation
Threat of new entrants	How can IS/IT build barriers to entry?	IS/IT changes the conditions which have to be met for a new firm to enter the market
Bargaining power of customers	How can IS/IT build in switching costs for customers?	IS/IT can expand the product or service which the customer buys so that any move to a rival will result in lower value from the new product or service
Bargaining power of suppliers	How can IS/IT change the balance of power with its suppliers?	IS/IT can change the relative bargaining positions in the market
Threat of substitute products or services	How can IS/IT generate new products or services?	The information on the IS/IT may provide new opportunities for new product development
The industry: jockeying for position among rivals	How can IS/IT change the basis of competition?	IS/IT can be used as part of re-engineering the business. The focus is on greater efficiency and effectiveness

Figure 6.5: Porter's five forces model and IS/IT opportunities. (*Source*: adapted from Ward and Peppard, 2003.)

and services may emerge that may completely change the basis of competition. All firms need to understand these interactions. In particular, they need to understand the role of IS/IT in managing them.

Analysis of the cases suggests that this model is invaluable in analysing business competitive drivers for SMEs. Porter's five forces model provides insights into an organization's strategic drivers. It has merit as it directs SMEs to look outside their own operational boundaries. Here, while there is a general awareness of the competition, it is held informally and the attitude towards competitors is reactive (Figure 6.6). Only three of the cases are presented here as Heath Springs is discussed in more detail in Chapter 8.

The analysis confirms the need for the SMEs to develop or maintain customer links through the use of EDI. It is also clear that competitive advantage is more likely to be sustained if CAD is integrated along the industry value chain. The model also indicates where competitive advantage is likely to be inhibited by inefficiencies in the organization.

Use of opportunity frameworks
The value chain and five forces model are invaluable in supporting an understanding of the potential of IS/IT to individual SMEs. They provided a means of highlighting key strategic areas where SMEs can reap benefits through the use of IS/IT. The technology fit framework and

Competitive force and IS opportunities	Light Assembly Co.	Precision Tool Co.	Clutch Assembly Co.
Threat of new entrants	• EDI system linked to customers • Design of lights through CAD or multi-media	• CAD used to design tools, library of designs available	• EDI ordering system linked to customers • Performance measurement systems in place • CAD used
Bargaining power of customers	• Improved design capability through CAD reduces customer power	• Design of precision tools integrated with manufacturer design process	• Design of springs integrated with manufacturer design process through CAD
Bargaining power of suppliers	• Better forecasting will enable planning of stock purchase	• Better inventory planning may enable reduction in stock holding	• Better forecasting will enable planning of stock purchase
Threat of substitute products or services	• Use of CAD or multi-media catalogues to help gain edge in light design	• Introduce EDI and integrate CAD with manufacturer	• Integration of CAD with manufacturing
The industry: jockeying for position among rivals	• Forecasting improved • Manage EDI links better • Better management information	• Better management information • Understand customer base better	• Improve forecasting • Quality performance information will exclude rivals

Figure 6.6: Application of Porter's five forces model to cases.

application search framework are found to be less useful here as the size of the case firms means that IT opportunities are relatively self-evident as a result of using the business strategy and systems analysis frameworks.

Positioning frameworks

Positioning frameworks consider the importance and effectiveness of existing IS to the business. The management of IS is also considered to determine whether it enhances or inhibits the value of IS. The relationship of IS structures in the organization is reviewed. Positioning frameworks help managers plan and respond to the future development of IS given a good understanding of the current situation. Three positioning subsets are now presented here: scaling frameworks, spatial frameworks and temporal frameworks.

Scaling frameworks consider the importance of IT to an organization and the management of its introduction or change. The McFarlan–McKenney strategic grid (Figure 6.7) provides a means of considering the value of both existing and proposed systems to the firm's strategic direction. The framework also aids managers' understanding of any organizational changes likely to be required. The vertical axis considers

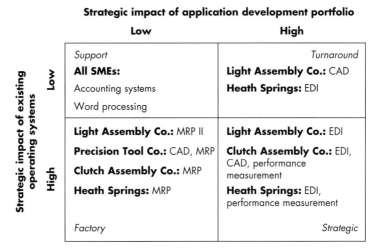

Figure 6.7: Scaling framework: the McFarlan–McKenney strategic grid for cases.

the strategic impact of existing IS in the organization. The horizontal axis reviews the strategic impact of planned systems. More usefully, the quadrants demonstrate the different types of systems that an organization requires and the relative strategic impact. Support systems are essentially secondary value chain systems that are valuable to the organization as they ensure the business runs smoothly, they include word processing, e-mail and accounting. Factory systems are primary value chain systems that are essential for the production of the service or product. The organization is dependent upon them but they may not offer future strategic impact. Strategic systems provide that strategic impact as they are outward-looking. They are likely to focus on developing industry value chain relationships. Finally, turnaround systems are investments in IT that may bring around future success but they are likely to be experimental and not integrated into business processes. The path followed for firms is likely to be from turnaround to strategic to factory systems.

The McFarlan–McKenney strategic grid shows that the SMEs focus on basic support systems such as word processing and accounting. They also invest in factory systems to manage production, all the SMEs having purchased an MRP system. However, the MRP systems are not used to manage the whole cycle of production from planning to finished product. For example, inventory is managed through the MRP system, but is not currently tied to production that leads to inaccuracies in stock maintenance. Production planning is carried out weekly and is done manually.

There is little evidence of the SMEs thinking about the strategic use of systems. Electronic data interchange is essential for Light Assembly Co., and Clutch Assembly Co. to maintain their preferred supplier status, yet they are not exploiting its full potential. It is primarily seen as a means of receiving orders and forecasts. However, Light Assembly Co. is aware of the potential to provide customers with a "virtual catalogue" that will enable more dynamic processing for the design of lighting assemblies. For Clutch Assembly Co. and Heath Springs, performance measurement is seen as a means of maintaining current strategic position with respect to competitors.

As identified in Chapter 5, customers are putting pressure on Precision Tool Co. to adopt EDI, but they are resisting. Ward and Griffiths (1996) place EDI in the turnaround quadrant for manufacturers. It would appear here that EDI will be an essential part of the future competitive business. Precision Tool Co. should consider it carefully as customers are likely to make EDI a requirement for preferred suppliers: it is already a requirement from at least one of Light Assembly and Clutch Assembly Co.'s major customers. For these, EDI has been placed in the strategic quadrant rather than in the turnaround quadrant as suggested by Ward and Griffiths. Earl argues that IT is strategic if the business is "dependent or shaped by IT"; in the Lighting Manufacturer, and Automotive Tube Manufacturer cases major customer requirements have made EDI strategic.

Time may be a feature of the difference in positioning of both MRP and EDI in different quadrants to those proposed for manufacturers by Ward and Griffiths. These technologies are not seen as an integral part of strategy. It is interesting that IS/IT plays little or no part in the strategic thinking of the firms. Only Lighting Manufacturer is thinking of moving into design using CAD as a strategic response to gain leverage over competitors. While Automotive Tube Manufacturer uses CAD as part of its current strategy, it is only because customers have demanded it.

Spatial frameworks address management of the information resource in the organization. The main issues here are the planning, organization, control and technology of the information resource, depending on the strategic context of the IS/IT (Earl, 1989). This may range from zero impact through operational support, to IS providing support for business strategies and ultimately, IS changing the business. They tend to be predicated upon large organizations with a separate IS department. Specialist IS staff are employed to develop organizational systems. There is an assumption in these frameworks that IS planning is linked to business planning. Most IS literature also separates management from users of systems, particularly with respect to planning. Spatial frameworks offer little added value as most of the features in their definition are absent in SMEs.

Information systems introduction in SMEs is often a reaction to a perceived need to improve efficiency and effectiveness. This leads to incremental introduction of IS (Hashmi and Cuddy, 1990), rather than a response to business planning. SMEs are cautious in their purchase of IS/IT.

It is a major investment that will be depreciated over a longer period of time than is generally expected. SMEs' choices focus on hardware and software that can grow with them and they perceive the investment as long term: 10–15 years. Implications for hardware providers are that they have to continue to support what they may consider to be obsolete technology.

In SMEs management rely on being as close to operational systems as users, hence the need for separate consultation is far less than in a large organization. The other critical issue is that the SMEs do not have staff whose core skill is IS. SMEs rarely have a fully developed IS department. There is considerable dependency on external consultants, for both purchase and implementation. This also highlights the limitation of temporal frameworks in analysing SMEs.

Temporal frameworks assist in identifying management issues at different stages of IS development. Stages models are used here to identify the current position of information management. These help identify issues that must be addressed before an organization can use information strategically.

Temporal frameworks consider the development of IS over time. Nolan's Stages of Growth model is probably the most commonly cited, although Galliers and Sutherland (1991) identify others (Figure 6.8).

Initiation represents start up computing, primarily to improve efficiency. Contagion occurs as more users in organizations demand IT and often have the budget to invest. However, this means that there is often a wide variety of IS and IT in an organization. Control occurs as management start to worry about the cost implications of IT. Often IT is brought under the auspices of the financial controller. These three stages are primarily about managing the technology. It is only once

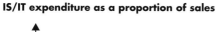

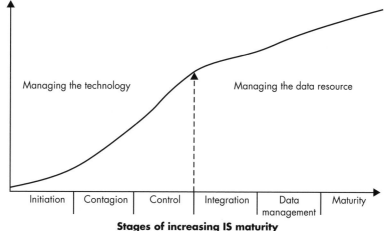

Figure 6.8: Nolan's stages of growth model. (*Source*: adapted from Ward and Peppard, 2003.)

organizations recognize the strategic role of IS that they can move forward to managing the data resource. Integration focuses on providing networks and developing shared databases. Once information becomes recognized as a strategic resource the firm moves forward to data management. Users understand the values and importance of sharing information throughout the organization. More than this however, business units recognize that information may change the way the business competes. Maturity is the stage when business strategy planning and IS planning are totally integrated.

Temporal models are predicated on the existence of an IS department within a functionally organized hierarchical structure. The models seem to imply an element of conflict in relationships between users and developers of IS. This attitude gradually changes as IS are recognized to have strategic potential. In the case of SMEs, the starting point for most is control, but this is in response to a business need not to contagion. The key difference between large corporations and SMEs is a concatenation of roles.

■ Towards a framework of frameworks for ISS in SMEs

Applying the frameworks to the set of SMEs reveals that most have some merit and, as such, can be taken to be relevant for all business sectors. As Table 6.4 shows, many of the frameworks are found to be of value in

Table 6.4: Useful Frameworks for ISS in SMEs

Awareness	Opportunity	Positioning
Refocusing frameworks: **Exemplar**: strategic opportunities framework (adapted from Benjamin *et al.*)	*Systems analysis frameworks:* **Exemplar**: value chain (Porter and Millar)	*Scaling frameworks:* **Exemplar**: strategic grid (McFarlan and McKenney)
Impact models: **Exemplar**: Porter's generic strategies	*Application search tools:* **Exemplar**: customer resource life cycle (Ives and Learmonth)	*Spatial frameworks:* **Exemplar**: sector information management grid (Earl)
Scoping models: **Exemplar**: information intensity matrix (Porter and Millar)	*Technology fitting frameworks:* **Exemplar**: industry dependent *Business strategy frameworks:* **Exemplar**: five forces model (Porter)	*Temporal frameworks:* **Exemplar**: stages of growth models

identifying strategic opportunities for the use of IS in SMEs. The increase in depth of shading indicates the reduction in usefulness in analysis.

Positioning frameworks offer least assistance to SMEs. The only positioning frameworks of value are scaling frameworks. The McFarlan–McKenney grid is useful in indicating the role of IS/IT and can provide a comparison with value chain analysis. However, again, the focus of the spatial and temporal frameworks is predicated on the existence of a separate IS department that are usually found in larger organizations and cannot easily be applied to the SME situation.

The role of the IS department in SMEs is effectively carried out by an external software provider. There are, therefore, far less control over systems maintenance activities. It is likely that once the initial IS planning has been done, any further development is reactive, driven by either software capability or a need from the business. This is unlikely to change. However, a more pro-active approach from the software provider could make the firm review its strategy and consider future IS/IT requirements. Another way would be to bring in a consultant to act as an intermediary between the firm and the software provider. In another case, Heath Springs, one person has the responsibility of reviewing IS needs and having discussions with the software provider. Senior management will need to be aware of the continuing need to provide input into the planning process.

Additionally, as customers insist on basic entry level IS/IT as a requirement for SMEs to remain preferred suppliers, it is important for SMEs to be aware of the externalities governing these relationships. The customer relationship is often seen as purely selling the product into the market. However, it is probably too much to expect strategic implications to be addressed by sales representatives. SMEs need to review their IS strategy in conjunction with the strategic direction of their customers. While it appears that the customers are extremely powerful, their dependence upon preferred suppliers continues to grow. This suggests that inter-organizational systems planning will become more important in order to maintain the industry value chain.

Awareness frameworks are as essential to the development of ISS for an SME as for larger organizations. An understanding of the business environment is critical. This provides the means for SMEs to address wider business objectives and the potential for change that IS/IT can provide. However, this needs to encompass the views of major customers. As far as it affects SMEs, efforts need be made to ascertain the customer information requirements and the compatibility of systems. Impact models are of slightly less value to SMEs than larger organizations. This might be due to the lack of a clear business strategy, although it is more likely due to a need to compete on both quality and price jointly.

Opportunity frameworks that focus on business strategy are most helpful. Application search tools and technology fitting frameworks have little relevance in the SME context, primarily because it is possible to gauge information requirements from the business strategy. Systems analysis and business strategy frameworks provide sufficient analysis to identify IS/IT opportunities for SMEs.

While the value chain is very useful, providing a view of current processes, it does not review the validity of the processes. There is a tendency for SMEs to focus purely on day-to-day issues without appreciating strategic management information requirements. Business modelling, including information flows, enables managers to see the progress of information through the organization. A potential flaw of the framework of frameworks is that it does not consider the opportunities that exist to review the business activities to see whether they address the business requirements, as is suggested by Galliers (1993).

■ Conclusions

This chapter has attempted to tackle two vital problems. One is the general need to validate ISS frameworks and the other is to assess the applicability of the frameworks in contexts other than those in which they were derived. The strengths and weaknesses of the frameworks in the context of SMEs have been demonstrated. The significance of the assumptions upon which the frameworks rest has also been emphasized.

The results show that many of the lessons from large organizations are relevant to SMEs. However, there are a number of key differences that arise because of the dependence of SMEs upon external agencies. The chapter has shown that awareness of IS potential for industry change is as important for SMEs as for their larger counterparts. Hence SME should consider IS as a matter of course in their strategic thinking. Also, there are opportunities for SMEs to use IS for strategic advantage, particularly in improving customer relationships and potentially in keeping out new entrants through IS. Strategic IS frameworks in these categories can, therefore, be seen as generic rather than only applicable to larger organizations.

The main failing for strategic IS frameworks are in the application of stages models for growth and the management of IS. This may be due to the absence of IS departments in SMEs. Additionally, senior management are closely involved in the purchase of IS because there are no real departmental heads to make decisions. Hence, it is necessary to question the general validity of these frameworks.

The frameworks identified in this chapter as having validity in the SME context provide the basic tools for SMEs to develop insights into the strategic use of IS. The next chapter develops these ideas further within the context of providing SMEs with a means of developing an ISS.

7 An organizational approach to IS strategy

■ Introduction

The previous chapter demonstrates the value of information systems strategic frameworks in the small- and medium-sized enterprises context. This chapter takes these ideas forward by reviewing and then developing an information systems strategy method for SMEs. The method is based on the contention of Chapter 6 that some existing frameworks can be used. However, the literature not only recognizes that technology is important, but that it is necessary to understand the organizational context in which it will be used (Earl, 1996a; Walsham, 1993; Galliers, 1991).

The characteristics of SMEs, particularly the informality of strategic planning, make this emphasis more critical in the development of an ISS (Blili and Raymond, 1993). An ISS approach from an organizational and cultural perspective is developed as a means of addressing this issue. The suitability of available analytical tools for ISS in the SME environment is discussed. The method described has been used in the 68 cases identified in the introduction to develop ISS for SMEs. Data from these cases are used to demonstrate the strengths of the method and to indicate further refinements that may be made.

This chapter first reviews ISS development in SMEs. It then critiques current tools and techniques. The use of corporate ISS models in SMEs is synthesized which leads on to reflection on the nature of ISS. This highlights the need for a multi-paradigm approach to ISS for SMEs. Such an approach is then developed based on theory extension and case research.

■ ISS in SMEs

As technology becomes more central to SMEs' products and processes, planning IS becomes more critical (Blili and Raymond, 1993). Planning IS in SMEs also needs to be integrated with business strategy. Yet, few SMEs plan their IS (Hagmann and McCahon, 1993). The limited planning that is undertaken tends to focus on operational systems to improve efficiency and effectiveness, and there is little concern with competitiveness. Firms can usefully reflect on the role of IS and adjust their IS planning process to match (Premkumar and King, 1991).

One reason for SMEs' limited view of planning is that, as discussed in Chapter 5, the incremental investment in IS usually in response to a specific identified need, particularly to improve basic administration and transaction processing. As stated in Chapter 3, SMEs often develop complex management reporting processes using simple IS. More importantly, once managers use the information available to consider strategic issues, benefits accrue. Once benefits arise, SMEs are more inclined to invest further in IS as was described in the case of Flower and Samios in Chapter 3. Information systems is central to their future success and growth, business strategy and IS strategy becoming intertwined. Indeed, SMEs that plan ahead and manage change are more likely to be successful in managing growth (Churchill and Lewis, 1983). They regard planning for systems ahead of the stage of growth for which they are required as particularly important. Additionally, highly competitive environments are also likely to drive SMEs to change business processes. Investment in IS increases survival rates of SMEs, supporting the contention that IS are vital to SMEs (Agarwal, 1998).

Hence, IS can have value for SMEs, and SMEs need to develop strategies for their IS. The key task for researchers and practitioners is to determine how SMEs may best develop ISS. While the field is under-researched, there is some work that has relevance. This chapter investigates this and builds upon it. It is vital that the outcome is an ISS development method that is both methodologically rigorous but also, crucially, operationalizable in the SME context. The research underpinning this chapter has two mutually supporting thrusts. The first is theoretical, critiquing existing ISS tools and developing new ones. The second is practical, using case analysis to test and amend the tools.

■ Approaches to ISS

As discussed in Chapter 6, one of the key roles for ISS is to identify systems that enable competitiveness. Competitiveness not only focuses on external strategic benefits, but internal process benefits through efficiency and effectiveness improvements. This is important for SMEs: in particular, is the need to use information technology as a means of integration within the industry supply chain (Blili and Raymond, 1993). As discussed in Chapter 6 business planning and ISS should be integrated. This supports the objective of developing systems with a strategic focus and ensuring that competitiveness is at the forefront of decisions to invest in IS.

While the strategic focus dominated ISS research in the 1980s, an organizational perspective is now evident. Information system strategy need to fit with the predominant organizational culture; hence there is a need to appreciate the underlying ethos and values in developing a suitable ISS (Earl, 1996a). Understanding the relationships in an organization are critical to the adoption of successful IS (Checkland and Holwell, 1998). It is important to recognize the difference between the "intended" ISS identified from the business strategy and the "realized" ISS that depends on appreciating organizational issues that inhibit success (Walsham, 1993).

A number of the key differences between SMEs and large firms are believed to influence strategic IS. These issues are first, uncertainty regarding IT and competition, where the limited knowledge of owners makes decisions on strategic IS difficult. Second, SMEs may not be able to respond to the introduction of strategic IS due to limited resources, including implementation and training. Finally, SMEs may not identify the potential from IT due to their operational focus. These issues need to be addressed for successful use of IT for competitive advantage (Blili and Raymond, 1993).

It is important for firms to measure the success of the business strategy and this can only be done through identification of relevant information (Galliers, 1991). This information forms the basis of the ISS. Galliers and Swan (1996) extend this idea, suggesting that ISS should *"place much greater emphasis on informal as well as formal information flows, both within and outside organizational boundaries"*.

Thus, while the focus of ISS is on alignment with business strategy, there is also recognition of the need to take account of culture and the role of information. These findings, while derived from research into large organizations, are relevant to SMEs. Crucially, ISS may provide a way to unlock the information available to SMEs and provide them with the means to be more competitive.

A multi-paradigm approach to ISS

Information system strategy is integral to business strategy, but an approach developed for SMEs needs to take account of their informal approach to business strategy (McKeirnan and Morris, 1994). SME owners usually have an implicit strategy but it is often not shared with other members of the management team. As outlined in Chapter 2, SMEs tend to be organic with informal management structures built round small management teams. Strategic information is usually held informally within that team. This suggests that any ISS approach for SMEs needs to take account of this informality. Therefore, a focus on information requirements is likely to be more appropriate than concentrating on IT requirements.

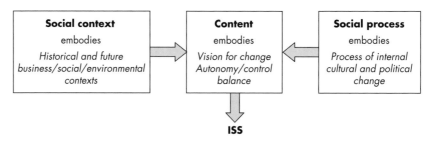

Figure 7.1: Themes in developing an ISS. (*Source*: adapted from Walsham, 1993.)

The main thrust of the organizational approach is to provide management with information to enable them to monitor efficiency and effectiveness, and to provide them with insights as to potential competitive advantage from use of IS. However, as discussed, ISS cannot be considered in a vacuum; business strategy and organizational structure need to be an integral part of the process. Organizational issues relate to the roles of individuals and their capacity for change, particularly when faced with the potentially radical change implied by the introduction of IS (Yetton *et al.*, 1994).

One approach to ISS considers the wider social, cultural and political environment of the organization may also influence the development of an ISS. The organization is viewed from various perspectives that add richness to the analysis, leading to more acceptable solutions as ISS as a process of change that must consider the social context and social process. It is the linkage between the two that ensures an effective solution. The third element to be considered is the role of IS in the firm, both organizational and technological (Walsham, 1993) (Figure 7.1).

Both Earl's framework of frameworks (see Chapter 6) and Walsham's social context/social process/content model assist in the development of an ISS for SMEs. The Framework of Frameworks helps in identifying the technology opportunities that are available to the industry and applicable to the SME. Walsham's model provides the organizational understanding essential for the successful adoption of IS through the vision of the owner, the social background of the firm and the industry and the firm's capacity to change.

These approaches to ISS are developed from different research paradigms. Earl's work draws on models that come from a positivistic stance, while Walsham is firmly located within an interpretivist perspective. The question must be posed as to whether it is possible to use such different methods. IS research approaches appear to fall into four categories that range from objective to subjective along one axis and unitary to pluralist along the other. Strategic planning has tended to be

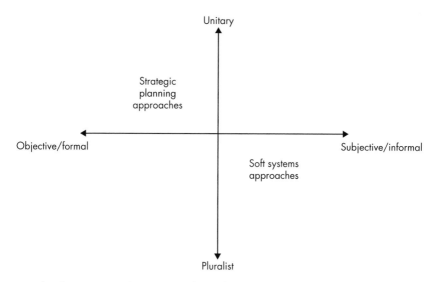

Figure 7.2: Classifying IS approaches. (*Source:* adapted from Gallier and Swan, 1997.)

in the unitary/objective sector, primarily because it has focused solely on the IS to support firms rather than consider the role of information. However, to understand the wider, possibly, more informal information flows, pluralist/informal approaches are likely to be better. The main one of these is soft systems methodology (SSM) (Checkland, 1981), which is discussed in more detail below. Critically, the different approaches should not be seen as conflicting, but as providing a means to understand the multi-faceted nature of information requirements in organizations (Galliers and Swan, 1997) (Figure 7.2).

Indeed, complex, multi-dimensional research situations, such as the organizational context represented by SMEs, require a "blend of methods from different paradigms" (Mingers, 1997). Mingers argues that "paradigm incommensurability" is no longer thought to be quite so firm and there are thought to be some bridges that can be made. This is particularly the case in IS research and a new paradigm, "critical pluralist" (Mingers, 1997) is proposed that suggests that multi-paradigm research focuses on three aspects. First, the "research content system" provides the real world situation within the research project. Second, the "intellectual resources system" enables researchers to draw upon the various theories and methods. The third aspect of the approach is the "research intervention system" recognizes that researchers use and approach to techniques may influence their use. This "critical pluralist" approach is used here to develop ISS for SMEs as it recognizes the need to deal with the formality of the competitive environment while recognizing the informality of management and organization within SMEs.

■ A multi-paradigm model for ISS in SMEs

The ISS framework (Figure 7.3) adapts Walsham's (1993) themes for IS strategy. There are three perspectives. First, the business context provides the understanding of the business environment within which the SME operates. This focuses particularly on the market and relationships with customers and suppliers. The owner's strategy for the business is elicited to aid identification of critical success factors (CSF). These provide the basis for strategic information requirements. The second perspective is business process. This focuses on understanding the work processes in the SME to appreciate whether information flows inhibit business activities, and also to identify changes that might be made as a result of the introduction of IS. Additionally, information available to the SME is identified. Finally, the strategic content embodies the vision for change from the owner and the practicality of its introduction given organizational circumstances.

Business context

There are three main aspects to the first part of the ISS development. First, the business strategy and objectives are identified. Second, the business environment of the SME is reviewed. Finally, the competitive environment is assessed.

A key issue for SMEs is their lack of an explicit business strategy but the owners' objectives are critical to the process of ISS (Blili and Raymond, 1993). Yet, many owners do have an implicit strategy and this can often be elicited. Critical success factors are a useful approach to determine whether strategic objectives have been met. Critical successs

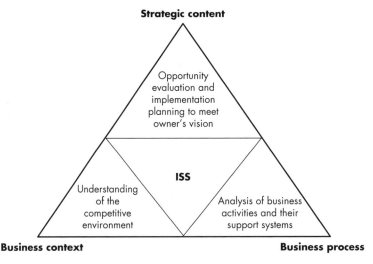

Figure 7.3: The ISS approach for SMEs.

factors are derived from the business objectives and represent the things that the business must get right in order to be successful (Boynton and Zmud, 1984). Performance measures are defined for each CSF as a means of determining whether they have been achieved. Performance measures always have a value associated with them, for example sales revenue will increase by 10% in the next year. Once performance measures are identified it is possible to determine the information that is required in order to know whether it has been met. This helps define systems requirements.

The balanced business scorecard (Figure 7.4) is a useful means of assessing whether a business has considered strategic objectives from customer, financial, organizational and growth perspectives (Kaplan and Norton, 1996).

The strength of the balanced business scorecard is that firms look at measures other than finance. The financial perspective is important as it addresses the question of how the firm appears to shareholders. The internal business perspective considers what has to be done well within the current operation to satisfy employees and others with whom the business interacts. Innovation and learning addresses the strategies required to grow and develop the business in the future. Finally, the customer perspective considers how the firm is perceived by customers in term of quality and service.

The business environment is assessed using standard analytical tools such as PESTEL (Table 7.1) and SWOT (Figure 7.5) for the overall context, while, as shown in Chapter 6, Porter and Millar's (1985) information intensity matrix provides a guide to the importance of information.

Strategic opportunities from IS, including emerging technologies, available to the industry in terms of production support

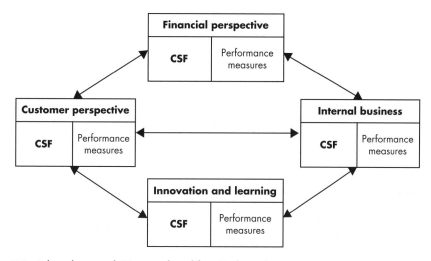

Figure 7.4: Balanced scorecard. (*Source*: adapted from Kaplan and Norton, 1996.)

Table 7.1: PESTEL analysis issues

Political	The political environment within which firms work may influence decisions that are taken. For example there may be tariff barriers in place. There may be particular issues relating to the global region within which a firm is situated. There may be restrictions on trade with particular countries
Economic	Costs are driving many firms, both large and small to relocate production to Eastern Europe, China and South America. As these areas are moving more towards free market economies, they are encouraging inward investment. This has many ramifications for firms as they have to consider the overall benefits of moving production. These include issues of managing quality, delivery and currency fluctuations
Social	The main focus here is customer values. There is a need to understand the demography of the customer base. In many Western European countries people are living longer, are fitter and have more disposable income. The "greying factor" is more important and older people are likely to wield more buying power in the future. Retirement is beginning to be seen as a voluntary activity. In contrast there are other countries, particularly in Africa where the population is much younger and has less disposable income. The gap between those who are information rich and information poor is widening
Technological	Technology has changed dramatically in the last 25 years since the introduction of the PC in the late 1970s. Microchip technology has revolutionized the development of computers. The Internet has dramatically changed communication. While the dot.com bubble burst rather quickly, many hi-tech SMEs are being started. New products and services using new technologies are being developed rapidly. It is important to understand whether the market is ready for the technology
Environmental	The discovery of the hole in the ozone layer, acid rain, nuclear waste in the sea, the extinction of many species have all led to a rise in concern among many people about the future of the world. Firms are expected to consider the impact upon the environment of the use of resources associated with their products or services. Technology-based companies in particular telephony companies are under scrutiny with regard to health issues associated with radio waves
Legal	Technology has made it possible to collect data on people to a much greater degree. Store loyalty cards enable purchasing patterns to be monitored. Internet shopping enables personal details including credit card details to be stored. The use of this information has been prohibited in many countries except for use by the firm collecting it and for the purpose for which it has been collected. There are also legal issues for product distribution as the music and video industries are finding as it is possible to digitally download these products without paying for them

(e.g. MRP) management support (e.g. financial analysis) and customer support (e.g. EDI) are useful to clarify this. Competitive forces analysis provides the basis for understanding the pressures on SMEs.

	Exploit	**Reduce**
Internal	**Strengths** *What the firm does well and can exploit to maintain and grow its market position*	**Weaknesses** *Understanding the products and processes within the business that are restricting growth*
External	**Opportunities** *Identifying future products and services or new markets that can be developed*	**Threats** *Knowing which competitors are likely to encroach on markets and identifying ways of reducing the threat*

Figure 7.5: SWOT analysis.

The business environment part of the framework encompasses industry awareness and an understanding of the firm's competitive position together with the vision of the owner.

Business processes

There are three activities in the business process element of the framework. First, understand the value-adding processes that contribute to the business. Second, identify whether the SME has the relevant systems to support both the business objectives and the value-adding processes. Finally, the extant IT is assessed.

The main issue here is to identify value-adding activities. To enrich understanding of these activities the organizational environment and the roles of the players involved need to be understood. The value chain identifies the key value-adding activities and the information flows between them. However, as discussed, ISS benefits from organizational fit. Soft systems methodology provides a means of analyzing organizational information flows and a comparison with the value chain. This comparison gives the means of appreciating how much of what the organization does adds value. The SSM analysis identifies issues in the organization that may need to be resolved for the value-adding activities to be effective.

The purpose of SSM is to enable the study of unstructured problem situations from a variety of viewpoints. Checkland's argument is that different people have different perspectives on a problem. The classic example he quotes is a prison; the prison officers seeing it as a place of restraint, the education officers, a place for re-education and the public as a place of punishment. The various perspectives lead to different views on the activities that should take place inside the prison.

There are several stages to SSM (Table 7.2). The most important aspect to the analysis is the constant iteration of the models developed. They are constantly compared with the real world so that the best fit is

Table 7.2: Description of SSM stages

SSM stages	Phases	Description
Finding out		This task is one that involves interviewing as wide a range of people as possible to identify the key issues. It may not be clear at this stage what the problem really is. This stage is the precursor to being able to express the problem situation clearly in both words and pictures
Expressing the problem situation		This stage is an opportunity to clarify with the problem owners the analysts understanding of the problem situation. The key technique that Checkland uses is the drawing of rich pictures (see Chapter 7). These are drawings that represent in an unstructured form the problem situation. They often take the form of elementary cartoon drawings (e.g. stick people, computers) that show the relationships between different aspects of the problem situation. They are useful for indicating contradictory information and highlighting communication problems
Deriving the root definition		A root definition expresses the central purpose of the system that is being modelled. There will be an over-arching root definition that encompasses the essence of the whole system under review. There will be a number of lower level root definitions that embrace the lower level activities that are the components of the total system
		There are a number of phases in this part of the analysis that enable the root definition to be developed. This is where SSM starts to put some structure into the analysis
	The transformation process	This process is about defining a set of transformations that will achieve the aims of the organization. Different people in the organization will have different objectives and therefore different transformation. While it is important not to disregard any transformations, there needs to be some reflection back onto the issues highlighted in the rich picture
	The root definition	Checkland argues that it is only when you have put a name to a system that its function or purpose becomes clear. The root definition does this in a structured way from the perspective of the main player in the problem. In the analysis it is important to consider the sponsor's objectives. The root definition takes account not only of the transformations itself, but also the people involved in different ways in achieving the transformation. The following aspects all need to be considered in defining the system: Customer: for whom is the system operated?

Table 7.2: (Continued)

SSM stages	Phases	Description
		Actors: which single group of people will perform the activities?
		Transformation: which single process will transform the input into the output?
		Worldview: what is the view that makes the transformation worthwhile?
		Owner: who has the power to say whether the system will be implemented or not?
		Environment: what are the constraints that may prevent the system from being successful?
Deriving conceptual models		This stage provides an ideal view of the various activities or business processes that have to be undertaken models to achieve the transformation. Checkland suggests that monitor and review is a useful activity to be included in all models. It is also possible at this stage to consider the information requirements that link the different activities
Comparison between the ideal and real word models		The next stage is to decide what actions need to be taken to address the differences between the ideal the ideal and real model and the real world. It is important to note that actions resulting form this analysis may not require word models technological solutions but may primarily require organizational change to exploit the use of current technologies more effectively

obtained to move towards changes in business activities or processes and information flows that support organizational objectives.

Organizational culture may determine the most appropriate IS (Checkland and Holwell, 1998). The analysis is undertaken through semi-structured interviews with the senior managers and the staff responsible for operations. The main outcome is a model of the key business activities essential to achieving the business objectives. Organizational inhibitors and enablers are identified. The information requirements for the business are also derived from this analysis.

Existing IS need to be assessed. This may be of more importance than for large organizations as SMEs' propensity to invest in IS is much lower. If current systems provide the organization with useful information there may be no need to change them and manual systems may be all that is required. The McFarlan-McKenney (1983) strategic grid (see Chapter 6) assesses the business value of the SMEs' IS. As Earl (1989) argues, organizations should regularly review their IS to see whether they continue to support the business objectives.

Information technology is also a critical part of an ISS (Earl, 1989). However, is shown in Chapter 4, IT in many SMEs inhibit precisely the flexibility for which SMEs are renowned. Most SMEs expect their IT to have a longer life than in larger firms, which means that many are locked into systems developed using third generation tools that may be unsupported or, at the very least, incompatible with current industry standards.

Strategic content

The strategic content stage compares the business strategy requirements with the organizational analysis to generate an understanding of the capacity of the organization to grow and develop from the use of IS. At this stage strategic alignment can usefully be considered (see Chapter 3). The MIT'90s strategic alignment framework reminds the analyst of the individual issues that affect performance in the firm. However, the real benefit of the framework is in recognizing and addressing how the impact of a decision in one aspect may affect the all the others.

There is a need to balance the ability of the organization to cope with change with the need to make strategic decisions on the use of IS. The owner's vision is revisited at this stage to ensure that recommendations fit. The 3D model of IS success provides a means for considering the ability of the SME to manage the relationships between technical development, deployment within the organization and delivery of business objectives (Figure 7.6).

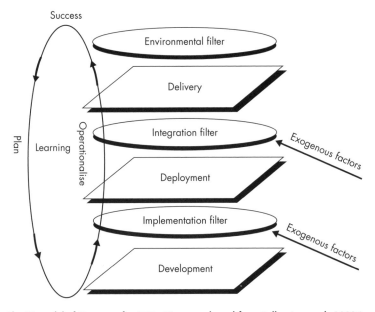

Figure 7.6: The 3D model of IS success for SMEs. (*Source*: adapted from Ballantine *et al.*, 1998.)

Success in IS can be identified at three levels (the "Ds"). First is the *development* level that addresses the technical development of a computer system for an SME. Second is the *deployment* level: where the system is used within the firm. The final level is *delivery* at which the contribution of the system to the firm's objectives as a whole are realized. Success at one level does not imply success at the next. Exogenous factors are those issues that can impede movement to the next level. For example, existing IS may be more comfortable for staff to use than new systems; this reluctance is demonstrated by the *implementation* filter. The *integration* filter is about the fit between the business strategy and use of the IS. Over and above the levels of achievement of success discussed, there is an issue of learning through time and experience, leading to better planning and knowledge of systems to grow the firm.

The ISS analysis identifies opportunities for best practice through the use of IS. However, as resources are tight SMEs will have to prioritise which systems they require. Systems may be organizational or computer-based. The analysis considers the contribution of systems to the business, the likely financial return from the systems, and the difficulty of implementation. For each system firms should consider the relative importance of market position, competitive advantage, financial return and the ease of implementation. They are unlikely to be of equal value to a firm and different firms will ascribe different weightings. It is useful to determine the contribution of each category to the business strategy (Ormerod, 1998). Ormerod offers a number of criteria that are shown in Table 7.3. These are examples; other criteria may be more relevant to the firm under study.

Systems are evaluated to ensure that they support achievement of the business strategy or that proposals are integrated into changes in the business strategy. The objective is to develop a set of recommendations that are practical, feasible and realistic in the SME context.

Figure 7.7 presents all the tools and techniques discussed above and in Chapter 6 within the context of the organization ISS framework. The next section considers the use of the ISS framework and the value of the models to the development of an ISS.

Table 7.3: Implementation decisions for proposed systems. (Adapted from Ormerod, 1998.)

	1 point	*3 points*	*5 points*
Market position	Nice to have	Build	Critical
Competitive advantage	Support	Primary value chain	Leverage (industry value chain)
Financial return	1–2 years	3–5 years	Unclear
Ease to implement	Enhancements	New system old technology	New system new technology

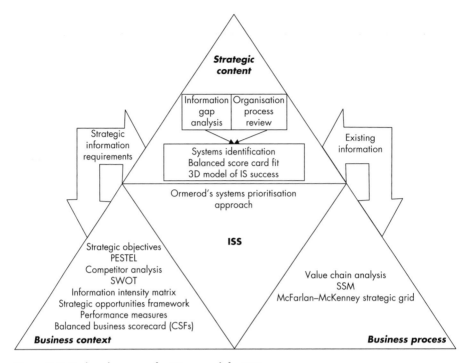

Figure 7.7: Tools and processes for ISS approach for SMEs.

■ Background to the case SMEs

This chapter presents data from 44 ISS developed for the case firms presented in Chapter 1 (Table 7.4). The outcome of the analysis is discussed below. The information is summarized and examples are presented rather than the complete set of results. Tables 7.5 and 7.6 show the industry sectors and size of firms used here to demonstrate ISS development. For succinctness, examples of the firms are provided as the others demonstrate similar outcomes.

The majority of case firms are small. They are currently in the position of considering their growth potential, hence these firms may have interest in using IS to manage growth.

There is no attempt to specifically select by industry groups. The contention of the ISS model presented in this chapter is that the focus of ISS is primarily on the role of information as a strategic resource, and that this is relevant to all industries. The process in developing the ISS is through interviews with the SME owner and staff as discussed in Chapter 1. In all cases the analysis is confirmed with interviewees. The synthesis of the ISS is also confirmed with the SME owner. The models and tools used to analyze the firm are those shown in Figure 7.7.

Table 7.4: ISS case firms

Name	Business	Ownership	Number of employees
Business services			
Public Sector Advocates	Community and public sector legal work	Partnership	108
Electrical Accreditation Agency	Electrical accreditation	Electrical industry	22
Soil Analysis Co.	Chemical analysis of soil	CEO	63
Energy Saving Co.	Environmental consultancy, energy maximization	CEO	17
Family Attorneys	Legal affairs	Partnership	20
Chemical Analysis Co.	Geotechnical and environmental consultancy	Family	38
Accountancy Firm	Chartered accountants	3 partners	23
Design and Marketing Co.	Marketing communications consultancy	Family	16
Events Management Co.	Conference organization	Partnership (3)	20
Mobile Phone Surveyors	Identification of land sites for erection of radio communication masts	CEO	6
Training Brokerage Co.	Management Training Agency	CEO	9
Seven Stars Printers	Printers of high quality colour work	Family, general manager introduced	10
Queensway Photographic	Development of window display photos	CEO	25
IT			
Biotechnology Software Developers	Development of software for scientific imaging analysis	Three directors	20
Manufacturing			
Light Assembly Co.	Assembly of light fittings	Family, general manager introduced	24
Epoxy Resin Co.	Development and manufacture of epoxy resins	Family	15
Enamel Box Co.	Manufacture of enamel gift boxes	Family and CEO	60
Car Paint Co.	Manufacture of car paints	Family, general manager introduced	36
Heath Springs	Coil spring manufacturer	Owned by Petersen group	112
Marine Cable Co.	Marine cable design and manufacture	Group autonomous division within multi-national	20
Burring Engineers	Manufacture of deburring machines	Family	24

(continued)

Table 7.4: (Continued)

Name	Business	Ownership	No of employees
Clutch Assembly Co.	Manufacture of automotive sub-assemblies	Family	285
Precision Tool Co.	Precision tooling manufacturer	Group	24
Car Sign Design Co.	Graphic design liveries for the automotive industry	CEO	15
Perforated Products Manufacturer	Manufacture of perforated products for the filtration industry	CEO	50
Wood Pallet Manufacturer	Wood pallet manufacturer	Family	44
Optical Lens Manufacturer	Manufacture of optical lenses	CEO and company secretary	10
Landfill Gas Co.	Production of equipment to extract methane from landfill sites	Family	40

Social services, education and not for profit firms

Name	Business	Ownership	No of employees
Recycling Training Co.	Training firm for people with disabilities using recycling	Owned by two partners	5
Skills Training Co.	Training provider	Family, not for profit organization	23
IT Education Charity	IT educational charity	Trustees	150
Tree House Health	Private high dependency care nursing home	Partnership	108
Garden Health Care	Private nursing home and sheltered accommodation	CEO	30
Rural Health Practice	Fund-holding general practice	Senior partner and four partners	22
University Arts Centre	Theatre, concert and conference complex	Non-profit organization	20

Wholesale and retail trade

Name	Business	Ownership	No of employees
Regional Travel Co.	Independent travel agent	Family	23
Holiday Coach Co.	Coach holiday and bus service providers	Family	48
Model Toy Co.	Supply and distribution of model car collectables	Two owner managers	5
Landrover Repair Co.	Renovation and repair of Landrovers	CEO	16
Wholesale Garden Nursery	Garden nursery wholesaler	Family	26
Heating Maintenance Co.	Heating systems maintenance	Family	14
Bird Designs	Design and manufacture of paper and wood goods	Family	16
Specialist Insurance Broker	Specialist insurance brokers	Two partners	27
Corporate Gift Co.	Design and manufacture of corporate gifts	Family	27

Table 7.5: Size of case firms

Firm size (employees)	Number
0–9	4
10–99	35
100–499	5

Table 7.6: Industry groups of case firms

Industry groups	Number
Manufacturing	14
Wholesale and retail trade	9
Business services	13
Social services and public administration	7
IT	1

The outcomes of the analysis are discussed and the value of the different tools and techniques reviewed.

■ Outcomes from the ISS

For many SMEs the process of developing an ISS is, in itself, of value. As discussed in Chapter 2, most SME owners do not have time for activities outside the day-to-day running of their operation. However, many owners recognize that growth means that they needed to systematize processes. Hence, having to articulate issues for the analysts gives owners the opportunity to reflect on their strategies to meet their objectives. The following discussion considers the outcomes of this research in the context of issues identified in the literature. These are, first, the operational focus of planning for IS (Hagmann and McCahon, 1993). Second, the use of IT to improve competitiveness is an issue that SMEs should consider (Blili and Raymond, 1993). Third, the relationship between the owner and strategy is important for growth (Storey, 1994). Finally, organizational culture may impact on the ISS as indicated by Walsham (1993).

Operational focus to IS

Not unexpectedly, the emphasis for IS in SMEs is directed to production operation systems and support for these activities (Figure 7.8). These can be quite sophisticated, for example, a design firm uses computerized designs linked to printing processes. However, often they are not used effectively. Manufacturers have been encouraged to purchase MRP systems by their customers. Yet, these SMEs have not changed their

	Strategic	**Turnaround**
	Customer databases (14) EDI (4) E-Mail (1)	
	Order processing (8) CAD (8) MRP (5) Job tracking (3) Job costing (2) Stock control (3)	Word processing (44) Accounting (35)
	Factory	**Support**

Figure 7.8: Distribution of IS in case firms using the strategic grid.

Table 7.7: Competitiveness of case firm markets

Competitiveness	Number of SMEs
High	34
Medium	1
Low	9

operational processes to use MRP effectively. This is demonstrated in the case of a spring manufacturer, Heath Springs, discussed in Chapter 8. The outcomes of the ISS in this study suggest the vision for IS is firmly directed at improving the operation with limited appreciation of the value of strategic information.

The analysis of the cases also indicates that there is little support for managers to measure the success of their business. For example, while the majority of the SMEs in the study have accounting packages, financial analysis is not carried out. There is no evidence of the wider measures advocated by the balanced business scorecard to monitor firm performance. For example, few SMEs monitor customer satisfaction formally, review employee satisfaction or consider innovation.

Competitiveness

Porter's (1980) five forces model is used to assess competitiveness. The results reflect the perceptions of the owners together with additional research on the industry sector. The outcomes were discussed with the owners. Thirty-four of the SMEs are in highly competitive industries with both local and national competition (Table 7.7).

Customer power is high in just over half the firms (Table 7.8). The pressures from customers tend to be for better quality products and reduced prices. However, for many of the firms operating in niche markets, they are the customers' sole source either because of the particular product or location of the firm. Despite the rise of the Internet, many customers

Table 7.8: Customer power in case firms

Customer power	Number of firms
High	24
Medium	3
Low	17

prefer to work with local firms as identified by Porter (1998) in his discussions on clustering.

Most of the SMEs are constantly striving to improve product quality and reduce prices, although only two firms (Design and Marketing Co. and Mobile Phone Surveyors) see a need to change business processes.

Case study 7.1

Design and Marketing Co. is an innovative, family-owned firm started in 1986. Designers work closely with clients to build an individual marketing and design message. The firm has 16 very loyal employees and is undergoing rapid growth. The management of the firm is still in survival mode, where all decisions and power is centred round the owner. The owner recognizes that he needs to both develop a small management team and to keep costs down, the designers need to work differently. As most of the designers work out of the office he wants to explore using IS to support changes in work practices. Installing a network is a priority for the firm. They will then be able to develop a database to support each design project, which will mean that designers will be able to access information from anywhere in the office and remotely. The firm will not require an increase in premises as urgently as workstations can be shared. Similarly, management IS will support the management team that is being set up to manage projects and finance. The owner recognizes that his role is more strategic.

This contradicts findings by Reid and Smith (1999). The reasons may be that most of the SMEs have owner-managers who tend to be more risk averse than general managers or empire builders (Hay and Kamshad, 1994).

Most owners do not think of using IS as a competitive weapon (Ryan and Hepworth, 1998). Primarily in the manufacturing cases, customer influence is critical to their approach to IS. In most of the others the response is to work harder at finding new customers and, to a lesser extent, to obtain more business from existing customers.

Owners

In a minority of cases the vision of the SME owner does extend to using IS as an integral way of running the business (Design and Marketing Co.

and Mobile Phone Surveyors). These owners are innovative and
knowledgeable about IS potential and are prepared to take risks to achieve
their objectives (Hay and Kamshad, 1994). They appear to be planning
their systems to manage future growth (Churchill and Lewis, 1983).
However, most owners acknowledge their limited knowledge of IS. This
often leads to concerns over whether they are being given good advice on
IS. Hence, there is a reluctance to spend limited resources in an area over
which many feel they do not have control.

Most owners focus on management IS that will help them control the
operational process rather than grow. Using the Benjamin *et al.* (1994)
strategic opportunities framework, as adapted by Earl (1989), Table 7.9
illustrates the limited management support provided by IS for a selection
of the case firms. The profiles of the other firms are similar. These

Table 7.9: Examples of current systems in case firms by function

Firm	Production	Management support	Customer relations
Manufacturing			
Perforated Products Manufacturer	Labelling system CAD	Accounting	
Wooden Pallet Manufacturer	OPERA order processing and production management	Accounting	
Clutch Assembly Co.	MRP CAD		EDI
Wholesale and retail trade			
Enamel Box Co.	Production control and information Sales order processing	Accounting	
Model Toy Co.		Customer database	
Bird Designs		Accounting (SAGE) Sales order processing	
Business services			
Regional Travel Co.	Ticket booking Customer database		
Mobile Phone Surveyors	CAD for plans Photo manipulation software	Accounting Work progress monitoring	
Chemical Analysis Co.	Report production Laboratory analysis		
Social services and public administration			
Rural Health Practice	Fund-holding system Medical system		
IT Education Charity	Project planning (needs review)	E-mail Sales system Finance system	Contact database Events database
Tree House Health	Nurse call	Accounting	

examples indicate that accounting systems provide the main management support. Wooden Pallet Manufacturer (Chapter 3), Clutch Assembly Co. (Chapter 4), Bird Designs (Chapter 2) and Mobile Phone Surveyors (Chapter 3) have been introduced earlier. Brief details are outlined of the other firms used as examples.

Case study 7.2

Perforated Products Manufacturer is a small family firm started in 1945 to manufacture combs. Today they manufacture perforated products for the automotive industry. They have developed process technology products with a US firm and are the only manufacturer in the UK. This is a growth area. The firm has been growing organically, with no clearly defined business strategy. They are starting to come under pressure from the automotive manufacturers to integrate systems to provide information on quality and accounting. The firm has no IT to support production scheduling or stock control. Their accounting system is only sufficient for basic statutory needs.

Case study 7.3

Enamel Box Co. is jointly owned by the original family and the new CEO. It manufactures high quality enamel giftware that is highly prized. The firm sells to major retailers. It has a loyal and dedicated staff, training takes at least 9 months and is a significant barrier to entry in the industry. The firm has invested heavily in production technologies, as plant and machinery to fire the product is costly. However, the management and process support is not sufficient to manage the growth. The firm has a number of standalone systems: stock control, pricing, order entry and accounting. The lack of integration means that there are growing inefficiencies in the firm that are leading to rising costs.

Case study 7.4

Model Toy Co. is a family-owned micro-firm run by the owner and his wife. The firm sells collectable model cars to both retailers and individuals. One of the owners has considerable experience in corporate IT and recognizes the value of using IT to manage the business. However, given the size of the business customer databases are the main application that has been developed. Customers are contacted regularly through a newsletter. Neither competitors nor suppliers use IT to any great extent, which makes it difficult for the firm to obtain information. However, they recognize the need to improve systems as inventory holdings need to be reduced. They also need more information on customers to increase sales.

Case study 7.5

Regional Travel Co. is a family run travel agency with seven branches in local towns. The firm specializes in the luxury end of the market providing tours to exotic destinations and providing support for independent travellers. The firm also has a business travel arm that it plans to extend. The firm has sufficient production technologies to book holidays and flights. However, they do not have management and support systems in place. For example, accounting has little IT support, which means that it is a time consuming operation for the firm. While they have a customer database it is not used greatly for marketing. There is no IT network between branches. Therefore all staff knowledge remains local. Knowledge is the key to growth: the firm needs systems that exploit it.

Case study 7.6

Chemical Analysis Co. is a small family-run firm that analyses soil samples for local authorities and utility industries. The firm was started in 1983 by the owner and his wife and grew steadily for 10 years. However, growth has declined since then and the business is in a steady state. The market is highly competitive, with price being the main driver. The firm is looking to improve efficiencies and reduce costs. Most systems are manual. For example, project costs are developed afresh for each. There is no costs database for engineers' time or materials. There is a standalone accounting package and spreadsheets are used by senior management. Analysis reports are produced using a specialist package. Other than this there is little management support.

Case study 7.7

Rural Health Practice is a five doctor medical practice in a rural area. It serves a large and dispersed community. The practice not only provides first-line health care from general practitioners but has developed nursing and ancillary care services alongside. Consultants from the nearest hospital also run clinics from the practice. The medical systems are good and provide the information required to manage the practice. These are standalone systems. However, they are not able to access information from hospital or central records for patients or to manage finances. The majority of systems to support the practice are paper based. The health practice recognizes the need to use IT more effectively and is actively looking at ways to achieve this.

Case study 7.8

IT Education Charity is a leading charity providing the education sector with knowledge about the potential from IT for learning. The charity works closely with government and education authorities in projects to develop understanding and use of IT. They are a medium-sized organization. The charity is poised to grow further and needs better management systems to achieve this. They have internal e-mail, which does not always work effectively. The contact database is critical to the charity as it holds all the information that enables it to develop and grow. The charity has developed sales, finance, planning (spreadsheets) and an events database. These are not integrated and do not provide the senior management team with effective reports. The charity recognizes that it needs to improve information flows to enable strategic use of the available data.

Case study 7.9

Tree House Health is a medium-sized firm that provides healthcare and long-term residence for the elderly. The firm is owned by six partners, of whom only one is actively involved in day-to-day management. The management team is small. The nature of the business is such that they need a large staff to provide quality care for the elderly patients. Again there are few management support tools used. A major problem for this firm is the high pressure from customers for price reduction and the competitive nature of the market. However, they have no systems in place that enable them to collect and analyze such information. The firm needs to keep costs down while maintaining quality. A financial costing system will help monitor costs and enable the firm to identify areas of potential reduction. More strategically, the firm could investigate working with local health service providers in using health extranets that are beginning to be developed by the health service.

However, the ISS process may elicit a number of other systems that owners believe will help them manage their business better (Table 7.10). It is interesting to note that these systems are still focused on supporting the effectiveness of the firm rather than competitiveness as identified through customer focus. For example, there is an emphasis on forecasting and sales order processing for many of the SMEs. Financial analysis is also recognized as important for managing future growth.

Organizational culture

Two models provide insights into organizational and cultural issues. Soft systems methodology provides insights into information flows within

Table 7.10: Examples of potential systems identified from ISS

Firm	Production	Management support	Customer relations
Manufacturing			
Perforated Products Manufacturer	Costing system; stock control; scheduling delivery	Financial monitoring; personnel performance monitoring	
Wooden Pallet Manufacturer	Costing system; CAD; part cost database		
Clutch Assembly Co.		Performance measurement; costing system; forecasting; skills database	
Wholesale and retail trade			
Enamel Box Co.	Production scheduling; raw material planning; Quality tracking; work-in-progress tracking; stock control	Sales costing; sales forecasting	Market information
Model Toy Co.	Stock control	Financial controls	E-mail; Internet
Bird Designs	CAD for design of new products	Performance monitoring	Integrated customer database and helpline
Business services			
Regional Travel Co.	Accounting; electronic bulletin; tour design	Management reports; performance monitoring; travel information system	Customer feedback system
Mobile Phone Surveyors		Resource planning; project management	Customer contact monitoring market intelligence
Chemical Analysis Co.	Project control; invoicing; inventory control; geological database	Tendering; resource utilization; forecasting; quality standards	Credit control; Internet
Social services and public administration			
Rural Health Practice		Electronic patient records; room planning (external consultants and services); personnel system to assist better skills knowledge and training recognition	EDI link to FHSA; EDI link to hospitals
IT Education Charity	Stock management; project tracking		
Tree House Health	Drug administration	Client database; quality/performance measurement	Competitor/market intelligence

SMEs and the way relationships in the firm enhance or inhibit this flow. The Seven-S model (Chapter 5) is used to analyze the owner's objectives and the ability of staff to respond to these. The ISS reports almost unanimously highlight organizational changes to improve business processes. Sometimes the changes are critical to survival as financial resources are involved. In the following cases, Burring Engineers, Skills Training Co., Family Solicitors, and Events Management Co., no computerized IS were identified. The recommendations in these cases are to make organizational changes to ensure that existing IS are used better to transmit information through the firm. Owners' attitudes to controlling their business also have a marked influence on organizational culture. Those who are prepared to trust their management teams and operatives use IS more effectively than those who try to keep full control.

The style of management in most of the SMEs tends to be directive, with the owner clearly leading the organization. The business and social services organizations differ slightly where professional staff have more autonomy, although administrative staff tend to be treated in the more directive way seen in the other firms. The structure of the SMEs tends to emphasize the management/operative divide. However, in the majority of cases staff are both loyal and flexible in the tasks they undertake. The strength of this approach is that staff can address many tasks in the organization. For example, both the garage staff and the administrative staff at the Landrover Repair Co. are encouraged to develop customer relationship skills. The weakness of this flexible attitude can be seen in the Training Brokerage Co. where all staff answer queries from existing and potential students, but only one or two people enter the data in the computer system, and information is lost through a plethora of informal notes.

Organizational structures and personnel tend to inhibit information flows. Soft systems methodology rich pictures provide graphic representations of where information blockages occur. An example of an organizational inhibitor is the Electrical Accreditation Agency where separate systems are set up in individual departments to record accreditation results that are also needed by another department. The information is printed out and sent to the second department who had to re-key the data. An example of personnel inhibiting information flows is in Light Assembly Co., where the operative in the warehouse does not see the value of keying in information about goods leaving the warehouse. Hence, the factory systems show more finished items than there really are, causing production problems. While other staff are fully committed to the system and relied on it, this individual was not involved in discussions over the reasons for needing the information.

Resources

Limited financial resources are a factor in final recommendations in many of the ISS developed. The social content aspect of the analysis identifies that only the more visionary owners are prepared to commit financial resources to strategic systems. The main objective for managers is to spend available financial resources on supporting management systems that would improve day-to-day operations.

Review of the ISS approach

The three-stage process has proved to provide a good framework for a thorough analysis of ISS requirements for SMEs based on feedback from users and SMEs. The main problem for the analysts is the difficulty in separating strategic from operational issues. The nature of SMEs means that the owner is intimately involved with all aspects of the business. The analysts have to unravel the different aspects. It is not uncommon for operational issues to impact upon discussions of business strategy and competitiveness. Models provide some clarity for the analysts. The positivistic or structural models (five forces, value chain) providing clear boundaries that can be reflected back easily to the SME to confirm understanding of strategic issues. Most owners had an implicit strategy, and analysts worked with them to elicit CSF. Standard models such as PESTEL and SWOT are useful to reflect back issues and understanding to owners. The strategic opportunities framework is particularly useful (Tables 7.9 and 7.10). However, the information intensity matrix is of limited value, merely flagging up the importance of information to the SME, but providing few other insights unavailable from other models.

Business process modelling proves to be more variable. There is more dependence upon the researchers understanding of the available tools. Generally, SSM is used in a partial manner to understand the problem situation, rich pictures being very informative. The later stages of SSM are used variably depending on the knowledge of the analysts. Value chain analysis is sufficient in many cases to identify systems requirements. In most cases, unlike large corporations, SMEs business processes are directly linked to value-adding activities with few superfluous activities. Thus, the problem becomes one of identifying systems to support existing processes, rather than devising new ones. Additionally, industry sector differences lead to some difficulties with use of tools. This is found particularly in knowledge intensive industries. Resource-based models such as core competences may be more relevant to these organizations (see Chapter 14). The strategic grid analysis provides some assistance in recognizing the limited role of IS in the SMEs and acts as a means of reflecting on the potential use of systems for business growth.

The use of CSF, particularly when linked to the balanced business scorecard is a means of demonstrating the management support systems requirements recommendations and their fit with organizational objectives. The 3D model is also useful as a means of reviewing the links between technical delivery, organizational deployment and strategic delivery to ensure that recommendations are practical and consistent.

Ormerod's approach to determining systems priorities is appropriate and helpful when determining systems priorities. However, it is clear that where the owner is closely involved with the final recommendations and action plan there is greater acceptance of the conclusions.

The SMEs involved in this research were revisited 6 months and 1 year after the ISS process was carried out. This reveals that the SMEs are using the recommendations from the ISS analysis in various ways. The ISS was used by the general manager of Seven Stars Printers to persuade the board that IS investment was required. At Landrover Repair Co the owner decided after 2 years that a networked management IS system would free him up to continue the development of his vehicle renovation business. He has now reduced management staff as a result of the system. After two ISS reports, Family Solicitors, which had a potentially fatal level of debtors, recognized that organization change was required. It was clear that their IS were sufficient, but the partners were required to act as debt collectors, a role they found incompatible with their activity as legal advisers. The ISS recommended that debt collection to be given to the accounts department and debt level reduced considerably.

The framework is robust, though unsurprisingly, models and tools used to analyze the situation are dependent upon the knowledge and stance of the analyst. There may be other tools that provide greater understanding in knowledge-based organizations (see Chapter 14). The involvement of the owner in the process enriches the understanding of both the owner and the analyst.

■ Conclusions

This chapter developed an approach to ISS in SMEs. It addresses the need for an effective ISS to focus on information and organizational issues not merely IT. The approach taken is one of "critical pluralism" enabling the adoption of tools and techniques from multiple research paradigms. The over-arching framework is supported, although there may be a need to review tools used within each aspect according to the knowledge of the analyst. The flexibility of such an approach suggests that it can be adopted in a wide range of different SMEs.

The practical implications of the ISS process as described for SME owners are threefold. First, it provides an opportunity for owners and senior managers to review their strategic direction and to identify their information needs. The owners in many of the SMEs have commented specifically on the value of the opportunity to articulate their strategy and the problems they perceive for their business. Second, business processes that inhibit the flow of information can become embedded in SMEs, as in larger organizations. The process has helped to identify those processes and propose alternatives. Finally, IS that provide the means of obtaining information to manage the business more effectively and competitively are identified. One of the main conditions in proposing new investment to SMEs is to recognize that they have resource constraints as well as limited expertise in IS.

However, as with most such interventions, they require the active participation of an external analyst and it is unlikely that owner-managers will have the skills or the time and motivation to take on the ISS development task.

The ISS process developed here has discussed and demonstrated the value of existing models within an overall framework that compares the external strategic environment and the existing internal operational processes. The process enables an analysis of the SME to be made that emphasizes the need for the effective strategic flow of information within the context of both the organizational and IS. The framework is not static. It allows for other tools and techniques to be introduced as they are developed, as will be shown later in Chapter 14.

This chapter has introduced the principles behind the organizational ISS approach and has outlined the rationale underpinning the use of a number of tools and techniques. To explain their use in more detail and how the whole process fits together a more detailed Case study is presented in Chapter 8.

8 Case example of ISS: Heath Springs

■ Introduction

This chapter demonstrates the use of the information systems strategy (ISS) framework presented in Chapter 7. The framework is used to develop an ISS for Heath Springs (introduced in Chapter 3), a small UK manufacturer of automotive components. The chapter describes the application of the method, its outputs and outcomes, and then assesses the value of ISS to the organization. This example demonstrates the detailed analyses that are undertaken for all the cases presented in Parts 2 and 3.

■ Case background

Heath Springs was founded in 1904 to manufacture expanding metal shirt bands, but later expanded into spring making of all kinds. The firm, acquired by the US-based Petersen Group in 1982, is now a major supplier of coil springs to the automotive sector. Ford and Rover are major customers and Heath Springs has an "open-book" partnership with Lucas Brakes meaning that the firms share information to ensure that the twin objectives of competitive pricing and reasonable profit margins ensue. The firm employs 112 people and has an annual turnover of £4 million of which £3 million is in the UK.

The Petersen Group comprises 18 autonomous firms, all, with the exception of Heath Springs, based in the US. Heath Springs can call on the group to secure loans but otherwise is autonomous, although the CEO is also a major shareholder in the group. The CEO, who is nearing his 50th birthday, is a leading light in the Confederation of British Industry and has been honoured in recognition of his services to the regional business community. Planning to retire soon, he has begun to groom a younger management team to take over. Amongst this team is a graduate of the firm's engineering apprenticeship scheme who has emerged as the information systems manager.

■ Business context
Market

Coil springs are a small, but crucial part of the automotive components market. Products are mainly fashioned from coiled steel although thin strips of metal are used to manufacture some types of spring. The products manufactured by firms, such as Heath Springs, are used in carburettors, brake assemblies and car bonnets. In essence, the coil spring has changed little since the early days of mass-production car manufacture but there are strong signs that ceramic technology may soon replace some functions currently performed by coil springs. It is virtually impossible to cost or price an individual spring since they are manufactured in bulk and the market is very price sensitive for bulk purchase. The scope for quality arises when firms, such as Heath Springs, can design and supply a spring to meet the precise technical needs of the customer at the right time and at the right price.

Customers

Around 60% of the firm's trade is secured by long-term contracts with customers, such as Ford, Rover and Lucas, though there are also foreign customers. The major customers are served in three main ways:

- Ford prefer the shortest possible lead time for orders. To help Heath Springs plan production, Ford supplies a 3-monthly estimate of anticipated needs. However, actual weekly orders often bear little resemblance to the medium-term estimates.

- Rover has a national distribution centre that orders parts from Heath Springs as the need arises.

- Lucas operates a kanban system so parts are not delivered until they are needed. Thus, Heath Springs are obliged to keep a stock of Lucas parts ready for immediate delivery.

As with other firms in the sector, Heath Springs has a well-developed relationship with its major customers. It has quality certification from Ford and Rover and works closely with the former on spring designs for new products. There is also a long-term agreement that Ford will assist Heath Springs to reduce prices by 1.75% per annum. A similar arrangement of co-operation to achieve long-term price reduction exists with Lucas. Heath Springs are also striving to reduce costs within its operations generally and has adopted an ABC accounting system to help it do so. However, it is hampered by concerted efforts by key suppliers to raise raw material prices.

Suppliers

Heath Springs is at the mercy of its suppliers for two reasons. First, manufacturers of metal coil currently find it more profitable to make coil rope, resulting in supplies of metal coil suddenly being constrained if increased demand is not met by the mills. Firms, such as Heath Springs, are too small to influence or deal directly with the manufacturers. Second, the output of metal coil from the mills is bought up by a network of small suppliers who then sell it on to firms including Heath Springs. However, the suppliers are often unable to meet a sudden surge in demand from Heath Springs.

Substitutes and entry barriers

Presently Heath Springs faces three forms of competition:

- *Local*: in the form of owner-managed firms with low overheads that mainly service the lock industry.

- *European*: especially German and Spanish firms that supply UK parts suppliers.

- *Overseas* (Far east): firms using technologically advanced processes to supply high specification assemblies.

Figure 8.1 uses Porter's five forces model to analyse Heath Springs. This demonstrates that IS are currently being used to mitigate competitive forces in at least two ways, although there are opportunities that are not currently being taken. First, Heath Springs has reduced the threat of new entrants by the use of EDI with its major customers, however, the potential from the use of this technology could be greater if there was integration with the MRP system. Second, the quality performance system provides a means to reduce competition from its

Competitive force	How IS/IT can create competitive advantage	What does it mean for Heath Springs?
Threat of new entrants	How can IS/IT build barriers to entry?	EDI ordering system with customers performance measurement system in place
Bargaining power of customers	How can IS/IT build in switching costs for customers?	Design of springs integrated with motor manufacturer design process through use of CAD
Bargaining power of suppliers	How can IS/IT change the balance of power with its suppliers?	Better inventory planning may enable reduction in stock holding
Threat of substitute products or services	How can IS/IT generate new products or services?	Primarily increase the use of CAD
The industry: jockeying for position among rivals	How can IS/IT change the basis of competition?	Quality performance information will exclude rivals Highlight inefficiencies in production

Figure 8.1: Porter's five forces analysis on Heath Springs.

rivals as it demonstrates the capacity for Heath Springs to produce high quality springs and reduce inefficiencies in its production processes. However, there are two opportunities where IS could be better utilized. First, in design where an integrated design process with customers would reduce their power and provide the information by which Heath Springs could estimate the costs of production earlier. Second, integrating the EDI systems with the MRP system may provide the opportunity to recognize inventory problems more quickly and thus enable raw materials to be ordered in a timelier manner.

Other competitive issues

Heath Springs is experiencing increasing pressure to expand its design function. However, if the firm were to go further along this road, it would be necessary to upgrade its existing CAD facilities that are currently described as "unsophisticated". But with a low margin, high volume product and further squeezes coming from rising supplier prices and long-term falls in customer prices, the incentive for expanding into a new area is small. Further, the technology of springs may be changing (for instance, the use of ceramics) and the nature of the motor trade may change in the wake of political concerns over traffic expansion and road building in the longer term.

Raw material and finished goods storage is beginning to pose a problem. Invariably, operators are forced to move several crates out of the way to reach the desired product. The need to store Lucas parts also results in large inventories. Many parts of the factory are using old but serviceable machinery.

Porter identifies three generic strategies by which firms compete. As discussed below, Heath Springs primarily competes on price but IS might offer them opportunities to compete in other ways.

Cost leadership

Heath Springs competes mainly on price. It mainly produces high volume, low cost products. The move into computerization arose from a need to be more efficient. Close monitoring of costs of production of machines is carried out in an effort to reduce wastage and determine the most efficient means of production. ABC accounting is applied by the firm, although the gains from this are offset by the operating decision to maximize production of the same spring design regardless of its production priority.

Differentiation

There is considerable competition in the industry. It is not clear what differentiates Heath Springs from other firms; indeed they are under serious competition particularly from firms that make locks, for whom

Perspective	Critical success factors	Performance measure
Customer	• Provide a quality service to customers • Improve time to get product to market • Become customers supplier of choice • Develop customer partnerships	• Reduce scrap rates by 10% • 95% delivery on time • Increase percentage of business by 5% • Increase number of co-operative design efforts by 30%
Financial	• To survive • To succeed • To prosper	• Improve cash flow • Increase sales growth by 5% • Increase market share by 3% • Increase return on equity
Organizational	• Manufacturing excellence • Increase employee satisfaction • Increase productivity	• Reduce cycle time by 5% • Reduce unit cost by 2% • Reduce sick leave by 3% • Increase training provision by 4% • Increase order throughput by 5%
Innovation	• Improve manufacturing learning • Improve research and development • Improve new product introduction	• Identify two new sources of steel • Identify ceramic spring potential • Identify new technology • Increase speed of design by 5%

Figure 8.2: Balanced business scorecard for Heath Springs.

entry barriers are not high. Service to the customer is the main differentiating factor.

Focus

Heath Springs see their future in the manufacture of springs for the motor industry. However, there are changes afoot from the development of ceramic technology. The firm could usefully be more pro-active in working with customers on research and design.

Achieving business strategy

Thus, Heath perceives their future business vision to be the main supplier of quality springs to the automotive sector throughout Europe. To achieve this, their business strategy is steady growth and improved profitability through improved efficiency and effectiveness. The balanced business scorecard (Figure 8.2) provides useful insights into the key areas that Heath need to address to remain competitive.

The advantage of using the balanced business scorecard is that Heath considers issues other than finance in achieving their objectives. The service–profit chain is achieved by ensuring that employees understand their tasks within the overall organizational framework. Positive employee attitudes are perceived by customers that ultimately brings financial reward (Heskett, *et al.*, 1994).

Heath are already being required by customers to improve quality. While they are measuring performance, it is helpful to have a goal and a performance measure. The performance measure leads to understanding of the information required for its determination. Thus, the balanced scorecard provides additional knowledge of what will be required by any IS.

■ Business process

Heath Springs produces springs to order. Products are usually designed by the customer and Heath Springs are asked to prepare an estimate of the materials, cost and time requirement for manufacturing. Estimates are mainly based on the experience of estimators. Manual records of previous jobs are kept, but are not generally consulted when preparing new estimates. The systems manager has spent some time with the estimating department designing a PC-based system that will store estimates. It is intended that this system will be integrated with the capacity planning (MRP) system. Apart from speeding up the estimation process, the new system will also improve the firm's pricing policy. In the past, estimates have been based on an assumed volume level. However, if subsequent orders are less than assumed at the estimation stage, under-recovery of costs ensues. In future, once the estimation system is linked to the sales department data, accurate and economic pricing should be possible.

Currently, capacity planning is carried out at a weekly, two hour meeting between the operations, logistics and sales managers. The prime object is to ensure that customers receive the springs that they order on time. There is also a need to ensure that setting up time on the machines is optimized. Setting up can take several hours, but varies according to the complexity of the spring and the age of the machine. The managers check to see if there are multiple orders for the same type of spring. This may mean that some orders rise up the priority list while others have their priority reduced and it can take 6–8 weeks to fill an order. Larger manufacturers are given priority, and machines often work overtime to fill these orders. The other parameter is that, to ensure that there is sufficient stock for the larger customers; 3 months advance stock is made. Heath Springs believes a full production run is the only way to ensure economies of scale.

All machines have to be set up individually for each spring. There is no facility to take a design and programing the manufacture of the spring. Indeed, the majority of machines have not changed since 1945, as a new machine requires a capital outlay of over £70,000.

Quality management	BS 5750, Ford & Rover quality systems			
Firm infrastructure	ABC management accounting; performance measurement systems to conform to major customers			
HRM	Staff training and development encouraged. Some resistance to IS introduction			
Technology development	Currently engaged in limited product design with major customers: under increasing pressure to increase design function			
Procurement	Obtaining raw materials is a source of continual concern: steel mills find it more profitable to produce steel rope not the steel coil needed for springs			
	Inbound logistics	**Operations**	**Outbound logistics**	**Marketing, sales and service**
	Taking advantage of availability and bulk discounts means that some raw materials must be stored for a long period of time Unavailability of steel a problem	The capacity and flexibility of processors can be a problem Relationship between estimates and true cost of orders is strained Forecasting is a problem Machine set-up an issue Prioritising work is a matter of the urgency of the order and the need to maximise the use of a particular machine set-up	Need to accommodate different customer systems (e.g. kan-ban, JIT) presents major storage problems	EDI available Computer analysis osales is done Integration of estimation process and sales office systems now being developed

Figure 8.3: Value chain for Heath Springs.

The business is modelled in two ways. First, using Porter's value chain (Figure 8.3) which provides a guide to importance of information for both primary and support or secondary activities. The value chain assumes that there are a large number of separate activities within the organization that contribute to the final product or service. An organization is profitable if the value it creates exceeds the costs of performing the value activities. To gain competitive advantage an organization must either perform these activities at a lower cost or in a way that leads to differentiation and a premium price.

The value chain for Heath Springs indicates that they can make more immediate gains by focusing on reducing costs, although in the long-term design integration with motor manufacturers may be more profitable. The primary value chain analysis indicates that inventory is a key area for cost reduction and IS can help achieve this through better forecasting information. Additionally, IS can assist the firm in developing a more accurate cost estimating system which will assist them in determining

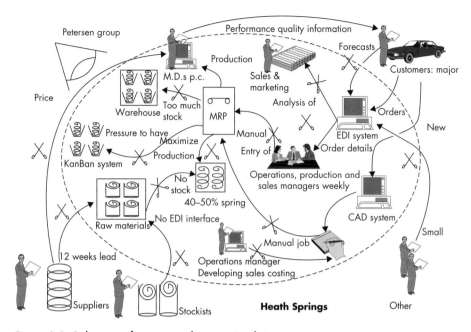

Figure 8.4: Rich picture of processes and issues in Heath Springs.

prices more accurately, thus providing them with more leverage over their customers. Again, IS assist the firm in sales analysis, however, better integration with costing systems will enable the firm to identify the percentage of queries being translated to firm orders.

At the secondary value chain level, the quality performance system permeates through the philosophy of the organization. However, there is a need for this system to be integrated with the MRP system as currently the data from production has to be re-entered for the CEO. Additionally, there is a change management issue that needs addressing, staff are nervous about the introduction of IS, particularly in the estimating department. While they have accepted the need for change and training as far as it affects production, it is not clear that the value of IS has been understood.

Second, the business is analysed using Checkland's (1981) soft systems methodology. This approach provides a number of alternative views of the firm that can then be modelled to identify potential problem areas. A rich picture (Figure 8.4) is developed to understand problem areas for the firm. The crossed swords that are shown in the figure demonstrate areas where either the business process or the information flows are not working effectively. The main issue which the rich picture highlights is the limited use within the firm of the MRP system. This suggests that while IS have been recognized by the CEO as critical to ensuring business success, the message has not permeated throughout the firm and affected work practices. The rich picture analysis thus enables the identification of

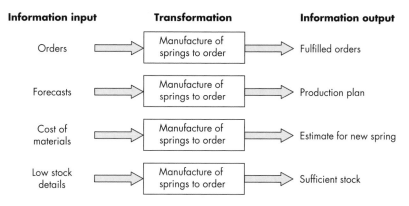

Figure 8.5: Key transformations for Heath Springs.

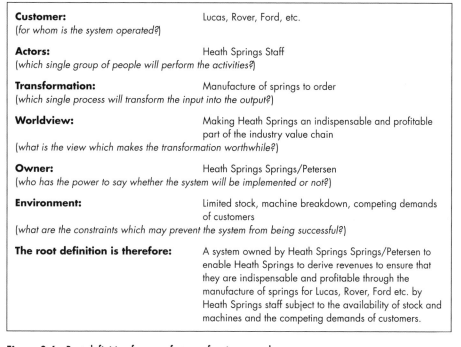

Customer: (for whom is the system operated?)	Lucas, Rover, Ford, etc.
Actors: (which single group of people will perform the activities?)	Heath Springs Staff
Transformation: (which single process will transform the input into the output?)	Manufacture of springs to order
Worldview: (what is the view which makes the transformation worthwhile?)	Making Heath Springs an indispensable and profitable part of the industry value chain
Owner: (who has the power to say whether the system will be implemented or not?)	Heath Springs Springs/Petersen
Environment: (what are the constraints which may prevent the system from being successful?)	Limited stock, machine breakdown, competing demands of customers
The root definition is therefore:	A system owned by Heath Springs Springs/Petersen to enable Heath Springs to derive revenues to ensure that they are indispensable and profitable through the manufacture of springs for Lucas, Rover, Ford etc. by Heath Springs staff subject to the availability of stock and machines and the competing demands of customers.

Figure 8.6: Root definition for manufacture of springs to order.

transformations (Figure 8.5): those areas that need to be improved for the business to be successful.

Systems are then defined which support the organization more effectively (Figure 8.6 shows a root definitions for the first transformation). These systems may not be computer-based but may, nevertheless, require organizational changes.

Conceptual models are then developed which are compared with the real world to highlight where there are issues that need to be changed in the organization (Figure 8.7).

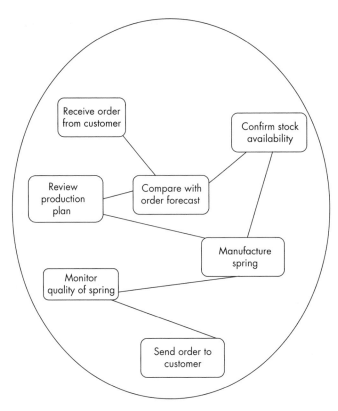

Figure 8.7: Conceptual model for manufacture of springs to order.

Table 8.1: Comparison of conceptual model and real world for manufacture of springs to order

Conceptual model	Real world
Receive order from customer	Order processing different for different customers. There may need to be a different transformation for Lucas
Compare with order forecast	This comparison is not really done in any detail. There is no clear process which links orders to forecasts and checks whether customers have got it right
Review production plan	Manual, time-consuming process which prioritizes orders on the basis of maximizing production runs not filling orders
Confirm stock availability	Stock is not always available, partly because of the production changes
Manufacture spring	Delays due to machine breakdown
Send order to customer	Small customers have to wait

The next stage is to decide what actions need be taken to address the differences between the ideal model and the real world (Table 8.1).

For example, if Heath Springs had a system to compare actual orders with forecast they might be in a better position to decide on the stock they

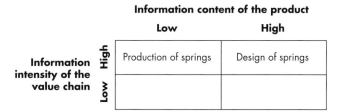

Figure 8.8: Information intensity matrix for Heath Springs.

required. There may be a case for setting up a separate process to deal with each car manufacturer if they require different delivery systems.

Information needs of managers

Order size is generally large, particularly from major automotive manufacturers and large orders are usually known in advance. Major customers use EDI for forecasting, order planning and invoicing, although no two systems are the same. A schedule of requirements is sent via EDI to Heath Springs, but the EDI systems are not integrated with Heath Springs' systems, so all data has to be printed and then re-entered into the local system. Actual orders do not always match the schedules, but in overall terms the scale of production is known. In addition, the lifetime of each product is known as it matches the lifetime of the automotive production. However, some customers have small infrequent orders that have to be fitted into the production schedule. The Information Intensity matrix (Figure 8.8) is used to identify the importance of information to the firm and where the emphases for its systems should lie. This analysis shows that IS play a key role in the production process for springs and that there is further potential for Heath Springs if it can automate design activities and integrates them with production.

There is a strongly felt need for more sales and marketing information. Currently the sales people are unable to identify trends or analyse sales. There is a need to hold data on sales history and perform forecasting. They are in discussion about a PC system that will enable them to download data from their AS400.

The MRP system is not really used to do more than identify stock and raw material availability. It is not possible to schedule the production or to carry out capacity planning using the MRP system. Indeed, 40–50% of the spring machines are idle at any one time, mainly due to a lack of raw materials.

Major automotive manufacturers place considerable emphasis on quality in products. Heath Springs has to demonstrate this through the introduction of a quality monitoring system which has been developed using an Excel spreadsheet which monitors costs per unit, scrap rates and machine utilization.

Table 8.2: Information requirements for core business activities

Information required to undertake the activity	Activity	Information resulting from the activity
Lead times from suppliers Current raw material levels Use of material for orders	Manage raw materials	Stock outs Re-order levels Exceptions between recorded and actual raw material levels
Forecasts from customers Orders from customers Machine availability Operative availability Raw material availability	Order processing	Completed orders Comparison between forecasts and orders
Staff skills and qualifications Training courses available Training requirements for Heath Springs	Staff development	Staff skills database Future training requirements
Invoice details Debtor details Order details Supplier invoices	Monitor cash flow	Cash flow forecast

These analyses enable identification of key information needs for managers (Table 8.2).

Existing IS and IT

The history of IS development in Heath Springs is recent. The CEO recognized that the firm had to bring in IS if it was to stay in business. Heath Springs has bought out a number of its competitors and the volume of work increased so that it was no longer possible to keep up using manual systems, particularly for accounting. In 1990 the CEO brought in a consultant to advise on introducing accounting systems. The systems were designed and developed in conjunction with a small local software house, Ace computers. The consultant had previously developed good relations with Ace, and Heath Springs has subsequently developed a strategic partnership with them. Ace use their contract with Heath Springs to learn about developing computer systems in a manufacturing firm. In return Ace provides their services at a reduced rate to Heath Springs.

The decision was taken to develop an MRP system suitable for spring manufacture. The system is not totally integrated but includes customer information, order information, stock information, product information, scheduling and resource planning. Currently, production and resource planning are the key systems which are not integrated and where the greatest potential for cost savings may occur. Production planning is done manually and is time consuming. However, they are developing

Strategic impact of existing operating systems	Strategic impact of application development portfolio: Low	Strategic impact of application development portfolio: High
Low	***Support*** Accounts system word processing	***Turnaround*** CAD
High	MRP ***Factory***	Performance measurement EDI ***Strategic***

Figure 8.9: Strategic grid analysis for Heath Springs.

systems to interface with the MRP system to enable it to be implemented in full.

During this time the operations manager has gained more expertise in computer systems and has begun to drive developments for the business with the consultant in a support role. There has also been less support required from the software house. Staff in Heath Springs were not involved in the introduction of the systems and there was considerable resistance, mainly due to inexperience with computer-based systems. The systems were developed first by the consultant and, to some extent, imposed on the firm because of their inexperience. There is little long-term planning of IS, the focus is primarily on improving operations.

The strategic grid (Figure 8.9) provides a view of both current and future opportunities for the use of information system/information technology. It also enables management to identify the appropriate way of managing IS/IT (Earl, 1989). By recognizing the purpose of the IS the best way of managing it can be determined.

Two systems are highlighted in the figure, MRP and CAD. EDI is put in as a strategic system. It would appear here that EDI will be an essential part of the competitive business of the future since EDI is a requirement from major customers. The MRP system is not yet fully developed as a factory system and might be considered as a strategic system, one that is critical for the achievement of the current business strategy. As discussed by Ward, this is to be expected. Similarly, Heath Springs does not currently use CAD to any great degree, but the analysis here suggests that it is a system that will assist them in their future strategy.

The firm has also initiated a performance measurement system that has been implemented on a PC. The system was developed as a response to customers for lower prices and higher quality. The systems enable Heath Springs to monitor productivity and identify where production costs are currently directed with a view to their reduction.

Attitudes and organization of IS

As discussed in Chapter 6, positioning frameworks provide little value to an understanding of information systems planning for small- and medium-sized enterprises, as most have limited sophistication in the use of IS. Initially it might appear that SMEs are in the initiation stage as identified by Nolan (1979) (see Chapter 6). As discussed, Nolan initially identified four stages which firms move through to approach maturity in their use of IS, though the model was later extended to six stages. The first three representing the data processing era while the last three are information management: firms having recognized the power of common data and the benefits from shared use of IS. Analysis of Heath Springs' approach to IS suggests that there may be some concatenation of the stages, primarily that control may well be the first stage due to the caution exhibited by the SME in its decision to purchase an MRP system as a means to improving efficiency and effectiveness. The need for common data is recognized by the firm, although it has only achieved limited advantage so far from the information it has.

As shown in Chapter 5 the Seven-S model provides a useful means of showing organizational relationships. The Heath Springs analysis first shown in Figure 5.3, is developed and expanded in Figure 8.10 and this provides a means of reviewing the potential use of IS from a number of different perspectives. The most crucial issue is the involvement of the CEO in the decision to introduce IS. His involvement is critical: he is both project champion and project sponsor for the introduction of IS in the organization.

	Heath Springs
Strategy	Production and performance orientated
Structure	Operations manager responsible for purchasing and on-going systems development
Systems	MRP package purchased; only partially implemented. Interface being developed with estimating system
Staff	Independent consultant and self-taught operations manager, additional support form software house
Style	Senior management are concerned to have the right operational support to improve efficiency
Skills	The operations manager has developed programming skills. Otherwise, spreadsheet manipulation is probably the only other skill, held by senior management
Super-ordinate goals	The whole organization is working together to improve efficiency and effectiveness. It is not thinking of using IS/IT to improve competitiveness

Figure 8.10: Seven-S analysis for Heath Springs.

For Heath Springs this indicates the focus of IS in the firm is directed at achieving greater efficiency and effectiveness in managing production. This focus is determined by senior management, using outside consultants. There is limited IS skill within the firm at all levels. The issue now is whether it is appropriate for the operations manager to teach himself how to develop IS for the firm or whether it would be better to continue using consultants. The positive side of his association is the continued involvement of senior management in the development of IS. However, it detracts from his role as operations manager that is a critical role as Heath Springs attempts to improve its operation.

In concentrating on the development of systems to support the business, limited time has been spent on some information management issues, primarily those of security and privacy of information, and disaster recovery. As the firm moves toward integrating its systems and becomes more dependent upon them it will be more critical that data is backed up and secured so that they can continue to work if there is any loss of data due to computer malfunction. This limitation highlights the difficulty facing firms in not having staff available with IS management skills either as consultants or employees.

■ Recommendations

The above analysis allows recognition of the key areas where IS can improve efficiency and effectiveness for the firm in line with their strategic objectives. It also allows them to progress to more strategic objectives. The balanced scorecard is usefully re-visited at this point (Figure 8.11).

Perspective	IS
Customer	Quality measurement EDI CAD
Financial	Financial analysis
Organizational	MRP Skills database Stock control
Innovation	CAD/CAM Market intelligence Improve new product introduction

Figure 8.11: IS recommendations for Heath Springs.

The systems may not be new to Heath Springs, but they all need improvement or integration with existing systems. The performance measurement system can usefully be integrated with the MRP system. The MRP system needs to be used more effectively with organizational processes being changed to acknowledge the contribution it can play. Financial analysis tools will help the CEO plan more effectively. Understanding employee skills will ensure that staff are contributing effectively; while stock control will assist in cost reduction. Heath Springs recognize they must work more closely with customers, hence the innovation recommendations, particularly CAD/CAM. It is important that they are aware of competition and also are able to identify market opportunities, thus market intelligence is important.

SMEs are resources constrained, therefore, it is unrealistic to expect all systems to be implemented immediately. Also, some require concomitant organizational changes to take place. Heath Springs recognized that market position was the most important factor for them. Competitive advantage and financial return were of equal importance, while the ease of implementation was the least important issue. They realize they have to change to remain competitive, thus systems changes would have to be borne. Ormerod's implementation analysis model, discussed in Chapter 7 (Table 7.3) is used with the firm to identify the relative importance to the firm of each of the identified systems. The values used are those presented in Figure 8.12 (see also Chapter 7). EDI is identified as the most important system and this concurs with the need to work more closely with

	Market position	5	Competitive advantage	3	Financial return	3	Ease to implement	1	Total
CAD/CAM	Build position	3	Leverage	5	3–5 years	3	New system, New technology	1	40
Accounting	Critical	5	Support	1	1–2 years	5	Enhancements	5	48
Performance measurement	Critical	5	Value chain	3	3–5 years	3	New system, New technology	1	44
EDI	Build position	3	Leverage	5	1–2 years	5	Enhancements	5	50
Stock control	Nice to have	1	Value chain	3	1–2 years	5	New system, Old technology	3	32
MRP implementation	Critical	5	Value chain	3	3–5 years	3	Enhancements	5	48

Figure 8.12: Importance of IS for Heath Springs.

customers. However accounting systems are seen as almost as important: a basic system that needs improvement to manage costs.

Discussion

The above analysis uses the ISS framework discussed in Chapter 7 to determine the potential from IS for Heath Springs. The usefulness and value of the various tools and techniques used in the analysis are reviewed here.

The information intensity matrix has shown that IS are useful for Heath Springs to co-ordinate processes as there is high information content in the firm's value chain, this is reinforced through the generic strategy analysis which highlights the need to follow a low cost strategy, currently. In the longer term, both models suggest that design of springs will provide greater opportunity for Heath Springs to gain competitive advantage over its customers. Thus, it can be seen that, in common with most SMEs, the current focus for IS planning is on improving efficiency and effectiveness (Sinclair, 1986). This is an essential requirement, particularly given the move by major automotive manufacturers to preferred suppliers. Unless the SME can demonstrate its ability to meet the requirements in quality of product and process of its customers it will lose them. Chapter 6 suggests that the use of Porter's generic strategy model is limited for SMEs; however, in conjunction with the information intensity matrix it highlights the difference between the current direction of ISP and the longer-term requirements for the firm.

The five forces model is invaluable in analysing IS opportunities for Heath Springs primarily in relation to its customers and suppliers. The provision of IS which more closely links the firm to its customers reduces the risk of other new entrants. The value chain is useful in highlighting the role of information in the primary process of spring production and indicates that information is important in the value chain. However, SSM has also been used here to analyse the role of information and shows that, as argued by Galliers (1993), there is need for a change management programme to ensure that IS are used to best effect. While the value chain shows the importance of information at a high level, the SSM analysis provides a means of indicating actions that can be taken to improve business processes.

The strategic grid does provide a useful snapshot of the role of IS in the firm. In conjunction with the other analyses it supports the contention that current ISP should be inwardly directed while the long-term ISP should be more towards customer involvement. In other words, there are competitive opportunities for Heath Springs from the use of IS.

These change the basis of competition and would move the focus of their strategy from one of low cost to one of differentiation. As a long-term strategy this is likely to be the direction which will bring them more success from the use of information. It will also have the value of more closely linking them in the industry value chain with their customers.

As discussed, there is limited value from the use of stages models for SMEs, however the Seven-S analysis indicates that Heath Springs should turn its attention to information management issues. There are three key aspects to IS planning, IS strategy, IT strategy and information management strategy (Earl, 1989). Heath Springs have successfully introduced the IS that they will need to be competitive and they have identified a technology platform that is robust. Information management is not an issue that has really been considered by the firm, beyond the need to have an integrated system. While it is unlikely to be a problem in the medium term, there is little thought given to system obsolescence and renewal. While the system is modularized, it is not clear that it will be possible to add new modules later. There is no policy on renewal of IT and whether the firm is locked into its existing supplier. Heath Springs could usefully discuss with the consultant and the software provider the policies which are required to ensure that the firm does not reach a point whereby it can no longer operate due to limitations of its IS.

■ Conclusions

This chapter demonstrates the development of ISS for a small manufacturing firm. It shows the potential value of information to the firm and hence the opportunities from IS/IT. The chapter illustrates the use of the ISS framework developed in Chapter 7.

Use of the ISS framework for Heath Springs reveals that in the short to medium term its ISS is correct to concentrate on improving efficiency and effectiveness. This is vital to achieve their main strategic objective of remaining as a preferred supplier to the major customers. These customers will continue to put pressure on Heath Springs to reduce costs and any improvements to the current processes which can be made should be made. Therefore, the objectives in the short to medium term are directed at the complete implementation of the MRP system with the additional need to consider organizational, human resource and training issues.

In the long term, the SME's success is likely to be guaranteed more from closer partnerships with its customers particularly from design integration. Hence, the firm will be in a stronger position if it seeks collaborative advantage with its customers, as identified by Kanter (1994), through the sharing of information. Discussions with the CEO in 2002 indicate he foresees radical change in the industry. While Heath is currently a first-tier supplier to the automotive industry, this may not last. The automotive industry is demanding sub-assemblies from its suppliers rather than components. This may mean that Heath becomes a second-tier supplier. Heath's CEO believes that it is vital for small suppliers to work together in a network to protect and develop products for the industry. He believes that flexible relationships between suppliers enabled by the Internet will help ensure their survival and possibly their growth. Inter-organizational systems planning is one mechanism by which this can be achieved.

Part 3 Strategic resource: attitudes to information

■ Part 2 argued that small- and medium-sized enterprises can reap the benefits of strategic information systems. Indeed, it is essential for them to plan their IS in order to compete effectively. However, SMEs cannot be considered as a homogeneous group. The dynamics of managing an organization of 30 people differ from that of managing 150. As discussed in Chapter 1, owners' reasons for being in business vary from setting up the pension plan to being the next Bill Gates. This leads to different attitudes to strategy and growth and hence investment in IS resources. The first two parts of this book have been largely exploratory, identifying the validity of extant IS frameworks and modes of analysis to the SME context. This part moves forward to consider the development of theory to understand IS adoption and use in SMEs. The part draws on the 44 cases introduced in Chapter 7 as a basis for theory development.

In Chapter 9 a framework is developed that articulates the different strategic opportunities for SMEs, and its attitude to IS may depend upon the direction they identify for business growth. As discussed in Chapter 3 some view IS as a necessary evil to improve efficiency, while others may recognize the potential of IS to help grow and develop the business. Two dominant factors are the role of the customer and of the market. The attitude of customers may also determine the necessary investment in IS in order to trade. These two dimensions, customer dominance and strategic focus, enable four potential IS investment scenarios (encapsulated in the focus-dominance model) to be developed.

Chapter 10 reviews the behaviour of SMEs' IS investment over time. Using the focus-dominance model developed in Chapter 9, this chapter demonstrates that there is a dynamic. SME growth has been the subject of debate, with some researchers presenting a staged approach to growth. Others suggest growth is a function of the relationship between the owner, business strategy and the competitive market. This chapter explores these dynamics. While there is little support for the stages of growth model, there appear to be a number of different growth paths taken. While many SMEs do not demonstrate radical shifts in their IS adoption, some do use IS to improve relations with customers or to reposition themselves in the market.

The following two chapters consider business transformation through IS. If SMEs are to use IS effectively as a strategic resource it is important to understand the transformation process, and whether it is possible to recommend alternative approaches to IS investment. Two models that have been shown to be of value in the large corporation environment are used. These models are the Venkatraman business transformation model and the Scott Morton MIT'90s strategic alignment framework. Using these models the two chapters seek to gain an understanding of the process by which SMEs may use strategic IS more effectively.

In Chapter 11 Venkatraman's business transformation model is used to understand the process by which SMEs change their use of IS as they grow and develop. The Venkatraman model suggests first, that IS may evolve and be used to improve internal business processes. Second, IS may be used in a more revolutionary way to change not only the business processes, but perhaps the very nature of the business. This chapter explores whether SMEs follow similar paths to large organizations or whether there are different paths to business transformation through IS.

Chapter 12 uses the Scott Morton MIT'90s framework to explore transformation paths from a consideration of relationships between strategy, technology, management structure, organizational processes and peoples' skills and roles. The argument is made for large corporations that there is a need for alignment of all these factors to enable the benefits of strategic IS to be achieved. This chapter explores the interaction of these relationships in SMEs and finds that there is only limited alignment in most cases, although alignment is achieved for those SMEs for which IS is clearly a strategic driver.

This part identifies four scenarios for strategic IS development for SMEs in the focus-dominance model. The paths for growth in strategic IS are identified and show that while there are opportunities for SMEs to use IS strategically, many of them stop short for a variety of reasons. The different paths for business transformation are then explored through each scenario, indicating the limits of potential change from a strategic alignment perspective.

9 Strategic context of IS investment

▪ Introduction

Part 2 demonstrated the value of information systems strategies to small- and medium-sized enterprises in developing their investment in IS. As recognized earlier, the heterogeneity of SMEs needs to be acknowledged, in no small part due to the different reasons owners have for being in business. Thus, SMEs approach to IS strategy, and hence their use of IS, needs to take account of the owners' different strategic objectives.

Strategically, IS are used either to lower costs of production, co-ordination and transactions, or to add value to the product, process or service. In general, large organizations have reaped the early gains from IS, though the well-publicized failures offer a note of caution. As IS costs fall and their use becomes more commonplace, SMEs have begun to exploit the potential of the systems. Much of this exploitation mimics the early cost reduction strategies of large firms. In addition, there is evidence that some SMEs use IS to add value. Information systems and technology can play a critical role in innovation (Yetton *et al.*, 1994). Yet, the tendency, at least in manufacturing SMEs, is still to view investment in IS as a cost.

This chapter develops a model of IS use in SMEs using multiple cases to explore it. The model, termed the focus-dominance model, proposes that investment in IS is influenced by an SME's strategic context defined by its strategic focus, either cost reduction or value added, and its market positioning defined by customer dependence, for example, few versus many customers.

The chapter initially investigates the ways in which IS contributes to performance in large organizations. This is followed by an analysis of competitive issues facing small businesses. An analytical model combining customer dominance and strategic focus is then developed. The model is tested and validated using the 44 case firms introduced in Chapter 7. Four exemplar cases are described to illustrate the four different IS profiles. Finally, the implications for research and practice are discussed.

▪ Developing the focus-dominance model

As discussed in earlier chapters the role of IS in organizations have ranged from operational efficiency through to adding business value.

Indeed, as outlined in Chapter 6, information can be used as a resource to measure the success of the business. The 'structuralist' competitive advantage debate over the use of information to enable firms to market new products or provide new services contains similar themes. Knowledge strategies to help firms compete depend upon their abilities to capture and use a wide range of internal and external information, both informal and formal.

Many organizations now view investment in information not only as a means to cost reduction but also as a way of adding value. As argued in Chapter 7, to achieve this, they need an IS strategy that is an integral part of business strategy. However, it is clear that, for many firms, IS strategy is reactive to business strategy and the potential advantages of using IS competitively are missed. Strategic alignment linking business strategy and technology is the key issue.

Management IS in SMEs

As earlier chapters have highlighted, management IS in SMEs tend to be based around operational support and transaction processing to improve efficiency. Management IS are often introduced as a response to a business need. For example, SMEs have been excited by the opportunities from the use of the Internet; but for many, this has translated into the development of brochureware web sites, with virtually none considering e-business by having online sales facilities (Poon and Swatman, 1999). In such businesses any competitive advantage is likely to be accidental. However, as discussed in Chapter 7, a few SMEs do plan the systems to manage growth, particularly the more mature and growing firms that need more formal management systems. Only those SMEs that see IS as integral to their business strategy may see strategic benefits, otherwise it is unlikely that there will be any (see Chapter 3). Indeed, it is likely that SMEs that adopt sophisticated management systems without thinking through the strategic implications will incur problems.

The limited IS knowledge of SME owners and managers can act as an inhibitor in investment. This occurs because there is often little time to consider strategic opportunities, additionally, there is a lack of trust of IS suppliers (Igbaria et al., 1998). Resource constraint is also a major issue affecting IS investment. This may lead to a low cost strategy towards IS investment, focusing on transaction processing. Whereas those SMEs that plan growth, or for whom the market demands investment may well see IS investment as part of a value-adding strategy.

SMEs and competitiveness

If the way that SMEs view IS is the first driver for change then a second key inhibitor or enabler of IS use in SMEs is market position. SMEs are driven primarily by the needs of their customers. As seen in Chapter 7, customer power is high for many SMEs. They are dependent upon customers who purchase large quantities and these customers are able to influence price (Reid and Jacobsen, 1988). In addition, the competitive environment in which SMEs operates increases the risk of failure (Storey and Cressy, 1995).

Against this, investment in IS increases survival rates (Agarwal, 1998). For example, in the automotive sector, the influence of the customer extends to ensuring that the SME can demonstrate quality of process and product (Reid and Jacobsen, 1988). This is usually achieved through the introduction of formal, computer-based performance monitoring systems. Additionally, as discussed in Chapter 5, information relating to operations (i.e. orders and accounts) and design is often expected to be transmitted electronically. Sometimes these interactions may be extended to develop collaborative advantages.

Successful SMEs cultivate their customers closely, monitoring individual requirements to keep their loyalty (Reid and Jacobsen, 1988). This occurs at both a social level and at an operational level. Not only are major customers courted, but also are smaller ones in order to maintain loyalty. Indeed, many SMEs see the size of their order books as a surrogate for success and neglect issues of order profitability. Advising customers of new products or services is seen as important. Consistent with this, SMEs are valued by their customers because of their ability to respond quickly to customers' changing requirements.

Information systems are one of the mechanisms by which SMEs are able to respond to the market. For example, EDI is used for production planning, while designs can be integrated through the application of CAD linked to the customers' IS (see Chapter 5). In general, there is a link between the innovative efforts of an SME and its competitive position (Lefebvre and Lefebvre, 1993).

Focus-dominance model

The two dimensions of strategic focus (cost reduction versus value added) and customer dominance (few versus many customers) define the strategic context, creating four competitive scenarios for IS investment in SMEs. They are efficiency, co-ordination, collaboration and repositioning (Figure 9.1). This model, termed the focus-dominance model, provides an analytical framework to explore the role of IS in SMEs within the strategic context of the business.

The categories of production systems, management support and customer relations (Chapter 6) can be used to align the IS to the business strategy in each quadrant of the focus-dominance model. Word processing systems and accounting packages are used by all SMEs to control costs with a focus on efficiency, and are categorized under management support. Customer databases fall within Earl's customer

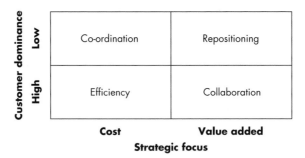

Figure 9.1: Focus-dominance model for SMEs.

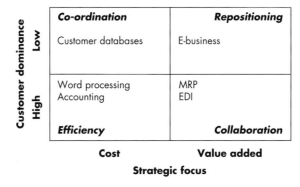

Figure 9.2: IS mapped onto the focus-dominance model.

relations category. Materials requirements planning and EDI systems form part of Earl's category of production, supporting planning and communications with customers. Thus, SMEs with systems restricted to word processing and accounting systems map onto the efficiency cell in the focus-dominance model. Those with customer databases map onto the co-ordination cell and those with MRP and EDI map to the collaboration cell. To complete the model's IS specification, the hypothesis is developed that innovative firms deploy interactive web sites, auction platforms and other e-business networking systems to reposition themselves in the market. The IS only used in each quadrant of the focus-dominance model are as presented in Figure 9.2.

The alignment of business and IS for SMEs in each of the four cells is described next.

Efficiency quadrant

The focus of IS use in the *efficiency* quadrant is for control of the business, primarily financial control. Information systems are concerned with improving the efficiency of internal processes, such as word processing and accounting spreadsheets. Information systems are, consequently, viewed as a cost to the business. This situation typically occurs where there is high customer dominance. This may be either because the business is starting up or because of the nature of the industry.

Co-ordination quadrant

In addition to the systems required to keep costs low in the efficiency quadrant, the primary use of IS in the *co-ordination* quadrant is to maintain customer relationships. This is a function of the larger customer base. Customer IS, holding basic data, are used. These may be supported by a local area network (LAN) to enable communication between different business activities. Internet access increasingly is common with external e-mail being exchanged with customers. The objective of the IS is to improve the effectiveness of business processes. Again, IS are viewed as a cost to the business, a necessity as manual systems cannot cope as customer numbers increase.

Collaboration quadrant

The third cell is the *collaboration* quadrant. Here, there is an increase in the sophistication of the systems used. SMEs in this quadrant need to communicate and exchange information with major customers in a cost efficient manner. Hence, there is more extensive use of systems such as e-mail and EDI. Manufacturing SMEs may be part of an Extranet. Often, customers are the driving force behind the introduction of new IS. SMEs begin to see the benefits of better management information particularly when negotiating terms with their customers. Information systems strategy is reactive to business strategy as SMEs attempt to capture value from having appropriate information when negotiating with major customers.

Repositioning quadrant

The final quadrant is *repositioning* – the integration of IS with business strategy (Yetton *et al.*, 1994). Here IS are an integral and tightly woven part of the business strategy of the SME. Therefore, IS influence the direction of business strategy as well as react to it. Strategic benefits are realized only when IS are seen as part of business strategy.

■ Exploring the focus-dominance model

Examination of each cell in the focus-dominance model shows how the business context influences the investment in IS. The adoption of

IS by SMEs is a function of the strategic context as defined by the focus-dominance model.

The case material used in this chapter is collected as described in Chapter 1 and 7. The 44 SMEs are those for whom an IS strategy is analysed in Chapter 7. The case firms use a wide range of IS. These are grouped using the three categories of production systems, management support and customer relations as presented in Chapter 7.

All the SMEs have word processing systems, and all but two have accounting packages. These are used to control costs with a focus on efficiency, and categorized under management support. Fourteen SMEs have customer databases locating them within Earl's customer relations category. Only five have MRP and, of these, three have EDI systems. As suggested earlier, these fall within Earl's category of production, supporting planning and communications with their customers. Finally, three SMEs have migrated into the e-business web-based economy. They have multiple systems in both management support and customer relations categories. Not all systems used by the SMEs are included in this classification framework. Those that have been excluded, such as e-mail, are discussed later.

The interview data from each SME also provided information on the number and importance of customers. A competitive force analysis was developed for each of the SMEs, which led to understanding whether customer dominance was high or low. This analysis combined with data from a Seven-S analysis (Chapter 5) enabled the identification of those SMEs that focus on cost reduction and those that focus on value-added strategies.

A two-stage procedure was followed. First, each SME was assigned to a cell in the focus-dominance model based on its strategic context (Figure 9.3). Next, the IS classification schema presented in Figure 9.2 was used to assign each SME to a cell in the focus-dominance model as a function of its IS profile (Figure 9.4).

Second, Figures 9.3 and 9.4 are then compared. If the strategic context is a powerful influence on IS investment, then the assignments will be similar, otherwise, the two patterns would be independent of each other. A comparison of the cells to which each SME is assigned in Figures 9.3 and 9.4 finds matches in all but eight of the 43 cases. The strength of the relationship is high, with 35 of 44 SMEs aligning their core IS strategy to their strategic context. There is a match in 80% of the cases. Therefore, the adoption of IS by SMEs is a function of the strategic context as defined by the focus-dominance model.

There are significant differences between the IS profiles for the SMEs in each of the four cells in the focus-dominance model. For an SME that started in the efficiency cell, a shift to the co-ordination cell as the number of customers increase is associated with the development

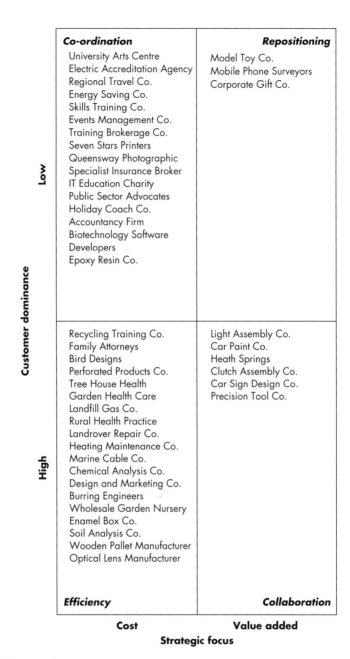

Figure 9.3: SMEs assigned by strategic context.

of customer databases. However, a shift to the collaboration cell is associated with the adoption of EDI and MRP to support an increased level of customer interaction. Each of the four profiles is illustrated here by a case SME from each quadrant in the model.

	Word processing	Accounting	Customer database	EDI	MRP	Performance measurement	Internet access	E-business
Efficiency systems								
Recycling Training Co.	X							
Energy Saving Co.	X	X						
Family Attorneys	X	X						
Bird Designs	X	X						
Chemical Analysis Co.	X							
Perforated Products Manufacturer	X	X						
Tree House Health	X	X						
Car Sign Design Co.	X	X					X	
Seven Stars Printers	X	X						
Garden Health Care	X	X						
Rural Health Practice								
Heating Maintenance Co.	X							
Marine Cable Co.	X	X					X	
Design and Marketing Co.	X	X						
Burring Engineers	X	X						
Wholesale Garden Nursery	X	X						
Energy Saving Co.	X	X						
Specialist Insurance Broker	X	X		X				
Public Sector Advocates	X	X						
Epoxy Resin Co.	X	X						
Enamel Box Co.	X	X						
Holiday Coach Co.	X	X						
Soil Analysis Co.	X	X						
Wooden Pallet Manufacturer	X	X						
Optical Lens Manufacturer	X	X						
Co-ordination systems								
University Arts Centre	X	X	X					
Electric Accred Agency	X	X	X					
Regional Travel Co.	X	X	X					
Skills Training Co.	X	X	X					
Events Management Co.	X	X	X					
Training Brokerage Co.	X	X	X					
Queensway Photo	X	X	X					
Landfill Gas Co.	X	X	X					
Landrover Repair Co.	X	X	X					
Biotechnology software	X	X	X					
IT Education Charity	X	X	X					
Accountancy Firm	X	X	X					
Collaboration systems								
Light Assembly Co.	X	X		X	X	X		
Car Paint Co.	X	X			X			
Heath Springs	X	X		X	X	X		
Clutch Assembly Co.	X	X		X	X	X		
Precision Tool Co.	X	X			X			
Repositioning systems								
Model Toy Co.	X	X	X				X	X
Mobile Phone Survey	X	X					X	X
Corporate Gift Co.	X	X	X				X	X

Figure 9.4: SME systems analysis.

Case study 9.1

Efficiency – Garden Health Care

Garden Health Care is a private health care provider for the elderly. It provides a home with round-the-clock care for frail people. Additionally, Garden Health Care supports people living in an integrated sheltered housing development. There is a management team of five, each responsible for a specific activity in the home, and 60 other staff. In common with many other health services providers, there is high turnover among care workers.

There are three main business processes: delivery of health care, facilities management and financial management. Delivery of health care is the organization of the day-to-day care of clients. This is managed by the matron whose duties include optimizing bed utilization, staff development, and training and monitoring quality of care. Data on clients and staff is maintained manually, as is cost information, budgets and income forecasts. Financial information is entered by the bookkeeper onto the computer.

Second, facilities management involves managing catering requirements, plants, gardening and transport. Rooms are also hired out to other organizations, such as government funded social services organizations. The final business process is financial management. The owner sets the annual budget with the management team. Budget performance is reviewed weekly and monthly using information from managers. The owner closely monitors and keeps tight control of all expenditure and variances.

The owner's objectives are to provide quality care and allow clients to maintain their dignity, to maximize financial return from the business and to retain control. The key success factors are high bed occupancy to keep costs down and quality of care. The owner is considering expanding the facilities, either on the current site or at other locations.

The market is competitive with a number of other similar services in the vicinity and there are low barriers to entry. Customer power, in the form of the government funded social services organizations that pays for 85% of clients, is high. The primary customer demands quality care and moderate pricing.

The major IS contribute to the focus on improving efficiency. These are an off-the-shelf accounting system for payroll and ledger activities; an invoicing system integrated into the accounting system; and spreadsheets used for managing various budgets. The focus of these systems is first, tight control of the finances as a means of monitoring efficiency; and second, good communication between management. The management style is formal, but the CEO tours the facilities keeping in touch with day-to-day activities.

Case study 9.2

Co-ordination – Training Brokerage Co.

Training Brokerage Co. started in 1989, offering project management consultancy and training mainly in Hong Kong and East Asia. The firm has since diversified into management training, led by a demand from overseas firms for UK management qualifications. Training Brokerage Co. co-ordinates and administers courses on behalf of two UK universities in several Asian regions. In 1997, they had a turnover of £0.7 million and employed 10 people in the UK. The espoused business strategy is to be the biggest provider of in-house management training in the UK. They are also planning to reduce their dependence on the two universities by developing relationships with others.

The firm has a large number of customers based mainly outside the UK. It views the students or end-users as its customers rather than the two universities. Therefore, customer databases and communication technologies are important to the business. Customer care has been identified as a major objective for Training Brokerage Co. This manifests itself in terms of improved marketing as well as support for existing customers undertaking distance-learning courses.

Training Brokerage Co. is pro-active towards IS, employing a manager with specific responsibilities for the systems. The system is networked so that all staff can access the three main databases: marketing, students and corporate clients. The system was developed by the IT personnel using Lotus Notes. E-mail is used to communicate with customers overseas. The firm has a separate PC-based accounting system while personnel and payroll operations are outsourced. The firm prides itself on being informal and responsive, with all staff able to undertake all business activities. While the systems are designed to aid co-ordination of business activities, the informality and lack of control mechanisms lead to incomplete data recording and lack of follow-up.

Case study 9.3

Collaboration – Car Paint Co.

Car Paint Co. is a manufacturer of paint for the automotive industry. The firm is the UK leader in automotive paint manufacture with 80% of the market. The firm is based on two sites that are largely autonomous as they make different products. Customers' demands for shorter lead times have impacted on the firm. There is pressure for just-in-time delivery of products and also smaller production runs are becoming more prevalent. Car Paint Co. has to be flexible and responsive to their customers needs. Collaboration takes the form of a representative of Car Paint Co. being based in the customers' warehouse where they store paint. Car Paint Co. has access to the automotive manufacturers' production schedule to determine future paint usage. Any issue of paint automatically triggers a new purchase order at Car Paint Co. While currently, they do not have an EDI system at least one of its major customers will make it a necessity in the near future.

Case study 9.4

Repositioning – Corporate Gift Co.

Corporate Gift Co. designs and manufactures corporate gifts for a wide range of internationally known firms. The firm also retails a range of gift items such as paperweights. It is based on a converted rural farm and most of its manufacturing is outsourced to South East Asia. Information systems have enabled the key stakeholders to live and work in a location of their choice and to manage the relationship with their customers and suppliers effectively.

The business strategy is tightly integrated with the IS strategy and the firm has invested heavily in IS, using Apple Macintosh systems. These systems were initially selected because of their strength in the core business competence of design, but all management systems have been built on this base. Corporate Gift Co. has a policy of open access to information (apart from accounts) to all employees. Management information is driven through the IT system with all staff understanding the need for accuracy.

Only IT literate staff are employed. The firm has a web site and is developing its e-business strategy in order to process customer orders online. Most communication with suppliers is already electronic. The intention is to integrate order processing with the back-office transaction processing system. This is seen as a key part of the business strategy to grow the business through identifying new markets. As a response to this change in strategy, Corporate Gift Co. also intends to bring some of its manufacturing back in-house The ability to link designs to orders, and thus to production, electronically is seen as a means of keeping costs down and quality up.

■ Non-strategic IS

The development of the focus-dominance model above is concerned with the strategic drivers of an SME's investment in IS. Of course, not all IS are strategic. To be strategic, the investment must be valuable, unique and difficult for a competitor to imitate (Feeny and Ives, 1990). For example, the usage of e-mail by Training Brokerage Co. is simply a tactical investment. It increases flexibility and is of lower cost than faxes but it does not change how Training Brokerage Co. competes and is easily copied by a competitor. Essentially, their customers are overseas; therefore e-mail is the easiest way to contact them. Taken together, the systems in Training Brokerage Co. are relatively simple, accounting, word-processing and customer databases.

Similarly, a number of other firms in the co-ordination cell have implemented LANs to access their customer databases. In themselves, these LANs are not strategic IS investments. They are complementary IS investments to the strategic investment in customer databases. Intranets and a number of other IS investments, also tend to fall into this category. Importantly, higher IS investment and investment in more complex IS are of themselves not strategic. Instead, only IS investments which are critically contingent on and aligned to the business strategy should be categorized as strategic IS. Research has tended to treat higher and more complex IS investment as a surrogate for strategic IS investment.

■ Implications for research

The key finding here, illustrated by the four cases, is that, in general, SMEs align their IS with their strategic context as defined by the focus-dominance model (Figure 9.2). In addition, the analysis distinguishes between strategic IS, which need to be aligned to the strategic context and other IS, such as e-mail, which are adopted for tactical rather than strategic reasons. Tactical IS do not need to be aligned to the strategic context.

The eight non-aligned SMEs raise questions about the dynamics of alignment. Do SMEs reposition themselves in the focus-dominance model and then re-align their IS or do they adopt the required IS before repositioning? For example, in Hong Kong some SMEs adopt IS before strategic repositioning while others align their IS after strategic positioning (Burn, 1997; 1996). Both dynamics appear to be viable.

Five of the eight non-aligned SMEs have IS which is inadequate to support their strategic position. Energy Saving Co., Seven Stars Printers, Specialist Insurance Broker, Public Sector Advocates and Holiday Coach Co. are located in the co-ordination cell in the focus-dominance model (Figure 9.3) but have IS consistent with the efficiency cell (Figure 9.4) and Car Sign Design Co. is located in the collaboration cell (Figure 9.3) but also has IS consistent with the efficiency cell (Figure 9.4). All three would benefit from developing IS to support their strategic positioning. For both Public Sector Advocates and Holiday Coach Co., this is increasingly critical as they are growing rapidly and need better strategic information.

Case study 9.5

Specialist insurance broker is owned jointly by the two CEOs. They bought the firm from its founder in 1996. The firm employs 27 people, grown from six within 5 years. The firm specializes in insurance for high-risk businesses. This is a growing niche market as the population moves towards a desire to undertake more high-risk sports (e.g. ballooning, white water rafting and bungee jumping). While the firm has only a small market share overall, in the high-risk area, particularly motor sports they are rapidly increasing their share of the market.

There is a fair amount of complexity in the business process to assess the risk of the particular sport. The process may require staff, often the directors, to physically visit locations to assess the risk. They prepare a report that sets out the situation that is agreed with clients before being passed to insurance companies to find the best quotation. Once the quotation is agreed, policy documents are issued. The knowledge and experience of the two CEOs and senior staff is an invaluable asset and a core competence of the firm.

There is a need for better management information to monitor achievement of critical success factors, particularly customer satisfaction, market intelligence and product innovation. Additionally, financial analysis is increasingly important to the firm. However, the systems in place were set up when the firm was in its infancy and do not meet all the management information needs. The firm is heavily reliant on paper-based systems, which leads to frustration as files are sometimes mislaid. Duplication of work is often found as client information is not held electronically and has to be retyped from paper files. The firm has already recognized the need to improve its accounting function and has purchased a new computerized financial system. However, there will be a need to change work practices as well.

In contrast, Landfill Gas Co. and Landrover Repair Co. have developed and implemented IS contingent on their relocation into the co-ordination cell before moving into that strategic context from their current location in the efficiency cell (Figure 9.3). Similarly, others, such as Perforated Products Manufacturer, that has implemented CAD as a first step in their espoused strategic intent of moving into the collaboration cell to become a preferred supplier to one of the large automobile assemblers, are developing their IS to support a strategic repositioning. For example, discussions on future plans for strategic use of IS suggest that the University Arts Centre and Training Brokerage Co. are building the IS infrastructures and competencies needed to move themselves into the repositioning cell.

Case study 9.6

Landrover Repair Co. is one of the leading suppliers in the Landrover after market. They refurbish Landrovers and also supply spare parts. The firm is owned by the CEO and employs 16 people. The firm has grown and is diversifying into conversion of automobiles to use liquid petroleum gas. The quality of their refurbishments ensures a steady stream of business, both new and repeat. The firm has taken a number of strategic decisions with regard to management information, particularly as the CEO want to grow the liquid petroleum gas conversion business. Accounting and payroll are both outsourced, which the firm finds increases the time that is available to focus on the business. They have developed a number of integrated databases to help manage the business: customer information, stock holdings and job planning. They have installed a network and the information is available to all staff who require it. The owner has also invested in e-mail so that he can receive management information when travelling abroad. Staff have been closely involved in the development of the systems and they are used effectively to manage the operation, leaving the owner free to focus on the new business.

This result also informs the existing record on SME investment in IS and organizational performance. As discussed in Chapter 3, there is limited use of management IS in SMEs. This is supported here if those SMEs in the efficiency and co-ordination quadrants that have accounting systems and, in some cases, customer databases, are seen to have limited management IS. In which case, 33 of the 44 SMEs in the sample have limited management IS. In contrast, SMEs in the collaboration and repositioning cells develop complex IS with which to manage the business. For example, advanced performance measurement systems are already in operation in Heath Springs, Light Assembly Co. and Clutch Assembly Co. that are all in the Collaboration cell (Figures 9.3 and 9.4).

In addition, given that the performance of IS investment is contingent on aligning the IS and the strategic context, few main effect benefits would be expected (Cragg and King, 1992). Further, the cost benefits for low investments in the efficiency cell are easier to realize than are the growth benefits contingent on the higher cost, and more complex IS required for co-ordination and collaboration. In which case, as Cragg and King report, firms with more sophisticated IS would tend to perform worse than these with more limited systems. However, the explanation here is not inadequate management competencies but the contingent nature of IS alignment benefits and the differential difficulty of realizing the IS benefits in different cells.

Finally, age and experience of the owner is frequently the most important factor in IS-based success (Chapter 2). To integrate that finding with the results reported here simply requires that business dynamism is also a function of age and experience. In which case, the successful owner both leads the strategic repositioning and adopts the appropriate IS as a joint event. Such entrepreneurs are unlikely to be constrained by either a lack of trust in external IS resources (Igbaria et al., 1998) or limited financial resources (Foong, 1999; Premkumar and Roberts, 1999).

Taken together, the above arguments show that the major finding reported here of focused, contingent IS investment by SMEs can be interpreted as consistent with the generally pessimistic literature in this area such as Cragg and King (1992). However, in contrast to those researchers, this chapter concludes that managers of SMEs do align their IS and strategic contexts with the expectation of collecting significant benefits. Of course, it is possible that the situation changed during the 1990s and a replication of Cragg and King's study would now report different findings. Against this explanation, Premkumar and Roberts (1999) reported limited IS investment by SMEs. The contingent model developed here combined with the frequency of SMEs in each cell accounts for their finding. The efficiency and co-ordination cells both specify limited IS investment relative to the collaboration and repositioning cells and occur more frequently.

■ Implications for managers

For managers, this chapter develops a powerful analytical model with which to frame their IS investment decisions. It both maps the fit between strategic IS investment and the SME's strategic context and illustrates with the four cases above the realities of the choices to be made. In this section, the strengths and weaknesses of the options in each cell within the focus-dominance model are examined to help further inform managers' IS strategic choice.

The Efficiency scenario strengths are improved control through simple IS focusing on cost reduction and improved efficiency. The main weaknesses are the internal and operational focus, rather than customer focus. The lack of any link between IS investment and the firms business strategy means that only limited benefits are likely to be achieved. The firm's IS goal is to realize IS-based cost benefits. For SMEs in this position this might well be the right strategy if growth is not planned. However, owners that are planning business growth should start to stand back from the operation and focus on the business strategy direction. It is likely that there will be two options, either

market development or product development. The first strategy is likely to need more knowledge of customers while the second requires a focus on market intelligence.

The co-ordination quadrant, which still has a cost focus, uses IS to improve communication and customer care, leading to improved operational effectiveness. The weaknesses here are limited integration with business strategy, and the need for better IS staff skills to work with more complex systems. The primary goal is improved customer relationships. For those firms planning growth, there is a real need to start looking at the value-adding benefits of IS. While firms have grown their markets, retention and development possibly through diversification may be looked for. However, even if firms are not planning further growth, greater benefits can be obtained from the use of IS if owners review their management information requirements to focus on success measures.

The collaboration quadrant focuses on value-added IS benefits. Business strategy is the driver here. The focus is on external relations with major customers. The critical assumption is that better information gives the SME the opportunity to add value for the customer through

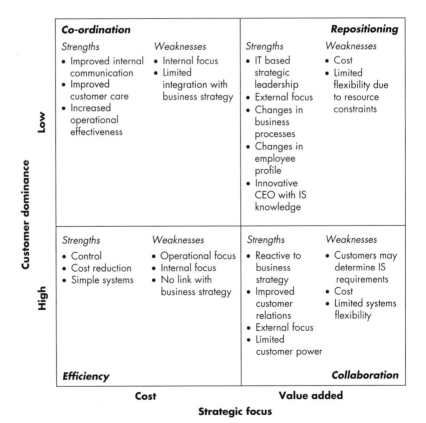

Figure 9.5: Strengths and weaknesses of SMEs in each scenario of the focus-dominance model.

collaboration. This emphasis on the joint creation of value-added limits customer demand for cost reduction. One major issue is the cost of the systems. This may lead to limited flexibility, as resource constraints limit upgrades and replacement. The other major issue is whether a major customer is tempted to use its power to maximize its own short-term profits rather than jointly create value for the partnership (Chatfield and Yetton, 2000; Webster, 1995; Reid and Jacobsen, 1988). There is often a steep learning curve for firms here, as customers demand fairly complex systems. Owners critically need good IS advice from trusted consultants and also need to involve the whole firm in business process changes that may be necessary.

Repositioning demonstrates strengths of integrated IS and business strategy that include both an internal and external perspective to the business. The owner is typically aware of IS-based opportunities for changes in business processes. The firm may require IS-literate employees to take advantage of the systems potential in providing knowledge. The weaknesses seen here are the potential cost to the business of the IS investment, its relationship to the business requirements, and the need for flexibility in order to manage continual change. Firms here need to be aware that IS is a means to an end not an end in itself and maintain a close eye on their future strategic direction. Figure 9.5 summarizes the strengths and weaknesses inherent in each scenario.

■ Conclusions

The existing research literature on SME investment in IS reports limited investment and weak or negative performance outcomes. In contrast, this chapter shows that SMEs' investment is strongly influenced by their strategic context. A contingent model of IS investment, the focus-dominance model, is developed in which investment is a function of the SME's strategy (cost reduction versus value added), and its market position (few versus many customers). SME behaviour is shown to match the model. The discussion shows how SME strategic, contingent behaviour is consistent with the typical null main effect findings in the literature. It also highlights the implications of the findings for managers.

The focus-dominance model forms the basis for the discussion of dynamics of IS development and SME transformation that follow in the next two chapters.

10 Strategic IS dynamics

■ Introduction

The focus-dominance model, introduced in Chapter 9, addresses fit between business and information systems strategies. As presented, the model appears to be a snapshot in time. However, it is the propensity to grow and develop that defines small- and medium-sized enterprises. The discussion in Chapter 9 suggests that there is an implicit dynamic embedded within the focus-dominance model.

The assumption underlying the focus-dominance model is that the initial strategic context of the typical SME is characterized by having a few dominant customers and a focus on cost, with IS investment supporting a focus on efficiency using spreadsheet and accountancy packages. The suggestion of the model is that a successful SME follows one of two trajectories. In one, the customer base increases and the information systems strategy changes from a focus on efficiency to one on co-ordination and IS investment in LANs and databases. In the other trajectory, the customer base does not increase significantly but collaboration between the firm and its few major customers improves, supported by IS investments in inter-organizational systems such as EDI.

Chapter 9 offered two propositions about the dynamics, or lack of dynamics, concerning IS uses in SMEs. The first is that an embedded stages model for IS use may exist. The second is that many SMEs choose to compete in one market and this tends to ossify their use of IS. Storey (1994) is critical of applying stages models developed from research on large firms to the behaviour of SMEs. He agrees with the second proposition that many SMEs do not progress from their initial start-up market position. When they do, Storey argues, growth is a function of the entrepreneur, the firm's industry sector, and structural characteristics such as location, rather than a progression through a series of predetermined stages as a response to emergent crises.

This chapter uses the focus-dominance model to examine evidence for the suggested trajectories. It uses the analysis to comment on the validity of the application of the stages of growth models to IS adoption in SMEs and the role of the entrepreneur and the strategic context, the basis of Storey's (1994) critique. An analysis of the outcomes of ISS development, undertaken for the 44 cases discussed in Chapter 9, follows, which provides support for all three analytical frameworks.

Integration is proposed and the implications for theory and practice
are explored.

■ Stages of growth

The concept that firms may develop following predictable, defined paths
or "stages of growth" has been proposed for some time. It has attracted
interest from those researching both large and small organizations.
Two of these models were introduced in Chapter 1. This chapter uses
Churchill and Lewis' five-stage model of growth for successful SMEs to
explore issues of IS investment.

As was shown in Chapter 1, Stage I is existence where the owner has
a clear business idea and closely manages all processes with a minimum
of staff. Investment is made in systems and equipment to carry out
operational activities. Stage II is survival and the business focuses on
managing operational activities with a simple organizational structure.
Funds are used to ensure there is sufficient stock to fulfill orders and
replace equipment. The firm may close when the owner retires.

Stage III is defined as "success". There are two parts to this stage.
Stage III-D is disengagement – the firm is profitable and has a reasonable
customer base. There may be some devolution of responsibility from the
owner to functional managers and there may be basic management IS in
place. Owners may decide to stay at this stage either because of the scale
of their market niche or because they look for a relatively risk-free
future. Stage III-G is growth – the owner has a clear strategy for growth.
Investment is made in additional resources including IS and personnel
to support growth. The owner is closely involved in the planning and
implementation strategies for growth.

The next stage, Stage IV is designated as take-off. The owner still
exercises power, but has functional managers directing planning. Growth
is likely to be rapid and cash flow is likely to be an issue as requirements
for resources increase. Information systems are used to manage increasing
business complexity. Stage V is maturity and represents a move to a
corporate style business where ownership and management are distinct.
The danger in this stage is that there may be little innovation and change,
and the firm may ossify.

Four firm-related success resources: financial, personnel, systems
and business (including customer and supplier relations) were identified
in Chapter 2. A key message is the need to plan for systems ahead of the
stage of growth for which they are required (Churchill and Lewis, 1983).
However, Scott and Bruce (1987) suggest it is unlikely that firms require
formal management systems until they reach maturity.

Four owner-related factors: business goals, operational skills, managerial
ability and strategic abilities were also identified in Chapter 1. However,
it is not critical for SMEs to use all these skills at all stages. For example,

owners' personal skills become less relevant as the SME grows. The importance of financial resources changes with business growth.

IS adoption and business growth

As discussed in Chapter 2, Storey (1994) is critical of stages of growth models being applied to SMEs. He suggests that many firms do not move beyond Stage I. As they have no desire to progress, a stages model, which implies movement to the next stage as the result of a crisis or other driver, is irrelevant. SME growth is actually achieved by a combination of the characteristics of the entrepreneur, the firm and its context.

The major factor in increasing investment in information systems and technology to manage growth is owner enthusiasm. An investigation of change in IS use over 4 years, reveals that hardware was not updated by 45% of SMEs, while others prefer to add to, rather than replace, existing hardware. Little change occurred in IS planning, although end-users were more involved in system selection. Some SMEs made IS/IT investments to improve operational effectiveness. However, any competitive advantage achieved was accidental, not planned (Cragg and King, 1993).

In contrast, in a study of 18 manufacturing firms over 8 years, the majority acquired new computers, although four did not. Most investment was in PCs and was directly related to growth in employee numbers. Spreadsheets for management reporting were adopted, although more complex analysis for forward planning was not undertaken. Databases were uncommon and were dependent upon individual users rather than management policy. A lack of trust of external IS sources inhibited IS growth and evolution, as SMEs generally do not have in-house IS skills. Limited financial resources are also cited. Again, it is the interest and enthusiasm of owners that primarily contributes to IS adoption (Cragg and Zinatellli, 1995).

In Storey's model, strategy is "*action taken by the firm once in business*". Market positioning, new product introduction and technological sophistication are the key drivers. Technological sophistication relates to product innovation and does not include management IS. The other two drivers that support growth are a willingness to borrow money to fund it and to devolve decisions to a management team. These reinforce the importance of the owner's attitude towards growth.

Investigating IS adoption and growth

There are a number of consistent criteria important for growth in SMEs. In terms of the entrepreneur, clear business goals and management experience stand out as essential. In respect of strategy, market positioning, financial resources and devolution of decision-making are important. Unless these are executed effectively growth will be inhibited. Not only must they all be executed well individually, but they must be aligned with each other. It is the alignment of strategy, market positioning and IS investment that is the basis of the focus-dominance model.

Stages of growth models suggest that there are SMEs for whom the key motivation is simply viability. There is little inclination to grow beyond the size required to ensure an acceptable level of profitability. In which case, IS investment is of limited importance. Only beyond this stage is there a requirement for IS to control the firm as devolution begins. However, some firms view this stage as an opportunity to prepare for further growth. These firms start early to invest in IS for the future.

Most of the research reviewed in this book concerns behavioural and strategic issues. However, some of the issues identified by Storey (1994) are structural. That is, the structure of the firm or of the industry or location enables or inhibits growth. Porter's (1980) work is archetypal of the structuralist school of competitive advantage. He argues that issues such as clustering may determine firm success. Firms that locate in a region where many similar firms are based will gain advantages over firms in remote regions. Similarly, there may be differences in SME success depending on their industrial sector, regardless of clustering. Other potential drivers include the role of IS/IT suppliers and the extent of formal sub-contracting networks to which an SME belongs. This chapter investigates these issues as well as the behavioural ones pertaining to the owner/manager.

The case firms used in this chapter are those introduced in Chapters 7. These firms have been followed for a number of years. The process of information gathering uses the approach described in Chapters 7 and 9. This has been repeated over time. Additionally, focus groups have been used to bring selections of the owner-managers and other senior staff together to discuss IS and business issues. This longitudinal analysis provides a rich dataset of the firms' past, present and intended uses of IS. The lengthy contact period enables the SMEs' plans to come to fruition and outcomes to be studied. The history of IS development and also the future potential for IS adoption is discussed with owners. Their strategy is further understood by the use of Ansoff's (1965) matrix to identify if the firm is looking to sell to new markets, develop new products or to diversify. This matrix is used in a later chapter to assess Internet developments.

In order to explore the potential importance of structural issues, owner-managers are asked about their relationships with IS/IT suppliers, their formal sub-contracting relationships and networks with other firms and the extent to which firms in their industry are clustered or geographically dispersed. In addition, the firms are classified by industry, though the fluid and entrepreneurial nature of some small firms makes discrete classification problematic.

The focus-dominance model is used to examine the adoption and use of IS over time.

■ Case analysis

The relative positions of the case firms 5 years prior to the ISS, at the time of the ISS and the planned future systems as identified from the ISS are modelled using the focus-dominance model. The firms are repositioned on the focus-dominance model on the basis of the strategic IS that they have at each of the three occasions: past, current and long-term plans (Table 10.1).

The past and the current state of the SMEs are presented in Figure 10.1. One element of the case analysis is the identification of future opportunities from IS/IT, some of which have now come to pass. Other opportunities are based on an understanding of the SMEs' future strategic growth plans and their IS requirements. These outcomes were discussed with the firms, enabling mapping of the growth paths for the 44 SMEs over the past 5 years and the next 5 years. These are presented in Figure 10.2.

Strategic positions

Chapter 9 argues that the efficiency quadrant represents the starting point for the most SMEs for whom IS/IT provides basic operational level support. Thirty-seven of the cases were located in the *efficiency* cell 5 years ago (Figure 10.1). The focus of IS/IT is primarily on cost reduction using IS/IT to improve management processes. There is no link with business strategy, and owners show little awareness of the wider possibilities from IS/IT. Only one SME chooses to stay in this quadrant using simple systems.

Current growth paths

A set of growth paths emerges from the mapping exercise (Figure 10.2). The simplest "path" is no change – the SME is content, or unable to move. The number of firms in these categories are represented by the encircled numbers. Other growth paths are vertical, horizontal, or both. The number of firms involved is shown at the arrowheads in Figure 10.2. The concern here is not only with the start and end point, but with the routes taken. Thus, the repositioning scenario can be reached from the

Table 10.1: Past, current and future growth focus-dominance model positions for case SMEs

Firm	Past				Current				Future growth			
	Effic	Co-ord	Collab	Repos	Effic	Co-ord	Collab	Repos	Effic	Co-ord	Collab	Repos
Recycling Training Co.	X				X				X			
Chemical Analysis Co.	X				X					X		
Bird Designs	X				X					X		
Family Attorneys	X				X					X		
Queensway Photographic	X				X					X		
Burring Engineers	X				X					X		
Marine Cable Co.	X				X					X		
Accountancy Firm	X				X					X		
Design and Marketing Co.	X				X					X		
Heating Maintenance Co.	X				X					X		
Landrover Repair Co.	X				X					X		
Electrical Accredit Agent	X				X					X		
Garden Health Care	X				X						X	
Tree House Health Care	X				X						X	
Rural Health Practice	X				X						X	
Perforated Products Manufacturer	X				X						X	
Precision Tool Co.	X				X						X	
Model Toy Co.	X				X							X
Mobile Phone Surveyors	X				X							X
Land-fill Gas Co.	X					X			Ceased trading			

Company	Effic	Co-ord	Collab	Repos
Coventry Training Co.	X	X		X
Optical Lens Manufacturer	X	X		X
Epoxy Resin Co.	X	X		X
Enamel Box Co.	X	X		X
Public Sector Advocates	X	X		X
Wholesale Garden Nursery	X	X	X	X
Events Management Co.		X	X	X
Soil Analysis Co.	X	X		X
Training Brokerage Co.	X	X		X
Seven Stars Printers	X	X		X
Henley Coaches	X	X		X
Biotechnology Software Developers	X	X		X
Specialist Insurance Broker	X	X		X
University Arts Centre		X	X	X
Regional Travel Agent		X	X	X
IT Education Charity		X	X	X
Corporate Design Co.		X	X	X
Heath Springs	X		X	X
Car Paint Co.	X		X	X
Clutch Assembly Co.	X		X	X
Light Assembly Co.	X	X		X
Car Sign Design Co.	X	X		X
Energy Saving Co.	X	X		X
Wooden Pallet Manufacturer	X	X		X

Effic: efficiency; Co-ord: co-ordination; Collab; collaboration; Repos: respositioning.

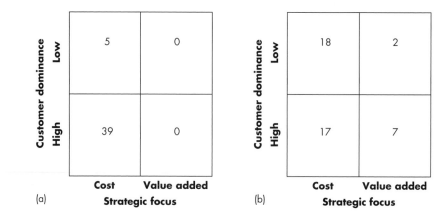

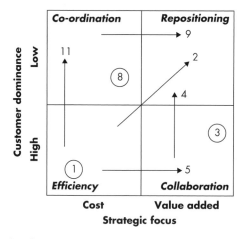

Figure 10.1: (a) Past (5 years ago) and (b) current strategic positions of case SMEs.

Figure 10.2: Current growth paths.

efficiency quadrant directly, or via co-ordination or via collaboration. The implications of each interim move are considered later in their role as potential stepping-stones to the final destination.

No change

One SME is comfortable remaining in the efficiency quadrant. Recycling Training Co. is a small charity, training people with special needs. For them, IS are for basic administration, and there is no further role for the information resources. There is a constant concern over viability and confusion over strategy. However, the owners do not want to change. They enjoy controlling the operation and have limited resources. They have word processing and spreadsheets but neither is really used. They are in Stage II of the Churchill and Lewis model and are likely to remain there until the owners close the business.

Case study 10.1

Recycling Training Co. is not result-oriented. Its main objective is training people with learning difficulties to achieve basic skills through the medium of waste recycling. The organization runs a paper waste collection service for local firms and also collects aluminium cans through special containers at waste disposal sites. The focus of the charity is the well-being of the trainees and its 10 employees. As with many charities a key concern is financial viability, as they need to be self-sustaining in the long-term. However, both of the business areas are highly competitive with many commercial firms in the waste disposal market. Currently, the organization benefits considerably from its charitable status, with local firms providing active support. The fees that the charity charges for collecting paper waste are not too uncompetitive. The charity managers believe that their time is best spent working closely with the trainees, helping them to improve their skills. This means that they spend very little time on managing the organization, beyond the day-to-day issues. The main concern is to have sufficient waste products coming in to provide trainees with material. There is relatively little management effort put into building relations with the firms that provide the waste or with organizations that commission training beyond what is necessary for the charity to continue to exist. This is a happy, easy-going and caring organization that sees little benefit from the use of IS.

Efficiency to co-ordination

The largest category is those SMEs moving from the efficiency quadrant to the co-ordination quadrant. These are firms that focus on increasing market share, and need to manage a large number of customers as they grow. Thus, in addition to existing efficiency-focused systems, they develop customer databases and recognize the need to improve internal communications. Local area networks begin to appear. For example, Regional Travel Agents, a travel agency specializing in independent travel, maintains a database to inform clients of holiday opportunities. Owners still look for operational improvement but recognize that IS/IT may enable a change in structure. There are limited links with business strategy in this move. Queensway Photographic recognizes the need to co-ordinate processing of jobs between departments as critical to survival. Communication is central to their systems requirements. Finally, Landrover Repair Co. has developed a customer database and job costing system to manage both its large customer base and its day-to-day operations more effectively.

Most of these firms are in Stage III-D of the Churchill and Lewis typology. For example, the owner of the Regional Travel Agents has appointed functional managers. There is cash for expansion, but the owners want to keep control and use the business to ensure their financial security. Landrover Repair Co. has gone in a different route using a management IS to refocus management requirements on key personnel. Yet, the aim is to keep control of the firm as a retirement plan. A moderately innovative strategy acknowledges limited resources. The key focus for IS is increasing efficiency and effectiveness. Queensway Photographic is a niche firm that employs a management team for day-to-day operation, but is closely managed by the owner. Controlling IS are being implemented for efficiency.

Case study 10.2

Queensway Photographic specializes in the development of large-scale photography for window and conference displays. The firm is owned by the CEO, who has a small management team. However, all decisions are made by the CEO, including costs of new commissions. The firm works in a specialist niche although it develops a wide range of photographs, what it is known for is the specialist skills in large-scale development. The owner has invested heavily in the technology to support this market niche. The owner is not planning further growth, beyond that which is sufficient to be in a position to sell the firm when he plans to retire. However, he wants to reduce overhead costs and recognizes that management IS might help. He is looking at automating job costing, so that the firm can use previous experience to inform future pricing. Additionally, he believes the process can be speeded up, improving customer satisfaction. Job tracking is also an issue for the firm and the owner believes that an automated system, possibly using bar coding, will help monitor progress, this will have the advantage of identifying bottlenecks in the firm as well as informing customers of job progress. However, there is little interest in the wider value adding potential from IS.

Co-ordination to repositioning

These firms are looking for growth, but demonstrate Stage III-G (growth) characteristics currently. Stage IV (take-off) is being planned. Biotechnology Software Developers is re-visiting its IS to enable them to manage growth more effectively. The owner is closely involved in growth planning and there is an emphasis on hiring effective managers. Holiday Coach Co. is looking at investment in IS to manage future growth. They have invested in a new building with networking capabilities. The owners perceive a future use of the Internet as critical to their business. They are in Stage III-G currently, looking to move to Stage IV.

Case study 10.3

Biotechnology Software Development is a highly innovative firm that was established in 1990 to provide digital imaging systems for scientific researchers. The firm has grown rapidly, it now employs 20 people, increasing revenue tenfold in 10 years. The firm has focused their business strategy on selling their product into new markets, particularly the USA and Germany. The market that the firm operates in is growing and developing, they are in a good position to increase their market share due to their lead position in product research. The firm is beginning to use the Internet as a means of updating software and customer relationship management. The firm's owners are well aware of their main competitors and are focusing on the best approach to increase market share. They are investing in the development of new products as digital imaging becomes more sophisticated. The owners also recognize that they need better management information as they grow the firm. Their management IS was set up when the firm started, but now they understand the need to improve knowledge exchange within the firm to improve customer relationship management and product development management.

Efficiency to collaboration

Efficiency to collaboration is a route taken mainly by manufacturing SMEs with one or two major customers. This is often the result of customer-pull. However, it does require a strategic decision by SME owners to make the necessary investments. Collaboration involves the addition of inter-organizational systems, particularly EDI, to communicate with customers. A consequence here is limited systems flexibility caused by SMEs developing systems to support one major customer. Other customers have different systems requirements that may be incompatible.

There is little evidence that the introduction of the inter-organizational systems changes the structure or staff roles. For example, while Heath Springs (Chapter 8), receives orders electronically, production planning is carried out manually rather than automatically entered into the MRP system. Garden Health Care, a nursing home (Chapter 9) sees the future as developing electronic links with medical practitioners and local pharmacists. This group of firms has a particular market niche that means that they tend to have a small number of major customers. Management looks to maintain and develop the relationships. Growth is sufficient to satisfy customer demands. Hence they are also likely to be in Stage III-D.

Collaboration to repositioning

These SMEs have already developed inter-organizational systems. Use of emerging technologies, such as the Internet, to extend and grow markets is seen as a natural growth path. Four SMEs are following this path. Energy Saving Co. analyses clients' gas and electricity use and provides advice on reducing consumption. They currently receive data electronically from the monopoly transmission supplier, National Grid. This data is analysed using IS/IT. Information systems and technology will allow them to work with customers fully electronically and they have invested heavily in IS. The interesting issue here is that the owner sees the Internet as a means of maintaining control. This raises questions over the stages model's insistence on devolution of power as important.

Case study 10.4

Energy Saving Co. is a rapidly growing, entrepreneurial firm owned by the CEO. There is a small management team of four, although the COE has a very hands-on management style. The staff (18) are highly qualified, with nearly a third having a second, higher university degree in a scientific specialism. The firm provides management and consultancy services on energy monitoring and efficiency improvement. Their success means that they are managing the business reactively, often fire-fighting, to ensure contracts are fulfilled on time. The business strategy is one of growth both by increasing market development and also to identify new opportunities for the high level of expertise in the firm by broadening their consultancy base into environmental issues.

The current IS is limiting future growth. The firm has a server and terminals, but these are mainly used for systems to support the operation. They have recognized the need to integrate finances, project management and customer relationship management. The firm sees the Internet as a means of enabling them to access information on customers to support their energy management policies more effectively. This will also support their objective of moving the business towards environmental consultancy.

Efficiency to repositioning

A further path has been identified – moving from efficiency directly to repositioning. This is evidenced in two cases. Model Toy Co. acts as brokers between manufacturers and designers of models and customers. They recognize IS/IT will change the nature of the business and enable them to be more responsive to customers and are moving to Internet selling of models. Mobile Phone Surveyors (Chapter 3) identify radio mast sites for mobile phone firms. They believe that customers value their ability to receive and act on information sent electronically.

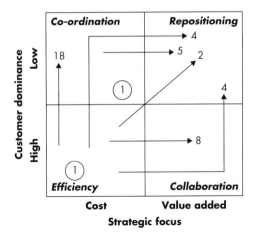

Figure 10.3: Long-term growth paths.

The CEO has invested heavily in IS/IT. The innovation here is in investment in a knowledge management system to change business processes. These firms are attempting to move to Stage IV (take-off) with a brief stay in Stage III-G. Their focus is on the owner maintaining control through the use of e-commerce.

Long-term growth paths

Twenty-eight of the 44 SMEs have adopted a co-ordination strategy, either as an end state or, for eleven cases, as a pathway on the way to repositioning as an end state. Few SMEs, only two, are attempting to move directly from the efficiency cell to the repositioning cell in Figure 10.3.

Twelve SMEs have migrated or are intending to migrate from the efficiency to the collaboration cell with four planning the *repositioning* scenario as their end state. Seven of these SMEs are manufacturers and suppliers to the automotive industry. The other five are in the social services and health sector. This reflects the need to work closely with customers, in the manufacturers' cases and with the wider medical services in the social service organizations.

It would appear that the move from efficiency to co-ordination with a further option to migrate to the *repositioning* quadrant is the dominant general growth path. This contrasts with the stages of growth model which does not distinguish between these different IS developments and alternative SME strategic pathways.

◾ Structural differences on IS adoption

In addition to the factors discussed above, Storey (1994) identifies structural issues including industry groupings, clustering, IS/IT

Table 10.2: Industry groups for case firms

Retailing and manufacturing	Service sector organizations
Land-fill Gas Extraction	Chemical Analysis Co.
Burring Engineers	Family Solicitors
Sea Cable Manufacturers	Queensway Photographic
Tritek	Coventry Accountants
Chemical Resin Co.	Coventry Designs
Enamel Jewellery Maker	Electrical Accredit Agent
Perforated Tubes Co.	Birmingham Solicitors
Precision Tooling Co.	Coventry Events Man
Heath Springs	Rural Health Practice
Car Paint Co.	Radio Mast Surveyors
Birmingham Clutches	Warwick Train Brokers
Solihull Lighting Co.	Seven Stars Printers
Wooden Pallet Co.	Warwick Ins Services
Bird Designs	Corporate Design Co.
Heating Engineers Co.	Stratford Signage
Landrover Repair Co.	Energy Usage Co.
Model Car Importers	Recycling and Training
Henley Coaches	Coventry Training Co.
Biotechnology Products	University Arts Centre
Regional Travel Agent	IT Education Charity
Wholesale Garden Nursery	Garden Health Care
	Tree House Health Care
	Soil Analysis Co.

suppliers and sub-contracting networks as critical drivers or inhibitors of growth. This section considers the influences of industry sector and business clustering on IS adoption and growth. Additionally three other structural variables are considered: informal network relations, sub-contracting and IS/IT suppliers.

Industry sector influences

The secondary analysis begins by examining the influence of the industry sector on the dynamics of growth. Table 10.2 dichotomizes the sample into service sector organizations comprising those SMEs engaged in business services, and social and public administration, and those involved in manufacturing and retailing. Manufacturing and retailing are combined as many of these SMEs engage in both or share similar characteristics. Figures 10.4 and 10.5 present the focus-dominance paths for the different sectors. While the small numbers and many paths through the focus-dominance model preclude any formal tests for difference, inspection of the figures reveal little difference between the two sectors.

Industry clusters

Industry clusters is a second potential structural driver. Only the seven manufacturing SMEs (Car Sign Design Co., Perforated Products

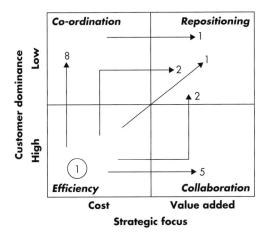

Figure 10.4: Sector effects on growth paths for manufacturing and retail SMEs.

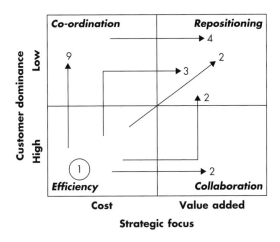

Figure 10.5: Sector effects on growth paths for service SMEs.

Manufacturer, Precision Tool Co., Heath Springs, Car Paint Co., Clutch Assembly Co. and Wooden Pallet Co.) that supply the automotive sector may be considered to be located in a cluster. Figures 10.6 and 10.7 group the firms by clustered and non-clustered SMEs. Extracting the automotive cluster SMEs from the full sample shows that all the clustered firms collaborate with customers and only two are planning to migrate to the *repositioning* quadrant. Here, it is unclear whether the factor is clustering or being a member of the automotive supply sector. Alternatively, it could be the relationship between the auto assemblers and their suppliers.

Strategic intent

Third, strategic intent is assessed by the Seven-S model. The analysis provides the information to position the firms using Ansoff's strategic

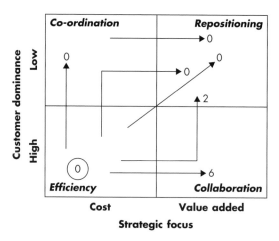

Figure 10.6: Automotive cluster SMEs growth paths.

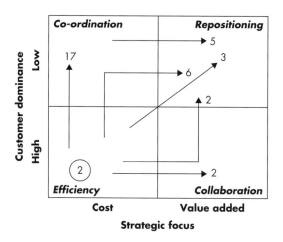

Figure 10.7: Non-clustered SMEs growth paths.

intent framework (Figure 10.8). This model is relevant to SMEs' strategic intent as it focuses on growth. The model uses the current growth strategies of the firm to consider the direction it is taking in relation to the current mix of product and market development. Understanding the growth direction enables business strategy to be better directed towards achieving growth. The strategic focus may either be towards product development or towards market development. The fourth strategy, diversification, is more difficult to follow as firms are moving into uncharted territories in both product and market development (Ansoff, 1965).

The strategic intent of the case firms is presented in Table 10.3.

Ansoff considers strategies involving staying in the current market (market penetration) (Figure 10.9), selling the same product to new

	Current product	New product
Present market	Market penetration	Product development
Future market	Market development	Diversification

Figure 10.8: Strategic intent framework. (*Source:* adapted from Ansoff, 1965.)

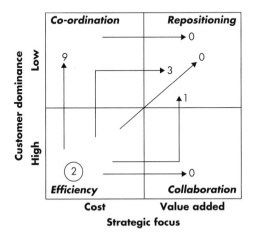

Figure 10.9: Market penetration as strategic intent.

Table 10.3: Strategic intent of case firms

Market penetration	Market development	Product development	Diversification
Recycling and Training	Chemical Analysis Co.	Bird Designs	Coventry Accountants
Land-fill Gas Extraction	Coventry Designs	Sea Cable Manufacturers	Model Car Importers
Family Solicitors	Landrover Repair Co.	Tritek	Warwick Train Brokers
Queensway Photographic	Radio Mast Surveyors	Chemical Resin Co.	Corporate Design Co.
Burring Engineers	Biotechnology Products	IT Education Charity	
Heating Engineers Co.	University Arts Centre	Perforated Tubes Co.	
Electrical Accredit Agent	Regional Travel Agent	Precision Tooling Co.	
Coventry Training Co.	Garden Health Care	Heath Springs	
Enamel Jewellery Maker	Tree House Health Care	Car Paint Co.	
Birmingham Solicitors	Stratford Signage	Birmingham Clutches	
Coventry Events Man	Energy Usage Co.	Wooden Pallet Co.	
Seven Stars Printers	Wholesale Garden Nursery	Rural Health Practice	
Henley Coaches	Soil Analysis Co.		
Warwick Ins Services			
Solihull Lighting Co.			

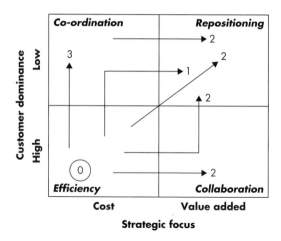

Figure 10.10: Market development as strategic intent.

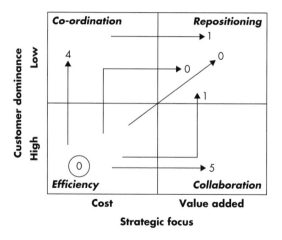

Figure 10.11: Product development as strategic intent.

markets (market development) (Figure 10.10), selling new products to the same market (product development) (Figure 10.11), and diversification (Figure 10.12). The growth plans of firms with the same strategic intent are modelled on the focus-dominance model to identify whether there are any structural issues to do with strategic intent.

This analysis shows that firms with market penetration as their strategic intent expect to move from the *efficiency* quadrant to the *co-ordination* quadrant as they expand their market and cope with more, similar customers. A few firms are planning to go on to *repositioning*, but the dominant strategy is *co-ordination*.

SMEs whose strategic intent is market development become innovators. These firms account for 12 of the 44 subject firms and 7 out of the 17 potential innovators.

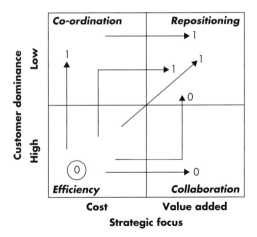

Figure 10.12: Diversification as strategic intent.

In contrast, product development as a strategic intent does not appear to be part of a repositioning strategy. This is possibly because the SMEs are selling into known markets and to known customers who are unlikely to require radical changes.

Last, diversification as a strategic intent tends to move the firms towards repositioning.

Informal network relations, sub-contracting and IS/IT suppliers

Three other structural variables, network relations, sub-contracting and IS/IT suppliers, which are important factors in the growth strategies of large firms, are reviewed here. Only three of the case SMEs have informal network relationships with other firms. The SMEs in the *repositioning* and *collaboration* cells have formal networks with customers. For example, Warwick Training Brokers has a partnership with a university, and Regional Travel Agents provides conference travel services to another sample firm, Events Management Co. In no case are these relationships IS-supported. Similarly, while there are formal supplier relationships, often preferred supplier status involving collaborators, only one other SME in the *repositioning* quadrant, Radio Mast Surveyors, is a sub-contractor. This suggests that it is difficult to be both an SME collaborating with a major customer and to pursue a repositioning strategy.

Last, all the case SMEs are serviced by reactive rather than proactive IS/IT suppliers. In some cases, this is in-house or from very small suppliers, mostly involving software packages. Even where the supplier is large, no strategic advice is offered in addition to satisfying the technical requirements. Hence, the role of the IS/IT supplier is not linked to movements within the focus-dominance model or changes in the stage of growth.

■ Discussion

The analysis here shows that most SMEs make one move only, from efficiency to co-ordination, or from efficiency to collaboration. These SME owners do not want to lose control and choose to remain in their current markets. This is particularly evident for firms in the *collaboration* quadrant that have a well-defined market niche.

The business strategy of these SMEs is directed at survival, possibly to ensure a retirement fund. There is some devolution of power, with functional managers employed for day-to-day operations in close liaison with the owner. There is evidence that for this group, Storey (1994) may be correct, there is little merit in considering a "stages of growth" model for these SMEs. The implications for IS is that they will look for the minimum necessary to improve efficiency and effectiveness, but are unlikely to see the value of IS as a means of growing. As Landrover Repair Co. shows, IS may help reduce overheads.

Only 17 of the 44 case firms wish to move to an innovative use of IS/IT. There are a number of reasons for this. The first concerns the SMEs' stage of development. There are a number of subsidiary processes involved in growth here. A key issue that affects IS/IT investment is the owner's objectives. Strategy development requires thinking about the future and this process may reveal a need for collaboration or co-ordination. It also means that the SME becomes aware of what others are doing by formal or informal environmental scanning, and may become sensitized to "best practice". SMEs that have a well developed and up-to-date business strategy are developing effective management teams that are involved in managing growth.

Examples for which the move to innovation makes business sense include Warwick Training Brokerage that is developing relationships with south-east Asia to broker training with UK institutions. Stratford Signage Co. designs signs for the automotive sector and has clients that demand fast turnaround, but they are also looking to expand their customer base. They see use of the Internet as satisfying both goals. Corporate Designs, located in a rural business park, designs and manufactures corporate gifts and has geographically dispersed customers and many overseas suppliers. These factors convinced them that innovative use of IS is the only way to grow successfully. Most of these firms show evidence of growth by stages, in both their business and in their use of IS.

A small, interesting group is the three SMEs that are moving directly to repositioning. The owners see IS as a means of radically changing their business while maintaining close control over strategy and operation. Model Toy Importers do not see the need to expand their staff or change their structure with their current move to a web-based organization. Radio Mast Surveyors is using Lotus Notes internally to improve knowledge management and the Internet to work more closely with its customer base. The owner is intimately involved with managing these changes. The management team is involved in some operational implementation but has no responsibility for the vision for growth. It is difficult to define a stage model for these, as they appear to bypass the planning for growth stage. In contrast, they do exhibit the key characteristics identified by Storey (1994) for success. The owners are older, well-educated, with some knowledge of the potential of IS. They have clear goals and are experienced managers. Owners are aware of the need to review the competitive environment to reposition the firm. They are prepared to invest for growth. The only issue is that they may not be as keen on devolving power to a management team.

In terms of the analysis of structural variables, these seem to be dominated by the behavioural ones. Information systems and technology supplier, informal networks, and industry groupings appear to have no impact on the sample. The effects of industry clusters and sub-contracting are similar. These variables only affect collaborating firms that are manufacturers and suppliers to the automotive industry.

The analysis of strategic intent is interesting. Market penetrators tend to adopt a co-ordination pathway. Six of the SMEs adopting a collaboration pathway also have adopted a product development strategic intent. Market development strategy is not associated with the adoption of particular pathways, while diversification is associated with innovation.

The above findings are subject to one major and one minor validity threat. The former is that the future pathways are strategic intentions that may not be implemented either due to internal or market constraints. In which case, the pathways developed here, while theoretically attractive are not practically feasible. The minor validity threat is that this sample is biased towards those SMEs which intend to grow and that therefore little can be said about those that are either content to stay small or that cannot grow. This may be the case for the majority of SMEs. It is therefore possible to say little about the propensity to adopt a growth strategy by the typical SME.

■ Implications for research

The findings in this chapter support, in part, all three models of strategic dynamics described at the beginning, namely the focus-dominance model, the stages of growth model and Storey's criticism of the stages model, labelled here the entrepreneur and the strategic context. The weakest support is for a stages of growth model. While up to 30% of the SMEs are following some kind of a stage model, it does not seem to explain either the enablers or the barriers to change. Further, it is only the transition from Stage II to Stages III-D and III-G that appear to be relevant. Both the predictive and prescriptive value of the theory applied to these SMEs appears weak.

The focus-dominance model does identify important strategic choices, and their IS components, that need to be made if a growth path is to be implemented. An analysis of the role played by IS suppliers suggests that an SME would need to build its own IS capability to support growth. The analysis within Storey's (1994) framework suggests that growth will depend on the owner's values and experience. In particular here, the owner's IS experience is a critical factor underpinning successful growth.

An analysis of industry sectors and strategic intent, as suggested by Storey, identifies the tendency for manufacturing suppliers to the automotive industry to follow a collaboration pathway and expand their initial efficiency strategy to include product development. Growth is then limited by the strategic agenda of the major assemblers who focus on capturing cost benefits from their small suppliers. An analysis of Honda shows that this is not a dominant strategy for the industry sector, but a strategic choice by a major customer (Chatfield and Yetton, 2000).

■ Implications for managers

For managers, the messages from this analysis are mixed. First, there is a large group of owner/managers for whom business growth is not an issue. However, these wish to maximize their profitability within the narrow bounds of the current business. Such SMEs are willing to introduce IS to control and manage operational activities. There is a need to review the operational processes with the owner to consider the best form these systems can take. As discussed in Chapters 7 and 8, there is a need for some business process change prior to introduction of IS. Yet, there is a dearth of independent advice for SMEs in this position. It might be possible to develop a checklist for them to review their requirements.

Approximately one third of the case SMEs are following a limited stages model of growth and investing cautiously to manage future growth. They are aware of the need to invest in advance of the stage of growth and are introducing IS to manage that growth. The owners recognize IS can change the way they compete, but are seeking incremental investment rather than a major push. For example, Regional Travel Agents has developed a web page with a booking form, but is not actively encouraging clients to book this way. The owners are reviewing business processes, but they need advice on IS capabilities before they will invest. The focus-dominance model suggests both IS investment guidelines and the elements to go on the above checklist.

The third group, those moving to repositioning, change perceptions of growth somewhat. Growth does mean more staff to run day-to-day operation, but the owner is closely involved with strategy and decisions on the direction of the business. The owner's knowledge is critical for development of innovative information solutions, but they must match the vision and strategy for growth.

■ Conclusions

This chapter sheds light on the process by which SMEs invest in, and gain benefit from, IS as they grow. It investigates whether an embedded stages model for IS use exists and, for SMEs choosing to compete in one market, if this leads to ossification in their IS use or whether SMEs followed the implicit pathways suggested in Chapter 9. An analysis of the outcomes of ISS development undertaken for the 44 SMEs provides weak and incomplete support for a stages of growth model. The evidence is stronger for the critique by Storey (1994) of stages of growth models and of the differential pathways identified by extending the focus-dominance model. These issues are explored further in Chapter 11.

11 Exploring business transformation through IS

▣ Introduction

Chapter 10 reviewed the growth strategies of small- and medium-sized enterprises and showed that there are different growth strategies followed by SMEs. The main finding is that the concept of a stages of growth model is not supported, while investment is essentially a function of the business strategy, the owner's knowledge and the firm.

This chapter investigates further, whether, and in what form, SMEs achieve business transformation through information system. Business processes and strategic intent affect achievement of transformation. It is useful to understand the underlying process that is adopted by SMEs in using and developing business transformation through IS. One classic IS business transformation framework is that of Venkatraman (1994), and this chapter assesses its suitability to SMEs.

Further investigation of the 44 case firms is undertaken to consider IS adoption over time. Organizational and management issues are assessed to consider SME approaches to transformation. Analysis reveals three paths or progressions through the transformation model, termed the *prescribed*, the *disconnected* and the *disjointed* rather than one. Finally, the discussion reflects on the drivers of these three paths and employs the focus-dominance model (Chapter 9) to shed light on them. Implications for management and research are presented at the conclusion of the chapter.

▣ Business transformation through IS

Venkatraman's (1994) framework (Figure 11.1) recognizes that information technology plays a major role in enabling business to respond to flexible and dynamic markets. The framework focuses on organizational and management process change required to exploit IT. Its central thesis is that IT benefits are limited unless organizational structures undergo commensurate change to manage the business response. While not proposing a "stages of growth" model, Venkatraman acknowledges that "potential benefits" increase from Level 1 (localized exploitation) to Level 5 (business scope redefinition). The costs associated with change at each level increase and firms need to consider their value. However, as competitive pressures increase firms will need to be proactive.

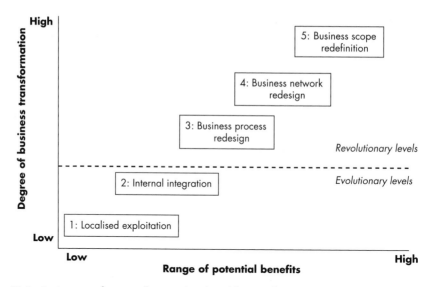

Figure 11.1: Business transformation framework (adapted from Venkatraman, 1994).

Localized exploitation improves "task efficiency" and IT has little impact on the business. Standard systems to support individual tasks are deployed. There is limited likelihood of competitive advantage as systems are easily imitated. The strengths for firms with this level of IS is that systems are usually simple and provide stand-alone support to individual managers. The weaknesses are the danger of duplication as similar sets of information are held in several locations in the firm. There is likely to be no impact on the organization from the introduction of IS. Knowledge cannot easily be exchanged and there is limited benefit from the IS investment.

Internal integration improves efficiency and effectiveness through firm-wide technical and organizational system integration. The focus is on "technical interconnectivity" rather than "business process interdependence". Integration benefits are only realized if the firm uses the information to improve customer service or efficiency. The strengths here include improved internal efficiency as information and knowledge can be shared. The improvement in internal communication often leads to improved customer service. However, potential weaknesses are that the IS system constrains business process change. The focus on internal efficiency may mean that external knowledge is not addressed, particularly there is no consideration of competitor changes.

Venkatraman calls these two steps evolutionary as they involve incremental change in business activities. Table 11.1 summarizes the strengths and weaknesses at each transformation level.

The next three levels are "revolutionary" as they require major process change to achieve competitive advantage. *Business process redesign* suggests firms question whether their structures enable them to

Table 11.1: Strengths and weaknesses of transformation levels

Transformation level	Major strengths	Potential weaknesses
Localized exploitation	IT easy to identify Organizational change minimal	Duplication Limited organizational learning Limited benefits from investment
Internal integration	Focus on internal efficiency Improved customer service	Imposed on existing business processes May not consider competitors changes
Business process redesign	Offers high value to customers New processes offer future potential	Benefits limited if viewed as merely corrective Include processes that should be outsourced
Business network redesign	Focus on core competences Streamline scope for flexibility Exploit opportunities of network	Poor co-ordination of network partners may inhibit benefits Limited IT infrastructure could inhibit learning
Business scope redefinition	Information as a strategic resource Build co-opetitive relationships between partners	Focus on network relationships not core competence Hollow factory may limit growth opportunities

Source: adapted from Venkatraman, 1994.

compete in a changing market. However, benefits are limited if firms only look at their own requirements and exclude those within the industry value chain. The strengths of this phase are that by refocusing on core business processes the firm can both offer better customer service and also position itself more effectively for future growth. However, benefits may not be achieved if the firm views this phase purely as a means of cost cutting or it does not recognize its core competences and outsource peripheral activities.

Business network redesign recognizes the need to exchange information across the value chain including managing relationship with collaborators. The solution is not merely technological, inter-firm relationships need to be developed to acknowledge network interdependencies. The strength of this phase is that the firm is focusing its business strategy through its core competences and develops IS to improve flexibility, particularly with customers and suppliers. The danger here for the firm is that network partners may not be as far advanced in managing the relationship, which might inhibit benefit achievement. All network players need to ensure that their IT architecture is sufficiently flexible and robust to deliver information to enable learning.

Business scope redefinition is the ultimate challenge, as firms exploit IT to change their business within an "extended business network". The focus is on the role of IT to develop greater co-opetitive relationships (where firms both compete and collaborate at the same time; see Chapter 13) within existing and new markets. The strength here is that information is clearly recognized as a strategic resource by the firm and key to partnership. Potential weaknesses are that the firm may lose sight of its core competences as it seeks to develop relationships. Outsourcing may increase dependency on partners and can potentially inhibit growth.

Managers need to review the level appropriate to their firm and consider their competitors' positioning in determining their response to change. Business process redesign is at the heart of all effective change. This can be achieved through two routes, first seeking efficiency, where process redesign is based on improving the quality of current strategies moving from evolutionary levels. Second is enhancing capabilities where changes in business scope require concomitant changes in business processes (Venkatraman, 1994).

Revolutionary level success depends upon a firm's Level 2 experience (Macdonald 2000; Venkatraman 1994); "*It is tempting to move directly from type I (Level 1) to type III (Level 3), but such a move may be risky given the absence of IT infrastructure linked to the strategic context*" (Venkatraman, 1994). Macdonald, reviewing experiences of success and failure of collaborative projects, writes that "management understanding and experience in respect of cross-departmental, cross-divisional and cross-functional integration have been consistently amongst the top three issues". He emphasizes the need to implement Level 2 projects, as management needs to understand integration issues, before they embark on higher levels. Neither Venkatraman nor Macdonald suggests that IS projects will follow a discrete path from Level 1 to Level 5. Indeed, in some parts of a business, a Level 3 process redesign may be followed by Level 1 exploitation in another. However, substantial learning derives from undertaking projects, so that lower level projects are likely to be enablers of higher-level ones.

As with much of the research reviewed in this book, these business transformation perspectives are outcomes from cases in large firms. There is little research on their applicability across all businesses. This chapter investigates if business transformation is applicable to SMEs. As IT becomes more accessible, understanding of how SMEs seek to exploit it for business growth and its role in enabling e-business is required.

■ Analysing business transformation

The analysis here is based on the same 44 SME cases used in the previous chapter to explore further the means by which they use IS to transform their businesses. Table 11.2 summarizes the different transformation paths followed by the case firms.

Table 11.2: Case firms and transformations

Localized exploitation	To internal integration	To business network redesign	To business scope redefinition
Recycling Training Co.	Family Attorneys	Regional Arts Centre	Model Toy Importers
Perforated Products Manufacturer	Land Rover Repair	Spring Manufacturer	Corporate Gifts
Lens Manufacturer	Bird Designs	Car Paint Co.	Mobile Phone Surveyors
Burring Engineers	Coventry Events Management	Wooden Pallet Co.	
Land Fill Gas Co.	Queensway Photographic	Light Assembly Co.	
Seven Stars Printers	Rural Health Practice	Tree House Health Care	
Chemical Analysis Co.	Soil Analysis Co.	Garden Health Care	
Epoxy Resin Co.	Energy Saving Co.	Clutch Assembly Co.	
Henley Coaches	Marine Cable Co.		
Electrical Accreditation Agency	Coventry Accountants		
Wholesale Garden Nursery	Coventry Designs		
Skills Training Co.	Heating Engineers		
Training Brokerage Co.	Biotechnology Software Developers		
Regional Travel Agent	Specialist Insurance Brokers		
Enamel Box Co.	Lubricant Wholesaler		
	Car Sign Design Co.		
	Precision Tool Co.		
	Public Sector Advocates		

Source: adapted from Venkatraman, 1994.

While the analysis that follows uses data from all 44 case SMEs, the transformations that they undergo is illustrated in each path by one exemplar. The discussion and conclusions reflect on all cases. The analysis explores transformation over a number of interventions, where researchers have carried out development of multiple IS strategies, and suggests paths the SMEs follow.

Localized exploitation

Localized exploitation is the starting point for all but five of the SMEs. This is not merely a reflection of a start-up position, but of the value of IS to the business. In most cases IS for managing and growth are seen as peripheral to the need for operational systems. However, at the second intervention 15 of the firms still used stand-alone systems – word processing and accounting. However, only one, Recycling Training Co. (Chapter 10), indicated they had no intention of altering this. The firm has two stand-alone PCs, one with word processing and a spreadsheet for accounts, while the other is used occasionally for training. At subsequent interventions the situation had not changed. Although it emerged that business processes needed to be changed to improve efficiency and to provide information on customers and trainees. Financial management remains a major issue. However, the owners are reluctant to alter processes as they are comfortable with the *status quo*, although they recognize it is not efficient.

Moving to internal integration

Revisiting opportunities for future development with owner/managers after a further time indicates that 16 SMEs do not wish major changes. Most of the owners of these SMEs are "life stylers" where the growth aspiration is to maximize value prior to retirement. Thus, owners focus on improving efficiency. Their ICT plans include investing in LANs to integrate systems to assist with managing growth, primarily supporting a growing customer base. However, there is little enthusiasm to invest further. These firms recognize the value of e-mail for external communication, although there is little development of Intranets or internal e-mail. Some SMEs have invested in web sites. These are primarily brochureware with contact to the SME by e-mail.

Case study 11.1

Family Attorneys has three partners, seven professional staff and 15 support staff in two branches. The firm provides a wide range of legal services, although much is based round land issues. Firm objectives are to grow through new customers and to increase margins by reducing costs. The structure means that partners have primary responsibility for all actions. The firm is traditional, although it started to change when a new partner joined. There is clear demarcation between professional and administrative staff leading to partners overseeing administrative activities, such as billing and debt collection. There is a small accounts department using an outdated accounting package. Secretaries use some PCs for word processing, and client records are stored manually. The major problem is cash flow, as partners act as debt collectors. They are reluctant to do this task while discussing clients' cases, but are also unwilling to delegate it to the accounting department. Client records are stored more than once – by the receptionist and by the solicitor responsible. Information is often only updated in one place having implications for billing, as the accounting department is not informed when this can be done. Processes need to be streamlined with internal integration of computer systems a priority to ensure common information access. However, Family Attorneys is not planning to develop its systems further.

At the subsequent intervention, little had changed in Family Attorneys, although debt collection was more problematic. The firm had not taken action on any of the recommended changes from the previous intervention. The SME was surprised to receive the same recommendations for change although the analysis revealed the same problems as on the previous occasion. These recommendations included a need for partners to review their roles with regard to administration by appointing an office manager. This was done and the IT provision reviewed. The PCs were networked and an integrated customer database developed. The accounts department was made debt collector, reducing cash-flow problems significantly. Thus, the firm moved from a position of localized exploitation to internal integration.

Moving to business process redesign

While Family Attorneys undertook minor changes in processes, they were primarily improving efficiency. None of the case SMEs reviewed their business processes as a precursor to investment in ICT, due perhaps to their operational focus and market niche positioning meaning that the businesses already focused on their core processes. However, there is a need to review these as SMEs grow. Yet, it is not clear that the owners believe that their structure inhibits growth.

Moving to business network redesign

Seven case firms have developed ICT with customers and suppliers. Four are manufacturers using EDI for orders and account processing. Additionally, CADs are transmitted electronically. However, the internal systems of these SMEs have not progressed beyond localized exploitation, leading to a need to re-enter data into internal systems to manage operations. It is only once the firm realizes there is benefit to internal systems improvement that they revisit internal integration. There is, again, little or no review of business processes. Two SMEs provide "social" services. Both are looking at improving services through electronic communication with external agencies such as pharmacies and medical practitioners. Again both have stand-alone systems to support operational processes. The owners believe their current processes to be efficient and effective. The Internet is recognized as a useful means of developing and managing the network relationship. The final organization is a regional arts centre that is building customer relationships through the Internet and contributing to an Internet-based regional arts network.

Case study 11.2

Wooden Pallet Manufacturer is a family firm started in 1972 by two brothers to manufacture timber casings. The firm's ownership has recently passed to the son of one of the founders who recognizes the need to reposition the firm for the future. While it is difficult to be innovative in the industry the firm wants to maintain its steady growth of between 10% and 15% annually. The market is fairly competitive and is highly dependent upon the automotive sector, with the top seven customers accounting for 83% of turnover.

The firm is looking to build relationships more closely with the automotive sector. Their investment in quality standards is important here, as customers demand more information about quality of process and product. This has led the new owner to actively review the IS within the firm as it has not been updated to acknowledge growth or changes in management. Thus, there are a mix of paper-based and stand-alone PC systems. These are clearly inadequate to develop relations with customers. Customers are working more closely with the firm in the design of the casings through exchange of CAD. The firm has invested in a new internal system that will manage the order process once the design has been agreed. Invoices and accounts are also now automated, with customers receiving information electronically. The introduction of the new IS has also highlighted the necessity for the firm to review its business processes.

Moving to business scope redefinition

Only three SMEs have changed their business scope. Two recognized e-business opportunities and refocused their strategy. The third implemented a knowledge management system to offer a new information-based service. All moved directly from internal integration to business scope redefinition. They recognize the role of information as a strategic resource and look to build partnerships. A knowledgeable owner who understands the potential of ICT, particularly the Internet, is key in identifying the opportunities from new systems. Venkatraman suggests a potential weakness of this stage is that firms focus on external relationships to the detriment of core competences. The SMEs here are clear about the need to develop core competences. Thus, they not only develop network relations but go onto review business processes.

Case study 11.3

Model Toy Co. was founded in 1986 to distribute toys. It moved into the more lucrative market of selling collectable model cars. Model Toy Co. supplies the specialist hobby market, 95% retailers and the rest private collectors. While they compete on quality and delivery speed, customers may wait some years for a particular model. One owner's background is corporate IT so Model Toy Co. has a small LAN and there are two stand-alone PCs bought as required with little strategic planning. However, the owners recognize the need for quality customer information and have a database and accounting system. All other systems are manual, including stock control. This causes problems, as Model Toy Co. need to manage cash flow more effectively. First recommendations included improving the customer database, automated stock management and a financial control system. E-mail would improve communication with customers.

By the second intervention, Model Toy Co. underwent a radical strategy review. The Internet revolution suggested to the owners that they could sell collectables online. They therefore set up a trading web site and collectable portal that was available to other collectable firms. The business focus has changed to one of attracting other collectable firms to be part of the portal, in other words selling space and getting commission. The retail arm continues but the dot.com is seen as the future. In the collectable business stock may not age, for example, the first item sold through the web site was an Ayrton Senna coaster. The SME still relies on its existing systems but plans include integrating the web site with operational systems.

■ Discussion

The analysis has identified four distinct transformation paths for SMEs, not one as suggested by past research in large firms. The first path (Figure 11.2) indicates that there are some SMEs for whom localized exploitation is the limit of their ICT investment. Owners are mainly concerned with life style, not developing the business. None of the SMEs wants to change their management approach, although the cases demonstrate the need for business process improvement.

The second path (Figure 11.3) is taken by the majority of case SMEs, localized exploitation is followed by internal integration, as owners recognize that they need to improve efficiency and reduce costs. However, there is little evidence of organizational change. These firms tend to be

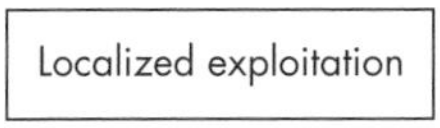

Localized exploitation

Figure 11.2: Prescribed path to transformation.

Figure 11.3: Second prescribed transformation path.

Figure 11.4: Disconnected transformation path.

Figure 11.5: Disjointed transformation path.

interested in, and achieve, steady growth by adding further, similar customers. Strategic opportunities from information are not recognized.

These two paths are "prescribed" Venkatraman progressions. SMEs either ossify at localized exploitation or internal integration. The SMEs are all well established and have considerable experience. In all the cases, there is evidence of the need to reconsider business processes prior, or as well as, developing IS. Yet, there is a general reluctance by owners to take this route perhaps due to resource constraints, fear of the uncertainty of changing processes, or a lack of vision.

The other two paths demonstrate that SMEs follow different routes to business transformation than suggested by Venkatraman. The third path (Figure 11.4) has SMEs moving to a form of business network redesign, primarily due to customer demands, but occasionally to provide better service. However, this is not integrated with internal IS due to conflicting customer demands, leading to data re-keying into local systems. However, process re-engineering is not considered. SMEs gain no benefit as they treat the networked systems as localized. This mentality is inconsistent with full exploitation of IS potential. This demonstrates a "disconnected" Venkatraman progression.

The final path (Figure 11.5) involves entrepreneurs driving innovative SMEs. They follow Venkatraman's suggested path of moving from localized exploitation to internal integration. They then make a step change and move to business scope redefinition. This is partly response to customer push, but also a recognition and desire to exploit the potential of IS and the strategic role of information. Innovation changes business scope, it crucially involves the roles and skills of individuals. However, innovation requires the redefinition of business networks and this, in turn, leads to business process redesign. For example, Special EFX is refocusing its business to become an e-retailer. To do this it is developing its network of suppliers to ensure quality production. It is also growing a new customer network through this change of business direction. At the same time it continues to grow its corporate business.

The move to business network redesign involves strategy changes, while the move to business process redesign is a structural change extending beyond that experienced in moving to internal integration.

Table 11.3: Strengths and weaknesses of SMEs approaches to IS

Cell	Strengths	Weaknesses
Efficiency	Control Cost reduction Simple systems	Operational focus Internal focus No business strategy link
Co-ordination	Improved internal communication Improved customer care Increased operational effectiveness	Internal focus Limited business strategy integration Improve staff training
Collaboration	Integration with business strategy Improved customer relations External focus Ultimately reduces customer power	Customers determine IS requirements Cost Systems flexibility
Repositioning	Changes/changed by business strategy External focus Changes business processes Changes employee profile	Cost Flexibility needed Knowledgeable CEO needed

This is a "disjointed" Venkatraman progression. All levels of the model are employed but not in the order envisaged.

These progressions or paths are better understood using the focus-dominance model (see Chapter 9). The strengths and weaknesses of each scenario were presented in Chapter 9 and are summarized in Table 11.3 allowing comparison with the business transformation enablers and inhibitors identified by Venkatraman (Table 11.1).

Comparing Tables 11.1 and 11.3 enables a review of the business transformation strengths and weaknesses for SMEs with those identified by Venkatraman. There is a clear correspondence between the evolutionary levels of Venkatraman's model with the efficiency and co-ordination segments for SMEs identified by the focus-dominance model. For example, localized exploitation and efficiency exhibit similar characteristics. Information technology is used locally to improve efficiency through the use of separate systems. With no link to strategy there is limited organizational learning or business benefits.

Use of systems in internal integration maps to the co-ordination approach, and recognizing the need for integration of systems to manage the business. In particular, improving customer service is common to both. The weaknesses are similar, as the systems are based on existing business processes with little business strategy integration. The focus is internal, with no consideration of market pressures. Again there are likely to be limited business benefits from Internet adoption.

Both collaboration and repositioning appear to map more closely with Venkatraman's revolutionary levels. Collaboration has similar strengths and weaknesses to business network redesign. SMEs following this strategy are primarily following a market niche strategy to a small range of customers. The emphasis here is on building relationships particularly with customers and focusing on core competences. Business processes are reviewed with external partners to build better relationships. There are three potential weaknesses of focusing on network growth for SMEs. First, the SME owner may concentrate more on building relationships, possibly at the expense of the operation. Second, partners may inhibit successful achievement of business benefits. Finally, there may be limited systems flexibility: this may inhibit learning. Internet adoption is likely to be of some benefit for external communication with customers. While SMEs here are aware of the potential there is still a need to reorient the business and the technology skills to achieve greater business value.

Repositioning and business scope redefinition have similar strengths. First, information is recognized as a strategic resource, hence the need for employees with different skills profiles. Relationships are built with external partners to develop the business strategy. The business strategy is seen as more externally facing with the focus on maintaining relationships. Business value is gained through use of knowledge with customer focus at the core. Thus, it is likely that these businesses are likely to achieve true "e-business" with the concomitant business value (Willcocks et al., 2000).

SMEs do not appear to undertake business process redesign as a formal development stage. There may be a number of reasons for this. First, SMEs operational focus and size may mean that they are already concentrating on their core competences. However, as earlier chapters have shown, there is evidence that information flows in SMEs can be improved through developing IS strategies. Second, SMEs tend to have a market niche serving a local market and owners often do not want to grow beyond what they can easily manage.

Moving between each stage is thus dependent upon the business strategy, knowledge of IT opportunities by the SME owner and an external customer focus. Figure 11.6 maps the four paths identified from the Venkatraman model onto the focus-dominance model.

The Venkatraman model is not prescriptive. However, the "prescribed" route through the levels as evidenced by the efficiency and co-ordination approaches is expected. The "disjointed" path involves a set of transformations that, while unexpected in sequence, are not completely unexpected in the Venkatraman model. This crucially rests on the experiences of internal integration as a precursor of higher-level changes. SMEs' size may enable this "disjointed" progression whereas cross-functional difficulties inhibit such paths in larger firms. Knowledgeable owners who recognize information as a strategic resource are critical here. The main difference in SMEs' actions is seen in the collaboration approach where systems use jumps directly from localized exploitation to business network redesign. Benefits may accrue from collaboration but none from internal IS integration. Both customer pressure and limited IT inhibit change. SMEs are unlikely to be able to move from network

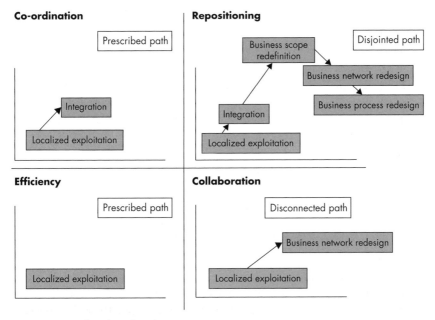

Figure 11.6: Growth paths and Venkatraman progressions.

redesign to process re-engineering. It may be that Schumpeter's (1962) notion of creative destruction is apt here as SMEs are loath to destroy in order to rebuild often due to resource constraints.

▪ Implications for research

Venkatraman's framework provides a useful means of assessing business transformation. However, its relevance to entrepreneurial firms may be open to question, with the majority not recognizing the value of IT to transform the business. The limited success and benefits from IS in many of the SMEs in both the efficiency and co-ordination scenarios does not give them much faith in future investments, hence they are unlikely to move towards revolutionary transformation. Thus, there is support for Macdonald's and Venkatraman's contention that poor experience is likely to inhibit future development. This may be due to limited business process redesign and this research concurs with his finding that it should be central to all change.

Enhancing capabilities is a critical part of taking advantage of business transformation (Venkatraman, 1994), thus it is not surprising that business process redesign follows from the "disjointed path". In this, SMEs would appear to be ahead of larger firms as this need is recognized. Size of firm may be critical here as larger firms may not be able to change processes or recognize competences as quickly as SMEs.

What is interesting is that business transformation may follow more than one revolutionary path in SMEs. The strategic intent of the firm and in particular its relationships with customers may well be a determinant of the path chosen. It would be useful to reflect on whether this is only an SME phenomenon.

■ Implications for managers

The message to SME owners is fairly clear from this analysis: business process review is at the heart of IS benefits. Figure 11.7 demonstrates the pivotal role of business process change in achieving transformation through IT. Improving efficiency means focusing on reducing current weaknesses in the organization and to attempt to achieve operational excellence within existing strategic boundaries. Improving capability recognizes that major strategic change will require different organizational competences to gain strategic advantage. For example, moving to business network redesign will change relationships throughout the value chain, which is likely to require a re-evaluation of business processes (Venkatraman, 1994).

Bearing this in mind, most SMEs can benefit by reflecting on the value to the firm of efficiency improvements at the simplest level. This could improve the limited learning that is seen at the evolutionary levels. As shown, there are a number of weaknesses inherent in many SMEs often due to limited management skills and because of the dependency on the owner for strategic decision-making. Reviewing current business processes can lead to cost reduction.

The role of information as a strategic resource is clear to SMEs that build relations with customers and are looking to use IS to develop the

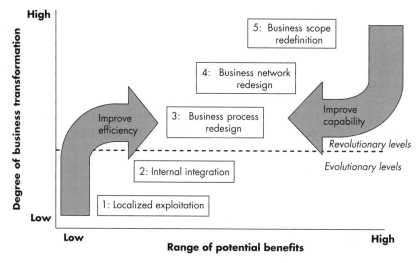

Figure 11.7: Business process change to achieve transformation (adapted from Venkatraman, 1994).

business. Those firms for which the business network is critical should also review their internal business processes as suggested by the case of Wooden Pallet Manufacturer, otherwise outmoded business processes may inhibit achievement of benefits. The position of the SME within the network of automotive suppliers is changing particularly with the adoption of CAD that may provide new opportunities that require enhanced business processes before they can be exploited by the firm.

■ Conclusions

This chapter investigates whether, and in what form, SMEs achieve business transformation. Using longitudinal case data from 44 SMEs, analysis reveals three distinct paths or progressions through the transformation model, termed the *prescribed*, the *disconnected* and the *disjointed*.

The prescribed path is seen in cost-focused SMEs. These firms are unlikely to gain benefits from the strategic use of IS as their focus is on control and improving efficiency through simple systems. The lack of any link to business strategy means that business benefits from IS are likely to be limited.

The disconnected path is tied in closely with high customer dominance while recognizing the value of IS to develop the relationship. The main issue to emerge is that there is little attempt to integrate internal systems to take greater advantage of the strategic opportunity from the development of the external network focus. While business strategy acknowledges the role of IS in partnership, the internal role is less clearly understood.

The disjointed path follows most closely the ideas of Venkatraman. SMEs here recognize and utilize the strategic power of IS to change their business. What is interesting is that it is only through the redefinition of the business that business networks are seen as important. Once that occurs, internal business processes need to be redefined. Venkatraman acknowledges that business process redesign is likely to follow business scope redefinition, not surprisingly as a new business is likely to develop new processes. However, what is different for the SMEs here is that they clearly recognize the need to develop their networks and integrate them within the business process changes.

It is helpful to understand this process as it provides a means of understanding the nature of IS investment in SMEs. From Chapter 9 it is clear that strategic IS investment has a number of different growth paths depending on the owner, the strategic context and the firm. This chapter extends this knowledge to consider the potential strategic use of IS in each of the focus-dominance scenarios and the likelihood of success in developing IS strategy for each of them.

12 Strategic alignment

▪ Introduction

The importance of strategic alignment was introduced in Chapter 3 using the MIT'90s model. The role of alignment in developing an information systems strategy was discussed in Chapter 7 where the integration of ISS with business strategy is essential for competitive advantage was emphasized.

Alignment is about achieving synergy between strategy, organization, processes, technology and people in order to sustain the quality of "interdependence" and thus achieve competitive advantage (Hsiao and Ormerod, 1998). Alignment of business strategy with, *inter alia*, information systems strategy is problematic for firms and is a key concern of senior management. However, alignment may be a moderating variable between IS use and firm performance (Chan *et al.*, 1997). Yet, little is known about the change processes in firms that lead to alignment or misalignment. The MIT'90s model (Chapter 3) identifies conceptual integration between the different change factors and demonstrates one "classic" route that firms may follow. However, Yetton *et al.* (1994) demonstrate three alternative paths while Hsiao and Ormerod (1998), taking a dynamic approach, suggest four further paths. There is, unsurprisingly, little research that considers alignment issues in small- and medium-sized enterprises.

This chapter investigates paths to alignment in SMEs. The chapter discuses the "classic" alignment model and the alternatives offered by Yetton *et al.* (1994), Yetton and Sauer (1997) and Hsiao and Ormerod (1998). Using the focus-dominance model four alignment paths for SMEs are identified. These are neither the "classic" model of alignment, nor the others suggested. The reasons for this mismatch are discussed and the chapter concludes with the implications for management and research of the new paths through the alignment maze.

▪ Alignment issues

Alignment is essentially about value realization from the inter-relationship of IS and business strategy. There needs to be recognition that organizations need to have the mechanisms in place to achieve strategic objectives through consistency between the external and internal business perspectives. Alignment is not static: for most firms there is a constant dynamic as they adapt and change (Henderson and Venkatraman, 1993). The business dynamic means that there is likely to be a need to transform the business processes as discussed in Chapter 11 to realign processes. The firm may be moved out of alignment by strategic choices, balancing swings need to be corrected to bring about the realignment. Strategic choice may be led by IS innovation, in which case business processes need to be aligned; or business change will lead to a reappraisal of IS to add value (Burn, 1997). Stagnation may occur when IS in not in phase with the firm or there is no capacity for it to develop (Sauer and Burn, 1996).

Strategic fit, when alignment occurs, implies convergence to a set of core values or competencies. There is recognition that the firm is focusing on what the firm does best. The organizational structure is changed to ensure that it "provides opportunities for the full use of peoples capabilities at all levels" (Miles and Snow quoted in Yetton et al., 1994). The need for change is obvious to all and is welcomed. Thus, fit may not be the outcome of rational strategic planning but can be seen as an emergent process shaping outcomes through incremental tactical decisions and ongoing practice. For many firms this may well be a useful approach to gaining competitive advantage, particularly when they have taken an innovative approach to IS, embedded in particular processes and learning that are unique to the firm (Yetton et al., 1994).

The firm can usefully develop capabilities to use technology as a differentiator. There is a need to be aware of IS opportunities, the skills that are required to drive them and the appropriate organizational structures to achieve value realization. As well as this external perspective, it is important to review fit with IS architecture, knowledge and skills within the firm to identify potential changes (Henderson and Venkatraman, 1993). Weaknesses in IS competencies can affect operational performance both in the business and within the IS department itself (Ward and Peppard, 2003). Change management becomes an important part of the alignment process (Earl, 1996). Strategic alignment is, therefore, not as clear cut as may be first thought. Alignment and fit is static for the relatively short time that a business strategy is in place. The dynamic nature of firms means leads to recognition that there is a dynamic in alignment. At times it is likely that firms will not have IS and business aligned and will need to take corrective action. Additionally, there may be different approaches to achieving alignment and fit that depend upon the nature of the firm. These different approaches are reviewed in the next section.

■ Opportunities for strategic alignment

The MIT'90s model argues that a successful organization has a high fit among its strategy, structure, roles and skills, management processes and technology, and between that configuration and its business environment (Scott Morton, 1991). The "classical" or conventional alignment model

(Figure 12.1) starts with a change in strategy. This changes structure, which in turn leads to change in processes, technology and individuals and roles.

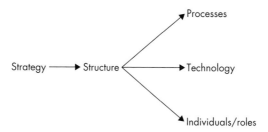

Figure 12.1: Conventional model of strategic alignment.

While Scott Morton suggests that there is one path for strategic alignment, Yetton *et al.* (1994) demonstrate that it is possible for technology to be the driver of change. For example, a firm of architects, Flower and Samios discussed earlier, transformed their business by adopting CAD tools (Figure 12.2). Their path was to develop individuals, then change the management structure. The strategic vision evolved dynamically and grew out of the changes made. Yetton (1997) argues that the adoption of technology led Flower and Samios to identify other uses, in particular as a means of cost reduction and improving efficiency. Competitiveness may depend on organizations' abilities to derive new competencies as much as the determination of strategic direction enabled by information technology (Craig and Yetton, 1997).

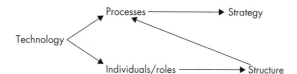

Figure 12.2: Architectural firm.

Yetton and Sauer (1997) demonstrate two further paths through the alignment elements. The first, technological determinism, commences with a change in technology that forces change in the other four elements (Figure 12.3).

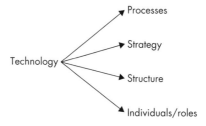

Figure 12.3: Technological determinism.

Figure 12.4: Lead-lag.

The lead-lag model (Figure 12.4) involves change in strategy, technology and structure but leaves processes and individuals and roles untouched. This model suggests that firms may start at any one of the three points, technology, strategy or structure. They may follow one of six paths and only touch each one of the three points once. Therefore, any one of the three may either lead or lag behind depending on the starting point. It is acknowledged that different roles/skills and management processes will be required depending upon the path selected. Therefore, it may be necessary to consider these issues as a precursor to change (Yetton and Sauer, 1997).

However, in one of the other major studies of alignment paths Hsiao and Ormerod (1998) find four different paths. Two planned paths where strategy determines change and two emergent paths which impacts upon strategy. In both planned paths strategy changes impacts upon the other four areas, technology, structure, processes and people. However the drivers of change and the levers that influence the final impact are different. The first planned path is structural reconfiguration (Figure 12.5). In this case the driver is structure; the levers are people and process which impact upon technology. New technology is required to implement planned change in processes and people.

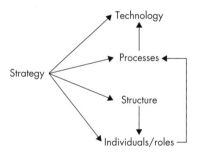

Figure 12.5: Planned: structural reconfiguration.

The second planned path is process engineering (Figure 12.6). In this case the driver is process change; the levers are technology and structure which impact upon people. This is a more traditional approach to strategic change from identifying the vision, goals and actions required for change.

The other two paths are emergent. In both emergent paths strategy is impacted by changes in technology, structure, processes and people.

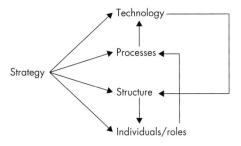

Figure 12.6: Planned: process engineering.

Again there are different drivers and levers for each and hence different impacts. The first emergent path is human renewal where individuals are the drivers of change (Figure 12.7). This process is a bottom up response to cultural change in the organization. Technology is seen as an enabler of that change which will in turn influence management processes.

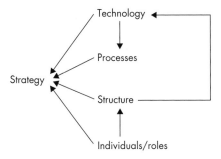

Figure 12.7: Emergent: human renewal.

The second emergent path is IT transformation that is led through technology (Figure 12.8). In this case the driver is technology, the levers are processes and people which influences structure. This path acknowledges the role of people and process change for effective IT adoption, hence it is emergent and ultimately will influence strategy.

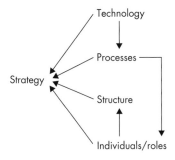

Figure 12.8: Emergent: IT transformation.

Thus, there are at least eight known paths that can lead to strategic alignment in organizations. While Flower and Samios is an SME, all the other research reviewed so far in this chapter is the result of work conducted in large firms.

There is only limited research on alignment in SMEs. In a study of Greek SMEs, there appears to be some correlation between value realization if IS adoption is linked to strategy. This is supported in a UK study (King *et al.*, 2002). Innovative firms are more likely to gain benefits. However, where IS not linked clearly to strategy there is likely to be mis-alignment and little benefit from IS (Spanos *et al.*, 2002). Perhaps not surprisingly the greatest alignment is seen in systems to improve efficiency and quality of product and service (King *et al.*, 2000). There is some evidence that incremental learning is the best way for SMEs to achieve alignment; suggesting a dynamic and emergent approach to alignment may be optimal. This may be best achieved through a CEO who is knowledgeable about IT opportunities; but focuses on the strategic context rather than technical detail (King *et al.*, 2002).

This chapter now investigates these issues to explore the potential for alignment in SMEs. Is there an inherent dynamic as suggested above? Is alignment emergent or planned? What are the benefits of alignment for SMEs? The next section considers strategic alignment using the 44 cases SMEs introduced in Chapter 7. The past, current and future intentions of IS adoption for the case firms were presented in Chapter 11. This analysis, combined with history of the management of the firm gleaned from discussion with the owner, management and staff as well as the ISS analysis is used to review the strategic use of IS. This analysis is used to model alignment paths in the SMEs.

■ Alignment paths in SMEs

It has been shown that SMEs either invest from necessity, the cost-focused approach or from an understanding of the potential to improve their market position by adding value. These are further divided depending upon customer dominance, leading to four different approaches for IS investment in SMEs: efficiency, co-ordination, collaboration and repositioning. Chapter 9 demonstrated that IS adoption in SMEs can be categorized using these approaches using the focus-dominance model. The current position of the case firms is reproduced in Figure 12.9.

The data analysis indicates that alignment in cost-focused SMEs is process driven. In contrast, alignment in value-added-focused SMEs tends to be strategy driven. Looking at the other axis, low customer dominated SMEs use IS to restructure, highly dominated SMEs cannot do this. This section presents the four alignment paths identified from the case analysis.

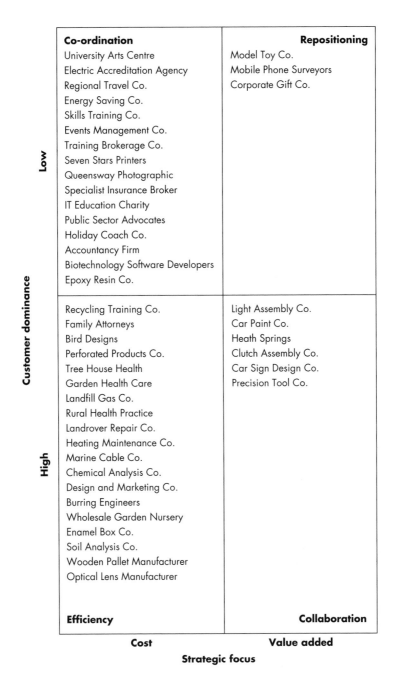

Figure 12.9: Current position of case firms.

Alignment issues in cost-focused SMEs

Both the efficiency and co-ordination cells reflect a low cost strategic focus with IS purely employed for efficiency improvements. As SMEs grow there may be a move from efficiency to co-ordination (see Chapter 10). However,

Figure 12.10: Efficiency path.

there is little attempt made towards alignment. In both efficiency and
co-ordination, SMEs are more concerned with delivery of their product or
service. The strategy of most of the firms is survival and achieving full
order books. There is also limited knowledge of the value of strategic IS.

Efficiency alignment path

It was argued in the previous chapter that SMEs in the efficiency quadrant
primarily invested in IS to automate systems. The aim is to reduce costs
and to have better control of processes. There is no link between IS and
strategy. There is also no attempt made to align skills of people in the firm
with either the management processes or with the technology. Thus, there
is only a link from management processes to technology (Figure 12.10).

This is illustrated by the case of Optical Lens Manufacturer.

Case study 12.1

Optical Lens Manufacturer has approximately 10% of the surface optical lens
machine manufacturing market in the UK. The firm is owned jointly by the
CEO and company secretary and employs 10 people. The firm has received a
major government grant to develop a new blocking machine. They sell the
surfacing machines to optical laboratories both in the UK and France. As
well as the development and manufacture of the surfacing machines, the
firm also offers a refurbishing service.

Optical Lens Manufacturer has traditionally targeted the 200 privately-
owned laboratories in the UK, but is now considering the major multiples
that offer fast prescription services.

Not surprisingly the CEO is at the hub of all decision-making in the firm.
The focus on the firm is on business growth, but management systems are
lagging behind. Staff work closely with customers to support their
requirements. While this makes them more responsive, there is very little
learning achieved as information remains with the member of staff. There is
no effective system of recording in the firm. Any customer and sales
information is stored manually. Pricing is calculated on an individual basis
by the owner. There is a manual system to plan production but the value of
this is limited as stock is not always available.

Figure 12.11: Co-ordination path.

The firm recognizes that it needs to put some automated systems in place to manage operational processes. They have installed an accounting package on a stand-alone PC. This has helped to record information about sales and allows control over cash and debtors. They have decided to install an inventory management system and production scheduling system to help manage the flow of work. Additionally, they see the need for an automated customer database in the near future. With a number of the processes in the firm, they are comfortable with existing manual processes and do not see the value of changing existing systems. It is only where efficiency and cost gains can be achieved that automation is sought.

The efficiency cell strengths are improved control through simple IS, while the main weaknesses are the lack of any link to business strategy and the internal and operational focus. However, it is appropriate for some SMEs to use IS in this limited way. The efficiency cell includes a number of SMEs whose owners are not interested in growth. Their objective is to manage the firm such that they can maintain control and enjoy doing what they are good at.

Co-ordination alignment path

The path in the co-ordination cell describes changes in management processes followed by changes in technology with changes in organization structure following last (Figure 12.11). The key difference that is found between the efficiency and co-ordination cells is the need to manage internal communications more effectively as the firm's customer base grows. Again, there is no link between IS and strategy. Neither is there any attempt to match the skills required to the technology investment.

Accountancy firm demonstrates this path.

Case study 12.2

Accountancy firm has three partners and 20 staff, of whom four provide administrative support. The firm was established in 1945 and has two offices in different towns. The client base is mainly SMEs in the local area. The firm has offered traditional accountancy services to these firms. One of the partners has identified a new strategic direction for the firm in offering business consultancy to support clients. He is pursuing this strategy with the support of the other partners. The aim is to grow the business to offer a broader range of services.

The two offices work in different ways, which partially reflects different business clients, although there are common activities and skills that could be shared. Within each office client files are stored manually. The system is effective, as staff can easily access client information. The firm uses automated systems to develop clients' accounts but systems are old and slow.

The firm has recognized that it needs to redevelop its systems so that existing processes can be made more efficient. The intention is to develop a client database that will be a starting point to develop customer relationship management as the firm looks to sell more services to clients. Upgrading accountancy software to run on the network is also a further priority. These are efficiency improvements that will position them to manage future growth. The partners plan to give staff more responsibility to manage groups of clients. Additionally, Accountancy Firm also plans to install a local area network and also to have e-mail communication between the two offices. This will enable exchange of knowledge and information between them and will reduce duplication.

Thus, for Accountancy Firm, the introduction of IT not only contributes to improving processes, but has enabled them to review the organizational structure to improve effectiveness.

SMEs in the co-ordination cell use IS to improve communication and customer care, leading to improved operational effectiveness. The weaknesses here are limited integration with business strategy, and staff needing better IS skills to work with more complex systems. This cell is made up of SMEs whose owners are interested in growth, but are less knowledgeable about IS and see it primarily as a means of improving efficiency in order to keep costs down as customer numbers increase. Again, IS are not seen as important to business strategy.

Alignment issues in strategic focus SMEs

The key difference between cost-focused and value-added SMEs is the recognition of strategy as the driver for change. In both the collaboration and repositioning cells the starting point for IS investment is strategy. However, there is considerable difference between the approaches taken by firms in these cells.

Collaboration alignment path

The level of complexity in the configurational fit required in the collaboration quadrant is the same as for co-ordination, but it takes a different form. Here, the critical issue is to respond to the needs of major

Figure 12.12: Collaboration path.

customers for production and quality control systems including, for example, EDI links and CAD. In this quadrant, the link is not across departments but via strategy. So the fit configuration spans strategy, management processes and technology (Figure 12.12).

This is illustrated by Car Sign Design Co.

Case study 12.3

Car Sign Design Co. was established by the owner in 1990 to produce graphic design liveries and signs, specializing in the automotive market. The firm employs 15 people and is planning to grow by increasing turnover by 25% in the next 5 years. Ten per cent of customers are in the automotive sector but they account for 80% of the firm's turnover. Car Sign Design works closely with these customers to ensure that orders are maintained in what is a competitive industry. The firm competes on quality and design innovation to develop and maintain the relationships.

The firm has invested heavily in design and production technologies and runs a very efficient operation. Work in progress is kept to a minimum, with order processing well organized.

The strategy of growth is based around relationship management of its large customers. Car Sign Design Co. recognizes the value of the Internet to do this, particularly in exchange of design information. They plan to reorganize the firm so that there are clear lines of communication, electronically, between order processing, accounts, design, production and delivery.

Car Sign Design Co. has identified its strategic growth objective and recognizes that technology will provide the means to be more competitive by developing relationship management with customers. In particular, they will be able to turnaround design information more quickly. Streamlining business processes will mean they will be in a position to continue to ensure order delivery on time.

The collaboration cell presents the first opportunity for a value-added focus for IS use. Business strategy is a driver here, although the main weakness is that customers primarily drive strategy. The focus is on external relations with the small group of customers for whom these SMEs provide goods. A potential strength for these SMEs, particularly because of the adoption of performance measurement systems, is that better information may give them some support to limit customer demands for cost reduction. However, a major constraint for these SMEs is the system cost, which may lead to inflexibility, as limited resources inhibit replacement. Investment in the collaboration quadrant does add value to the SMEs. However, it is reactive to the strategy of being a preferred supplier to a major manufacturer.

Repositioning alignment path

The repositioning cell is the only one that recognizes the need for full alignment. The issue of critical importance is the knowledge of the owner about the opportunities from IS and the potential to exploit it.

Owners in this quadrant demonstrate an excellent knowledge of the role of technology in managing and growing their firms. They recognize that investment in technology is vital to manage growth. Their enthusiasm for technology often means that the investment is done prior to changes in organizational structure, management processes and skills. This is possibly unsurprising as they are deliberately planning growth (Figure 12.13).

Three firms introduced earlier demonstrate this path: Mobile Phone Surveyors (Chapter 3), Model Toy Co. (Chapter 7) and Corporate Gift Co. (Chapter 9).

Case study 12.4

The owner of Mobile Phone Surveyor recognized the growth of the mobile phone market and has developed his expertise in this area. His decision to adopt Lotus notes as a knowledge management system to provide a repository for the surveyors' knowledge was designed to plan for growth. The organizational structure changes required staff to work more as a team not as individuals, sharing knowledge. Management processes were put in place to facilitate this. The owner recognized that he needed to train staff to use the system or to employ staff that know how to use technology and who believed that it would provide a means for the firm to grow.

Repositioning demonstrates strengths of integrated IS and business strategy that includes both an internal and external perspective to the business. The owner is aware of IS and the opportunities for changes in business processes. The weaknesses seen here are the potential cost to

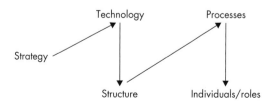

Figure 12.13: Repositioning path.

the business of the IS investment and its relationship to the business requirements, and the need for flexibility in order to manage continual change. The importance of the owners' knowledge of IS coupled with their ability to integrate this with the business strategy is only understood by a few SMEs.

Both the collaboration and repositioning scenarios demonstrate a strategic focus to IS adoption, whether from an external driver, as in the collaboration quadrant, or internally, based on the owners' knowledge, as seen in the innovation quadrant.

Differences in alignment

As discussed at the start of this chapter alignment is dynamic, dependent on the development of business strategy. Firms need to recognize the need to realign their IS and business when this occurs. This leads to the potential for misalignment while the firm is in flux. The danger for many firms is that lack of alignment may lead to stagnation.

In the majority of the cases SMEs are looking for growth, although in some cases, in a limited way. Thus, they have either reviewed or are in the process of reviewing strategic choices. As the cases demonstrate this leads to different imperatives impacting on alignment. The individual alignment paths presented may be usefully summarized by mapping them together using the MIT'90s model (Figure 12.14).

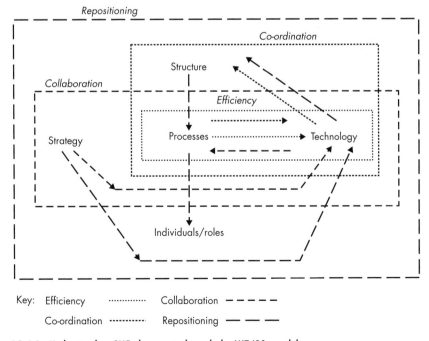

Figure 12.14: Understanding SME alignments through the MIT '90s model.

As shown by the cases alignment for the efficiency scenario involves technology investment driven from process change. In the case of the co-ordination scenario this lead to structural changes as organizational learning develops. Strategic issues emerge in the value-added scenarios of collaboration and repositioning, although they follow different routes. While strategic drivers mean that investment in technology is essential, the major organizational change is in management processes to take advantage of better communication. In repositioning strategy and technology are closely linked as a means of changing the firm. However, owners recognize the broader imperatives that are involved in change and review the structure, management processes and roles. What is interesting is that SMEs do not appear to follow the traditional alignment path in any of the scenarios. There is no direct link between strategy and structure, or between strategy and management processes.

■ Implications for research

As discussed in Chapter 9, IS investment in SMEs can be seen as either a low cost response to provide efficiency savings, or as a strategic response either driven by necessity or due to innovative owners seeking growth. A major barrier to the use of IS to support innovation is the leadership and technical knowledge of the owner and/or management team.

SME management has insufficient time to spend on future business developments, and management teams have little experience, skills or interest in exploiting technology (Rothwell and Beesley, 1988). There is often little attention paid to developing products or services as firms are comfortable with existing market situations. Hence, there is a tendency for SMEs to invest only in the IS necessary to carry out individual activities, particularly those that involve basic administration and transaction processing. Few SMEs have the motivation and/or capacity to introduce the integrated systems needed to support IS-based innovation. Developing these capabilities in top management groups in SMEs is a critical precursor to long-term success of a repositioning strategy.

Strategic use of IS is becoming more important in flexible and dynamic markets (Ciborra, 1997). Improvisation is a way of responding to this market and the innovative use of resources, such as IT, is critical (Ciborra, 1997). However, while SMEs are an innovative sector, their use of IS is relatively inflexible (see Chapter 3). This tends to lead to a fairly traditional view of IS where it is used as a means of support (Yetton and Sauer, 1997). For SMEs, the use of IS in cost-focused strategies mainly supports existing management processes with little strategic input. This is a different path from those identified by previous researchers and reflects the limited strategies of many SMEs, particularly those in business for lifestyle reasons.

The need to develop new competencies is often a driver for change. For many cost-focused SMEs, their market niche may not be under threat and, therefore, change is unnecessary beyond efficiency improvement. However, the Internet may impact on this as larger firms are enabled to threaten these niches as e-commerce systems make it easier for them to deal directly with customers (Rhodes and Carter, 2000). However, Croteau et al. (2001) suggest that this type of firm adopts a strategic choice that inhibits the effective use of IS. For efficiency-focused SMEs, as demonstrated by the MIT'90s model, technology is primarily used to support existing management processes, but there is likely to be little influence on strategy, organizational change, or individuals' roles and skills. Mapping co-ordination-focused SMEs to the MIT'90s model suggests that the adoption of technology will, in addition to supporting management processes, have some effect on organizational structures as information exchange is improved. Strategy might be influenced to a limited extent, but different skills are not a requirement.

The value-adding strategic focus shows closer similarities to paths that have been identified previously. The difference between collaboration and repositioning may depend on the ability to improvise in varying market situations. The more formal response of the collaboration quadrant is a result of the SMEs close links with major customers. Therefore, strategic IS responses are planned top-down. SMEs are locked into relationships that make it unlikely that they will be in a position to, or will need to, develop new competencies. Hence, there is little emphasis in developing individuals' roles and skills. The difference between SMEs and larger firms is that the former are not changing their structure to take advantage of the strategic value from IT. This may be because these SMEs tend to be manufacturers and have fairly defined activities. For collaboration-focused SMEs, there is some similarity with the lead-lag model, with technology supporting strategy. The difference is that it is management processes that change rather than organizational structure. This may reflect a need for more formal management to manage customer relationships more effectively. For repositioning SMEs, success is only likely to be assured providing the SME considers changes across all the elements of the MIT'90s model. Technology investment is a response to change in strategy, with this scenario following the lead-lag view more closely although recognizing the need for processes and roles to change.

The development of new competencies as a strategic response is seen in the repositioning quadrant. Owners here appear to fulfil Ciborra's observation of the need to be aware of the dynamic market. New competencies are developed that are enabled by IT, thus supporting Craig and Yetton's contention that competing differently requires all aspects of the MIT'90s model to be considered.

For growth-minded SMEs the strategic use of IS is important. However, most SMEs start in the efficiency quadrant. Growth may move them to the co-ordination quadrant, but further moves may depend upon the owner's attitude to change and their knowledge of IS.

Hsiao and Ormerod (1998) identify four archetypes for alignment. For each change path there are three major components, a driver, two levers and an impact on the MIT'90s elements. They identify two modes: planned and emergent. In focus-dominance terms collaboration and repositioning scenarios map onto planned modes as both are strategy driven. Efficiency and co-ordination scenarios are emergent. However, none of the four quadrants demonstrate the paths suggested by Hsiao and Ormerod. As only one SME path, repositioning, employs all the elements of the MIT'90s model, SMEs do not have drivers, levers and impacts. In efficiency there is a driver, processes, that has an impact on technology but the levers are missing. Similarly in co-ordination, the driver is process change and this is leveraged by technology that has an impact on structure. However a second lever is missing, presumably damping down the effects of the technology lever. Again, in collaboration, the single lever is technology driven by a change in strategy affecting processes. Only in repositioning are two levers employed.

The lack of levers may help to explain why SMEs fail to get the benefits expected from IS. Firms need to manage strategic coherence and synergy relationships. Strategic coherence involves technical and organizational coherence. Technical coherence maintains an appropriate fit between technology and management processes while organizational coherence requires symmetry between structure and people. Strategic synergy is achieved through alignment of another two relationships – synergy of internal and external infrastructure. Synergy of internal infrastructure refers to integration of management processes and people while synergy of external infrastructure demands the integration of technology and structure (Hsiao and Ormerod, 1998).

SMEs, in most instances, are not managing coherence or synergy. This results in either little, or wasted, investment in IS. One of Hsiao and Ormerod implications is that if firms use a planned mode of change they need to bring together the four change elements (technology, structure, people and processes) under the guidance of business strategy. Here, only repositioning firms do this.

■ Implications for management

The discussion about strategic alignment is not just of theoretical interest. It does raise issues for SME owners planning to use IT to change their firm. The limited change observed in firms in the efficiency scenario is that technology is only used to improve management processes. Thus, there will be no impact on strategy, structure or people. This severely limits the benefits or opportunities to change the business.

While this might be fine for lifestyle firms it will limit the aspirations of those who seek to grow. This links closely to the prescribed path found in the previous chapter. SME owners need to be aware of the limitations of not using IT to integrate processes. The likelihood is that there will be duplication and gaps in information provision.

Alignment for co-ordination scenario firms is also limited to current strategy. Again, IT is largely seen as a means to improve efficiency. SMEs in this quadrant recognize the need to change structure to enable a more effective flow of information. However, there is still no consideration of strategy or whether different people might be required to make effective use of the IS. Again, while many owners will be content with their current strategy, those that are looking to reposition their firms will need to consider the potential for change from IT and whether they have the people in place to make it happen. Again this matches the prescribed path found in Chapter 11. SME owners need to be aware of the limitations of not planning for IT and its potential impact upon growth.

The two value-added focused scenarios present more considered perspectives on the role of IT. Both recognize the centrality of strategy in business growth. However in the Collaboration scenario technology affects processes, unlike the lead-lag model which affects structure. There is no influence on either structure or people. Technology is adopted but there is no recognition that organizational structure may need to change to take advantage of the opportunity to improve the flow of information to enable people to be more effective. The problems here are that strategic change is not thought through. While IT is recognized as enabling change SME owners need to be more aware of the day-to-day impact. Otherwise it is unlikely that they will reap the rewards of their investment. The disconnected path that epitomizes the actions of collaboration scenario SMEs is clearly in evidence here.

The repositioning scenario is the only one that clearly demonstrates that owners recognize the need for strategic alignment that encompasses all of the MIT'90s factors. Owners have a clear business strategy that they want to see enabled by technology. However, they are clear that this will require a change in structure to make it happen. This may also lead to a change in process as the previous business strategy has been radically changed. Finally, there is also an understanding that different skills will be required. Again, this supports the arguments in the previous chapter for the disjointed path in the repositioning scenario. Business scope redefinition is central to the change process for these firms. Developing close links with customers and suppliers is seen as integral to change through IT. Finally, the need to change business processes to manage the highly innovative strategic change is seen. Thus, SME owners who are looking to reposition their businesses using IT understand the need for inclusion of all the five MIT'90s factors. Those owners who seek to emulate these firms need to recognize this.

■ Conclusions

This chapter has sought to understand whether and in what way SMEs consider strategic alignment, a process that enables firms to realize value form there is investment. Existing research on large firms uses the classic MIT'90s model to explore alignment. This useful approach is repeated for the 44 case SMEs whose growth plans have been explored. The existing evidence from large corporations identifies eight paths for strategic alignment. However, none of these are found to be valid in the SME context. What is clear is that there are four different paths followed by SMEs that are partial in considering alignment issues. These paths show that cost-focused SMEs begin with technology, but do not consider that IT can either affect or be affected by strategy. The prescribed approach to business transformation identified in Chapter 11 may be a reason for the limited alignment in cost-focused SMEs. Both value-added focus scenarios are strategy led. There is some similarity with the lead-lag model of alignment. The disconnected progression identified for collaboration scenario SMEs can be understood more clearly as these firms move to improve IS and management processes to build the network relationships that customers demand. Disjointed progression is seen for repositioning SMEs, similarly, the desire to invest in IS is central, but owners recognized the need for change. Indeed, it is only in the repositioning scenario that the full impact of technology is understood, although through a different path to any identified for large organizations.

Part 4 Knowledge and development of IS

This part looks at the issue of managing and planning knowledge and of re-engineering processes in small- and medium-sized enterprises. Part 2 demonstrated that SMEs need to plan their information systems if they wish to grow and to develop more effective relationships with their customers. An organizational IS strategy framework was developed and assessed to achieve this objective. The data from the cases was then used to develop a theoretical model to understand IS adoption in SMEs. Part 3 developed four different scenarios for IS investment using the focus-dominance model. Business transformation and alignment are shown to be different in SMEs than in large firms, with a limited focus on organizational and management process change being the found. However, SMEs that are looking to reposition themselves in the market do recognize the need for business process re-engineering (BPR) to realign themselves to realize benefits and gain competitive advantage. Part 4 takes these ideas forward by exploring these issues from a number of different aspects.

The strategic use of information is shown to be increasingly important for firms with a value-added strategy towards IS investment. For these firms, particularly, the development of business networks enabled by IS is increasingly important. Chapter 13 investigates the role of knowledge sharing in SMEs, especially in respect of their formal trading relations with customers. Knowledge sharing provides organizations with a means of developing partnerships where benefits accrue to both parties. However, while there is little evidence of knowledge sharing in SMEs, the chapter suggests ways that this might be achieved. The focus-dominance model is used to underpin the investigation into knowledge sharing.

Chapter 7 suggested that understanding knowledge-based SMEs through value-adding processes might not be the best approach for information systems strategy. Therefore, Chapter 14 investigates if a resource-based view provides a richer analysis than the contingent models proposed in Chapter 7 for developing an ISS in knowledge-rich SMEs. This is demonstrated through an in-depth case study of a knowledge-based SME. Finally, business process change was introduced in Chapter 11 as essential for firms to gain the benefit of efficiency improvements or to take advantage of business scope redefinition. Chapter 15 explores BPR through eight Taiwanese cases. These cases provide insights into the key factors that need to be in place for SMEs to undertake successful BPR.

13 IS role in co-opetition and knowledge sharing

▓ Introduction

The concept of knowledge was introduced briefly in Chapter 3. Knowledge was shown to be dependent upon some kind of human intervention. Knowledge can be understood in more detail as formal (explicit) or informal (tacit) and understanding and using these different forms of knowledge is essential for organizational learning. Firms work closely with other players in the industry value chain, and organizational learning needs to take cognizance of the relationships that develop from this. Skills in managing inter-organizational knowledge flows are a source of competitive advantage (Dunning, 1988) and managing co-operative relationships clearly involves managing knowledge flows. Information systems and information technology play a paramount role in co-ordinating and controlling joint ventures and in learning from them (Birnberg, 1998). Further, IS is an enabler of new organizational designs (Osborn, 1998). Hence, IS is a key tool in the management of knowledge sharing. Co-opetition (Brandenburger and Nalebuff, 1996), or simultaneous co-operation and competition, may aid competitiveness by knowledge sharing, but any exchanged knowledge may also be used for competition. Firms therefore have to manage "knowledge sharing" under co-opetition.

This chapter analyses the role of IS/IT in the context of co-opetition using a game-theoretic model to identify the effects of knowledge sharing under co-opetition. The opportunities for knowledge sharing are assessed by an analysis of IS use in SMEs. This analysis demonstrates the opportunities for co-opetition. The chapter first introduces the concept of knowledge and its role in organizational learning. It then presents the background to SMEs' uses of knowledge. A description of co-opetition is given and the game-theoretic model is presented. The chapter posits a relationship between knowledge sharing and SMEs' attitude to the use of IS, and tests it through an analysis of the 44 case SMEs presented in Part 3.

▓ Defining knowledge

Knowledge is a dynamic concept that changes over time as it is assimilated into organizational learning. Much knowledge is tacit, it is personal, not easily expressible or visible. Tacit knowledge is often hard to formalize. Much expert knowledge falls in this category: for example, skilled craftspeople are not often able to express the principles underpinning their ability. The emphasis in many IS is towards explicit knowledge that can be codified and expressed through rules or principles. Tacit knowledge is difficult to share which means that organizations need to put mechanisms in place for its exchange (Nonaka and Takeuchi, 1999). New knowledge has to find its place in the organization. This takes time, as new knowledge has to be assimilated, which can be a slow process. It is important for organizational learning that this process occurs and change emerges (Sauer and Yetton, 1997).

Sharing knowledge within organizations provides the basis for the development of new rules. Experience and understanding enables judgements to be made that lead to workable guidelines that eventually become accepted rules (Earl, 1996). This is not only valid within organizations but throughout the value chain. Thus, knowledge sharing between firms working together is essential to network learning. Partnership conditions involved in collaborative working require understanding between all players at all levels for networks to be effective (Kanter, 1996). In many networks exchange of structured data (transaction, inventory information) is the starting point for relationship development, but to attract increasing business benefits it becomes important for firms to review business process relationships and expertise. Benefits include improving operational efficiency, market positioning, partnership trust and innovation (Venkatraman, 1990).

Many SMEs have not moved beyond operational efficiency involving sharing little beyond some information about transactions. The main benefit of this is cost saving and is usually achieved through exchange of structured information between partners. SMEs in the collaboration scenario in the focus-dominance model benefit from sharing inventory information. This enables better planning within the SME, again leading to efficiency benefits. Information for this task is relatively structured. Firms focusing on operational efficiency may also benefit from shared expertise through sharing knowledge about design, where it is important for firms to facilitate exchange of the complexity of knowledge networks (Venkatraman, 1990). Information exchange in this scenario is unstructured and tacit. As Chapter 11 showed it is only those firms in the repositioning scenario that recognize the importance of business process change. Integration through the Internet is a major contribution to process change in networks. The information exchange here is relatively unstructured and may provide opportunities for improved market positioning through differentiation (Venkatraman, 1990).

Non-bureaucratic organizations, such as SMEs, should excel at knowledge generation (Spender, 1996), though only firms able to protect knowledge have incentives to innovate, while a major problem for many firms is knowing what knowledge is valuable (Liebeskind, 1996). Thus, while the organic structure and culture of SMEs may foster knowledge innovation, many structural features suggest they are unable to obtain sustainable competitive advantage from that innovation. Yet, as with most issues addressed in this book, knowledge management research focuses on large firms, even though SMEs are likely to be knowledge generators.

Knowledge management in SMEs

SMEs present a curious position with regard to knowledge management. They face the emergence of world markets and the need for quality, fast delivery and partnerships, just as their larger counterparts. As shown in previous chapters and demonstrated by the focus-dominance model, collaboration between SMEs and with large firms is common. The ability to share resources is important to SMEs that are seldom able alone to participate globally. Alliances encourage innovation, expand product portfolios, and forge new supplier relationships (Maynard, 1996). However, the scarce entrepreneurial resources available to SMEs restrict their activities (Dyer, 1996).

Many SMEs wish to share knowledge, as they see co-operation with customers as a route to survival, for example firms such as Heath Springs (Chapter 8), Precision Tool Co. (Chapter 4). For example, SMEs are frequently involved in product design for larger customers (e.g. Light Assembly Co., in Chapter 4). Design involves innovation and understanding customer needs; yet this knowledge is seldom integrated into a wider strategic perspective, due to SME preoccupation with day-to-day viability. Knowledge-intensive SMEs are often employed as constituents of larger project teams. Even non-knowledge-intensive SMEs may compete on knowledge – this is often explicit knowledge of a local market or product. SMEs can gain from knowledge sharing (by collaborative design, cost reductions strategies, and guaranteed orders). For example, Car Sign Design Co. works with Queensway Photographic utilizing their skills and technologies on occasions. However, there are dangers in knowledge sharing unless guarantees of use are agreed between partners. Increasingly, firms work together to develop products and markets. These feed off each other and support areas of business growth. The personal computer industry is a case in point. Twenty-five years ago, no one could have imagined that many homes would have 120 gigabytes PCs with peripherals such as printers, webcams, wireless networks and CD rewriters. The industry has emerged with many firms supporting and developing these complementary and essential products. The firms involved in the developments had to work together to ensure that their devices were compatible with each other. Understanding this process, how firms can work together and yet compete is termed co-opetition.

■ Towards a theory of knowledge exchange

Co-opetition involves the recognition that firms may benefit from working together. It provides a means to explore the roles and relationships of all players involved in the market. The relationship between them can be seen as a value net (Brandenburger and Nalebuff, 1996) (Figure 13.1).

Complementors are those firms whose products add value to the firm's product; such that customers value it more highly than if they bought the firm's products alone (Brandenburger and Nalebuff, 1996). For example in the automotive industry, car safety has become an important issue. Acknowledging this, insurance firms reduce premiums on safer vehicles which encourage customers to buy them and brings insurance firms more customers. Firms may also be complementors when suppliers find it beneficial to supply both players, not just the one firm. These firms are likely to share knowledge informally.

A competitor is a firm that leads customers to value your product less when they have the competitor's product than when they only have yours. For example, having just had an excellent meal in a gourmet restaurant, it is unlikely that you will manage another, even if it has an unenviable reputation. On the supply side, another firm may be a competitor if it is better for the supplier to supply them than when it is supplying you alone. Firms may be both competitor and complementors with regard to suppliers. For example, Compaq (now HP) and Dell are competitors for Intel's limited supply of microchips, but complementors when working with Intel to develop the characteristics of the next generation of microchips (Brandenburger and Nalebuff, 1996). In the network society it is important to recognize the symmetries between players in the value net to gain a win-win situation for all players. A key issue for co-opetition is the notion that *"there is duality in every relationship – the simultaneous elements of co-operation and competition"*

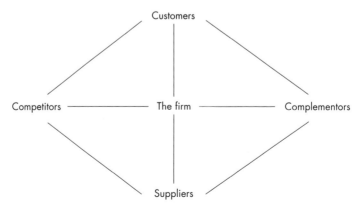

Figure 13.1: The value net for co-opetition. (*Source*: adapted from Brandenburger and Nalebuff, 1996.)

(Brandenburger and Nalebuff, 1996). Under co-opetition, *what to share, with whom, when*, and *under what conditions* is paramount. For SMEs this is unexplored, but a game-theoretic approach may offer insights.

Game theory enables analysis of situations where outcomes are interdependent. It provides a systematic approach to strategy development when decisions depend upon the actions of others. Game theory acknowledges the role of partial knowledge and also attitude to risk in decision-making. One of the most important aspects of game theory is that it considers issues from a variety of perspectives, not only yours (Brandenburger and Nalebuff, 1996). Knowledge and knowledge sharing is central to this process.

There are three aspects by which knowledge exchange may benefit players in co-opetition (Loebbecke and van Fenema, 1998):

1. *Synergy*: the extent to which co-operation yields additional value beyond the sum of the parties' individual knowledge. Synergistic value only exists if both players exchange knowledge.

2. *Leverage*: the potential of the "knowledge receiver" to increase its value by exploiting the shared knowledge individually beyond the co-operation.

3. Use of "received" knowledge may have a *negative reverse-impact* (NRI) on the "sending" party. NRI is the extent to which a receiver's use of the knowledge lowers the sender's original value. The exchanged knowledge may be used by competitors and, thus, weakens its value to the original owner.

The proposition is that the impact of knowledge sharing under co-opetition will vary depending on the synergy of co-operation and the leverage by the receiving party. Additionally, NRI may have an adverse influence on knowledge sharing despite the benefits of synergy and leverage (Figure 13.2).

		Leveragability by receiving party	
		Weak	**Strong**
Synergy of co-operation	**Weak**	Ambiguous attitude towards knowledge sharing	Negative attitude towards knowledge sharing
		Effect of NRI: Negative attitude towards knowledge sharing	Effect of NRI: Reinforced negative attitude towards knowledge sharing
	Strong	Positive attitude towards knowledge sharing	Ambiguous attitude towards knowledge sharing
		Effect of NRI: ambiguous attitude towards knowledge sharing	Effect of NRI: Negative attitude towards knowledge sharing

Figure 13.2: Synergy, leverage, NRI and knowledge. (*Source*: adapted from Loebbecke and van Fenema, 1998.)

Under conditions of weak leverage and weak synergy, from the sender's perspective there is little to gain or lose from knowledge sharing. Where there is weak synergy but a strong risk the receiving side may leverage the knowledge, propensity to share knowledge is low. Strong synergy and weak leverage describes a situation in which a firm would be eager to share knowledge in a "co-opetitive" environment since there is more to gain from synergy than the other party might derive from leverage. However, with strong synergy and strong leverage, the expected synergy may be offset by the expectation that the other party may gain additional value. From a sender's perspective, strong NRI lowers the interest in sharing knowledge. If *both* parties can translate the knowledge into adjacent business capabilities, they can exploit opportunities beyond the co-operation. This suggests partially diverging interests, typical of co-opetition, and the derivation of competitive advantage requires careful management of knowledge sharing.

While these theoretical positions are intuitively appealing, there is little work that investigates empirically how co-opetition operates. This chapter concentrates on the use of received knowledge by SMEs. In particular, the focus is on use that SMEs make of this knowledge to develop their businesses. Thus, the role of synergy and leverage for the SME is explored; the role of NRI is left to one side for now. The chapter does not consider the impact of the sender of the knowledge exchange. Further research is required to identify the role of NRI on customers. The chapter first sets out the theoretical impact of synergy and leverage on SMEs using the focus-dominance model. This establishes *a priori* expectations that are tested using case data.

The chapter uses outcomes from 44 of the SME cases to assess management actions that influence how co-opetition may operate, and how knowledge sharing may be managed. This chapter considers four questions:

▓ Is co-opetition an issue for SMEs, and for what types?

▓ What is the role of IS in managing knowledge in SMEs?

▓ How the three co-opetition forces manifest in SMEs?

▓ How may SMEs attempt to manage the knowledge sharing process?

The next section reviews the use of IS for managing knowledge in SMEs.

▓ Managing knowledge in SMEs: role of IS

SMEs use knowledge to manage day-to-day operations. The knowledge may be explicit and held on IS, or tacit and held by management. As shown in Chapter 3, IS adopted by SMEs tend to be simple. Most SMEs view IS as a cost, and is reluctant to invest after start-up. However, growth minded SMEs recognize the potential of IS to change their business. The customer is important in decisions on investing in IS. Customer influence is paramount at start-up when SMEs need to attract and keep customers and so are extremely flexible, and when the SME is established as a preferred supplier to a major customer. Otherwise, customer power is weaker. The focus-dominance model, introduced in Chapter 9, that compares customer dominance with strategic focus, is used here to consider the contribution of IS to knowledge sharing. Figure 13.3 maps the types of information used in the different cells. This provides a background to identify when SMEs may find knowledge sharing and co-opetition pertinent.

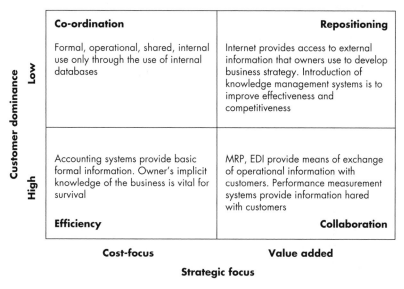

Figure 13.3: Information use in SMEs.

Cost-focus on managing knowledge

The two cost-focused cells, efficiency and co-ordination have limited use of knowledge. In the efficiency cell IS are concerned with improving the efficiency of internal processes. Hence, knowledge is mainly used to manage day-to-day operations.

In addition to the systems used for cost control in the efficiency cell, in the co-ordination cell the main use of IS is to improve customer care due to the larger customer base. The objective of the IS is to improve the effectiveness of business processes but the focus remains internal. Again, the primary use of knowledge is to manage internal operations.

Co-opetition is unlikely to be an issue for those SMEs with a cost-focus strategy. Their systems are primarily internally focused. Chapter 10 showed that the primary growth path for SMEs is from efficiency to co-ordination. Information is used to manage the business. In the efficiency cell the tendency is to provide sufficient information to satisfy basic record-keeping only. Co-ordination is an extension of this, with increasing firm size making it necessary to develop databases to provide information access. In neither cell is information shared with customers to develop the relationship further. Therefore, the main use of information in the efficiency and co-ordination cells is to support internal day-to-day operations. Hence, the expectation is that both synergy and leverage will be weak, leading to an ambiguous attitude to knowledge sharing.

Value-added focus on managing knowledge

The collaboration cell demonstrates an increase in the sophistication of the technology used. SMEs need to communicate and exchange information with customers in a cost efficient manner by using systems such as e-mail and EDI. The use of IS is integrated with business strategy, particularly when dealing with major customers. Often, customers are the driving force behind the introduction of new IS. Knowledge transfer and sharing is seen in this quadrant, while much of it is related to operations, exchange of performance management information provides some value to the firm.

In the repositioning cell IS is an integral and tightly woven part of the business strategy of the SME. Therefore, IS influences the direction of business strategy as well as being reactive. The role of information changes to how the firm may grow and learn rather than maintaining current direction. The need is for systems to support a performance-focused management style. Knowledge is critical in enabling the owner to manage business growth. Thus SMEs can be considered to be *repositioning* themselves for future growth.

The value-added focus suggests co-opetition may benefit SMEs that are either required to share information with their customers (collaboration cell) or that use IS as a means of changing and developing the business. Information exchange may become core to business strategy (repositioning cell). SMEs in the collaboration cell have a few key customers that expect information on product and process quality. This exchange is critical to the relationship; hence synergy tends to be strong. Few SMEs use information to exploit knowledge on their own, and hence leverage is likely to be weak.

The expectation for co-opetition forces in the collaboration cell is that synergy is likely to be strong as the co-operation may lead to additional value from information to both parties. For example, SMEs that engage in co-operative design are likely to gain synergy as they learn from customer requirements, and reuse the knowledge in other projects, increasing interdependency between SMEs and their customers.

Large customers encourage SMEs to focus on a narrow product range, to hone their skills and reduce costs progressively. SMEs are encouraged to enter open-book arrangements where both parties have full access to product data; but this usually end up as a form of control not an exchange. However, the SME is less likely to be able to increase the value of the knowledge outside the relationship, hence leverage is likely to be weak. SMEs often possess weak leverage due to their poor ability to manage both the knowledge exchange process and the outcome, while larger firms are more able to lever the knowledge gained.

The co-opetition framework (see Figure 13.2) suggests that overall there will be a positive attitude towards knowledge sharing in those SMEs in the collaboration cell.

The repositioning cell contains dynamic SMEs that recognize the value of information and knowledge as a strategic resource to enable change. The businesses often concern information exchange, and there is an expectation of strong synergy. The SMEs use information to improve, grow and attract other customers, indicating leverage is likely to be strong.

A similar analysis of co-opetition in the repositioning quadrant suggests that synergy is also strong as information is recognized as a strategic resource by both parties. However, as indicated in Figure 13.3, repositioning SMEs recognize the need to exploit shared knowledge to develop their business strategy. Hence leverage is likely to be strong. The game-theoretic framework indicates that there will be an ambiguous attitude towards knowledge sharing.

To explore the potential of SMEs for knowledge sharing under co-opetition, the game-theoretic and the focus-dominance model are integrated (Figure 13.4), first, to shed light on whether co-opetition is an

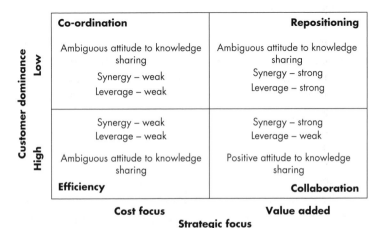

Figure 13.4: Co-opetition in SMEs.

issue for SMEs and for what types of SME. Second, to identify how synergy and leverage forces might manifest in SMEs.

The other issue of concern here is how any knowledge transfers, and hence, co-opetition forces are managed by SMEs.

■ Managing knowledge transfer

This chapter focuses on explicit knowledge sharing through the use of IS in SMEs. It considers how SMEs may manage explicit knowledge exchange either to exploit or to mitigate the co-opetition forces. Managing explicit knowledge sharing requires; contractually defined *quid pro quo* knowledge exchange contents and procedure, and inter-organizational co-ordination, and planning and control procedures. Explicit knowledge can be readily assembled and exploited; yet the stickiness of tacit knowledge engenders synergy, leverage and NRIs less likely. The literature focuses on tacit knowledge transfer, control and use problems. Yet, for many SMEs, theirs is explicit knowledge of markets and customers, and the problem is guarding easily transferable information since small incremental knowledge can distinguish a firm (Cohen, 1998).

SMEs are typically in a poor power position vis-à-vis their larger counterparts. Thus, in terms of explicit knowledge, SMEs are poor at recognizing the value of their knowledge but are often forced to "exchange" it. Further, their lack of strategic or external focus, coupled with poor IS, makes them poor at monitoring large firms' or competitors' performance. SMEs are also poor at the contractual aspects of knowledge exchange. They are resource poor, so cannot retain adequate legal advice, and large firms are, in any case, disinclined to negotiate. The primary mechanisms by which firms may manage co-operative knowledge exchanges include *inter-organizational co-ordination by mutual adjustment*, and *intra-organizational co-ordination*, and *planning and control procedures*. Explicit knowledge allows comprehensive contracts to be developed that specify the contents and procedures for knowledge transfer.

Successful SMEs usually cultivate their customers to maintain loyalty. For example, in the automotive sector customer influence extends to ensuring the SME can demonstrate quality of process and product by formal, computer-based performance monitoring systems. SMEs try to gain leverage by using performance information to limit price reductions, but the cases suggest success is limited. Information on operations and design are expected electronically, which may bring collaborative advantage. Operationally, firms need to screen their partner's performance and adjust accordingly. Formal planning is uncommon in SMEs leading to outdated management practices and autocratic management that may limit the ability to take advantage of knowledge from customers. SMEs' management structures are flatter and less bureaucratic than in large firms encouraging team and cross-functional orientation and efficient and informal communications. However, this may militate against formal planning and control procedures.

■ Exploring knowledge transfers

This chapter attempts to operationalize two constructs: co-opetition and knowledge sharing. Neither of these has well-developed definitions or dimensions in the literature. Therefore, the approach taken to understand the role of knowledge sharing in SMEs is to revisit the case study SMEs presented in Chapter 7 and analysed using the focus-dominance model discussed in Chapter 9. Figure 13.5 shows the positions of the firms in the focus-dominance model.

The case analysis is a useful means of discussing the role of synergy and leverage and the role of explicit knowledge. The models identify what the firms exchange and the systems they use to exchange them. It also identifies the competitive forces at work in the SMEs' sectors. Soft systems analysis (Chapter 8) reveals if the exchanges are easy or problematic and the form that the exchanges take. The notion of co-opetition is taken here to refer to SMEs' interactions with their major customers. For some SMEs they will compete with their own customers – "classic co-opetition" – while other SMEs face the prospect of their dominant customers grabbing value from the exchange for themselves. Further, large firms often encourage their suppliers through information exchanges and the dissemination of "best practice". If the knowledge SMEs exchange with their customers is explicit (as is focused on here), then this knowledge is less sticky and can leak to competitors. Thus, even when competition is not dyadic, explicit, component or public knowledge may escape to other SME competitors. For Dyer and Singh (1998) explicit knowledge may just be information. For Cohen (1998) knowledge is information in context. It is not the intention here to enter the knowledge versus information debate. Rather, to accept that the boundaries between information and knowledge are blurred and porous and that knowledge typically derives from information. While some of the material exchanges by case SMEs is information, some other, designs and formulations for example, is clearly knowledge. As discussed, explicit information is valuable to SMEs.

■ Analysis

The analysis is undertaken from the perspective of SMEs as knowledge receivers to consider the resultant actions and the role of co-opetition. Each of the cases presented in the focus-dominance model in Chapter 9

Co-ordination	Repositioning
University Arts Centre	Model Toy Co.
Electric Accreditation Agency	Mobile Phone Surveyors
Regional Travel Co.	Corporate Gift Co.
Energy Saving Co.	
Skills Training Co.	
Events Management Co.	
Training Brokerage Co.	
Seven Stars Printers	
Queensway Photographic	
Specialist Insurance Broker	
IT Education Charity	
Public Sector Advocates	
Epoxy Resin Co.	
Holiday Coach Co.	
Accountancy firm	
Biotechnology Software Developer	
Recycling Training Co.	Light Assembly Co.
Family Attorneys	Car Paint Co.
Bird Designs	Heath Springs
Perforated Products Co.	Clutch Assembly Co.
Tree House Health	Car Sign Design Co.
Garden Health Care	Precision Tool Co.
Landfill Gas Co.	
Rural Health Practice	
Landrover Repair Co.	
Heating Maintenance Co.	
Marine Cable Co.	
Chemical Analysis Co.	
Design and Marketing Co.	
Burring Engineers	
Wholesale Garden Nursery	
Enamel Box Co.	
Soil Analysis Co.	
Wooden Pallet Manufacturer	
Optical Lens Manufacturer	
Efficiency	Collaboration

Customer dominance — Low / High

Strategic focus — Cost / Value added

Figure 13.5: Focus-dominance case analysis.

are reviewed by considering the different IS in the SMEs: production, management support and customer-focused systems. Interviews on the use of information to change and develop the business are used to determine whether and in what way synergy and leverage occurs.

Knowledge sharing in efficiency-focused SMEs

Table 13.1 shows the systems that are used by each of the 13 firms in the efficiency quadrant and the synergy and leverage associated with the use of those systems from the perspective of the SMEs as knowledge receivers.

Table 13.1: Synergy and leverage in efficiency cell firms

SMEs	Production systems	Management Support	Customer focused
Recycling Training Co.	None No synergy – no information is exchanged No leverage – no information from customers is used to improve the production process	None No synergy – no information from customers is collected No leverage	None No synergy – no information is used to develop a better service for customers No leverage
Family Solicitors	None No synergy – no information is exchanged No leverage – no information from customers is used to improve the production process	Accounting No synergy No leverage – accounting information is not used	None No synergy – no information is used to develop a better service for customers No leverage
Bird Designs	None No synergy – no information is exchanged No leverage – no information from customers is used to improve the production process	Accounting Sales order processing No synergy No leverage – neither accounting nor sales order information is used explicitly	None No synergy No leverage
Perforated Products Co.	Labelling system CAD Strong synergy – design information exchanged with customers is an integral part of working with customers Weak leverage – the production process is not being developed from knowledge gained	Accounting No synergy No leverage – accounting information is not used	None No synergy No leverage
Tree House Health	Nurse call No synergy – internal system No leverage	Accounting Strong synergy – information exchanged with health authority to	None No synergy No leverage

(*Continued*)

Table 13.1: (Continued)

SMEs	Production systems	Management Support	Customer focused
		plan care, helps SME improve efficiency. Weak leverage – some use of information to plan business growth	
Garden Health Care	Catering budget Personnel reporting	Accounting Invoicing Budget monitoring	None
	No synergy – internal system No leverage	Strong synergy – information exchanged with health authority to plan care, helps SME improve efficiency. Weak leverage – some use of information to plan business growth	No synergy No leverage
Landfill Gas Co.	Job costing CAD No synergy – internal use only No leverage	Accounting Project management No synergy No leverage – neither accounting information nor project management is used	None No synergy No leverage
Rural Health Practice	Fund-holding system Medical system No synergy No leverage	None No synergy No leverage	None No synergy No leverage
Landrover Repair Co.	None No synergy No leverage	None No synergy No leverage	None No synergy No leverage
Marine Cable Co.	CAD Production, purchasing and inventory management (not used) Strong synergy – design information exchanged with customers to improve designs Weak leverage – not really used to develop other relationships	Sales order processing, orderbook analysis (unused), accounting No synergy – information not part of customer exchange No leverage	None No synergy No leverage

Table 13.1: (Continued)

SMEs	Production systems	Management Support	Customer focused
Chemical Analysis Co.	Report production Laboratory analysis	None	None
	No synergy No leverage	No synergy No leverage	No synergy No leverage
Heating Maintenance Co.	Work scheduling	None	None
	No synergy No leverage	No synergy No leverage	No synergy No leverage
Design and Marketing Co.	CAD	Accounting	None
	Strong synergy – close relationship with customers to develop marketing strategies Strong leverage – information used to market firm to other businesses in the same industries	No synergy – only internal use No leverage	No synergy No leverage
Burring Engineers	None No synergy No leverage	Accounting No synergy – only internal use No leverage	None No synergy No leverage
Wholesale Garden Nursery	Production planning	Accounting	None
	No synergy No leverage	No synergy – only internal use No leverage	No synergy No leverage
Enamel Box Co.	Production and control information No synergy No leverage	Accounting No synergy – only internal use No leverage	None No synergy No leverage
Soil Analysis Co.	Laboratory IS	Accounting	Brochureware web site
	No synergy No leverage	No synergy – only internal use No leverage	No synergy No leverage
Wooden Pallet Manufacturer	OPERA order processing and production management No synergy No leverage	Accounting No synergy – only internal use No leverage	None No synergy No leverage
Optical Lens Manufacturer	CAD Bill of materials check No synergy No leverage	Accounting No synergy – only internal use No leverage	None No synergy No leverage

It is evident that knowledge sharing is not an issue for most SMEs in the efficiency quadrant. The likely explanation is that these SMEs are primarily "lifestyle" firms that are not looking for growth beyond selling into their existing products into existing markets.

The expectation from the theoretical model is that both synergy and leverage in this quadrant are likely to be weak. However, the evidence for the five SMEs in Table 13.2 suggests that synergy is strong. This is explored in more detail by considering the contractually defined information flows, the processes by which information is exchanged and the nature of inter-organizational co-ordination, and planning and control procedures employed by the case SMEs.

The cases in Table 13.2 have strong synergy and weak leverage, apart from Coventry Designs. Knowledge exchange is formal, though often there are no planning and control procedures. Firms have close customer relationships, but these are usually formal and limited to information supporting contracts. The game-theoretic model suggests that SMEs would benefit from knowledge sharing, although owners might be concerned about its implications. The formality argues for more structured systems to assist SMEs in managing knowledge exchange more effectively. Perhaps unsurprisingly, Design and Marketing Co. stands out as having more informal relationships as it is in a sector where creativity is

Table 13.2: Explicit information transfer in efficiency quadrant SMEs

SMEs	Contract-defined information	Process for exchange	Inter-organizational co-ordination	Planning and control procedures
Perforated Products Co.	Design Performance Measures Orders Accounts Invoices	Manual Formal	Formal process	Defined by customer
Garden Health Care	Patient cases Budgets/account Medical	Formal process with social services	Formal process for exchange	Tight, clear structure for delivery of information
Tree House Health Care	Patient cases Budgets/account Medical	Formal process with social services	Formal process for exchange	Tight, clear structure for delivery of information
Marine Cable Co.	Designs	Formal meeting	Limited	None
Design and Marketing Co.	Design information Costs	Meetings with clients	Informal meetings	None

important. Marine Cable Co. lacks planning and control procedures as it is young, and systems are being developed.

However, the benefits of the exchange vary depending on the focus of the exchange. For Perforated Products the focus is in the production area, helping them to improve their product. The focus of Garden Health is in the management support arena; synergy is weak currently as the systems are still being developed. Marine Cable Co. exhibits strong synergy. A reason for this might be that the business depends on working closely with its customer base to develop new products. While the firm is currently in this quadrant it is intending to grow through building relationships with customers.

Overall there is little evidence of knowledge sharing in this quadrant. For those that do share knowledge it is only done in a limited form, and leverage is limited. These firms are likely to have a negative or limited view of knowledge sharing.

Knowledge sharing in co-ordination-focused SMEs

SMEs in the co-ordination quadrant are those that are growing steadily and have some investment in IS. The outcome of the analysis on these is shown in Table 13.3.

Again, there is a range of different information exchanges undertaken by these SMEs. For many there is no synergy or leverage, while for other it is weak. For four SMEs co-opetition forces are an issue.

Knowledge sharing is not an issue for the majority of the firms in the co-ordination cell. The low customer dominance coupled with a focus on existing markets means that information exchange is not an issue. The other four SMEs all have strong synergy and strong leverage. The main difference between this group and those in the efficiency quadrant is that the latter lack formal planning and control procedures. The game-theoretic model suggests that these firms may be unsure of the benefits of knowledge sharing. Therefore, owners may wish to explore business possibilities beyond the limitation of current customer relationships. Table 13.4 presents the explicit information transfer in co-ordination cell firms.

Warwick Training Brokerage (Table 13.4) has a close relationship with a university to provide services to support a distance learning MBA programme. The firm is using the knowledge gained to develop its own management education services. Similarly, IT Education Charity is using the knowledge it receives from government to develop its products and services further. Government supports the charity as it follows the political philosophy of devolving services rather than providing them itself. It is interesting to note that all the SMEs that exhibit strong synergy and leverage are in knowledge-intensive industries. The SMEs growth and development are based on interpreting and developing ideas from customers.

Table 13.3: Synergy and leverage in co-ordination cell SMEs

SMEs	Production systems	Management Support	Customer focused
Regional Arts Centre	Customer database Ticketing system No synergy No leverage	None No synergy No leverage	None No synergy No leverage
Electric Accreditation Agency	Engineering product databases No synergy No leverage	None No synergy No leverage	None No synergy No leverage
Regional Travel Co.	Ticket booking system Customer database No synergy No leverage	None No synergy No leverage	None No synergy No leverage
Energy Saving Co.	Envirotrak CAD No synergy No leverage	None No synergy No leverage	None No synergy No leverage
Skills Training Co.	Trainee recording Claim system Time reporting Strong synergy – information on students, courses, costs exchanged with council Strong leverage- information used to develop new markets	Accounting Environmental monitoring e-mail No synergy – information primarily for internal use No leverage	No synergy No leverage
Events Management Co.	Events management No synergy No leverage	Accounting No synergy – only internal use No leverage	Contact database No synergy No leverage
Training Brokerage Co.	Customer database Strong synergy – information on students, courses exchanged with university Strong leverage – information being used to develop management courses and identify new customers	None No synergy No leverage	None No synergy No leverage
Seven Stars Printers	Estimation and job costing No synergy – internal activity No leverage	Accounting No synergy – only internal use No leverage	None No synergy No leverage

Table 13.3: (Continued)

SMEs	Production systems	Management Support	Customer focused
Queensway Photographic	None	Accounting	None
	No synergy No leverage	No synergy – only internal use No leverage	No synergy No leverage
Specialist Insurance Brokers	Financial services quotation package No synergy – mainly internal use No leverage	Accounting No synergy – only internal use No leverage	None No synergy No leverage
IT Education Charity	Project planning IT information services database Strong synergy – research-based information database depends on government project priorities Strong leverage- the charity uses the information to develop and expand its project base	E-mail Sales system Finance system No synergy No leverage	Contact database Events database Strong synergy – government/ other agencies share information Weak leverage – the charity uses the information to identify new customers
Public Sector Advocates	None No synergy No leverage	Financial management No synergy – only internal use No leverage	None No synergy No leverage
Epoxy Resin Co.	Stock control Order processing No synergy – not particularly customer focused No leverage	None No synergy No leverage	None No synergy No leverage
Holiday Coach Co.	Coach management system No synergy No leverage	Payroll Accounting No synergy – only internal use No leverage	Passenger booking system Private hire system No synergy No leverage
Accountancy Firm	None No synergy No leverage	None No synergy No leverage	None No synergy No leverage
Biotechnology Software Developers	Price codes Software development tools Strong synergy – knowledge of software performance and utility exchanged with customers Strong leverage – software development makes the product more marketable	Order records Accounting No synergy No leverage – information not used to identify growth opportunities	Customer records Weak synergy – no systems to support customers

Table 13.4: Explicit information transfer in co-ordination SMEs

SMEs	Contract-defined information	Process for exchange	Inter-organizational co-ordination	Planning and control procedures
Warwick Training Brokerage	Student details Course details	Formal process with University	Formal process for exchange	None
Coventry Training Co.	Course details Student details Costs	Formal process with council	Formal meetings	Clear structure
IT Education Charity	Research	Formal meetings	Formal meetings	None
Biotechnology products	Software Design	Send software Meetings	Informal	None

However, in all cases apart from the IT charity, the focus of synergy and leverage is in production. Management information is not used to support growth and development. Thus, an ambiguous attitude to knowledge sharing is demonstrated as proposed in Figure 13.4. There are three causes. First, owners are primarily concerned with core daily operations. Second, they have insufficient resources. Third, they do not have IS to identify areas where they could challenge the customers who supply the shared knowledge. However, the four SMEs that exhibit strong synergy and leverage are making resources available, are looking at new markets and new products for future growth. These SMEs may be persuaded that a value-adding focus for IS is important to growth.

Knowledge sharing in collaboration-focused SMEs

It has been shown that there are limited opportunities for knowledge sharing amongst SMEs with a cost-focused strategy. The next part of the analysis considers those SMEs that have a value-added strategy, where information is already regarded as an asset. Table 13.5 presents the analysis for those firms in the collaboration cell. These SMEs have high customer dominance and are primarily manufacturing.

The SMEs all exhibit strong synergy and weak leverage, particularly in production. These SMEs are looking to build relationships with existing customers and see this as best done through identifying new products. However, there is some nervousness about their exposure to few customers amongst the SMEs. Hence some are starting to develop new relationships with other firms. Light Assembly Co. (Chapter 4) has already experienced this and had to identify new customers when their main customer decided they were overexposed. Heath Springs (Chapter 8) has recognized market changes and is building relationships with sub-assembly manufacturers in anticipation of no longer being a first-tier

Table 13.5: Synergy and leverage in co-ordination cell SMEs

SEMs	Production systems	Management Systems	Customer support systems
Clutch Assembly Co.	MRP CAD	Accounting Performance measurement	EDI
	Strong synergy – design information exchanged with customers Weak leverage – design information serves mainly to improve existing relationship	Strong synergy – information on performance exchanged with customers Weak leverage – information used to limit price reductions with existing customers	Strong synergy – exchange of information to provide JIT service No leverage – exchange here mainly focused on improving relationship with existing customers
Heath Springs	MRP CAD	Accounting Performance measurement	EDI
	Strong synergy – design information exchanged with customers Weak leverage – design information serves mainly to improve existing relationship	Strong synergy – information on performance exchanged with customers Weak leverage – information used to limit price reductions with existing customers	Strong synergy – exchange of information to provide JIT service No leverage – exchange here mainly focused on improving relationship with existing customers
Light Assembly Co.	MRP (sales and production) Strong synergy – mainly for order processing weak leverage – design information serves mainly to improve existing relationship	Accounting No synergy – information only used internally no leverage	EDI Strong synergy – information exchanged to enable forecasts of product requests no leverage
Car Paint Co.	MRP Strong synergy with customers designing paint requirements Weak leverage – design information serves mainly to improve existing relationship	Accounting Sales forecasts No synergy – information only used internally No leverage	EDI Strong synergy – not systems based, operatives based at manufacturer Weak leverage – knowledge used to improve service delivery

(Continued)

Table 13.5: (Continued)

SEMs	Production systems	Management Systems	Customer support systems
Car Sign Design Co.	CAD/CAM Signflow	Accounting	External e-mail
	Strong synergy – design information exchanged with customers Weak leverage – design information serves mainly to improve existing relationship	No synergy – information only used internally No leverage	No synergy No leverage
Precision Tool Co.	CAD system MRP system	Accounting	None
	Strong synergy – design information exchanged with customers Weak leverage – design information serves mainly to improve existing relationship	No synergy No leverage	No synergy No leverage

supplier. Car Sign Design Co. is looking to build a wider local constituency to provide a cushion against loss of major customers.

The SMEs in Table 13.6 have strong synergy and weak leverage primarily as they are preferred suppliers. This is the first grouping to use IS, usually EDI, for knowledge exchange. Use of electronic systems forces exchanges to be formal and structured. This confirms the contention that these firms will have a positive attitude to knowledge sharing, though there might be concern that the knowledge provided might be used negatively. Customers define what is exchanged, but there are examples of SMEs refusing knowledge sharing requests, which is the case for Precision Tool Co. Their main concern is more to do with the cost of introducing the required systems rather than not wanting to exchange knowledge.

However, there is a mixed response to information exchange in both management and customer support. For some, performance measurement is essential to be a preferred supplier, leading to strong synergy in management information. Customer care and relationship management is critical and synergy is strong in customer support. Car Paint Co. differs as they have an operative on the client's premises, relying on a personal touch rather than systems. There is some evidence

Table 13.6: Explicit information transfer in collaboration cell SMEs

SMEs	Contract-defined information	Process for exchange	Inter-organizational co-ordination	Planning and control procedures
Birmingham Clutches	Design Performance measurement Orders Invoices	EDI	Formal	Defined by customer
Car Sign Design Co.	Design Orders	Internet E-mail	Formal	Defined by customer
Heath Springs	Design Performance measurement Orders Invoices	EDI	Formal	Defined by customer
Solihull Lighting Co.	Design Performance measurement Orders Invoices	EDI	Formal	Defined by customer
Car Paint Co.	Orders Invoices	Manual Fax	Formal	Defined by customer
Precision Tool Co.	Designs	Formal	Formal process	None

that information is exchanged but this is primarily used to improve the relationships with current customers, thus leverage is limited. Hence, knowledge sharing is of value to SMEs in the collaboration quadrant.

Knowledge sharing in repositioning-focused SMEs

The final analysis is of the three SMEs in the repositioning quadrant (Table 13.7).

An entrepreneur seeking the next growth area in mobile communications runs Radio Mast Surveyors. He uses customer-derived knowledge to plan and develop applications for radio masts and identify opportunities overseas and growth areas such as WAP phones. He views the information and knowledge he gains from existing customers as a means to expand the business into overseas markets. He is also exploring other opportunities for his services given the different forms of mobile communication that are emerging.

Corporate Gift Co. uses the knowledge it gains from working with corporate customers to develop a retail business online. The knowledge about sales is being used to reduce the product range and reposition the business. The CEO sees the firm's future more in the retail arena.

Table 13.7: Synergy and leverage in the repositioning cell SMEs

SEMs	Production systems	Management Systems	Customer support systems
Radio Mast Surveyors	CAD for plans Photo manipulation software	Accounting Work progress Monitoring	Lotus notes E-mail
	Strong synergy – plans exchanged with customers Strong leverage reuse of information to learn and develop	No synergy – information only used internally No leverage	Strong synergy – building up knowledge base with customers Strong leverage – information used to expand into new markets
Corporate Gift Co.	CAD	Accounting Sales order processing	Online sales
	Strong synergy – design information is exchanged with customers Strong leverage – design information is used to develop new products for new markets	No synergy – information only used internally No leverage	Weak synergy – Knowledge Base is built on products and customer preferences Weak leverage – information is primarily used to review product base
Model Toy Co.	E-portal Strong synergy – knowledge of customers purchasing objectives is collected Strong leverage – knowledge used to grow and develop e-portal	Accounting No synergy – information only used internally No leverage	None No synergy No leverage

Model Toy Co. has completely repositioned itself based on its knowledge of the collectable market. The firm developed a web portal that now offers a service to other firms selling collectables. The knowledge they receive from the use of the portal is used to continue portal development and attracting new businesses.

Hence, all the SMEs in the repositioning quadrant value exchange of information to grow their business. However, as with all the other SMEs the primary area for this is in production systems. The entrepreneurial nature of these businesses means that, while as knowledge receivers they use information effectively, there might be some reluctance to share knowledge. In particular, if it affects the potential for development.

All these SMEs have strong synergy and leverage. Yet, information exchanges are fairly formal (Table 13.8). There are no planning and control procedures that enable greater freedom for growth, as in the

Table 13.8: Explicit knowledge transfer in repositioning cell SMEs

SMEs	Contract-defined information	Process for exchange	Inter-organizational co-ordination	Planning and control procedures
Radio Mast Surveyors	Site information Planning information	Report delivery Formal process	Due date Formal	None
Corporate Gift Co.	Orders Designs Accounts Invoices	Formal process	Due date Formal	None
Model Toy Co.	Orders	Formal	Formal	None

co-ordination quadrant. Additionally, there is significant use of IS to manage and disseminate knowledge. The attitude and knowledge of the owner determines the approach. The game-theoretic model suggests that firms with these characteristics may have an ambiguous attitude to knowledge sharing.

The main message is that SMEs have greater freedom to plan and develop their own growth and leverage the use of information when there are limited planning and control systems. IS are important in managing customer relationships when SMEs take a value-added view of IS investment.

■ Implications for research

The role of knowledge in organizational learning and innovation is recognized by many authors. However, there is virtually no research within the SME context. This chapter establishes that SMEs need to manage knowledge sharing and that they are often players in a co-opetitive game. Game theory is shown to be useful to analyse the role of knowledge sharing under co-opetition and identifies three co-opetitive forces, two of which, synergy and leverage, are used in the analysis. Using the focus-dominance model, theoretical expectations of the impact of synergy and leverage on SMEs are set up.

Contrary to expectations, there is evidence of synergy and leverage in some cost-focussed SMEs. The game-theoretic model engenders expectations of knowledge sharing opportunities and co-opetition in value-added focussed SMEs. The theoretical proposition outlined is that SMEs with a cost-focused strategy are likely to have weak synergy and leverage and hence an ambiguous attitude to knowledge sharing. However, the analysis demonstrates that where synergy exists it is strong. This appears to be because of the strong relationship between the SME and its customers in the production area. The exchange of information, particularly in product design is critical to both businesses. However, leverage from the information is only evident in the co-ordination quadrant, where firms are looking for growth often through new markets for existing products. Thus, there is some confirmation of that benefits arise through improvements in operational efficiency and market positioning, although the benefits to strategic capabilities are not found as identified by Venkatraman (1990).

For value-added SMEs, the analysis supports the proposition that those in the collaboration quadrant exhibit strong synergy and weak leverage, while repositioning SMEs exhibit both strong synergy and leverage. In these cases process and expertise exchange provides benefits. What is not clear is that the collaboration quadrant SMEs are enhancing their strategic capabilities to any great extent from the knowledge exchange, as suggested by Venkatraman. This may be because of the weak leverage because of relative size. However, it might be argued that if SMEs spent more time codifying information and formalizing the knowledge within the firm that they might gain these benefits.

Further research needs to be done on the role of tacit knowledge in SMEs to understand its use and role in organizational learning.

■ Implications for management

SMEs need to consider how to make themselves receptive to exchanged knowledge, and flexible and responsive enough to gain competitive advantage, if this is ephemeral. It may be that knowledge is bundled with other physical assets and that there are prerequisites for using the knowledge fully. SMEs are knowledge creators, but are poor at knowledge retention. Part of the resolution of this lies in the SMEs' own hands. They need to be proactive in knowledge sharing agreements, to recognize knowledge has value and the value added derived from knowledge exchange. While some SMEs here expect new technology to open up global markets, their collaborations are essentially local. SMEs will be more vulnerable as inter-organizational IS spread and the world gets more information exchange intensive. At minimum, SMEs need to recognize that these forces exist. Recognition is the first step in management, though often the SMEs cannot mitigate the forces, especially from major customers. They may however, be able to gain more value internally from the knowledge they are forced to share. As with many issues in SMEs, the owner-manager attitude is paramount. That most of the knowledge shared by SMEs is explicit, suggests that some management of the sharing process is within the hands of the SMEs.

The strength SMEs have is that they are repositories of a considerable resource of tacit knowledge. SMEs need to recognize that as they grow the need to formalize this knowledge will enable them to strengthen their relationships throughout the value net. Management IS can assist in this process.

■ Discussion and conclusions

To date little is known about how co-opetition operates in the real world and still less of its impacts on SMEs. Researchers are still debating on issues of the role of knowledge and knowledge sharing in organizations. This chapter attempts to add to this debate by understanding the context of co-opetition in SMEs, the role of IS in managing knowledge, how the co-opetition forces of synergy and leverage manifest themselves and how SMEs attempt to manage the knowledge sharing process. Managing inter-organizational knowledge processes play a prominent role in sustainable competitive advantage. The game-theoretic analysis provides a structure for modelling knowledge sharing under co-opetition.

Co-opetition forces do impact on SMEs, though the context is significant. Some SMEs employ tactics, sometimes through the use of IS, to mitigate and exploit these forces through knowledge sharing management, though their efforts are largely unsuccessful. However, in the majority of cases SMEs fail to exploit knowledge explicitly in either managing the business or in providing customer support. Both of these areas need to be developed further if SMEs are to grow and develop.

As has been emphasized, knowledge needs to be assimilated over time to become effective within the firm. Over time, this knowledge becomes the competences or capabilities of the firm. The "unique blend of resources" leads to differentiating characteristics of firms that enable them to gain strategic advantage (Sauer and Yetton, 1997: p. 17). The concept of firms as collections of resources has led to the resource-based view of strategy that is discussed in the next chapter.

14 Role of core competencies in developing ISS in knowledge-based SMEs

■ Introduction

Research into the sources of competitive advantage identifies two views (Dyer and Singh, 1998). The first, exemplified by Porter (1980) concerns industry structure. The role of information systems in enabling competitive advantage in this type of world is about lower cost, building barriers to entry and tying in customers and suppliers. The second, more recent, view is resource-based. This argues that competitive advantage arises from the ability *"to accumulate resources and capabilities that are rare, valuable, non-substitutable and difficult to imitate"* (Dyer and Singh, 1998: p. 660). The resource-based view of the firm emphasizes the resources firms need to develop to compete in the environment. Miller and Shamsie (1996) identify two forms of resources, property based and knowledge based. They argue that property-based resources contribute most in stable settings, while knowledge-based resources have the greatest utility in uncertain environments. Any resource of either type must be difficult to create, buy, substitute or imitate. Knowledge-based resources are difficult to imitate because they are subtle and hard to understand. Property-based resources are about control, while knowledge-based ones are enablers of adaptation. Each category of resource comes in two varieties – discrete and systemic (or bundled) involving things such as teamwork. Miller and Shamsie state what IS researchers have shown for a long time without ever really formalizing it, that *"whether or not an asset can be considered a resource depends as much on the organizational context as on the properties of the asset itself"*. This reinforces the IS view that it is the use and management of IS that confer advantage not their mere existence.

While the resource-based view of the firm has substantial theoretical support, it has not been empirically tested to any great extent (Miller and Shamsie, 1996). The little testing that has occurred is in large US firms. While the resource-based view in the context of small- and medium-sized enterprises has been explored, for example by Rangone (1999) with respect to strategic planning, the role of information systems strategy is unexplored.

This chapter takes the first step towards filling this void. It discusses the role of IS as firm resources and the role of such resources in SMEs. It uses as a vehicle the identification and development of an ISS in a knowledge-based SME. This type of firm should have systemic, knowledge-based resources as its prime competitive tools. As Andreu and Ciborra (1996) suggest, resources used in context can develop into core competence capabilities that can differentiate. The use of core competencies or capabilities, a key aspect of resources, as a basis for an ISS is contrasted here with the use of a structural approach exemplified by the value chain.

There is much in the resource-based view that is intuitively appealing for understanding SMEs' use of IS. SMEs are typically unable to restructure the industry to gain competitive advantage, as they are often small producers in near perfectly competitive markets unable to influence price or quantity. While IS do enable some competitive advantage from collaboration with customers and suppliers as Porter suggests, the structural view does not explain why some SMEs are innovative with IS and others in the same market conditions are not. The resource-based view suggests context is vital – for instance, the SME's owner-manager's attitude and experience of IS will impact heavily on the role of IS. Further, as discussed in Chapter 13, SMEs are generally poor at knowledge sharing and management. In part this is a structural constraint – SMEs in homogeneous markets do not have knowledge that confers competitive advantage and are poor at contractual relationships due (primarily) to resource poverty. The latter limits SMEs use of property-based resources and the former will temper their ability to use knowledge-based resources. However, SMEs are not a homogeneous group and there is an identifiable subset that may be characterized as "knowledge based". These are the most interesting place to explore the application of the resource-based view of the firm to SMEs' use of IS. Using participant observation research in a not-for-profit organization, Housing Consultancy, which provides consultancy in social housing, this chapter investigates these issues.

■ SMEs, ISS

As discussed in Part 2, SMEs have much to gain from strategic IS. However the methods used in ISS planning are primarily 1980s strategic models applied from an IS/IT perspective. As demonstrated in Chapter 6, much of the strategic thinking embedded in strategic information systems planning (SISP) processes is derived from the work of Porter and Millar (1985) who highlight the transition of IT from support service to strategic resource, and explicitly connect information with creating and sustaining competitive advantage. Using the value chain and five forces models, they show how IT can change the nature of competition by altering industry structures, supporting cost and differentiation strategies, or even spawning new businesses. While this structural view has proven beneficial, insights from a resource-based view involving core

Table 14.1: Value chain analysis applied to knowledge-based firms

Characteristics of value chain analysis	*Characteristics of knowledge-based firms*
Orientated towards the production of goods rather than services	Produce intangible services based on knowledge and experience
Implicit primacy of primary activities over support activities	Support activities have a much greater importance, directly adding value through human creativity
Uni-directional, following the flow of physical materials	Operate a feedback loop mechanism, continually gathering information, developing skills and using experience to enhance the service product
Reflects capital investment priorities of plant and machinery	Human assets are more important than capital assets

competencies may be of more value to knowledge-based small businesses. Information system can be an integral part of core capability development in two ways. First, by improving work practices and communication to ensure resource-based capabilities are understood and used across the organization. Second, by considering the differential advantage that can be leveraged through making capabilities "rare, valuable, difficult to imitate and with no strategically equivalent substitutes" (Andreu and Ciborra, 1996). At this point it is worth considering some of the limitations of structural analysis.

■ Limitations of structural analysis

Value chain analysis (Porter and Millar, 1985), a key tool of structural analysis, is almost ubiquitous as an exemplar framework for use in the SISP process (Ward et al., 1990; Earl, 1989; Synnott, 1987). However, there are difficulties in applying it to knowledge-based firms. Knowledge-based firms are those who deliver a service based around the strategic use of information or knowledge held within individuals and systems. These firms include consultants and professional services firms such as accountants and attorneys. Law firms and financial services as environments do not easily lend themselves to value chain analysis (Doyle, 1991). Table 14.1 summarizes the difficulties in applying value chain analysis to knowledge-based firms.

Table 14.1 suggests that knowledge-based SMEs may need to use other processes to develop effective SISP. There are two reasons for this. First, the iterative nature of the process means that the added value is difficult to gauge at any one stage. In other words, the value chain is less than clear in knowledge-based firms. Second, the importance of the people in the process means that core knowledge tends to be held informally. A knowledge-based SME is likely to use systemic resources as identified by Miller and Shamsie (1996) as their strategic advantage is in being able to leverage the knowledge of individual experts through collaboration. Rangone (1999) suggests that a resource-based view of strategy is appropriate for small businesses. The focus of the strategic analysis should only be on those resources that are critical for the achievement of sustainable competitive advantage. Three core capabilities are identified as suitable for SMEs. These are, first, innovation, the ability to develop new products and services. The second is production capability, the ability to make and deliver to customers. The third core capability is marketing. The extent of these capabilities in small businesses depends upon their strategic direction.

Thus, SMEs may develop resource-based core capabilities that cannot easily be imitated, a prime requirement for resource-based strategy. An alternative approach may be needed for the development of SISP in knowledge-based organizations.

IS and knowledge-based SMEs

Sveiby and Lloyd (1987) describe knowledge-based firms as those whose services are heavily customized to their clients' needs. They are characterized by non-standardization, creativity, high dependence on individuals and complex problem solving. They are firms in which the key resources are people. Positioning such firms on the information intensity matrix (Chapter 6) reinforces this view (Figure 14.1).

The positioning of consultancy, essentially a knowledge-based activity, is informed by Ward's (1988) positioning of legal services and education, although amended by Doyle's (1991) suggestion that an information-rich process is necessary to build an information-rich product. The information intensity matrix suggests that possibilities

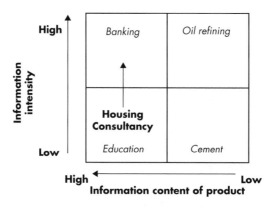

Figure 14.1: Porter and Millar's information intensity matrix (*Source:* adapted from Earl, 1989).

exist for knowledge-based consultancies to use IS/IT as a competitive weapon, not only for the product itself but also within the production process of the product, as proposed by Andreu and Ciborra (1996).

While the structural view and its concomitant strategic management tools can be used advantageously in the SISP process, the resource-based view of strategy also yields benefits. Competition in the 1990s requires firms to identify, cultivate and exploit "core competencies". Core competencies are the collective learning of the organization. In particular, they involve the process skills of co-ordinating a diverse range of competencies directed towards a market segment. Core competencies should constitute the focus for strategy at the corporate level (Prahalad and Hamel, 1990). This principle is appropriate for a knowledge-based organization.

Extending the concept of competencies, Sanchez *et al.* (1996) suggest the obsolescence of existing perspectives on strategic management. Concepts of industry structures and portfolio analysis are being replaced by emphasis on intangible concepts of skills, technologies and competencies. Many of these intangible assets are capabilities and knowledge, that when deployed in a co-ordinated manner, become the core competencies of the firm. These core competencies are the real area of competition rather than end products that are merely their expression. While Porter argues that competitiveness could be gained through structuring within an industry framework, the resource-based view argues that it is variety created by individual firms that increases competitiveness (Dyer and Singh, 1998).

Firms exploit their existing capabilities through "competence leveraging"; attacking new markets or strengthening positions through focused deployment. They can engage in "competence building", creating new capabilities or developing new abilities to co-ordinate existing ones.

As Sanchez *et al.* (1996) observe, this theory is developing. Its vocabulary and theory are not well defined; interpretation is idiosyncratic. There are no well-tried tools or frameworks to assist strategic management from a competence-based perspective. Not surprisingly, no SISP tools or frameworks have been developed. Managers therefore have three alternatives. First, use of conventional tools and frameworks of SISP, with their acknowledged limitations. Second, identification of tools more closely aligned with core competence theory and third, to derive new tools from the theory.

◼ Tools for competence-based analysis for ISS

Insights gained from the use of the conventional tools are not invalidated by a focus on competencies. However these insights need to be relevant in terms of competence-based strategy. Questions such as "what does this say about the firm's competencies and its learning processes?" and "how does this assist competence-leveraging or competence-building activities?" help reinterpret the outcomes in terms of competence-based strategy. Dyer and Singh (1998) observe that the industry view of competition can be useful in providing insights, particularly in collaborative ventures. They recognize the need for both resource-based analysis and industry analysis in managing firm growth.

Existing tools

Whilst there are no tools specifically addressing competencies, there are a number of methods derived from a systemic view of problem situations that may generate insight. One used with some success in the development of IS is SSM used to help analyse the Heath Springs Case in Chapter 8. From both a competence and an IS perspective, SSM has a number of positive features as:

- It is systemic and, hence, accommodates feedback loops and learning processes.

- It allows investigation of competence-leveraging and competence-building activities through root definitions of suitable systems.

- It allows the derivation of information needs through development of conceptual models.

- It is applicable in problematic situations where conventional strategy tools are less useful.

Although SSM can be adapted to investigate information needs, it cannot of itself draw out strategic opportunities that still remain the province of the structuralist strategic management frameworks.

New tools

The firm grows through its core competencies and these enable the development of core products. Core products will be used by business units in the firm towards the development of their individual end products. As discussed in Chapter 13, competencies form the basis of organizational learning. By knowing its core competencies the firm has a better understanding of its capacity to innovate (Prahalad and Hamel, 1990). Prahalad and Hamel propose a hierarchical model of core competencies (Figure 14.2) that are made manifest in core products, and, in turn, contribute to end products, flexibly constructed, to target specific market segments. Core competencies may be used by more than one core product.

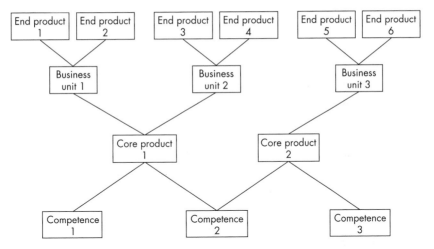

Figure 14.2: Core competence framework. (*Source*: adapted from Prahalad and Hamel, 1990).

Within this model are three criteria are by which core competencies can be identified as:

■ Potential access to a wide variety of markets.

■ Significant contribution to perceived customer benefits of end products.

■ Difficult for competitors to imitate.

Application of these and the hierarchical model give insights into the competence structure of the firm, and the strategic opportunities for competence leveraging and competence building.

■ Using IS/IT to support learning processes

Andreu and Ciborra (1996) consider the development of core capabilities to be a fundamental learning process. They explore how IS/IT can contribute to the learning aspects of competence development by taking a resource-based view of the firm, where IT aids the transformation of standard resources into core capabilities.

From a competence-based strategic perspective IS/IT applications need to be identified that support competence leveraging (Sanchez *et al.*, 1996) and competence building (Andreu and Ciborra, 1996). The next part of this chapter describes an in-depth case study in a knowledge-based small business, Housing Consultancy. The background to the case is described followed by the SISP process undertaken with the organization.

Case study 14.1

Housing Consultancy provides consultancy and associated services in social housing. It has a turnover of £3 million and employs around 40 people. Housing Consultancy has around 250 clients: local authorities, housing associations, resident groups and local housing firms. It supplies a wide range of services in compulsory competitive tendering, tenant participation, estate management and the right to manage. Housing Consultancy also runs training courses, seminars and conferences. The organization works in a politicized environment, relying on government funding of housing projects. The structure of the social housing industry is fragmented with a few national agencies like Housing Consultancy and hundreds of local consultancies.

Housing Consultancy has active projects throughout the UK. They are organized into three Regional Teams, based in London, Birmingham and Manchester, that are self-managing and autonomous, with responsibility for their own financial and operational performance. The Regional Teams decide their own strategic priorities and construct their own business plan. They are managed by a Regional Co-ordinator assisted by a business manager who handles day-to-day interactions with the consultants. Consultants work from home, spending most of their time on-site with clients. They are self-managing and have almost complete control over their working time. Each month every consultant submits a paper document containing details of client hours worked, expenses incurred and other activities. They receive feedback including chargeable hours worked and expenses incurred to facilitate their workload management. This is called the project progress report (PPR) system and is at the heart of operational management of Regional Teams.

■ SISP process in Housing Consultancy

The SISP process began with a presentation to the Senior Management Team on the concepts of core competence, their relevance to the SISP process, and a discussion about what might constitute the competence set for Housing Consultancy. Over a period of 4 weeks interviews were held with key staff in London and Manchester. Three SSM workshops were held with the Promotions and Marketing manager, the Northern Team Leader and business manager, and the Southern Team Leader and business manager, respectively. Another three informal workshops were held with team business managers and the finance manager to assess the relevance and applicability of emerging themes.

Interviews with key personnel in Housing Consultancy, and analysis of reports and documentation associated with management of the Regional Teams are the data sources for the core competence and SSM analyses. Soft systems methodology analysis leads to the identification

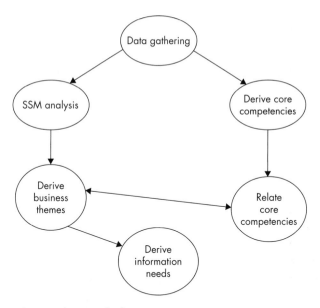

Figure 14.3: Deriving business themes and information requirements.

of business themes that are essential for leveraging competitive advantage through IS/IT. Business themes encapsulate the current business direction as a means of determining implementable strategies (Earl, 1996b). While core competence analysis identifies the critical resources that Housing Consultancy exploits in its chosen market place. Prahalad and Hamel's model is used to explicate the core competence structure of Housing Consultancy within the context of its core products, finance and customer perspectives. Information requirements are defined for those business themes identified as being essential for core competence leverage. This is shown diagrammatically in Figure 14.3.

Data gathering

A series of semi-structured interviews covering the full range of Housing Consultancy staff were used to gather data (Table 14.2). The interviews focused on eliciting information needs for current operations and attempted to identify the key organizational competences required for Housing Consultancy to compete effectively in current markets and exploit strategic opportunities in the future.

The interviews generated, at the operational level, a detailed list of information needs that would allow staff to manage, administrate or deliver services better. At the strategic level a number of issues emerged:

■ The accounting system could be enhanced to give more appropriate financial analysis to Regional Teams and senior management. This also presented the opportunity to build financial models of the Regional Teams and Housing Consultancy as a whole.

Table 14.2: Interviewees and indicative content

Position	Interview content
Senior Director and Consultant	Mission, objectives, strategy. External environment – political and economic; Housing policy, trends; Housing Consultancy as an organization
Senior Director and Consultant	Mission, objectives and strategy. Structure of Housing Consultancy business, customers, products, services and skills; Selling process; Possibilities for IS/IT
Regional Co-ordinator, Consultant and Regional Business Manager	Financial aspects of Regional Team management; Project management and resource scheduling; Selling process; Marketing and central Resource Library
Regional Co-ordinator and Consultant	Project management, resource scheduling. Marketing and tendering; Shared budget management information, client communications; Electronic Resource Library and communication
Finance Manager	Corporate Finance and Regional Team finance requirements; Budgeting and business planning; Housing Consultancy business model
Consultant	Field work – nature of, use of IS/IT; Selling process; Training materials, team working, communications, and products; Potential for Knowledge Base, organizational learning
Manager Promotions and Marketing	Marketing, market analysis; Mailing lists and promotions; Competition; P&M function within Housing Consultancy

■ Regional Team management was compromised by inefficient data collection mechanisms, and by inadequate analysis and reporting. Feedback to consultants was slow and unpredictable.

■ There was no effective method collecting and collating marketing information about clients that, in principle, was available from a variety of sources. Marketing and selling were *ad hoc*, undertaken by Regional Teams or individual consultants.

■ There was general frustration that despite the quality of consultants, there was a failure to gather and disseminate their experience as training materials, templates for presentations, survey questionnaires, etc. A "Resource Library" fulfilled this function, in principle, but was rarely used or updated.

■ As a major symptom of the last two points was a general conviction that "Promotions and Marketing" (P&M) was insufficiently integrated into the information flows of Housing Consultancy and was not providing the service required of it.

■ Generally communications within teams, between teams and with the Senior Management Team was considered cumbersome, untimely and inefficient, reinforcing the difficulties of consultants working remotely.

In addition, three management perspectives became apparent from the interviews. First, there is a customer-orientated perspective that attempts to identify sets of customers with common attributes or interests. This perspective is required as a basis for making promotional initiatives. Second, there is an income perspective that categorizes different types of payment regime or income categories (e.g. Section 16 Promotion – grant funding from the UK Government for seed corn promotion of participatory tenant management) and is the perspective through which the financial performance of Housing Consultancy is observed. Finally, there is a product perspective that attempts to identify common products that are supplied to customers. Products and services delivered are frequently tailored specifically for the customer and are consequently diverse.

The relationships between Housing Consultancy's customers, the products and services they take, and the income category through which they take them, are complex. Interestingly, these are identical to those identified by Rangone (1999).

Strategic analysis and debate is dogged by indiscriminate use of these different perspectives. The end result is that the debate is confusing and a common understanding of strategic approaches is hard to establish. The approach taken to reconcile these conflicting perspectives is, first, to identify the core competencies for Housing Consultancy and, second, to analyze them using SSM.

■ Core competence analysis

The Prahalad and Hamel model provides the only means to date of modelling core competencies. The model has its basis core competencies that are defined as the critical resources found in the business and are embodied in core products. Finally, they are delivered through strategic business units to customers.

The core competence model of Housing Consultancy can be mapped directly onto the Prahalad and Hamel model, other than the income category replacing the strategic business unit component. This is done because Housing Consultancy differentiates its activities by the nature of the type of business and the way it is commissioned. This leads to differential charging to support different grant regimes. However, all staff are involved in all the various income generating activities. Hence, while the activities are distinct, the size and structure of Housing Consultancy suggests that strategic business units are inappropriate and income categories will be more meaningful.

Table 14.3: Housing Consultancy core competences

Housing Management theory and practice
Research (interviewing, designing and conducting surveys) skills
Group work skills/community work skills
Event management skills
Training skills
S16 and other grant regime procedures
Project Management skills
Communication (writing/publicity/etc.) skills

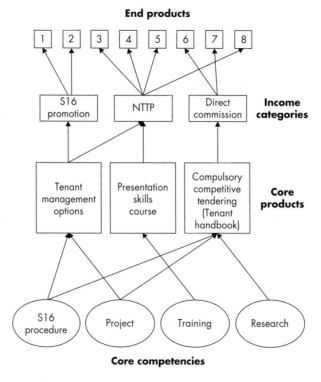

Figure 14.4: Model of a selection of competencies/product/income for Housing Consultancy.

Using the working definition of core competencies/capabilities as "those competencies that management perceive as of central importance to the company's goals and strategy" (Lewis and Gregory, 1996) all interviewees were asked about what they considered to be the core competencies/capabilities of Housing Consultancy. Table 14.3 represents a broad consensus of these views.

The Prahalad and Hamel model for core competencies is adapted for Housing Consultancy. A selection of the core competencies and products is presented in Figure 14.4. Rather than business units Housing

Consultancy has separate income categories that are distinct. Strategic opportunities for competence leverage and building may now be identified. This is done using SSM analysis.

■ SSM analysis in Housing Consultancy

The SSM analysis was developed from the interview material and workshops with managers to verify and develop the analyst's understanding. A key issue for the analysis is that the resulting rich picture is a composite of different views of the situation in Housing Consultancy. The model acknowledges the different roles, norms and values found in Housing Consultancy and develops a model of the perceived "social system" (Checkland and Scholes, 1990). This "Analysis Two" mode of SSM is rarely complete because of its reliance on perceptions from different actors. Checkland and Scholes acknowledge the difficulty of identifying norms and values, particularly from interviews. The action research approach provides a means of developing additional understanding of these norms and values by involvement in the business. In Housing Consultancy the roles for the consultants were professional in that their knowledge in the housing field brought respect from their peers. The values found in Housing Consultancy are those of social justice and commitment to social housing. The norms in Housing Consultancy show a situation where independence is valued. However, management now finds this inhibits effectiveness as the organization grows. Figure 14.5 shows the resultant rich picture.

Three major issues emerged from the analysis:

■ The difficulties of Regional Co-ordinators in obtaining operational and financial reports from the PPR and Finance Systems.

■ The lack of client information flows into promotion and marketing, preventing marketing analysis.

■ The inability of consultants to contribute their own materials and experience to the Resource Library, and to access and retrieve material.

These problems suggest the need for three key transformations (Figure 14.6).

Each of these key transformations was examined through root definitions, conceptual modelling and comparison with real world feasibility. An example conceptual model of a marketing analysis and support competence is shown in Figure 14.7.

In addition the analysis identified two issue-based systems that cause concern among some actors in Housing Consultancy. First, *control and*

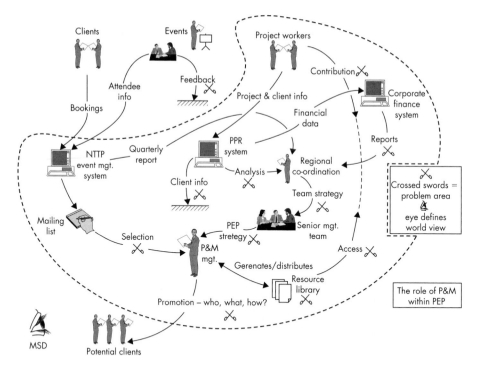

Figure 14.5: Rich picture of key processes and interactions in Housing Consultancy.

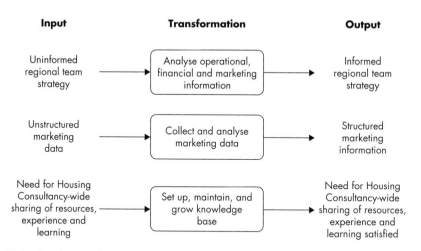

Figure 14.6: Three key transformations.

planning is seen as difficult in Housing Consultancy, primarily because of its loose network structure as well as the independent nature of consultants. The problem owners particularly perceive that growth is inhibited by a lack of business and financial planning. Second, *communications* is recognized by many of the players to be an inhibiting factor in disseminating knowledge throughout the organization, making it less effective in carrying out its primary role.

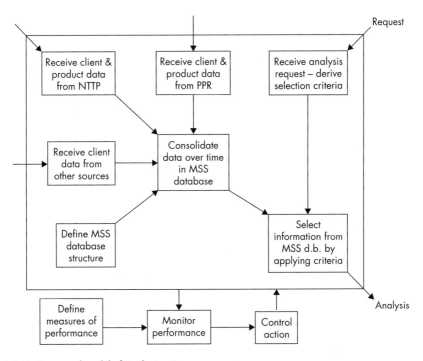

Figure 14.7: Conceptual model of Marketing Support competences.

Table 14.4: Emerging business themes for Housing Consultancy

Operations Management	Means by which the operations of Regional Teams are planned, managed and accounted for, within the Team, and also communicated within Housing Consultancy
Marketing Support	Accumulation and structuring of all client data, operational and qualitative, to provide analysis to support operations, marketing, strategy formulation and planning
Knowledge Base	Institutionalization of firm-wide experience as standard documents, training courses, project experience etc. to enable access and sharing by Housing Consultancy personnel to facilitate and enhance their activities in the field and within Housing Consultancy
Communications	Mechanisms by which communications of tangible and intangible information and knowledge is facilitated throughout Housing Consultancy regardless of structure or geography
Control and planning	Financial control and analysis throughout Housing Consultancy, together with the formulation of Business Plans both short and longer term

These five systems can be considered in Earl's terms as business themes. They represent key areas of capability or competence in which Housing Consultancy need to excel to meet their strategic objective (Table 14.4).

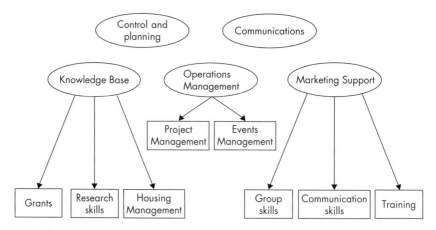

Figure 14.8: Relationship between business themes and core competences.

■ Relating core competences to business themes

The earlier core competence analysis highlighted eight areas that are thought critical for success by Housing Consultancy staff. As Rangone (1999) indicates, core competence leverage is key to the development of strategic growth in SMEs. The five business themes highlighted by the SSM analysis provide the means by which these core competencies can be leveraged to enable strategic growth in Housing Consultancy. Figure 14.8 demonstrates the connection between core competencies and business themes.

The three primary task business themes map directly onto the core competencies. However, there are no core competencies that connect either to control and planning or communications. These two business themes are derived from issue-based systems and represent skills that are needed throughout the organization. Thus, they are critical to enable effective leverage of all the core competencies.

■ Matching information needs to business themes

Information needs of managers were identified through the interview process. The SSM analysis and core competence analysis allows refinement of these information needs through identification of those that are necessary to support business themes. Table 14.5 indicates the business themes and their associated information requirements.

Table 14.5 suggests that not all core competencies are being used in Housing Consultancy. For example, events management is not included in any of the information issues raised in Operations Management. In the Knowledge Base area all core competencies are used, which is not

Table 14.5: Business themes and information needs-related core competences

Business theme	Information need	Core competence
Operations Management	Resource schedules and diaries	Project Management
	PPR – resource, expenses and money equivalents against budget	Project Management
	Team performance – time usage, chargeable and non-chargeable, expenses, utilization, and realization	Project Management
Knowledge Base	Access to Regional Team and/or Corporate Resource Library	Housing Management Grants Research skills
	Access to Housing Consultancy corporate Knowledge Base	Housing Management Grants Research skills
	Access to personnel Knowledge Base. Templates for responding to invitations to tender	Research skills Housing Management Grants Research skills
Marketing Support	Customer/Contact Database	Communication skills
	Access to Tendering Results Analysis	Communication skills
	Broader and deeper marketing information about attendees and their organizations	Communication skills
	Clear up-to-date information on Housing Consultancy clients and services being provided	Communication skills
	Clearer information on target audiences.	Communication skills
	Feedback on initiatives, monitoring of results	Communication skills Training
	Skills and Materials versus Products	Group work skills
	Products versus Customers	Group work skills
	Products versus Margins	Communication skills
	Customer Identification and Contact Points	Communication skills
	Customer needs and perceptions	Group skills
Communications	Access to Regional Team and/or Corporate Resource Library	
	More effective/less time-consuming inter-Team, intra-Team, and Corporate communications	
Control, planning	Margin analysis by sales category.	
	Financial reports – team performance against budgets	
	Corporate financial reports	
	Restructure of Nominal Accounts with respect to sales categories and overheads	
	Contribution by sales category	
	Housing Consultancy financial model	

surprising, as these are the critical activities for Housing Consultancy. Again in Marketing Support, communications appears to be most important. There are no clear core competencies indicated for the two issue-based themes. The reason for this is that, these business themes and information needs are those that all businesses require for effective management.

■ SISP recommendations

The SISP process identified areas of key capability (or core competence) that Housing Consultancy needs to establish to fulfil its strategic objectives. Table 14.6 tabulates the three primary task business themes with a summary of information needs. These, in turn, require actions to

Table 14.6: Business themes, information needs and consequential actions

Business theme	Information implications	Actions
Operations Management	Requires accumulation and analysis of project related data over time Needs Marketing Support through analysis of existing information and projections for future initiatives	Enhance PPR system to provide required analyses Provide channel to input project related data into Marketing Support system
Marketing Support	Requires structured analysis of data sets to create and maintain support database Requires defined inputs from NTTP and PPR systems to maintain database over time Marketing Support initiatives driven by operational strategies	Explore and build on competence orientated model of Housing Consultancy's products and services Design and implement Marketing Support system Include input channels from NTTP and PPR
Knowledge Base	Requires structured view of what constitutes a Knowledge Base. Suggestions might be: • Standard material for recurrent training courses • Procedure guides for regulatory schemes such as Section 16 etc • Experience guides to managing meetings, conducting surveys etc • Personnel skills/expertise base • Discussion groups on topics of interest	Initiate exercise to derive requirements for Knowledge Base Set out parameters for creation and management of Knowledge Base Select "experts" to contribute standard material by topic

satisfy these needs that, in essence, define the application development portfolio as a deliverable of the SISP process.

The initial outcome of the models is a developed set of short- and long-term business themes as advocated by Earl (1996). This approach recognizes that ISS are only one of the resources required for flexible strategy development. Thus, business themes have some correspondence with competence-leveraging and competence-building activities.

Recommendations for IS/IT developments in Housing Consultancy

The recommendations were incorporated in an "Implementation Schedule for Business Themes". This outlined a timetable for the implementation of first, *IT Infrastructure and Communications*, then the business themes of *Control and Planning* and *Operations Management*. These are to be followed in the longer term by the themes of *Marketing Support* and *Knowledge Base*.

Information systems and information technology applications are developed within the context of business themes following Earl's (1996) organization approach to ISS. The proposals for an improved IT infrastructure are also discussed, particularly its contribution to the business themes of communication, and control and planning.

Communications

Communications is essential for achievement of all core competencies. As such, it becomes an infrastructure issue, not only involving connectivity but also the medium of information transfer. Thus, development of an Intranet would facilitate file transfer throughout Housing Consultancy. It would also enable the support of the Knowledge Base through the use of search engines. Additionally, Internet facilities would enable improved marketing facilities. For example, hypertext can be used to structure complex networks of home pages, indices, documents, pictures, sound and video. File transfer protocols allow distribution and contribution mechanisms.

Control and planning

The main objective here is to improve financial planning and control. The accounting system needs to be improved to be able to report in a more detailed format to satisfy business requirements. There is also a need to improve financial analysis capabilities for Housing Consultancy. In particular, it would be helpful to construct a financial model of Housing Consultancy. This would allow investigation of sensitivities to changes in grant regimes, sales mix and cost structure. It would facilitate the development of the annual business plan and allow financial projections on the basis of performance variations against budget.

Operations Management

Managers have identified a need to monitor projects and financial progress more effectively. The PPR systems needs to be re-developed to allow more detailed and frequent reporting, particularly to satisfy the regulatory needs of the Department of the Environment.

Additionally, there is a need to review the financial system to enable managers to have access to the information they require to support their PPR.

Marketing Support

The case analysis has identified that Marketing Support is a critical area for Housing Consultancy if it is to grow. Marketing is a new area for Housing Consultancy but one requiring a major investment from Housing Consultancy and is unlikely to be undertaken soon. However, the importance for Housing Consultancy of being able to undertake client analysis to assist in future strategic plans and their marketing makes it an important area for consideration. A marketing system would facilitate competence-leveraging activities by applying core competencies and products to new market segments and also identify segments for which new competencies are required with implications for competence building.

Knowledge Base

The concept of a Knowledge Base for Housing Consultancy is highly strategic. In essence, the organization needs a knowledge management system to capture the corporate experience, information, capabilities and materials that are essential for the future of Housing Consultancy. The Knowledge Base will also provide an environment and engine for organizational learning. This supports the strategic learning loop by building competencies that will differentiate Housing Consultancy (Andreu and Ciborra, 1994). For example, the ability to bring national experience to bear on local projects, the development of libraries of standard procedures, the ability to consult across the organization are all differentiating competencies for Housing Consultancy.

Summary

Five business themes have been identified for Housing Consultancy. Three are directly linked to core competencies that can assist in leveraging the business. Two, communication, and control and planning, are over-arching themes that are necessary for managing business growth. Systems are also identified to assist Housing Consultancy in both areas.

ISS implementation

The SISP analysis enables Housing Consultancy the impetus to build on the momentum for developing IS/IT following the successful implementation of a computerized accounts system. With the help of an external IT consultancy, Housing Consultancy have put in place an IT infrastructure to support the organization. The London and Manchester offices are fully networked with all employees having PCs and each office having a file server. The two offices are connected via an ISDN line. Remote workers have dialup access to their servers and hence have e-mail provision and the ability to up- and download files. Housing Consultancy have standardized their software and have developed a productive relationship with a supplier of IT hardware and software capability.

Operations Management

The reporting of consultant time and expenses against projects is now undertaken entirely electronically, and consolidation is achieved through a complex spreadsheet program. Consultants can monitor their performance and that of their projects through access to a variety of reports. Considerable time was spent in an abortive effort to make use of a commercial package, but this failed due to emerging inadequacies of the package and a lack of support from the vendor. A custom-built database solution has been designed and awaits development by the IT consultancy.

Knowledge Base

The provision of IT infrastructure has facilitated several developments towards an organizational Knowledge Base. Tendering for projects now has a centralized database of all past tenders, invitations to tender and information relating tenders to consultant's expertise. Standard pro-formas for all tenders and e-mail have facilitated the tender build process by multiple consultants.

Training course materials have been captured for all the key repeated courses. Consultants access these remotely and customize them. There is a library of news updates, reports on social housing and research documents accessible to all the members of Housing Consultancy. A bulletin board has been set up to encourage the sharing of expertise, knowledge and experience, and promote debate and discussion. Housing Consultancy are planning to reorganize their Knowledge Base to allow a web style browser interface.

Marketing Support

As indicated in the recommendations this was seen as a long-term activity and radical change was not expected. Indeed, little progress has been made, although all training course customers are now recorded on a database.

The Internet

Housing Consultancy now has a high quality web site, developed through the IT consultancy that presents a comprehensive view of the organization, its capabilities, projects and news, and contact details. Both offices have Internet access which is used for researching government databases, and arranging and purchasing travel and accommodation requirements.

■ Discussion

The discussion reviews core competence theory for ISS in the light of the experience at Housing Consultancy. The literature on SISP in SMEs suggests that SMEs differ from large organizations and, hence, so must SISP processes. While also observing the large variation in the impact of IT in SMEs (Naylor and Williams, 1994; Cragg and King, 1993; Doukidis et al., 1996), the implicit assumption is that the generic term SME is adequate for discussion of SISP.

This chapter questions this view and highlights a category of SME, knowledge-based firms, in which IS/IT has a large potential impact. The chapter shows that these firms might benefit from analysis through a competence-based view of strategy. Knowledge-based firms are characterized by the intangible nature and high information content of their product, and its significant customization for the client. This has been demonstrated through the analysis of Housing Consultancy for whom information about housing issues, grant requirements and client needs is critical.

Other examples of knowledge-based SME include IT consultancies, advertizing agencies, graphic designers, HRM consultancies and solicitors. These types of firms proliferate in an environment where large organizations outsource non-core capabilities. The non-core capabilities of large firms are becoming core competencies of knowledge-based firms and so a competence-based view of strategy may be appropriate for them.

This perspective has particular benefits in the environment of SMEs that are dominated by larger customers over whom they have little influence. The politicized context of Housing Consultancy is a good example. Their need for improved strategic planning in order to respond to changes in government policy, particularly with regard to grant regimes is seen as critical. In such circumstances the competence focus elicits strategic decisions in terms of competence building and leveraging with a view to generating strategic options (Sanchez *et al.*, 1996). Increasing flexibility is inherent in this approach which is beneficial in uncertain environments. Where explicit strategic direction is difficult to determine, focus on competencies allows progress to be made in contexts of environmental complexity.

Limitations of value chain analysis

Value chain analysis would have identified operations management, and control and planning themes that are primarily concerned with efficiency and effectiveness. Although consideration of the primary activity of sales and marketing may have suggested uses of IS/IT, value chain analysis would not have provoked the insights with respect to core competencies provided by the application of the Prahalad and Hamel model. The potential strategic impact of the marketing support system might have been overlooked. Table 14.7 compares the generic value chain activities with the emergent business themes in Housing Consultancy. This table indicates that there are some value chain activities which are not central to a knowledge-based organization.

The most important business theme that would not have emerged from value chain analysis is that of the Knowledge Base. This theme occurs several times in the information needs analysis, but the value chain model has no component that reflects the feed-back learning processes associated with developing core capabilities (Andreu and Ciborra, 1994) inherent in knowledge-based firms. From a competence-based perspective the value chain analysis offers only opportunities for deriving competence-leveraging applications, but does not address the possibilities of competence building.

The strength of SSM over the value chain as a means of analysis lies in the comparison of ideal business process (conceptual) models with

Table 14.7: Comparison of value chain generic processes with business themes in Housing Consultancy

Generic value chain activity	Business theme
Primary value chain	
Inbound logistics	
Operation	Operations Management, Knowledge Base
Outbound logistics	
Marketing and sales	Marketing Support, Knowledge Base
Secondary value chain	
Firm infrastructure	Control and planning, communication
HRM	Control and planning, communication
Product and technology development	
Procurement	

the real world. This, together with the information needs analysis, provides a means of determining the information implications inherent in the main business themes and the actions that are needed to ensure that the information is available to managers.

Competence-based view of strategy

The justification for SISP is predicated on the recognition of information as a strategic resource and that IT is increasingly pervasive in all aspects of business activity. The intent of SISP is to align IS/IT with business objectives and to search for competitive advantage through its use. A competence perspective on strategy does not invalidate these considerations but rather re-interprets them. Core competencies, especially in knowledge-based firms, increasingly have information at the heart of their content and directing their deployment. Business objectives are realized through exercising competence leveraging and building, while core competencies become the locus of competitive advantage. In Housing Consultancy it was recognized that an Intranet and also development of Internet facilities would improve information access. Thus, the competence-based view of strategy is vital to SISP, and the methods employed need to incorporate this perspective. The task of SISP then becomes one of searching for opportunities of competence leveraging and building, and investigating the ways in which IS/IT can facilitate and enable these.

Tools for competence-based SISP

There are, as yet, no SISP tools or frameworks derived from a competence-based view of strategy, and this exercise has been conducted largely through conventional frameworks, interpreted from the competence perspective. The Prahalad and Hamel model is beneficial in several respects as:

- It illustrates the locus of competition as core products and core competencies.

- It gives direction to the analysis of a firm's competencies.

- It gives structure to the analysis of raw market data that relate to end products.

- It highlights the development of a competence in market data collection and analysis.

Its key limitation is in the process of how to assess, from all the firm's capabilities, those that meet the Sanchez *et al.* (1996) tests for core competence. This requires a filtering process such as suggested by a more sophisticated approach to competence analysis which produces a competence map for the business. A major practical benefit is claimed to be that of "providing the management team with the ability to add consideration of competence building and competence leveraging into their strategic formulation process" (Lewis and Gregory, 1996). Tools are needed to establish the competencies of the firm, those required in the market, both now and in the future, and to consider the options for competence leveraging and building.

Role of SSM

SSM played a significant role in this exercise; rich pictures are able to illustrate problem areas, which may be interpreted as competence deficiencies. Having posited such deficiencies, conceptual modelling was successful in investigating idealized systems for competence leveraging and competence building. While drawing out the implications for real-world action, these models cannot test the validity of the competence identified with respect to the market.

The potential of SSM in a competence-based view of strategy is as a meta-tool for building further tools to facilitate the competence analyses of firms and their environments. For example, the Lewis and Gregory process of competence analysis could be described with a SSM conceptual model. Comparison of competence sets would lead to specific direction as to competence leveraging and building possibilities. Figure 14.9 shows opportunities for competence building and leveraging derived from comparison of competence sets.

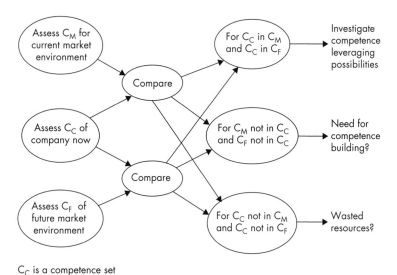

C_C is a competence set

Figure 14.9: Opportunities for competence building and leveraging derived from comparison of competence sets.

Table 14.8: Competence interpretation of business themes

Business theme	Competence interpretation
Operations Management	Quantitative change in ability to manage many projects in the field seen as competence leveraging improving the effectiveness of interaction with the Department of the Environment and allowing potential application across new markets (e.g. national Housing Associations)
Control and planning	Not really competence building or leveraging since it does not result in any offering of product to the market. Developments in this theme are directed towards evaluating strategic options generated from competence-building and leveraging activities
Marketing Support	A competence building activity which would facilitate Housing Consultancy's deployment and co-ordination of resources in offering products to the market
Knowledge Base	Again a competence building activity enabling new ways of creating product offerings facilitates new ways of deploying resources, and representing a new medium through which new competence building activities could take place
Communications	Not a competence building activity in itself. Effectively subsumed within the Knowledge Base theme
Business Theme	Competence interpretation

Business themes as competence leveraging/building

Having adopted a competence-based view of strategy, the SISP exercise struggled to apply the theory directly due to lack of tools, and had to rely on the interpretation of conventional frameworks. However, if SISP under this perspective is to have credibility then the outcomes must relate to competence leveraging and building, since these are the focus of strategic analysis. The outcomes of this SISP exercise are a number of business themes, some of which have a close correspondence with competence-building or leveraging activities.

Table 14.8 demonstrates that, whilst a business theme may be concerned purely with efficiency and effectiveness, those of truly strategic nature will correspond to competence-building or leveraging activities.

■ Conclusions

Strategic thinking has moved from a structural view of competitive advantage to a resource-based view. The resource-based view of the firm emphasizes the resources firms need to develop to compete. Two forms of resources exist, property-based and knowledge-based. Property-based resources contribute most in stable settings, while knowledge-based resources have the greatest utility in uncertain environments.

While the resource-based view of the firm has substantial theoretical support, it has not been subject to much empirically testing. The resource-based view in the context of SMEs is largely unexplored and the role of IS is likewise untested.

This chapter discusses the role of IS as firm resources and the role of such resources in SMEs. It uses as a vehicle the identification and development of an ISS in a knowledge-based SME. Systemic, knowledge-based resources are likely to be the prime competitive tools of this type of firm. The use of core competencies or capabilities, a key aspect of resources, as a basis for an ISS is contrasted with the use of a structural approach exemplified here by the value chain. This chapter has described a SISP exercise which, informed by a core competence perspective, was hampered by the lack of tools and frameworks explicitly embodying these concepts.

From an organizational learning perspective Housing consultancy's understanding of its core competencies has enabled it to recognize the core knowledge that resides within it. This understanding provides the basis for development of new competencies that will support innovation and growth in the organization. However, to reap the benefits of any potential change it is important to consider the need for business process change. The next chapter explores business process re-engineering within the SME context.

15 Exploring business process re-engineering in SMEs

▓ Introduction

Business process re-engineering (BPR) is recognized as a means of either improving efficiency or of enabling full value-added changes to be achieved in firms (Chapter 11). The main focus of BPR is on process change to improve customer value. This chapter explores BPR concepts and issues within the small- and medium-sized enterprises context.

As discussed in Chapter 11, competition and globalization have led to enterprises restructuring and focusing on managing change more effectively. Business process re-engineering is advocated as the main approach to business transformation. Enabled by information technology and emphasizing a customer-driven, process-oriented management practice, BPR has delivered to some large firms great business gains in quality, cost, speed and efficiency. Paradoxically, high failure rates of BPR projects also indicate that BPR is risky if undertaken improperly since transformation involves a complex interaction of people, IT and new skills.

The BPR literature has focused on large firms, yet small firms have attempted to re-engineer. SMEs, like larger firms, face challenges as they react to the changing environment such as the emergence of world markets and needs for better product quality, faster delivery and closer business partnerships (Mahesh and Garret, 1996). It is arguable if SMEs have more flexibility and adaptability due to their structure, ability to respond to market, and team-based nature, to enable BPR (see Chapter 4). As Hale and Cragg (1996) point out, there is a need to investigate the small firm arena to determine whether the same principles for BPR that apply to large organizations are suitable for SMEs, or if a different approach needs to be taken by small businesses looking for radical change. It is important to investigate whether SMEs can benefit dramatically, like larger firms, by undertaking BPR, or if their limited financial and human resource, information systems and technology and BPR expertise, inhibit BPR performance. However, the need is to avoid the anecdotal or descriptive nature of much BPR research and to take a holistic view of its impacts.

This chapter uses a framework developed by Chang and Powell to explore BPR in SMEs. The chapter then considers a case analysis of eight Taiwanese SMEs and investigates their responses to BPR. The inclusion of Taiwanese SMEs provides a useful counterpoint to the predominately UK-oriented cases that have been explored so far in this text. As will be demonstrated, while some of the context is different for the firms analysed in this chapter, many of the issues resonate with the experiences of the UK case SMEs.

■ Nature of BPR

Business process re-engineering is *"the fundamental re-thinking and radical redesign of business processes to achieve dramatic improvements on critical measures of performance"* (Hammer, 1990). This definition implies a discontinuity in the performance of an organization and implies that *"incremental changes are no longer enough"* and that *"transformation cannot be achieved without fundamental change"* (Coulson–Thomas, 1992). However, a radical strategy such as "starting over" is not necessarily essential because *"if a company is in business today, it must already offer some kind of value to its customers"* (Manganelli, 1995). Indeed, *"starting with a clean sheet of paper results in abolishing existing systems, skills and structures which can lead to expensive rebuilding efforts"* (Jennings, 1996). Davenport (1993) suggests process innovation and sees re-engineering as a strategy for change that must carefully consider complex implementation issues involving understanding the workforce, technology and culture. While many argue that BPR is not new, it is the integration of process, IT and business transformation that differentiates BPR from past initiatives (Earl, 1989).

As outlined in Chapter 11, business process redesign can be approached from two directions. First, it can be used to improve operational efficiency within the firms existing boundaries, which is often a consequence of reviewing processes as a result of internal IT integration. Operational innovation, new approaches to work, is seen to bring strategic, market and operational benefits. These changes are emergent, identified through an open organizational culture that values change and innovation (Hammer, 2004). Second, the firm can enhance capabilities by reviewing external relationships and repositioning itself within the business network (Venkatraman, 1994). It was argued in Chapter 11 that SMEs in the repositioning scenario of the focus-dominance model take this route.

The main elements of BPR are characterized as fundamental work process redesign, adding value to final customers, the integration of cross-functional specialization and exploitation of IT (Figure 15.1).

As Figure 15.1 demonstrates, re-engineering focuses on *customers*, emphasizing "value-addedness" from their perspective as the key to

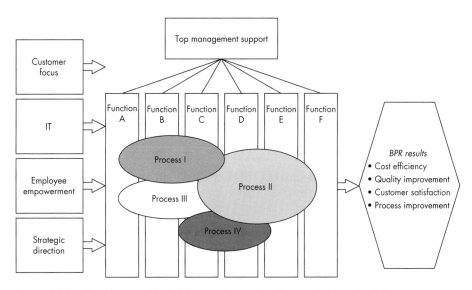

Figure 15.1: Main elements of BPR. (*Source*: adapted from Chang and Powell, 1998.)

competitiveness (Talwar, 1993). As Skrovan (1995) puts it, "improvements in execution must start by clearly focusing on the consumer value chain. Changes must add significant value from the consumer's perspective in order to deliver any meaningful increases on the top line".

Business process re-engineering focuses on *process*, defined as "set of logically related tasks performed to achieve a defined business outcome" (Davenport and Short, 1990). Entailing both physical and informational aspects, BPR involves functional integration. Stewart (1993) indicates that process management differs from function management in three ways: it focuses on external customers; employees with different skills are grouped together to accomplish a complete set of work (process); and information moves to where it is needed without passing through the management hierarchy.

Increasingly, there is emphasis on IT to integrate re-engineered processes. Firms can approach process redesign from two different perspectives – "seek efficiency" (localized exploitation and internal integration) and "enhance capabilities" (business network redesign and business scope redefinition) (Venkatraman, 1994). Correspondingly, IT's role has evolved from operative efficiency to become an *enabler* in creating and maintaining flexible business networks (Tinnila, 1995). Thus, IT infrastructure can be a *facilitator* as well as an *inhibitor* in re-engineering (Zairi and Sinclair, 1995). IT can be used to "hasten" work rather than to "transform" it.

Re-engineering also places a major emphasis on employees and their role in resolving problems. While IT is central in BPR initiatives (Flynn, 1992), most researchers agree that process improvement involves changes to jobs and the social structure to increase motivation, reduce stress and improve performance by empowerment (Wastell *et al.*, 1994).

Commitment from top management is regarded as important for re-engineering (Barrett, 1994). This encompasses both participation and involvement, and is strongly associated with technical innovations (Jarvenpaa and Ives, 1991). Vision and perspective from executives are needed to keep the re-engineering initiative on track. It is their time and energy that keep BPR efforts moving (Holland *et al.*, 1995).

The traditional approach to BPR suggests that a strategic approach and the development of a BPR strategy is key (Talwar, 1993). Critical inputs from both corporate and IT planning should be incorporated in BPR planning (Teng *et al.*, 1994). However, there are dangers with this approach as there is an assumption that once there is a fit between strategy and organizational structure, alignment of process, people and IT will necessarily follow. However, as BPR involves changing the firm's competences, it is more likely to be successful if it is emergent, benefiting from organizational learning (Craig and Yetton, 1997).

■ BPR framework for SMEs

Chang and Powell (1998) suggest a framework that can be used to consider BPR in SMEs. They draw on the BPR literature and consider the issues in relation to the management issues that affect SMEs in developing the framework (Figure 15.2). This section elaborates on the components of this framework.

Culture

Business process re-engineering does not work without profound cultural change: "a cultural transition is needed to move from traditional command and control mentality to a style that features leadership, teamwork, empowerment, entrepreneurship and risk taking" (Tersine *et al.*, 1997). As discussed in Chapter 9, the majority of SME strategies tend to gradual incremental change, rather than radical innovation. The risk-taking attitude to radical change, however, is related to the owner-managers' personality and the organizational climate. In addition, a lack of management at many small companies often allows employees to make decisions for themselves (Brady and Voss, 1995). This affords a fast response to internal problem solving and provides ability to reorganize rapidly to adapt to change in the external environment (Goss, 1991). However, decision-making in SMEs is often dominated by the CEO, which may hinder top-down communication, while making it easier to implement forced change (Chapter 2).

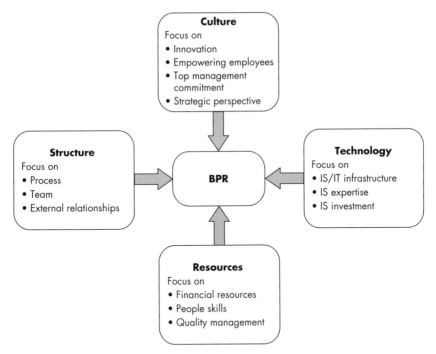

Figure 15.2: BPR framework for SMEs. (*Source*: adapted from Chang and Powell, 1998.)

As shown in Chapter 2, innovation is one of the cornerstones of SME growth. SMEs are often perceived as more fertile than larger firms in terms of innovation (Carrier, 1995). There is scant evidence of strategic thinking in SMEs. Survival is the main strategic objective for most firms (Chapters 2 and 9). The lack of strategic business planning in SMEs, as Clayton (1996) points out, leads to outdated management practices and an autocratic style of management.

Structure

Business process re-engineering emphasizes horizontal integration that involves cross-organizational boundaries – the analysis and design of workflows, and processes within and between organizations (Davenport, 1993). As discussed in Chapter 2, management structures of small firms tend to be relatively flat and middle management plays a minimal role. Thus, they do not suffer from bureaucracy and cumbersome organizational systems. This organizational flexibility should lead to a greater ability to respond to change within the market. However, as discussed in Chapter 4, SMEs are often reluctant to adapt their structure, until growth makes it imperative to change. Small businesses also encourage team and cross-functional orientations – it is suggested that every small business starts as an empowered team (Kinni, 1995). The lack of bureaucracy makes for efficient and informal internal communication networks. SMEs are considered adaptable, able to respond readily to changing customers' needs. Further, the owners have deep knowledge of their business and the firm's capabilities. Due to the lack of management layers, small businesses are closer to their customers (Brady and Voss, 1995). However, there is considerable dependency upon maintaining the contracts with large corporations (the "hollow factory" concept).

Resources

Businesses are trying to do more with less and so they have re-engineered corporate resources (or eliminated them) in order to reduce operating costs (Witherill and Kolak, 1996). They declare that financial resources are already limited in SMEs and thus SMEs' management of cash is more efficient and flexible than large business. However, *"restricted access to finance is potentially a significant constraint on the growth of small businesses"* (Binks *et al.*, 1996). Two of the most serious problems SMEs may face when trying to implement quality management are the owner/manager's lack of business experience and knowledge, and the shortage of financial and human resources required (Haksever, 1996). Thus, while survival is the first concern in SMEs, financial insufficiency or constraints may significantly inhibit SMEs undertaking BPR. Almost 60% of owner-managed businesses fail due to the owner's lack of appropriate management experience (Nash and Rock, 1996). Owners of small firms caught up in day-to-day operations often lack perspective on the kinds of problems that can threaten the business (Woods, 1996). SMEs are at a greater disadvantage than larger firms because they typically have few in-house technical experts to deal with new developments (Ferrell, 1996).

IS and IT

Information technology infrastructure can be a significant enabler or barrier on the practical options available to planning and changing processes for BPR (Grover *et al.*, 1993). However, most re-engineering efforts are technology driven, with the role of IT changing from producing data to integrating new ITs and assisting people to become independent information gatherers (Ribbler, 1996). However, SMEs are not likely to employ IT staff and the general level of IS skills within the firm is likely to be limited. Additionally, IS investment is often seen as a necessary evil which leads to a reluctance to invest.

This analysis suggests consideration of the following questions in relation to SMEs and BPR:

■ Why and when do SMEs undertake BPR?

■ What are the benefits, if any of BPR for SMEs?

■ What are the enabling and inhibiting factors for SMEs of success in BPR?

■ Research background

Chang (2001) undertook case studies of eight Taiwanese SMEs that had undertaken BPR. Three of the firms are small with fewer than 50 employees and five are medium-sized firms with 50–500 employees. The data was gathered through semi-structured interviews with the CEO and management team from each SME. In order to attempt to mitigate contextual biases, the cases include four SMEs operating in manufacturing and four in the service sector. SMEs' perceived BPR satisfaction is a surrogate for BPR success or failure. For each sector, two successful and two failure cases are selected. This enables a comparison to be made, and the success and failure factors discussed. The characteristics of the SMEs are shown in Table 15.1.

In Taiwan, SMEs constitute 95% of total enterprises in some sectors (Lee and Chen, 1992). Between 1972 and 1989, the average cash turnover of SMEs in Taiwan was 25 compared to 16 of large business (Lee and Ho, 1992) indicating that SMEs' management of cash is more efficient than large business. Due to insufficient capability to secure market information, most SMEs attempt to join in formal sub-contracting or "sourcing systems" to ensure stable orders. Taiwanese SMEs, as in the rest of the world, are confronting dramatic changes in the general environment. Export-oriented SMEs are restricted to labour-intensive and mature-technology industries that restrain them from upgrading their technology, enlarging their scale of operations and promoting their marketing (Wu and Chou, 1992). Severe labour shortages and the rapidly rising wage rates have further made SMEs lose competitiveness. Financial problems have been a major obstacle for SMEs to develop. Macro-environmental transition and changes have forced SMEs to investigate their internal operations and management. Accordingly, new approaches to efficient operations and effective management, such as BPR, have become popular.

Most of the SMEs are seeking to grow by business expansion, for example, Telecoms Supplier is enlarging its sales division to target more market segments and product diversification, while Supersonic Machinery is developing technology to manufacture semiconductors. In contrast, Automatic Assembling and Freight Shipping tend to have steady orders and loyal clients. The business strategies are reflected in the firms' risk-taking attitudes and market competition. Five of the firms are in intensely competitive markets. For example, Telecoms Supplier competes with over 400 firms that sell telecommunication devices, while Financial Institution is protected by the government, and Shoe Trading are content with their current business performance and focus their BPR on functional integration and internal efficiency. Automatic Assembling and Shoe Trading are sub-contractors. This secures regular orders but they have no power to influence market prices. A common feature of the eight SMEs is

Table 15.1: Characteristics of BPR case firms

Cases	Number of employees	BPR outcome	Industry	Strategy	Market	Sub-contractor
Automatic Assembling	10	Success	Manufacturing	Market segmentation	Steady	Yes
Supersonic Machinery	40	Success	Manufacturing	Diversification	Growing	Yes
Geodetic Surveying	15	Success	Service	Expansion	Steady	No
Freight Shipping	150	Success	Service	Market penetration	Competitive	No
Shoes Trading	100	Failure	Manufacturing	Market penetration	Growing	Yes
Telecoms Supplier	300	Failure	Manufacturing	Expansion	Competitive	No
Financial Institution	200	Failure	Service	Market development	Steady	No
Retail Grocer	200	Failure	Service	Product development	Competitive	No

Table 15.2: The purpose of BPR in case firms

Purpose of BPR	Case firms	Number
Process improvement	All firms	8
Cost reduction	Telecoms Supplier	3
	Retail Grocer	
	Shoe Trading	
Customer satisfaction	Supersonic Machinery	4
	Automatic Assembling	
	Freight Shipping	
	Financial Institution	
Quality	Geodetic Survey	3
	Freight Shipping	
	Financial Institution	

that their purpose in adopting BPR is derived from a desire either to improve efficiency or to enhance capacities, rather than from a "crisis situation" (Kinni, 1995). The reasons given for undertaking BPR vary between the firms, but mainly focus on process improvements (Table 15.2).

Case analysis

The main findings from the cases are organized around the four classifications: structure, culture, resources and technology presented in the Chang and Powell model. The cases enable a modification of the framework and an investigation of the success factors that influence BPR performance in SMEs.

Culture

SMEs with ambitious business strategies and less risk-averse attitudes are more likely to benefit from undertaking BPR. Such firms, for example, Geodetic Surveying and Supersonic Machinery do not confine their re-engineering to functional areas but extend it to include the entire business network. The cases reaffirm that while SMEs are growing, either through business expansion or product diversification, it is more likely that a radical re-engineering approach will be adopted. The findings also support the notion that when owner-managers adopt highly centralizing, autocratic stances, it is difficult to produce a conducive environment in which to re-engineer (Hirschfield, 1994).

Innovation

Innovation is positively related to IT tools and IT performance, in particular when firms are expanding. Rapid growth leads to product innovation taking precedence over process innovation. Since the rapid growth case firms, in particular, are technology oriented, use of the latest IT tools and applications in support of product innovation is common.

Consistent with the assertion that innovation is fostered in decentralized, highly integrated, informal organizations (Teng *et al.*, 1994; Wind and West, 1991), the cases suggest that innovation is positively correlated with a team-based orientation. For example, Retail Grocer encouraged "unconventional ideas" among project members when creating the firm's new image.

The cases also reveal that a positive attitude to risk may lead to increased BPR satisfaction. This is demonstrated in the cases by the willingness to make radical change, which is largely dependent upon the owner-managers' perceived benefits and related to the current growth strategy. For example, Telecoms Supplier is engaged in large-scale functional integration as part of their expansion strategy in a belief that simpler business processes will benefit the firm and its distributors. Similarly, Supersonic Machinery recognizes a need to re-engineer its R&D in order to use its expertise to manufacture semiconductors.

Empowering employees

The cases support the notion that employee empowerment and top management commitment are critical elements of successful BPR (Janz *et al.*, 1997; Janson, 1993; Hammer, 1990). Higher employee autonomy is more likely to occur in decentralized SMEs, such as Automatic Assembling and Supersonic Machinery. These firms demonstrate that small businesses operate as an empowered team (Kinni, 1995) where knowledge workers are greatly involved in decision-making and product discussion.

Top management commitment

Management support, coupled with good top-down communication, is considered by all the SMEs as the most critical factor in BPR success (Janson, 1993; Stevenson, 1993). Direct involvement appears to be an effective approach, given the owner-managers' knowledge of the business. For example, the owner of Freight Shipping has been in the business for over 10 years, and oversees several functions such as personnel, sales and finance. In Automatic Assembling, the owner was enthusiastically involved in developing the integrated ordering system, and at Geodetic Surveying the owner-manager took charge of establishing the link to its clients using IT. These owner-managers are familiar with both the business and the technology, thus they are capable of leading BPR and conducting process change. However, due to a lack of management support, Telecoms Supplier has experienced difficulties in obtaining sufficient financial backup and launching a process change programme as part of the strategy.

All but one of the BPR initiatives in the SME cases are CEO-led. Direct involvement by owner-managers may increase the chances of successful

BPR. This is illustrated in Geodetic Surveying where the owner participated in building its business network with clients. Having been in the business for over 10 years, he has established a good relationship with several clients. Similarly, Automatic Assembling represents a case of applying a "top-down" approach to BPR. The owner-manager oversees several functions – personnel, finance and accounting. Led by the owner, the firm's re-engineering project integrating several functions encountered few difficulties. Such direct involvement tends to occur in smaller firms where the structures are less formal and communication lines shorter.

Only Telecoms Supplier indicated that the ideas of process change, such as streamlining workflow and office work, and eliminating non value-adding activities derived from departmental managers. In keeping with the survey, the R&D director from Telecoms Supplier commented that functional managers have a better understanding of processes and adequate knowledge of process improvement. However, he questioned the owner's commitment. A lack of a commitment from top management is an important failure factor for most firms. Many authors have stressed the importance of obtaining management support (Drucker, 1996; Stoddard *et al.*, 1996; Stevenson, 1993). The cases investigate the extent to which the owner-managers' attitudes and perceived benefits of BPR affect how re-engineering is implemented. In most of the case SMEs consider commitment from senior management to be very important. A lack of top-down communication and an autocratic management style can significantly affect the outcomes.

Strategic perspective

Strategic thinking and planning is usually limited in SMEs. However, five case firms are re-engineering their core processes, which suggests some recognition of the need for strategic thinking. For example, Geodetic Surveying's firm–client interface is largely involved with customer services and product development. Automatic Assembling's integrated IS comprise three major processes: ordering, client/supplier database and manufacturing. However, long-term planning is required to ensure that business gains from re-engineering can be sustained. For example, Retailer Grocer soon lost competitive advantage due to a lack of long-term business planning, a focus on short-term pay-off and a failure to implement process change on a continuous basis.

The cases provide a clear indication that re-engineering firms' core processes and transforming key processes into strategic capabilities increases the chances of BPR success, supporting Wastell *et al.* (1994), who argue that BPR initiatives should take place within a strategic business context. Geodetic Surveying's customer system and Automatic Manufacturing's combination of ordering system and client/supplier's databases are examples of this. The main processes considered for re-engineering are shown in Table 15.3.

Table 15.3: Processes to be re-engineered

Case	Targeted business processes to be re-engineered
Geodetic Surveying	Firm–client link for technical support and information sharing
Supersonic Machinery	Integration of R&D, product development and sales
Telecoms Supplier	Office workflow and management hierarchy
Retail Grocer	Integration of design, planning and marketing departments
Automatic Assembling	Integration of ordering, product line and supplier/client databases
Freight Shipping	Integration of R&D and IT departments and firm–client link
Financial Institution	Online Internet banking system
Shoe Trading	Integration of design and sales divisions

There is a high degree of agreement on the alignment of BPR strategy and business direction. The lack of a strategic vision as guidance of BPR implementation made Retail Grocer realize that their BPR interventions were based on intuition not analysis and could not be justified financially. Limited results from BPR are also experienced by Shoe Trading, whose main focus was on process improvement. They put this down to their lack of competitive power due to their position as a sub-contractor. Most of the unsuccessful cases demonstrate a lack of managerial knowledge and strategic vision. Little consideration is given to what customers really need and want. For example, Telecoms Supplier has focused on expanding its distribution channels and improving efficiency of its sales network while paying little attention to the competition and the latest products it sells. Retail Grocer is engaged in establishing its reputation and business image while ignoring quality issues. Similarly, Financial Institution launched its Internet banking without considering possible resistance from its clients due to security concerns. The IT department at Telecoms Supplier is building a web site that features a wide range of products as part of their re-engineering. A similar situation exists in Financial Institution. The online banking system was created by an external IT support firm without careful planning and management backup.

Structure

Sia and Neo (1996) assert that re-engineering may lead to flatter and leaner structures, while the cases reveal that the formal and hierarchical structure found in some SMEs, such as the Telecoms Supplier, can impede successful implementation of BPR.

Process

The cases suggest that a more formal and hierarchical structure may inhibit BPR. This occurs in larger firms, such as Telecoms Supplier, that indicate that a major purpose of their BPR is to de-emphasize divisions of labour to streamline processes and reduce administrative costs. BPR is seen to be overwhelmingly top-down, being led by the CEO. Telecoms Supplier is the only case of re-engineering launched by functional managers but without top management support.

Teams

Team-based operations bring greater involvement and motivation. In keeping with Stanworth and Curran (1973) and Frohman (1996), the cases reveal that this depends largely upon whether owner-managers are willing to relinquish control. At Automatic Assembling a senior technician describes their environment as "like a family", while in Shoe Trading, the owner is seen as a "dominant boss". The owner's style is an important determinant of team efficiency.

Team-based operations are more likely to occur in smaller businesses, for example, Automatic Assembling and Geodetic Surveying, due to their decentralized structure and shorter lines of communication. While the literature suggests that cross-functional teams ensure that the process is viewed and understood comprehensively (Sellers, 1997), in SMEs, a major benefit from team-based operations is to bring greater involvement, increased motivation and communication, and enhanced job performance.

External relationships

Good relations with their customers and other firms for support and information sharing is a major benefit. This aids SMEs in gaining access to benchmarking and networking. External relations can be reinterpreted from two perspectives. First, as SMEs normally operate in only a few markets, social ties and their relationships with suppliers are important. The owner-managers of Geodetic Surveying, Automatic Assembling and Shoe Trading claim to have a steady market share, and loyal customers. They have been in the business for a long time during which they have developed a distribution network that is attributed to relations with suppliers and retailers.

Second, many of SMEs are sub-contracted to larger firms and in some cases SMEs are themselves sub-contractors that farm out jobs to satellite manufacturers. Thus, the relationships of SMEs and their sub-contractors become quite sophisticated. For example, the focus of Shoe Trading's BPR was to improve communication with its 150 contracted manufacturers while building up relationships with foreign clients to secure regular orders. Automatic Assembling is sub-contracted to several major clients while at the same time acting as a sub-contractor for about 50 satellite manufacturers. As their products are highly technology-oriented, the firm has to ensure the accuracy of the materials provided by its suppliers. Thus, their re-engineering project intended to deal with the complexity of business processes by integrating its ordering system, production line and supplier/clients databases.

Brady and Voss (1995) suggest that SMEs are close to their customers. This is not so for the case firms as the majority operate internationally. For example, Supersonic Machinery's sales reach several countries in south-east Asia. The major clients of the Shoe Trading are American and Australian.

Cross-functional integration can be expanded to inter-organizational co-operation (Davidow and MaLone, 1992). Chapter 11 suggests that relatively few SMEs are involved in such a level of business network redesign, although collaboration among SMEs, such as partnership and cross-border alliances, is more common (Bonk, 1996; Rosenfeld, 1996). Geodetic Surveying built up an integrated IS with a customer interface to link its major clients. This enables mutual information sharing and facilitates online inquiries. The firm also provides its clients with technical support and the latest information about surveying tools. The owner is conscious of the advances of IT and offers employees, most of whom specialize in surveying, opportunities for further training to ensure they are familiar with the systems. Their clients, mainly civil engineers, have similar IT infrastructure. Otherwise, the costs for establishing such a network would be prohibitive.

The cases reinforce the view that strategic behaviour is the main reason for building relations. Geodetic Surveying's client-oriented interface and Automatic Assembling's integrated ordering system are both highly related to the firms' core processes. The social ties evident in the sub-contracting relationship supports the literature that they are one of the factors that explain SMEs' network structure (Baker, 1990; Holt, 1987; Mitchell, 1973).

Resources

Most of the cases indicates that BPR is a reflection of a current strategy to reduce operating costs. This is especially so when SMEs hope to grow (Binks et al., 1996). Restricted finance, as illustrated by Retail Grocer, poses a significant constraint.

Financial resources

The cases concur that a lack of capital poses a constraint on SMEs for BPR. Financial deficiency restricted Shoe Trading and Retail Grocer from advanced use of IT for functional integration and inter-organizational linkage. Larger SMEs are more likely to establish a budget for consulting, while Financial Institution provides an example of relying too much on external support and losing control. In other cases, the financial issues centre on IT investment since most of the firms are technology-oriented and functional or firm-wide integration largely involves IT. In this regard, the cases suggest that the extent to which SMEs spend on IT for BPR depends on the owner-manager's perceived benefits to individuals and the firm (Cragg and King, 1993). For example, the use of IT for BPR at Geodetic Surveying results from the owner's awareness of technological advances. A large investment in IT has been made so as to serve clients better.

People skills

Most of the SMEs are technology-oriented and employ skilled staff. The main focus of staff is towards product innovation. In most of the cases, the organization structure is sufficiently flexible to promote innovation.

As discussed above and in earlier chapters, SMEs' managerial skills are often limited. Therefore, management may not be able to provide support when radical process change is undertaken. For example, Shoe Trading has difficulties in retaining its talented designers after radical process change. However, the potential of IT use may be restricted by poor IT capabilities.

Quality management

Quality is seen by the case firms as providing excellent service to customers. Quality management is recognized by the firms as important in achieving this. The literature argues that quality management techniques help to sustain and build on the improvements gained through successful re-engineering (Davenport, 1993; Niven, 1993; Knorr, 1991). However, BPR needs to be strategically driven (Guha *et al.*, 1993; Talwar, 1993) and requires a plan to ensure that changes will be consistent with the business goals (Hale and Cragg, 1996). The lack of strategic direction in most of the case firms limits the benefits from quality initiatives. Retail Grocer had difficulty in sustaining their initial benefits from re-engineering and failed to deliver "core value" to their customers due largely to a lack of strategic vision and long-term business plans. Similarly, the absence of a BPR plan rendered Shoe Trading unable to deal with the consequences of radical process change. A major problem was its inability to retain the firm's main designers, since it could not provide sufficient support for them and establish a proper reward system to deal with workload problems.

Technology

Innovation is mostly likely to occur in the SMEs that are currently growing. Innovation tends to be interpreted as using IT for "product innovation". In growth conditions, IT is most likely to be applied to product development, usually coupled with R&D functions. Innovation achievement is best when there are both sufficient IT tools and good IT performance. Additionally, innovation in SMEs is significantly related to team-based operations and efficiency.

IS/IT infrastructure

The potential of IT as an important supporting role in eliminating time and distance, and integrating functional units is demonstrated in the cases.

The Internet, particularly e-mail, is extensively used for linking firms with customers, suppliers and others. Automatic Assembling combined three major functions: the ordering system, clients and supplier databases, and production lines. This was achieved by using several IT tools such as spreadsheets and workflow software. The firm feels they have increased speed and flexibility in customized production and improved customer satisfaction. Information technology helped create an efficient communication network with customers and satellite manufacturers.

The case firms appear to use IT widely for process integration and product innovation. However, many of these provide technology-related products or services. The extensive use of IT applications, such as spreadsheets, databases and document imaging for inter-organizational linkage is evident. However, the application of workflow and knowledge software to "process innovation" is comparatively rare. This contradicts the suggestion that BPR is exclusively driven by IT (Venkatraman, 1994; Gant, 1992; Alter, 1990). Rather, IT plays an important supportive role as a tool in eliminating time and distance for process integration (Carr and Johansson, 1995; Talwar, 1994). However, a lack of IT tools, as in Financial Institution and Shoe Trading, is an inhibitor to functional integration. In regard to inter-organizational linkage, Geodetic Surveying provides an example of successfully establishing an integrated system between the firm and its clients for mutual support and information sharing, while the non-standardized IT platforms between Supersonic Machinery and its 200 contracted satellite firms demonstrates an obstacle to successful implementation.

Adequate end-user training and alignment of IS/IT strategy with business strategy appear to be key factors in the use of IS to facilitate BPR in SMEs. Existing IT infrastructure can be a significant barrier, limiting the practical options available for planning and changing processes in BPR (Grover *et al.*, 1993). In the case of SMEs, this usually refers to poor end-user skills, and a lack of funds. With few in-house technical experts, Financial Institution relied heavily on vendor support resulting in a loss of strategic control. Lack of finance inhibited Shoe Trading from advanced use of IT to support their re-engineering.

IS expertise

Business process re-engineering is a management issue where re-engineering solutions involve more organizational and cultural elements (Wastell *et al.*, 1994). The cases support this and reveal that process change, either functional integration or inter-organizational co-operation, must be accompanied by end-user training. SMEs typically have fewer in-house technical experts to deal with new developments (Ferrell, 1996). Financial Institution sought assistance from consultants due to a lack of IT skills, while relying too much on external IT vendors resulted in a loss of control.

IS investment

Financial constraints may significantly inhibit firms from investing in IT, as in Retail Grocer. The cases reinforce the view that IT investment should be aligned with firm's strategic IT planning and business strategy. For example, the investment in IT for the Internet banking system at Financial Institution based on a suggestion from IT consultants rather than firm's planning, only to reveal that the time and costs could not be justified. Similarly, Shoe Trading's re-engineering efforts were doomed as the purchase of IT tools was merely for integrating some "supporting processes" that yielded little value to customers.

Success and failure factors for case firms

The major BPR success and failure factors demonstrated from the cases are summarized in Table 15.4.

BPR as an ongoing effort towards a learning organization

The principles of BPR emphasize horizontal integration across functions (Davenport, 1993; Harrington, 1991; Hammer, 1990). The cases support this and demonstrate a potential for SMEs to expand from functional integration to inter-organizational co-operation, which Venkatraman (1994) refers to as "business network redesign". As the owner of the Geodetic Surveying and the general manager from Supersonic Machinery admit, this is dependent upon their IT infrastructure. Five case firms focus their re-engineering on operational processes, implying that they are re-engineering core processes that deliver value to customers (Champy, 1995; Johansson *et al.*, 1993; Meyer, 1993; Rockart, 1988).

Among the eight firms interviewed, only Financial Institution formally sought advice from external IT professionals and consultants, although a lack of strategic control made the firm unable to align the BPR and corporate strategy.

Business process re-engineering needs to be strategically driven (Guha *et al.*, 1993; Talwar, 1993) and requires a plan to ensure that changes will be consistent with the business goals (Hale and Cragg, 1996). Retail Grocer had difficulty in sustaining their initial benefits from re-engineering and failed to deliver "core value" to their customers due largely to a lack of strategic vision and long-term business plans. Similarly, the absence of a BPR plan rendered Shoe Trading unable to deal with the consequences of radical process change. A major problem was its inability to retain the firm's main designers, since it could not provide sufficient support for them and establish a proper reward system to deal with workload problems.

Retail Grocer is an example of failure to implement BPR on a continuous basis. They redefined their business with a view to gaining dramatic results. They invested in marketing and refurbishing the shop. Although the owner is open to ideas, he is the dominant decision-maker.

Table 15.4: Success and failure factors for BPR

Classifications	Elements	Success factors	Failure factors
Culture	Innovation	• Product innovation (Supersonic Machinery) • Innovative environment (Retail Grocer)	• Autocratic management style (Financial Institution; Shoe Trading)
	Empowering employees	• High employee autonomy (Geodetic Surveying; Supersonic Machinery; Automatic Assembling)	• Lack of management support (Telecoms Suppliers)
	Top management commitment	• Top-down approach (all cases expect Telecoms Supplier) • Direct involvement (Geodetic Surveying; Supersonic Machinery; Automatic Assembling) • Good top-down communication (Automatic Assembling)	• Poor top-down communication (Retail Grocer; Financial Institution; Shoe Trading)
	Strategic perspective	• Strategic thinking and customer focus (Geodetic Surveying; Supersonic Machinery)	• Lack of strategic vision (Financial Institution; Telecoms Supplier; Retail Grocer)
Structure	Process Teams	• Teamwork efficiency (Automatic Assembling; Geodetic Surveying)	• Formal hierarchical structure (Telecoms Supplier)
	External relations	• Good relations with customers and suppliers (Supersonic Machinery) • Good relation with suppliers (Automatic Assembling) • Good relation with customers (Freight Shipping; Shoe Trading)	
Resources	Finance		• Lack of funds (Retail Grocer)
	People skills	• Knowledge workers (Geodetic Surveying; Supersonic Machinery; Automatic Assembling)	• Lack of managerial skills (Telecoms Supplier; Retail Grocer; Financial Institution)
	Quality management	• Integrating total quality management (TQM) and BPR within the strategic context (Geodetic Surveying; Supersonic Machinery) • Organizational learning (Automatic Assembling)	• Lack of long-term business plans (Retail Grocer; Shoe Trading)
Technology	IS/IT infrastructure	• Applying IT to core processes (Freight Shipping; Automatic Assembling) • Inter-organizational co-operation (Geodetic Surveying)	• Lack of IT tools (Shoe Trading)
	IS expertise	• Skill Training (Geodetic Surveying)	• Lack of IT expertise (Financial Institution; Shoe Trading)
	IS investment	• High IT spending (Geodetic Surveying)	• Lack of funds for IT investment (Retail Grocer)

A question of how SMEs can sustain the benefits of process redesign and learn from experiences emerges, since most SMEs have limited financial and human resources (Binks *et al.*, 1996). Some technology-oriented SMEs, for example, Geodetic Surveying and the Supersonic Machinery claim regularly to attend seminars provided by government and universities. Automatic Assembling provides an example of empowering employees to create an environment of "ownership" and offers training so that technological and managerial skills can be transformed into "knowledge" and accumulated within the firm.

A holistic view of strategic BPR planning recognizes that the factors that result in a desire for process re-engineering manifest themselves internally and externally. External factors may include customer needs, market trends and competition, technological opportunities, and the relations with suppliers, sub-contractors or other SMEs. The owner-managers have to decide how radical their re-engineering efforts will be and the level of functional or inter-organizational integration. The study reveals that SMEs are at the disadvantage of less strategic thinking, while the strong social ties and sound relations with customers, suppliers and other firms (Holt, 1987; Mitchell, 1973) imply a potential for SMEs to attain more integration along the process improvement continuum. This can be facilitated by the use of technology and telecommunications. Internal factors concern resources, including financial and human capacities. A review of firm's strengths and weaknesses enables the CEO to determine the core competencies and select the major processes to re-engineer. The need of a fundamental process change, though, is dependent upon the owner-managers' risk attitudes and perceived benefits from BPR.

■ Implications for management

Once the targeted processes have been chosen, SMEs need to examine whether they are culturally and structurally ready for re-engineering. Specifically, re-engineering requires a strong commitment from owner-managers since they play a decisive role in determining strategic direction. Full support from employees cannot be neglected. Change issues, such as resistance and lack of required skills, may arise and need to be tackled at two levels: organizational and technological. Employees have to be motivated and empowered in order to increase top-down communications and responsiveness to customers. Training is an effective approach to enhancing managerial knowledge as well as inter-functional work skills. The role of the IS function has to be repositioned to facilitate BPR by investing in IT tools and provide required end-user skills. Change has to be managed as a strategic project. This is to ensure that re-engineering efforts are implemented as planned and assessed by new performance standards and targets. Conducting pilots and measuring results regularly may significantly increase efficiency. While lack of a project team is ranked as a major factor in BPR failure, the survey reveals that, however, forming a project team for some SMEs may not be necessary nor financially feasible. Due to the team-based nature of small firms, the majority of re-engineering initiatives are led by owner-managers. This acknowledges the importance of top management support at all stages from BPR planning to evaluation.

Despite much debate on whether IT is a necessity for BPR, this research shows the powerful potential of IT in re-engineering. The role of IS/IT has evolved from automating existing outdated processes to providing firms with an array of opportunities by shortening communication lines and eliminating space and time. This is achieved, in essence, by the innovative use of IT. Firms' IT capacities are significantly correlated with innovation in BPR SMEs. However, the focus has to be on the alignment of IT strategy and BPR strategy derived from a strategic vision. This is to ensure that the investment on IT and any required end-user training can be evaluated by internal and external customers, or "process outputs," rather than by functional performance or cost savings. Given the often limited financial and human resources in SMEs, the knowledge and experiences accumulated from the innovative use of IT and the efforts of R&D provide a valuable basis for continuous process improvement towards a learning organization.

■ Implications for research

Business process re-engineering was introduced as requiring top management support, customer focus, IT, employee empowerment and strategic direction for it to be successful. The Chang and Powell framework (Figure 15.2) is used as a basis to consider whether these issues are valid in the SME context. The cases demonstrate that the main issues for success in BPR for SMEs are the strategic direction of the firm, top management commitment and external relations with customers.

Where top management commitment extends to empowering employees, this is likely to lead to success. In the cultural context, the cases suggest that those SME with a positive attitude to risk are more likely to benefit from BPR. While a more ambitious business strategy usually refers to large-scale functional integration that may involve downsizing, adopting a radical approach as recommended by many BPR proponents (e.g. Johansson et al., 1993; Kaplan and Murdock, 1991) is not evident in the cases. Thus, SMEs tend to engage in more incremental process change methods to cope with reality. However, a strong commitment from the top management is essential. In keeping with Tushman et al. (1986), the cases indicate that direct involvement is strongly related to strategic control and project efficiency. Lack of owner support or an autocratic style, as in Financial Institution and Shoe

Trading, can hinder re-engineering. Employees need to be empowered and motivated in order to take greater responsibilities and adapt to new performance standards and requirements. However, the final structure factor, that of process is less relevant, possibly due to the flexibility inherent in SMEs.

IS investment is also seen as necessary to success. However, it needs to be integrated with strategic direction for success. The cases provide a clear indication that IT has powerful capacities to eliminating time and distance to help the firms to achieve functional integration and improve cross-firm linkage. Several firms, such as Supersonic Machinery and the Telecom Supplier, are applying IT largely to product innovation as they manufacture or provide technology-based products/services and, at the same time use IT to improve client and supplier relations. Geodetic Surveying provides an example of expanding IT use to establish a firm–client interface for mutual support and information sharing, although the successful implementation of such system is largely due to the similar IT infrastructure between them and their clients. For either functional linkage or inter-organizational co-operation, firms need to have sufficient funds for IT investment and provide training to ensure that employees are capable of new tasks. Apart from the integrated system at the Automatic Assembling that combines ordering system, production and client/supplier databases, the use of IT for "process innovation" is relatively rare. Information technology plays an essential supporting role in SMEs' re-engineering.

The other technology factors are less important. Financial resources are also seen to be the main constraint for SMEs. The other resource issues are not as influential on BPR in SMEs. This leads to a revised model for assessing BPR in SMEs (Figure 15.3).

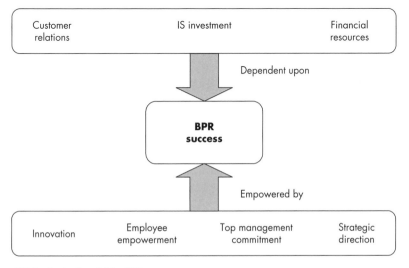

Figure 15.3: Revised model for BPR.

■ Conclusions

Business process re-engineering initiatives can be classified by two dimensions: scope and scale (Levene and Braganza, 1996). *Scope* includes the number of functions integrated to form the process (Rockart and Short, 1989). *Scale* is the extent of change in terms of how radical the BPR project is (Hagel, 1993). Davenport and Short (1990) identify types of processes as inter-personal, inter-functional and inter-organizational. Broadbent *et al.* (1994) contrast approaches to process redesign as simplification and innovation. Based on the strategic nature and radical orientation, Childe *et al.* (1994) depict a spectrum of process improvement activities, from personal/group improvement, quality improvement teams, process simplification, process re-engineering, business integration, to business re-engineering. While Craig and Yetton (1992) argue that process simplification offers firms the potential to capture some performance advantages and to minimize risk factors, higher levels of BPR, such as business integration, involve organizational and job redesign and new developments in IT. The higher levels of BPR are, in turn, viewed as more strategic and radical with the potential for substantial gains. Therefore, BPR projects in SMEs will involve lower scale and less scope, for example, individual/group improvement and process simplification, as SMEs' policies are more conservative and owners try to avoid risks.

The motivations and purposes for SMEs to re-engineer may be different from those for larger firms. In SMEs re-engineering is often a response to positive trends – they tend to re-engineer from a position of strength (Kinni, 1995). Two reasons are cited: first, small firms are already short of the time and resources needed to re-engineer and it is unlikely that a small firm that is faltering can muster the required energy; and second, the by-products of success – rapidly increasing volume, straining processes and increased profits are the impetus for small companies to re-engineer. They need to counter fast growth with processes improvement. Perry (1986) indicates that most small firms grow fastest from start-up until a "comfort" stage is reached. From an organizational life cycle perspective, firms pursuing a growth strategy tend to re-engineer in order to enhance their external flexibility, that is relations with customers and suppliers, and internal efficiency, that is quality and production (Dodge and Robbins, 1992).

Part 5   Future: Internet adoption and strategy

Part 5 explores e-business opportunities for small- and medium-sized enterprises. Internet technologies are changing approaches to business in the market. Supply chain relationships are changing as firms develop e-business systems that reduce transaction costs. Not only are existing firms exploring business opportunities from the use of Internet technologies, but entrepreneurial opportunities are being identified directly because of these technologies. Since the comet-like performance of dot.com firms, more thought has been put into developing serious business propositions that utilize fully Internet technologies rather than firm existence simply due to the technologies. The development of e-business is dynamic and moves from simple use such as e-mail and a web presence, through to working with customers before considering full transformation of business activities. Few firms of any size in any sector have achieved such radical change.

For SMEs the Internet both looks exciting and frightening as the basic rules of business are being rewritten. While many are embracing the new technology and see it as a means of repositioning their business, others find it has little to offer, particularly as their customers do not demand its use. SMEs have tended to adopt the simpler e-business technologies, such as e-mail and brochureware web sites, often as a result of public sector intervention. However, there are few SMEs that have moved beyond these systems to investing more fully in transactional e-business. Customer pressure tends to drive these more advanced firms. The lack of strategy may also inhibit development as e-business is most successful when integrated with strategic direction.

Chapter 16 reflects upon the value of stages models of e-business adoption for SMEs. In comparing existing research a composite model is developed. The chapter considers the different factors that are thought to influence Internet adoption decisions. These include perceived benefit, which encompasses issues, such as image and cost reduction; organizational readiness, usually personified in the owner and external pressures which are usually from customers. Case analysis suggests that steady development of e-business is unlikely to occur, instead it is found to be a function of the business value of the Internet and business growth plans.

These issues are explored in more detail in Chapter 17, which unusually for this book, draws on a survey, to understand whether strategic intent influences e-business decisions. The chapter considers whether e-business adoption is a factor of market position or product innovation. SMEs' strategic intent is explored through Ansoff's model for growing firms. This book has argued that the strategic use of information does not depend upon industry. This chapter considers whether there is any sector difference for e-business adoption. The final issues addressed here are whether the enablers and inhibitors of e-business adoption influence strategic intent and industry adoption. The evidence is mixed, although product development is found to be a key driver for e-business, rather than market development. SMEs value the opportunity to find new suppliers, while still preferring to work within markets with which they are familiar. Overall, SMEs are found to be cautious in their adoption of e-business.

Governments throughout the world believe that their economies will benefit from local firms utilizing e-business. Concern about the speed of e-business investment has led many governments to develop promotion and support schemes for firms. The SME sector is actively being supported through local schemes and agencies that provide advice and access to Internet technologies. The final chapter in this part considers the macro-economic competitiveness factors that potentially influence SMEs decisions to invest in e-business and compares them with institutional factors, such as government support. Customers are again found to be the main driver of change from a market perspective. SMEs also value local independent advice through intervention projects, while remaining unaware of national schemes.

Overall, this part shows that SMEs are cautious in their adoption of e-business. The decision to invest needs to show a clear business benefit as with all other information system investments. The supply chain and markets are not yet demanding more sophisticated systems; most SMEs are content to wait and observe what the future brings.

16 Exploring e-business in SMEs

◼ Introduction

Extant theory suggests that businesses reap the greatest benefits from the Internet by integrating business systems and by changing business processes. Indeed, such integration is the final outcome of growth models that postulate businesses move in stages from one use to another. However, there is little evidence that small- and medium-sized enterprises do more than develop web sites and adopt e-mail. In this chapter case studies of 12 SMEs are used to explore the adoption of Internet technologies. The strategic issues limiting Internet adoption are considered. A strategic model is then developed that suggests the criteria for adoption are dependent upon SME owners' attitude to growth. This leads to the development of a contingent (or "transporter") model rather than a "stages" model of Internet adoption. This research has important policy implications as, at least in the UK and in Europe, government SME e-business adoption facilitation is predicated upon an adoption "ladder". If no ladder or stages model is appropriate for SME then government encouragement to move from one level to another is misguided. The transporter model identifies four roles for Internet technologies in SMEs – brochureware, support, opportunity and network. These are driven by business growth planning and perceived Internet value.

The chapter first introduces the main issues involved in e-business from its simplest to most complex forms. The current state of knowledge concerning SMEs adoption of the Internet is then investigated. The research approach and background to the cases is then provided. This leads to consideration of competitiveness, growth, and Internet adoption in SMEs. The contingent model is developed and its implications discussed.

◼ Defining e-business

E-business has grown rapidly over the last few years. The Internet and the development of the World Wide Web have opened up the potential of the global information society. Growth is driven by accessibility of the Internet; firms using the Internet for electronic transaction; digital delivery of informational goods and services, such as, music and finally retail sale of tangible goods (Currie, 2000). E-business is seen as a

Table 16.1: E-business stages models

Costello and Tuchen (1997)	Currie (2000)	Willcocks and Sauer (2000)	Teo and Pian (2003)
			Level 0: E-mail adoption
Publish Web presence	*Publish* Web presence	*Web presence*	*Levesl 1: Internet presence*
Interact Customer relationship management Internal management of knowledge resource	*Interact* (Intranet, e-mail)	*Interact/transact* Some customer/ supplier interaction and internal support	*Level 2: Prospecting* Customer support through e-mail
Transact Customer order processing and tracking	*Transact* Customer order processing and tracking Supplier electronic transactions	*Integration* Organizational business process transformation	*Level 3: Business integration* Productivity improvements through service integration
	Integration (Full supply chain integration)	*Leverage* Customer focused; transformation through knowledge as a strategic resource	*Level 4: Business transformation* (Development of new business models)

broad generic term for the development of strategies for firms to use the Internet (Sauer, 2000). There are three main aspects to e-business: intra-organizational (internal to the firm); inter-organizational (between firms in supply chain) and e-commerce (customer to firm). Both intra-organizational and inter-organizational e-business are usually developed to improve productivity through better internal communication and processes. E-commerce is seen as providing an alternative route to market for both tangible and intangible goods.

Precise Internet benefits remain unclear, but speculation suggests that greatest benefits occur under full supply chain integration (Currie, 2000). Implementation is thought to progress through several stages and evolves as businesses recognize the benefits. Table 16.1 presents a summary of four stages models.

These different stages models suggest that firms progress e-business through stages as they identify the benefits. They all follow a similar path suggesting a web presence is found early on in the decision to adopt e-business. The only difference is in the Teo and Pian (2003)

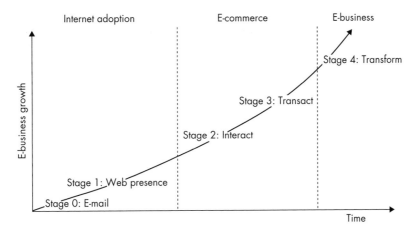

Figure 16.1: E-business stages model summary.

model, perhaps due to its recency, when the hype of having a web presence has died down, alternatively there may be demographic factors as the study was carried out in Singapore. It is also interesting to note that both Willcocks and Sauer (2000) and Teo and Pian (2003) recognize the power of e-business for business scope redefinition. However, integrating these models leads to a summary model (Figure 16.1).

While Internet systems are necessary to develop these processes, value arises once businesses use the knowledge and experience to produce outputs accessible through the Internet. The potential for transformation is thought to emerge once businesses recognize the need to reorganize processes and focus on core competencies (Willcocks and Sauer, 2000). Currently, many firms do not progress further than Stage 2, as they achieve no benefits.

Opportunities for e-business transformation require visionary changes in four aspects of the business: communication, information, transaction and distribution. Communication includes relationship building between strategic partners through new channels offered by the Internet. Information distribution is defined as accessibility of knowledge within and between firms and market enabled by the Internet. Transactions are considered as electronic order processing and tracking. Distribution is the ability to use the Internet for delivery, and support of goods and products (Angehrn, 1997). These need to be seen within the context of an "e-vision" (Feeny, 2000) that identifies new business opportunities within a dynamic market that focuses on customer needs.

■ E-business and SMEs

SMEs believe that the Internet will enable them to reach wider geographical markets and increase customers (Lunati, 2000). However, e-business adoption is often reactive and opportunistic rather than strategic (Quayle, 2002; Sadowski *et al.*, 2002). There is little evidence of business strategy driving Internet adoption among SMEs. However, strategic commitment is critical in Singaporean SMEs (Kowtha and Choon, 2001). Indeed, Internet adoption is faster when SMEs recognize a business need (Kendall *et al.*, 2001).

In common with most large businesses, SMEs have embraced the use of e-mail (Poon and Swatman 1999), with 90% of SMEs using it regularly a year after its introduction to the business (Chapman *et al.*, 2000). There is evidence that many have also developed "brochureware" web sites. However, there is little indication that many SMEs have integrated their web sites with their back-office systems. While many see value in e-mail and web sites, there is scant evidence of decisions to invest in internal networks or e-business systems (Santarelli and D'Alti, 2003; Keindl, 2000). Currently, the e-business growth path for SMEs appears to stop at Stage 2 (interaction) with only a few progressing to Stage 3 (transaction) (Figure 16.1) (Lawson *et al.*, 2003; Poon and Swatman, 1999). Stage 4 is only recognized once SMEs identify business benefits. However, as shown in Chapters 11 and 12, innovative and entrepreneurial SMEs will change to take advantage of Internet opportunities.

Influencing factors

One Internet adoption model (Mehrtens *et al.*, 2001) suggests there are three main factors that influence SMEs' decisions – perceived benefits, organizational readiness and external pressures. There are three aspects to perceived benefit. First, efficiency benefits arise from improved communication using e-mail; this is also identified by Poon (2000). Second, effectiveness benefits obtain from the ability to gather research and competitor information, also identified by Poon. Third, use of the Internet presents a modern image and improves SME promotion.

Organizational readiness for Internet adoption is personified in the SME owner. SMEs do not see Internet adoption as an information technology issue, but as a business one. SMEs that are attracted to Internet-based commerce tend to be more entrepreneurial, risk takers, innovative and invariably, creative (Poon and Swatman, 1999). A second organizational readiness factor is the requirement for SMEs to have adequate information system in place to access the Internet (Mehrtens *et al.*, 2001).

The final factor, external pressure, is primarily from customers, though suppliers and employees are also influencing factors. While Poon (2000) recognizes that customer pressure is influential, there is evidence that a lack of customer use is an inhibitor, particularly of e-mail (Sillence *et al.*, 1998).

A study of e-business adopters and non-adopters in Chile found that organizational readiness is the most important factor in the decision to adopt. Organizational readiness implies adequate technological and financial resources to enable e-business adoption. The effectiveness perceived benefit of managerial productivity was found to be next important, with external pressure third (Grandon and Pearson, 2004).

Thus, current research suggests that a number of factors influence Internet adoption and development in SMEs. Business need and perceived benefits figure prominently in SME Internet development. However, despite their popularity in early IS adoption research and their intuitive appeal, there is little evidence that SMEs follow a "stages of growth" model for Internet adoption. A contingent model that involves "transportation" from one use to another without the implicit idea of growth may be more useful for understanding SME Internet adoption. One explanation for this lack of evidence is the propensity of past research to consider SMEs as homogenous group. However, as shown in Chapter 9 in developing the focus-dominance model, SME research needs to recognize heterogeneity. It is known that owner attitude and business strategy influence IS adoption, and may do the same for Internet adoption. Hence, this chapter seeks to determine whether SME Internet adoption strategies are contingent on factors, such as owners' attitude, business strategy, perceived benefits and customer influence.

■ Research approach

This chapter seeks to determine whether approaches to Internet adoption are dependent upon contingent variables. Therefore, it is first necessary to understand the reasons for SME Internet adoption. This chapter analyses the approach to Internet adoption taken by 12 case firms. The background to these firms is shown in Table 16.2.

Semi-structured interviews lasting between 1 and 2 hours were held with SME owners to discuss approaches to Internet development. Interview reports were sent to the owners subsequently for validation and refinement. The issues are divided into four sections: business objectives, business strategy, competitive environment, and technology and e-business. The questioning on business objectives and strategy identifies whether different strategic approaches lead to differences in Internet adoption decisions. The competitive environment discussion enables consideration of the influence of customers, competitors and suppliers on Internet adoption. The questioning on technology and e-business provide a means of identifying the level of knowledge about the potential role of information and communication technology and the Internet for the business and the way in which it relates to business strategy.

Table 16.2: Background to case firms

Firm	Product	Ownership	Turnover (£s in million)	Employees
Heath Springs	Design and manufacture of springs	Owned by CEO, part of US group	7	100
CAD Service Co.	Laser scanning for CAD software support	Owned by CEO	2	14
Corporate Gift Co.	Design/manufacture of corporate gifts	Family-owned	6	50
Curtain Material Wholesale Co.	Curtain materials and accessories to trade	Family-owned	0.8	7
Equipment Hire Centre	Hire of builders' equipment	Family-owned	0.4	7
Garden Pottery Co.	Design/manufacture of ceramic pottery	Family-owned	1.1	30
IT Services Co.	Systems development/ training ICT solutions	Owned by CEO	n/a	13
Oil Flow Co.	Consultancy services to oil and gas industry	Jointly owned by Chairman and CEO	n/a	20
	Design/manufacture of flow equipment to oil industry			
Patent Attorneys	Registering patents	Partnership	n/a	21
Epoxy Resin Co.	Development and manufacture of advanced polymer resin technology	Family-owned	n/a	22
Reduced Power Co.	Design and manufacture of energy saving devices	A number of equity partners including the CEO	1.2	14
Savoury Pie Manufacturer	Manufacturer of Savoury Pies	Family-owned	4.5	75

n/a: not available.

■ Growth, competitiveness and the Internet

The case analysis is summarized in Table 16.3. The analysis reviews the business strategy and attitude to growth of the owner. In most cases, this is one of staying in existing markets with existing products. While some

Table 16.3: Strategic alignment and Internet adoption in case firms

Firm	Business strategy	Competitive influences	Future Internet potential	Internet technologies				
				E-mail	Web site	Internal network	E-business	EDI
Heath Springs	Same products, new markets, double turnover	High rivalry between firms Competition from overseas markets Customer pressure on price Customer dominance – high	Strong, enabling networks between customers and suppliers to develop	Internal and external	Brochureware	LAN		Used extensively with customers
CAD Service Co.	Existing products into new market Looking for business growth	Customer pressure on quality	Would like to use, but customers resistant	External	Interaction with customers	LAN		
Corporate Gift Co.	New products into new markets Looking to grow business	High rivalry between firms Corporate customers pressure on price	Critical to future development	Internal and external, used extensively	Online sales available	Intranet	Under development	Internet EDI being introduced with major customers
Curtain Textile Co.	Existing products into existing markets Life style, therefore not looking for growth	Suppliers influence product availability; no pressure from customers	Seen as irrelevant	External, but not used	Use discontinued	LAN		
Equipment Hire Centre	Existing products into existing markets Life style, therefore not looking for growth	Some rivalry between firms	Not seen as important, but owner enjoys IT	External	Brochureware	LAN		

(Continued)

Table 16.3: (Continued)

Firm	Business strategy	Competitive influences	Future Internet potential	Internet technologies				
				E-mail	Web site	Internal network	E-business	EDI
Garden Ceramics	Existing products into existing markets Not looking for growth	Highly competitive industry Focus on quality	Not seen as important	Not used	Brochureware			
IT Services Co.	Existing products into new markets Focus is on survival	Customers pressure on price	"Must have" as others do	External and internal	Brochureware	LAN		
Oil Flow Co.	New services into new markets Business survival through diversification	Declining industry has led to diversification: offering consultancy services to the industry Customer dominance – high	Not seen as important	External	Brochureware	LAN		
Patent Attorneys	Existing product into existing markets Not looking for growth	Competition between existing firms	Important to manage business more effectively	External	Under development	WAN		
Epoxy Resin Co.	New products into existing markets Survival is main objective	Customers demand high quality and innovative products Customer dominance – low	Not seen as important	External	Brochureware			
Reduced Power Co.	Existing products into new markets Steady growth	Customer pressure on price Customer dominance	Not seen as important	External	Brochureware	LAN		
Savoury Pie Manufacturer	New products into existing markets, but not looking for growth	High rivalry between firms	Not seen as important	Not used	None	LAN		

owners are looking for growth, there are a number that are in business for life style reasons, which impacts on their strategic intent. Additionally, owners were asked about the business value of the Internet for their firm. This ranged from high future potential to many who saw little value. For example the owner of Curtain Textiles said *"I deal with major manufacturers of curtain materials, I've known them for years, and we talk on the phone. I don't see that situation changing"*. However, the opposite view holds in the automotive spring manufacturer who has a clear vision for the future *"The automotive industry must work more closely together in the future otherwise suppliers won't survive, I see networks using the Internet as the way forward in the future"*.

All the case firms bar Garden Ceramics have Internet access and e-mail. In the UK these usually occur together due to the way Internet service providers (ISPs) operate. Curtain Material Wholesale Co. was provided with e-mail as part of an EU funded project, but once this finished no longer uses it. Three firms have internal e-mail as well. Two are larger SMEs that use ICT to manage their businesses. The third, CAD Services, started as "dot.com" where staff expected to be able to use e-mail internally.

Nine firms have web sites. Most are brochureware, providing limited information about the firms and their products or services. Only Corporate Gift uses its web site as part of its strategy to develop its e-business markets. CAD Services developed its web site as part of its business, but customers do not use it, primarily because of security

Case study 16.1

Curtain Material Wholesale Co. sells curtain materials and accessories to the wholesale trade. It is the only wholesale curtain retailer in Birmingham. The firm is family owned and the whole family works in the business. Turnover has remained fairly static over the last 3 years, although recent months suggest an upswing in the market, with 7% growth in customers.

Curtain Material Wholesale Co. customers include curtain makers and small retail outlets and contractors. Its markets are all the smaller traders that larger manufacturers do not wish to trade with. There was a shake up in the market a number of years ago and large manufacturers decided that they only wanted to trade with 250 customers rather than the 2500 with which they had been trading. Thus, the firm became a key customer to the manufacturers.

The market is contracting, as there is an oversupply in curtain manufacturing. However, Curtain Material Wholesale Co. competes on quality and service, often guaranteeing next day delivery. The firm does not try to compete on cost. It has a policy of not allowing one customer to become dominant and they estimate that the top 5 customers account for 15% of sales. The core business area is within 30–40 miles of Birmingham. Most new business is found through word of mouth.

The business strategy is one of consolidation within its existing products and markets. The owner is focusing on succession planning, to be able to pass on a viable business to his sons. Thus, a major focus in recent months has been on cutting costs and improving margins while offering quality products.

The firm has three networked PCs. They process orders electronically and do accounts using SAGE software. This provides all the reports that the owner requires. The firm also uses banks automated clearing system to pay bills and to do its payroll. The owner sees no need for cash-flow forecasting. A member of the family puts in the first system. It was subsequently upgraded on advice from the firm's accountant. The firm uses a sole trader hardware specialist to maintain and support the system.

Curtain Material Wholesale Co. has access to e-mail. However, it is rarely used as very few of their customers or suppliers use it; it is not checked regularly. Personal contact is valued in this industry. The development of relationships with both customers and suppliers is seen as vital. Hence most contact is either face to face or on the phone. A personal business adviser from Business Link persuaded the firm to participate in a European-funded scheme to develop a web site. However, the firm then found that they would have to pay to have the web site hosted. They could not see the relevance to the business and declined to go further. The owner does not believe that the Internet offers the best way to sell his product currently. However, he does believe that the market will change in time, but not for many years.

concerns, and also because of data file size. There are difficulties over the time it takes to download files and the danger of file corruption. Hence, CAD Services finds that it is becoming more a brochureware site. Again, Curtain Textile decided not to use its web site once it had to pay for it to be available. Garden Ceramics web site was developed by an employee and is hosted by the employee's ISP, it is not seen as relevant to the firm. None of the firms has an Intranet, although Corporate Gift is considering the further development of its system. Patent Attorney's wide area network development will be using Internet technologies.

Overall, so far this chapter provides some support for the current literature, as there is only limited Internet development in the case SMEs. E-mail and web sites are common. What is of greater interest is whether the firms perceive that the Internet holds future benefit, either to mitigate competitive pressures from competitors or customers, or to grow the business.

■ Business growth and the Internet

Analysis of the interview data reveals that two drivers are key in determining SME use of the Internet. The first driver is business growth. In some firms business growth is planned and investment made ahead of need. In many other SMEs growth may occur but it is not as a result of planning. Attitudes to business growth often determine whether SME owners consider resource investment in the business. IS investment is traditionally restricted in SMEs, with many investing at start-up, but no further investment is usually made until the business outgrows existing systems. Therefore, it is plausible that attitudes to growth will impact SMEs' decisions to invest in the Internet. The second driver is business value from use of Internet technologies. Business value of the Internet is identified through response to the firms' competitive positioning and their knowledge of what is happening within their industry.

The analysis indicates that SMEs have considered the role of the Internet for their businesses. Their approach is generally cautious. Most firms do not see the value of the Internet to their growth strategy. However, a number of visionary owners believe that they can change their business through the use of the Internet. What is striking in discussions with the SME owners is that they are not Luddites, but are very knowledgeable about their industries. They also appreciate the tight resource constraints they are under and, as with ICT investment, Internet investment has to have more than a perceived benefit.

Interaction of the two drivers allows the identification of four groupings or SME segments. These are brochureware, business opportunity, business network and business support (Figure 16.2). The characteristics of these groupings and some exemplar SMEs are discussed in the next section.

Brochureware

Those firms that do not plan business growth and see the value of the Internet as low all have e-mail and have experimented with web site development. The owners have thought about the Internet, but cannot see its relevance to their business. Among the reasons for this is the nature of the industry. Savoury Pie Manufacturer said (as he presented a large, well-thumbed black tome) "*This is my bible, I can't take my computer to bed with me, this tells me everything I need to know and I can't see it changing*". Not only did he not need the Internet for information,

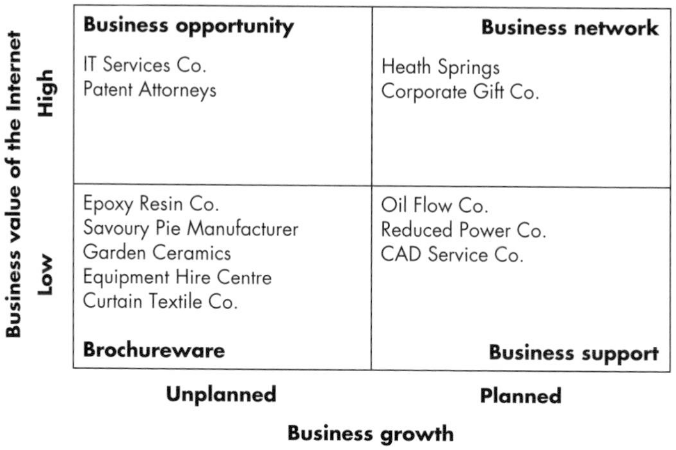

Figure 16.2: Segmentation strategy for SME Internet adoption.

but he said "*I have a close relationship with the managing director of* (major regional supermarket), *we prefer to meet regularly to discuss orders and promotional activities. Neither of us wants to change this*". Curtain Textile expresses similar sentiments.

Case study 16.2

Savoury Pie Manufacturer is a family-owned firm that has been established for approximately 30 years. The main business is the manufacture of savoury pastries. They also buy in sausages and beef burgers to sell on. The senior management team consists of three advisors in human resources, food technology and finance, the CEO and co-director who co-ordinates the key accounts. The advisors meet once a month and are on call as required. The firm sells to both wholesale and retail food distributors including football clubs and cafes. The CEO believes the market is a mature one, he has no intention of expanding into other areas, however, he is looking at new products within what he considers to be a mature market.

The firm has a computer network with 14 PCs and a separate server. They have had to upgrade their accounting systems as it was not Y2K compliant and they have now have got Sage Line 100. All van drivers have a hand-held computer that holds details of customer accounts information and stock details. New order information on the hand-held computers is uploaded to the main computer when the drivers return. There is no pressure from their major supermarket customer to use EDI or e-mail to receive orders; negotiations and discussions on orders are undertaken in person.

The firm has access to e-mail but it is not really used either internally or with the customers. However, the accountant does use online banking to download data to Excel. The accountant prepares profit and loss accounts and sales figures from the data from the bank. There is no electronic system of stock control it is all done manually by a stock controller. There is no automated production planning, this is a full-time manual task.

Garden Ceramics believes that their customers would not buy online, they tend to sell to the quality end of the market and sales are made through garden exhibitions. In contrast, Equipment Hire Centre has invested heavily in IT, but mainly because the owner enjoys using it. It is not seen as a means of growing the business. For example, the owner decided that mobile toilets were a useful addition to his hire range and was pleased to advertise them on his web site, but when asked whether he would deliver them to a town about 80 kilometres away said "*No, I only want to trade locally*". He is a "life style" owner not looking for growth.

Case study 16.3

Equipment Hire Co., has been in business since 1976. It is a small business primarily hiring out a wide range of tools. It has recently diversified into toilet hire and the sale of gases, which are both seen as growth areas. In addition, a second firm was formed in 1996 to sell motorcycles. The tool hire market is highly competitive and fairly local, not more than 30 miles from the business. The owner has identified a number of competitors, both local and national. He believes that the quality of service that he offers to customers is better than his competitors. He also believes that the tools he offers are maintained at a higher quality than the National competitors. The business growth areas have been identified with this in mind. Twenty-five per cent of business is from the general public while the majority comes from construction firm and large manufacturers.

The firm achieved 50% growth last year and the owner plans to continue growth through profitability. Staff are being included in the vision for business growth through the development of a profit sharing scheme. The owner has a well-developed and clear business plan. The firm has made considerable investment in upgrading its site and systems to ensure that it provides a high quality service to customers and to support the business objectives.

The system consists of a server and five PCs running Windows NT. There is an automatic back-up system on the server. Two modems provide Internet access. Cabling has been carried out to enable the network to be expanded into the shop and the workshop, which is across a large courtyard. The firm uses word processing, a publishing package and an accounting package.

Data is entered manually onto Excel to prepare management accounts. Autoroute is used to plan delivery routes. The quality system has been developed using Lotus approach, but there is some concern that this is not the easiest of systems to manipulate. The owner has developed the majority of the systems in-house to his own requirements. He received some assistance from his accountant in setting up the management accounts. Currently, the firm is reviewing the possibility of developing a front-office system that will write out contracts and track the history of all tools to improve productivity.

E-mail is used to communicate with the main overseas gas supplier. The Internet is not used extensively. The firm has recently developed a brochureware web site. The web site is promoted through headed paper and mouse mats and is registered with the top ten search engines. While the firm believes that about 25% of its current customer base has access to the Internet, they believe it is important to be prepared for the future. The relationship with the overseas gas supplier is being nurtured and customers will have access to their web site from the Equipment Hire Co. web site.

Case study 16.4

Epoxy Resin Co. was established by the CEO in 1987 to develop manufacture and sell advanced polymer resin technology products. The firm serves a range of industries with materials that are used in the development of prototypes, resin tools, patterns, models and pre-production items. The UK customer base consists of approximately 2000 firms, of which 40 are key accounts. Three salesmen cover all UK customers while export sales are achieved through a network of agents.

The market is fairly competitive, although the level of competition varies within the product ranges. Differentiation in the industry is achieved through different firms focusing on different product characteristics. There is some concern that the cost of production is increasing.

The owner's strategy is to grow the firm by size rather than focus on profitability initially. This will be achieved through management and development of customer relationships through the provision of high quality products.

The operational management systems show a sophisticated use of the Sage Line 50 accounting package. However, there is little management information available to the firm to help develop its strategic direction. It has a web site but it is mainly used to promote products. The firm does not wish to sell online. The web site is maintained regularly. Prices are not available on the site as it is thought this information might be used by competitors. The firm uses the Internet for research purposes.

This group contains the largest proportion of case SMEs. They have all investigated the Internet and taken what they consider to be the most useful parts, e-mail and web sites, in some cases, and made a decision not to invest further. Hence, there is a role for the Internet for these firms but it is restricted to the presentation of online firm information or brochures.

Business opportunity

Two SMEs perceive the Internet to offer high business value but are not planning business growth. Patent Attorneys is looking for business efficiencies from the use of Internet technologies. In particular, access to international patent information is faster using the Internet. Otherwise they primarily see it as a tool to obtain advice from their experts located in different offices. They foresee the Internet as a key medium for information and research for their industry. The current systems development is being planned to support this future growth. However, the firm does not yet envisage a need to move into e-business.

Case study 16.5

Patent Attorneys are part of an international group of firms that specialize in Intellectual Property Law which covers patents, trade marks, designs and copyright law. Its client base covers the spectrum from International corporate clients to individuals with about one third being overseas clients, including other patent attorneys ensuring that their clients' patents are covered in Europe. The firm has three branches.

The firm uses e-mail extensively with clients, with one client requesting invoicing through the Internet. Clients expect a quick response to queries, because of e-mail. Managing expectations is an issue. E-mail is however, seen as a positive approach to offering a better service to clients. The firm strategy is one of growth, with the Internet seen as a means of offering added value to clients. Patent Attorneys believe that there is an expectation from clients that a progressive firm will have a web site and use the Internet for trading. A web site is under development and will go live shortly. The Internet is used extensively by professional staff to contact worldwide patent offices and also to access commercial search databases. The firm finds that databases are updated more quickly than the paper-based information they are subsequently sent. The firm does not consider security to be an issue. This is primarily because it is being addressed as part of the web development and encryption facilities are being included.

The drive for use of the Internet and IT has been led directly by a senior partner who has considerable expertise and knowledge in this area. The main focus for the adoption of IS is to improve the service to clients by improving efficiency and reducing costs. Patent Attorneys is currently putting in a wide area network that will enable all the group branches to communicate with each other. The wide area network technology is being implemented by the group, thus reducing the risk to Patent Attorneys. The system will enable all data to be held in common across all three branches of the firm. This will enable staff to undertake tasks remotely without having to travel to another branch. It is seen as a way of reducing costs, minimizing duplication of resources and improving efficiency for the benefit of their clients.

IT Services has been using the Internet for some time to provide information on its services and products. The firm provides training services, employment services and systems development opportunities. It sees the Internet as a means to promote employment and training services. Systems development is declining as business investment in IT is generally slowing. The SME does not see the Internet playing a role here. Its main function is to manage the business internally and to communicate with customers. Therefore, the main issue for IT Services is to maintain its presence with its current Internet service provision, and plan for the future.

Case study 16.6

IT Services Co. founded in 1994, provides recruitment, training on IS and also develops ICT solutions including e-commerce solutions. It currently employs 13 people, down from 30 in the last year. This reflects a downturn in the market for systems development. The firm works primarily in its local region. They are in a highly competitive environment as they also compete with other local firms.

IT Services believed that they would be able to increase their e-commerce development arm. However, when the dot.com bubble burst many businesses questioned the viability of e-commerce. This led to far less business in this area than they had expected. Additionally, the firm decided to focus on one development platform for its e-commerce solutions. This platform has proved less popular than was envisaged. This combined with a general downturn in the market has led to some concerns about the viability of systems development. The SME is considering to increase its recruitment and training arms to manage this situation. However, they believe it is important to maintain the systems development section as this is likely to be more profitable in the longer term.

Staff are highly skilled, which has benefits and limitations. Staff turnover is high, but systems development for customers and IT Services itself is well managed. Government policies on allowing skilled overseas workers into the UK have helped the firm.

Not surprisingly there is a local area network that is used by all staff. The system is both used for management support as well as systems development. The firm uses SAGE for accounting and Payroll. They have a customer database as well as a recruitment database. They also have a timesheet reporting system. The current economic downturn has led IT Services to focus on improving its internal systems particularly marketing and financial analysis. The firm has a marketing web site that is updated regularly. However, there is no intention to offer online services due to the economic downturn in the market.

This group of SMEs recognizes that the Internet has some value to them, in the future. However, it is limited to improving efficiency internally, customer communication and research. The contrast between this group and the brochureware group is that owners recognize the business value of the Internet and although not seeking growth, recognize that competitive pressures demand investment. These firms see a business opportunity from use of the Internet.

Business support

Firms using the Internet for business support are planning growth, but currently see little future for their businesses from the Internet. All the SMEs here are innovative firms seeking to grow. Oil Flow Services is undergoing a major change from providing a key product to the oil industry to providing global consultancy services. They believe this will provide them with growth opportunities. As the patent on their key product is expiring shortly, diversification is seen as a means of leveraging the knowledge within the firm. However, while the Internet is used for research and e-mail is used extensively, they do not believe that it will change the way they do business in the next 3 years. Although the use for customer communication will increase. Similar sentiments are expressed by Reduced Power. They have a number of innovative products that are sold into large firms, so personal contact is regarded by customers as important and there is little indication that the Internet is of value.

Case study 16.7

Oil Flow Co. was started 20 years ago to provide products and services to the oil industry, 80% of which is export trade. The main product allows improved flow of liquid through pipes. In 1998 a new CEO was appointed while one of the original owners is still closely involved as chairman. Their five largest customers account for 80% of sales, with the largest customer accounting for 25% of sales. However, product orders have declined recently, as the industry is in decline, which has led to the decision to diversify and refocus the business.

The firm has reorganized itself to extend the market into the far east, south east Asia and Australasia, and the USA and to provide a wide range of consultancy services to the oil and gas industry. The firm sees the consultancy arm as having high growth potential.

They have a PC network; all members of staff have computers. The systems have been set up in-house by staff. Maintenance is also managed by staff. The firm uses Word, Sage, Goldmine, a sales contact database, for managing customer information. Management information from the systems is limited. There is no internal e-mail, although it is available for communication with customers. Much of the communication with customers is still via fax. The firm has a brochureware web site that was developed in-house. The Internet is used for research. The firm is also considering developing a CD brochure for customers.

In terms of future systems development, EDI is likely to be of greatest importance to Oil Flow Co. It does not consider that trading over the Internet will be important in the next 3 years.

Case study 16.8

Reduced Power Co. design and sell advanced electronic control systems to reduce power use both for industry and the home. The firm has been in business for 15 years. Growth has been slow during this period partly due to limited finance, although, the firm has recently achieved 30% growth. In 1996 the previous owners were bought out and a good relationship has been developed with the current financier, a Saudi Arabian businessman. The CEO owns 38% of equity in the business. The firm has been profitable since 1996, with most of the profits being reinvested in the business for research and development purposes. Reduced Power Co.'s products are developed with UK government and EU funding as they are highly advanced technology. The firm subcontracts all its manufacturing and works closely with the university sector on product development.

The product requires little maintenance once it is installed, is 99.5% reliable over a 5 year rolling period. It has a minimum lifetime of 15 years. This means that the firm has little repeat business unless it can attract major firms and organizations that have multiple outlets. They have to target new markets for the products. Contracts can take up to 2 years to be agreed with new customers, who can expect a return on their investment in 2–5 years.

Reduced Power Co. has just upgraded its computer network. There is a separate server and nine PCs. Technology and systems development is regarded as integral to business strategy. Systems have been developed in-house by sales managers using Lotus approach. All managers are experienced in using databases and the systems satisfy their information requirements. The firm purchase targeted databases to help with marketing. They have an accounts system that is primarily used for bookkeeping. Data is downloaded to a Lotus spreadsheet to prepare monthly management accounts. The firm also has systems to plan routes and schedule installations of equipment for technicians. Internet access is available on three PCs, and a web page has recently been developed. The Internet is mainly used for research purposes. Competitor and customer information is identified through the web. External e-mail is used mainly to contact overseas customers with phone and fax being the preferred means of communication in the UK. The firm checks e-mail daily. The web site is seen as a means of attracting more overseas customers.

This contrasts with the experience of CAD Services that developed an e-business web site to provide services to customers for their CAD systems. However, their experience is that customers prefer personal contact and that traditional marketing techniques are more effective. While CAD Services uses the Internet, it does not plan to develop it further as part of its growth plans.

Case study 16.9

CAD Service Co. is an umbrella firm for two subsidiaries; it has been in business for 6 years. The first subsidiary provides an advanced scanning service to the automotive industry, primarily. The firm has developed a laser scanner that can digitize a 3D model and send the information directly to a computer. This service is used extensively by car designers. The firm is looking for other markets for this product as they believe that this is a highly innovative product with considerable market potential. The second subsidiary provides a consultancy service for firms that are having problems with their CAD software. This firm was originally set up as a dot.com. The concept was for customers to e-mail files with problems to the firm, these would then be repaired and sent back to customers. The service was seen as a low cost solution for customers. However, customers prefer personal service rather than purchasing electronically, partly because of security concerns.

The firm recognized 4 years ago that e-mail would be useful for them and made the investment in the technology. The staff, who are very knowledgeable about IS, use internal e-mail to communicate through networked PCs. External e-mail is used extensively to communicate with customers. The firm also has a brochureware web site. The scanning subsidiary web site has proved useful to identify new customers, while customers prefer a more traditional approach to marketing for the CAD support subsidiary. E-commerce is not likely to be used to any great extent primarily because of customer concerns about security.

Customer products are leading edge and are focused on future markets; hence there is a high degree of confidentiality about the work being done. Customers prefer to trust delivery to couriers rather than the Internet. Another limitation of the Internet is the speed of file transfer as the scanning subsidiary's data files are too large to easily be transmitted over the Internet without data corruption. Hence, CD-ROM is the preferred medium to ensure quality and to satisfy customers. The firm sees this situation continuing for the foreseeable future.

These SMEs are seeking to grow, but do not believe that the industry demands investment in Internet systems to support that growth. These SMEs see the worth of the Internet as a business support medium.

Business network

Opportunity from the Internet is seen as key to the development of the two SMEs in the final grouping. Both see their future tied into using the Internet. Corporate Gift is furthest ahead in its development with a strategic decision to diversify its business from its corporate customer base. It is building on its core competencies of design and quality manufacture to develop online retail sales. The firm has always developed its IT strategy alongside its business strategy. Hence, it is well positioned to take advantage of e-business. Corporate Gift has an effective internal network that is accessible and used by all staff as means to manage the business processes. The firm is integrating online sales with their back-office systems. Additionally, they are introducing Internet EDI systems to work more closely with their major corporate customers.

Case study 16.10

Corporate Gift Co. designs and manufactures corporate gifts. The firm has experienced about 20% real growth in the last year and is planning to continue its growth through increasing market share in retail, corporate and consumer markets. The industry is highly competitive with companies targeting both the retail and corporate markets. However, there is no one firm that is a direct competitor. Corporate Gift Co. believes that it is better than its competitors in a number of key areas, particularly, innovation, design, customer service and use of technology. Success depends upon product innovation and quality. Growth is mainly financed through factoring of the sales ledger.

The firm usually subcontracts manufacturing, much of it overseas. However, quality control has led it to consider bringing most (about 85%) of the manufacturing back to the UK. It has also purchased laser-cutting equipment to help develop prototypes. The firm is extending its facilities on site to prepare for this development. Currently, it sources its raw materials and manufactures in the far east. The Internet is used extensively to find sources, although the information provided by web sites is not always sufficient to decide whether a potential supplier is adequate. The difficulty of managing quality control has led to the firm considering sourcing more materials in the UK.

The firm has an extensive network of Apple Macintosh computers with 27 users. The business system is integrated, providing order processing, financial analysis, customer database and both internal and external e-mail. It is regarded as critical for the business. Microsoft Office is also used. Production planning and return monitoring is carried out using a spreadsheet. Apart from accounting, all other business systems processes are accessible to all members of staff. There is some concern that the software may not be supported in the long term. Corporate Gift Co. is already considering its long-term options for the future, changing infrastructure platforms is not one they wish to consider.

The SME has a web site that is mainly used to advertise products. Online sales order processing is available for personal shopping. This is a new business opportunity for Corporate Gift Co. External e-mail is used extensively. Internal e-mail is also used to transfer data between departments. The firm is looking at introducing Internet EDI with its major retail customers. There is recognition of the need to develop and e-business system to integrate web-based order processing. The firm would like to have open Internet access all the time, but the cost makes this prohibitive.

Heath Springs is, in contrast, at the planning stage of its Internet development. Currently EDI is used to deliver order processing information from customers. Design material is also delivered electronically. The firm is not yet using the Internet to any great extent, but the CEO foresees major industry restructuring that will require the formation of strategic partnerships among suppliers. He is focusing on changing the business strategy to develop the network partnership he sees as important for future development.

These two firms plan their growth and perceive value from the Internet. Its role, therefore, is in supporting a business network.

▓ Discussion

This chapter investigated the role of the Internet in 12 case SMEs. A model of Internet use, driven by perceived value and growth planning, is derived. The message from this chapter is that, overall, there is little sign that SMEs see the Internet as being a major future change agent. However, there is evidence that the owners' attitudes to growth and their

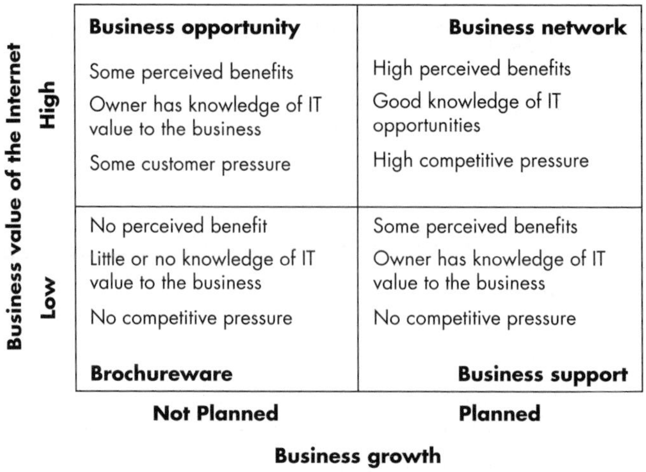

	Business opportunity	**Business network**
High	Some perceived benefits Owner has knowledge of IT value to the business Some customer pressure	High perceived benefits Good knowledge of IT opportunities High competitive pressure
Low	No perceived benefit Little or no knowledge of IT value to the business No competitive pressure	Some perceived benefits Owner has knowledge of IT value to the business No competitive pressure
	Brochureware	**Business support**
	Not Planned	**Planned**

Business value of the Internet

Business growth

Figure 16.3: Segmented Internet adoption patterns in SMEs.

understanding of the business value of the Internet are instrumental in their decisions to adopt. There is scant support from these cases for a stages model of development, as the SMEs appear to consider the role of the Internet as they would other technology investments: if it supports the business then the investment will be made. Thus, this chapter supports Kowtha and Choon (2001) as strategic commitment is essential. There is some confirmation here too for the concept of perceived benefits as articulated by Mehrtens *et al.* (2001). However, it is important to note that those SMEs in the brochureware quadrant perceive little or no benefits. Organizational readiness as indicated by level of Internet knowledge among SME owners is a factor in adoption, although as has been shown, it is also a factor in the decision not to adopt. There is only limited evidence of external pressure for change in this group of firms. Only one case firm sees the need to refocus due to industry pressure, Heath Springs. Figure 16.3 summarizes the adoption issues and demonstrates that different types of business will view Internet adoption in very different lights. This suggests that SMEs are unlikely to follow a stages model. Rather, they will focus on what is best to meet the owners' strategy for business growth. Internet development in SMEs is likely to be slow to reflect this approach to resource investment.

The issues in this chapter have implications for policy development. In the UK, policy guidelines from the Department of Trade and Industry are developed around the stages of growth concept for SME Internet development. The government expects all SMEs to follow this path and directs its policy to achieving this objective. This chapter suggests that Internet adoption policies should more closely reflect the four segments identified here, recognizing that the Internet is a business tool for some but not all SMEs.

17 Strategic intent and e-business

◼ Introduction

As the previous chapter shows, the development of e-business in small- and medium-sized enterprises is slow. The limited research into this issue identifies perceived benefit as the major driver. However, other factors may influence SMEs' decisions to invest in e-business. For example, SMEs' adoption of information systems to manage and grow as either cost or value adding largely depending upon the firms' strategic intent. This chapter investigates whether, and in what way, strategic intent affects SMEs' attitudes to Internet adoption. It also considers drivers and inhibitors of e-business adoption to determine any relationship between these and strategic intent. Here, strategic intent encompasses two dimensions: markets and products as identified by Ansoff (Chapter 10). Most SMEs plan growth through a combination of these (Storey, 1994).

This chapter differs from most in this book as it presents the outcome of a survey of SMEs in the UK West Midlands to investigate these issues rather than using case analysis. The value in using a survey here is that it allows comparison between industrial sectors and strategic intent. While it is suggested earlier that industry sector is not an factor in IS adoption, it is only with a larger sample that this can be demonstrated conclusively. The first issue discussed in the chapter is the relationship between growth strategies and strategic intent. Drivers and inhibitors of e-business are then identified. The chapter investigates three research questions; does strategic intent drive e-business adoption and is it a factor of market position or product innovation? Is this consistent across sectors? And how is strategic intent and industry adoption influenced by the enablers and inhibitors of e-business adoption?

◼ SMEs and strategic intent

While the focus-dominance model (Chapter 9) is concerned with investment in information and communication technology to manage the business, the different scenarios clearly suggest diverse strategic intents. The efficiency scenario is found when SMEs are starting up. However, as discussed in Chapter 2, in some SMEs the owners are in business for "life style advantages". In particular, they like the freedom to pursue a business interest, and to produce sufficient income to have a comfortable life. They are only interested in selling their current products into existing markets. Their firms' use of IS mirrors this. These organizations usually have simple standalone systems possibly with a simple web site.

The co-ordination scenario is found as businesses grow. The businesses here are increasingly looking to sell their products into new markets. They are looking for steady growth for their existing products. They utilize more sophisticated IS to allow them to do this including the development of Intranets and often external e-mail to work with customers.

Product development is the focus of the collaboration scenario. This group of SMEs is usually closely allied to a few major customers and develops new products to support their requirements. These SMEs seek growth, but through the development of customer relationships. Information systems here includes use of EDI and often Extranets.

While the SMEs in the co-ordination and collaboration quadrants often seek steady growth, the final group in the repositioning scenario sees diversification as the way forward as they are looking for rapid growth. This often means different delivery means for products but also developing new product to satisfy their markets. This group is likely to put IS at the centre of business growth strategies.

Strategic intent for growth is modelled using Ansoff (1965) as discussed in Chapter 10. Comparing strategic intent strategies and the focus-dominance IS growth model suggests that there is a one-to-one mapping between the two models. Figure 17.1 demonstrates the relationship.

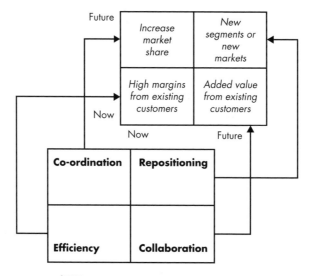

Figure 17.1: Strategic intent and SMEs.

The analysis in Chapter 10 confirms that firms in the collaboration scenario focus on product development as their strategic intent. Similarly, firms in the repositioning scenario generally diversify. Market penetration is found in the efficiency scenario. The main difference with the above proposition is that market penetration is still the initial strategy pursued by growing SMEs planning a move into the co-ordination scenario. There is no clear direction for a market development strategy. It was argued that this might be because of the practicality of achieving the espoused strategic intent. Alternatively, while all the firms analysed in Chapter 10 are growth firms, they might not have reached the stage in their growth where they can confidently move from the current strategic intent to the future.

Chapter 10 considered IS investment in the broadest sense in comparing strategic intent with focus-dominance IS strategy. Chapter 16 recognizes that there is little evidence of strategic planning for e-business in SMEs. The focus of this chapter is whether, and in what way, strategic intent drives e-business adoption. This is explored further by considering the enablers and inhibitors of e-business adoption. The knowledge gained through this analysis may also enable confirmation or refuting of the hypothesis that the strategic intent of SMEs maps to the IS investment strategy as indicated by the focus-dominance model.

Drivers and inhibitors of e-business in SMEs

This section reviews the current knowledge of drivers and inhibitors of e-business in SMEs. This provides the basis for the development of a survey instrument to consider the relationship between them and strategic intent.

Previously it was shown that the key enablers of e-business in SMEs are perceived benefit, organizational readiness and external pressure. The different aspects of these enablers are summarized in Table 17.1.

Perceived benefit was identified as a key driver for SME e-business adoption. Efficiency benefits include reducing operating costs including

Table 17.1: E-business enablers

Perceived benefit	Efficiency improvements due to better communication
	Effectiveness benefits use of external information
	Image
	Identifying new business opportunities
Organizational readiness	The SME owner recognizes business value
	Adequate Internet access
External pressure	Customer requirements

transaction costs involved in sales and purchasing. Effectiveness benefits include improved market intelligence and ability to identify suppliers for product development purposes through the Internet. Additionally e-business is seen as improving trading relationships. Image is seen as important, for two reasons. First, it helps to maintain market share and second, to increase it. Improved customer service is seen as a key driver by most researchers in this area, not merely as an external pressure, but also in improved effectiveness, for example, in increased service delivery such as dispatch of goods and online support. Table 17.2 provides a summary of the issues identified by those researching e-business adoption in SMEs.

For many SMEs, failure to plan the introduction and exploitation of new technology stems from management limitations (Klein and Quelch, 1997; Premkumar and Roberts, 1999). One issue for many SMEs is that

Table 17.2: Drivers for Internet adoption in SMEs

Driver	Authors
Reduced operating costs	Standing *et al.* (2003); Quayle and Christiansen (2004); Quayle (2002); Kendall *et al.* (2001); Riemenschneider *et al.* (2003)
Sales and purchasing cost reduction	Quayle and Christiansen (2004); Jeffcoate *et al.* (2004); Tse and Soufani (2003); Riemenschneider *et al.* (2003)
Improved range and quality of services to customers	Quayle and Christiansen (2004); Jeffcoate *et al.* (2004); Tse and Soufani (2003); Mehrtens *et al.* (2001); Teo and Pian (2003); Sadowski *et al.* (2002); Santarelli and D'Altri (2003); Ramsey *et al.* (2003); Quayle (2002); Daniel and Grimshaw (2002); Riemenschneider *et al.* (2003)
Increased speed in dispatch of goods	Tse and Soufani (2000)
Finding suppliers	Dandridge and Levenburg (2000); Teo and Pian (2002); Santarelli and D'Altri (2003)
Avoiding loss of market share	Santarelli and D'Altri, (2003); Kendall *et al.* (2001); Riemenschneider *et al.* (2003)
Increase market share	Standing *et al.* (2002); Quayle and Christiansen, 2004; Ramsey *et al.* (2003); Daniel and Grimshaw (2002); Kendall *et al.* (2001)
Market intelligence	Quayle and Christiansen (2004); Jeffcoate *et al.* (2004); Ramsey *et al.* (2003); Mehrtens *et al.* (2001)
Improved trading relationships	Quayle and Christiansen (2004); Mehrtens *et al.* (2001)

they have already invested heavily in communication and data exchange systems with their major customers. For example, many SMEs have invested heavily in EDI and their current dilemma is whether to fulfil customer demands to move to Internet-based systems. This is in part due to SMEs' concerns about e-commerce that inhibit future development (Van Akkeren and Cavaye, 2000). Table 17.3 summarizes the factors inhibiting e-business adoption in SMEs.

Thus, a range of issues may affect SMEs decisions to invest in e-business and to take advantage of future opportunities. This chapter considers whether these factors affect all SMEs, or if strategic intent acts as a moderator of the enablers and inhibitors. As discussed previously, there is evidence that strategic intent drives SME IS adoption.

Table 17.3: E-business inhibitors

Cost	Implementation costs	Santarelli and D'Altri (2003); Kendall *et al.* (2001); Grandon and Pearson (2004); Van Akkeren and Cavaye (2000); Lawson *et al.* (2003)
	Limited financial resources	Sharma *et al.* (2004); Chapman *et al.* (2000); Ramsey *et al.* (2003); Riemenschneider *et al.* (2003)
	Need for immediate return on investment	Van Akkeren and Cavaye (2000)
Security	Concerns about confidentiality	Santarelli and D'Altri (2003); Quayle (2002); Kendall *et al.* (2001); Lawson *et al.* (2003);
	Fear of fraud	Van Akkeren and Cavaye (2000)
Management	Insufficient time spent on planning	Bianchi and Bivona (2002); Grandon and Pearson (2004)
	Insufficient knowledge or experience of IS	Klein and Quelch (1997); Premkumar and Roberts (1999); Zhu *et al.* (2003); Sharma *et al.* (2004); Kowtha and Choon (2001); Ramsey *et al.* (2003)
	Inexperienced owner	Van Akkeren and Cavaye (2000); Klein and Quelch (1997); Premkumar and Roberts (1999)
Technology	Complexity requiring new skills	Kowtha and Choon (2001); Van Akkeren and Cavaye (2000); Riemenschneider *et al.* (2003)
	Existing IS limiting future development	Van Akkeren and Cavaye (2000); Zhu *et al.* (2003)
	Lack of trust in external IS suppliers	Chapman *et al.* (2000)
	Limited in-house IS skills	Santarelli and D'Altri (2003); Kendall *et al.* (2001); Poon and Swatman (1999); Sharma *et al.* (2004); Chapman *et al.* (2000); Ramsey *et al.* (2003); Lawson *et al.* (2003); Riemenschneider *et al.* (2003)

Therefore, this chapter considers three essential questions about SMEs attitude to e-business:

■ Does strategic intent also drive e-business adoption, and is it a factor of market position or product innovation?

■ Is this consistent across sectors, given research suggesting that sector is not a determining factor in ICT adoption?

■ How is strategic intent and industry adoption influenced by the enablers and inhibitors of e-business adoption?

■ Research approach

These research questions can only be answered by considering a large sample of SMEs. In particular, these questions seek to map out the terrain through analysis of tends and patterns. Thus, a survey is the most effective means of achieving this. The survey instrument is designed to capture information about the strategic intent of the SMEs, as defined by the Ansoff framework. Additionally, information about the current and future use of the Internet is collected. The importance of e-business to the SMEs is determined and the drivers and inhibitors of e-business identified.

Data collection and analysis

The survey is designed as part of a major study into e-business undertaken throughout the UK West Midlands, a region regarded by the EU as in need of development. The data was collected by telephone with the respondent being the SME owner who is knowledgeable about strategic intent.

A total of 1403 firms responded. This was reduced to 354 usable responses here for a number of reasons. Some responses were obtained from firms that could not be considered to be SMEs. They were often small business units operating within larger organisations (the 136 responses from the Education and Health Sectors were examples of this). Also excluded are micro-firms that had no intention of using technology to grow their business, those that did not use PCs, and those sectors that displayed little evidence of strategic intent. For example, the construction industry was removed from the sample as 80% of the firms aimed to stay within existing markets and existing products. This contrasted with other sectors that had over 50% of SMEs moving towards new products and new markets.

Dimensions of analysis

The two dimensions used in the analysis are shown in Table 17.4.

SMEs that are content to stay with existing markets and products are likely to take a more conservative strategic stance than those who are either selling new products into existing markets or selling existing products into new markets. The most radical strategic stance is seen in those SMEs aiming to diversify, by selling new products into new markets.

Strategic intent patterns

Respondents are asked where they expected most growth, in current or new products/services, and whether the growth would be in new or existing markets in order to assess strategic intent. The market penetration category accounts for 172 (49%) of firms; product development for 82 (23%), market development for 43 (12%) while diversification accounts for 56 firms (16%). Figure 17.2 presents the strategic intent by industry of the case firms.

Table 17.4: Dimensions of analysis for assessing strategic intent and e-business

Dimension	Characteristics	Description
Business sector	Manufacturing	
	Wholesale/retail	
	Business services	
Strategic intent	Market penetration	Selling existing products into existing markets
	Product development	Selling new products into existing markets
	Market development	Selling existing products into new markets
	Diversification	Selling new products into new markets

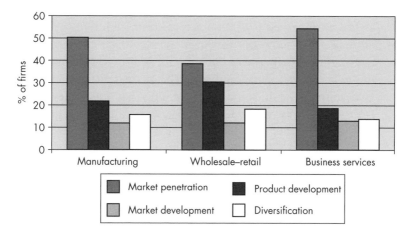

Figure 17.2: Strategic intent by industry.

Many SMEs start as a result of identifying a market niche for one or two products with which the owner is familiar, has knowledge to develop and possibly initial contracts. Many stay within the comfort zone of their knowledge and experience, preferring not to grow beyond a certain size.

The wholesale/retail sector provides a slightly different pattern of strategic intent to the other sectors (Figure 17.2) perhaps reflecting market volatility, as this market requires new products more frequently. A further reason may relate to the SME–customers relationship. As many manufacturers are tied in with customers, their products are more clearly defined by a preferred supplier relationship. Given the strategic intent of most firms is limited, it is likely that the main focus of ICT will be on systems that reduce costs. Owners are less likely to invest for future growth.

Current use of the Internet

Eighty six per cent of SMEs have Internet access, with little industry variation; all use e-mail. Forty per cent of these firms use e-mail internally and externally, suggesting there is some recognition of Internet value in managing internal efficiencies as well as external communication. Fifty three per cent of the SMEs have a marketing web site, with 56% of these updating it at least once a quarter. While there is little cross-sector difference, strategic intent does appear to drive development with over 63% of firms that are looking to introduce new products to existing markets having marketing web sites.

Importance of the Internet in achieving business growth

SMEs were asked about the importance of the Internet in achieving business growth over the next year and the responses analysed by strategic intent and business sector jointly (Table 17.5).

Some important distinctions emerge: firms in business services show a clear and marked gradation across strategic intent types. While 27% of market penetration business services see the Internet as very important, this increases to 35% for those whose strategic intent is towards product development; 47% in market development; and to 59% in the diversification category. This may reflect new opportunities emerging because of the Internet. Delivery of products and services and development of new services may be more likely in business services.

Somewhat counter-intuitively, the reverse is found for manufacturers: while 25% of market penetration manufacturers view the Internet as very important, this declines to 24% in the product development category; to 19% in market development and to 9.5% in diversification. However, this might reflect the well-developed relationships with customers driving Internet adoption for market penetration, while new markets are found in other ways.

Table 17.5: Importance of the Internet for growth by sector and strategic intent

Strategic intent	Sector	Unimportant	Marginally important	Moderately important	Very important
Market penetration	Manufacturing	25.4	28.4	20.9	25.4
	Wholesale–retail	21.1	28.9	21.1	28.9
	Business services	6.0	23.9	43.3	26.9
	Average	*16.9*	*26.7*	*29.7*	*26.7*
Product development	Manufacturing	6.9	27.6	41.4	24.1
	Wholesale–retail	13.3	23.3	43.3	20.0
	Business services	4.3	17.4	39.1	34.8
	Average	*8.5*	*23.2*	*41.5*	*25.6*
Market development	Manufacturing	18.8	43.8	18.8	18.8
	Wholesale–retail	0	58.3	33.3	8.3
	Business services	20.0	13.3	20.0	46.7
	Average	*14.0*	*37.2*	*23.3*	*25.6*
Diversification	Manufacturing	23.8	38.1	28.6	9.5
	Wholesale–retail	22.2	27.8	27.8	22.2
	Business services	5.9	17.6	17.6	58.8
	Average	*17.9*	*28.6*	*25.0*	*28.6*

The wholesale and retail sector shows more market penetration firms consider the Internet as important for strategic growth. However, market development firms present little interest in the Internet. It is surprising that the Internet is not seen as a distribution method for products, although it may reflect the type of products for which the Internet is not a suitable distribution mechanism. Alternatively, it may reflect a desire not to trade outside a limited geographic area.

Importance of e-business

SMEs are then asked about their attitude to e-business and its importance in three years. Fifty one per cent of survey SMEs regards e-business as essential or very important. The cross-sector patterns are similar. E-business is less important for manufacturers than for the other sectors, with only 45% of SMEs considering it either essential or very important. One explanation may be the perception that e-business is about consumer trading rather than supporting customer requirements through business-to-business exchanges. This is somewhat surprising, given the emphasis placed on the importance of EDI by many major manufacturers. However, the other sectors are only slightly more optimistic suggesting that there is still a need to educate owners about future Internet potential (Figure 17.3).

Table 17.6 shows analysis by strategic intent of firms that see e-business as essential or very important.

Clearly, firms that are most strategically conservative are less likely to see e-business as essential or very important. For example,

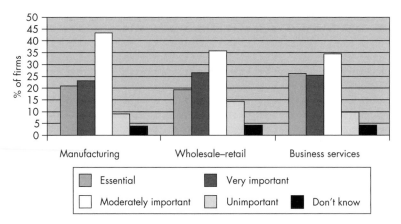

Figure 17.3: Importance of e-business by sector.

Table 17.6: Importance of e-business by strategic intent

Strategic intent	Essential	Very important	Both
Market penetration	23	17	40
Product development	17	38	55
Market development	23	28	51
Diversification	29	25	54

manufacturers in the market penetration category are least likely to see it as essential or very important (34%). Interestingly, firms that intend to develop new products are more likely to see the future importance of e-business. This suggests that, contrary to current thinking, the use of technology is triggered more by a new product orientation in firms than by a new market orientation. For example, business services firms in the diversification category are most likely to see e-business as essential or very important (65%). Thus, while many SMEs can be criticized for having a too one-sided perspective on strategic development, there is a need to encourage SMEs to take a more simultaneous view of new product development *and* new market development.

Drivers for e-business
SMEs are asked the importance of the following issues in encouraging them to use e-business:

■ customer demand;

■ reduced operating costs;

■ reduction in costs associated with sales and purchasing;

- improve the range and quality of services which can be offered to customers online;

- increase in speed of dispatch of goods;

- increase in speed by which suppliers are obtained;

- avoiding loss of market share to competitors already using e-business;

- increase market share.

Table 17.7 shows the percentage of firms in each of 12 categories that replied "very important" to each.

The different drivers have differing effects on different categories of firm. Customer push/demand is highest for manufacturers in the market penetration, product development and market development categories but particularly pronounced for wholesale/retailers that are looking to diversify.

Reducing purchasing cost and operating costs are most prevalent for firms in the product development category, perhaps indicating a heightened need to reduce the cost-base of products to win market share for new products in existing markets. The need to use e-business to reduce purchasing and operating costs is particularly prevalent among market penetration wholesale/retailers – again there may be a strong emphasis on the need to reduce costs to continue to survive with existing products in existing markets. Firms looking to develop new markets seem less concerned about the use of e-business to reduce costs, perhaps this might arise after new markets are penetrated and firms need to compete more on cost than on "novelty" and innovation.

Improving the range and quality of services delivered online item is most pronounced in business services across all strategic intent categories and in wholesale/retailers looking to diversify.

The speed of dispatch driver is strongest for business services in the product development category and for diversifying wholesalers. The increased speed of supply items is most prevalent in the product development strategic intent category as is concern about the loss of market share and winning new customers. Clearly, the product development category emerges as a class of business with a specific and pronounced set of needs and concerns about the move to e-business. Firms in this category have a great interest in e-business given their need to:

- reduce operating costs and costs associated with sales and purchasing;

- increase speed in doing business (important in generating customer satisfaction/lock-in);

Table 17.7: Drivers for e-business adoption

Strategic intent		Customer demand	Reduced operating costs	Reduced sales/ purchasing costs	Improve services online	Speed of dispatch	Increased speed supplies	Avoid losing market share	Winning new customers
Market penetration	Manufacturing	47.5	13.1	9.8	19.7	16.4	19.7	16.4	24.6
	Wholesale–retail	37.5	34.4	31.3	34.4	28.1	21.9	37.5	40.6
	Business services	30.0	25.0	15.0	40.0	20.0	15.0	23.3	40.0
	Average	*38.6*	*22.2*	*16.3*	*30.7*	*20.3*	*18.3*	*23.5*	*34.0*
Product development	Manufacturing	50.0	38.5	38.5	30.8	26.9	30.8	46.2	57.7
	Wholesale–retail	38.5	30.8	26.9	26.9	34.6	38.5	30.8	46.2
	Business services	40.0	40.0	35.0	45.0	40.0	35.0	55.0	55.0
	Average	*43.1*	*36.1*	*33.3*	*33.3*	*33.3*	*34.7*	*43.1*	*52.8*
Market development	Manufacturing	40.0	20.0	13.3	33.3	20.0	26.7	20.0	20.0
	Wholesale–retail	33.3	8.3	8.3	8.3	8.3	8.3	33.3	25.0
	Business services	30.8	30.8	23.1	46.2	23.1	15.4	38.5	53.8
	Average	*35.0*	*20.0*	*15.0*	*30.0*	*17.5*	*17.5*	*30.0*	*32.5*
Diversification	Manufacturing	26.3	21.1	21.1	26.3	10.5	21.1	36.8	42.1
	Wholesale–retail	64.7	41.2	23.5	41.2	41.2	17.6	35.3	52.9
	Business services	37.5	12.5	18.8	31.3	18.8	18.8	25.0	25.0
	Average	*42.3*	*25.0*	*21.2*	*32.7*	*23.1*	*19.2*	*32.7*	*40.4*

▓ win new customers;

▓ avoid losing their existing customer base.

Inhibitors of e-business adoption

Respondents are asked whether, and to what degree, they agree with nine statements that may discourage them from adopting e-business. The statements involve:

▓ concerns about confidentiality;

▓ concerns about the risk of fraud;

▓ technology costs associated with e-business development being too high;

▓ poor public telecommunications infrastructure inhibiting technological development;

▓ obtaining authorization for credit card clearance;

▓ IT skills shortages amongst the workforce;

▓ lack of management willingness to adopt IT as an obstacle to further e-business development;

▓ further e-business development offers no tangible benefits;

▓ further e-business development is not relevant.

Respondents were offered five categories of response ranging from totally agree to totally disagree. A "net agree" score is calculated for each category of firm on each factor. The net score adds together those agreeing or strongly agreeing and subtracts those disagreeing or strongly disagreeing (Table 17.8). Thus, the higher the number, the more respondents agree with the statement.

There is a net positive view that firms are concerned about confidentiality and fraud over the Internet, and these views are most pronounced among diversifying SMEs. The net agree score for confidentiality and fraud in firms in the market development category is 36.5 and 42.3, respectively and these are higher than any other strategic intent category. There are particular concerns about confidentiality and fraud among business service SMEs in the market development, diversify and market penetration categories, together with wholesale/retailers in market development (confidentiality only). Business service firms in the

Table 17.8: E-business inhibitors by sector and strategic intent*

Strategic intentions		Confidentiality	Fraud	Technology costs too high	Poor telcomms	Credit card clearance	Skill shortages	Management unwilling	No benefits	Not relevant
Market penetration	Manufacturing	29.5	32.9	0.0	−13.1	−18.1	−50.9	−32.9	16.4%	−27.8
	Wholesale–retail	3.1	−3.1	−31.2	−21.9	−18.8	−18.7	−43.8	−15.6	−31.3
	Business services	36.7	25.0	13.3	−13.3	−20.0	−28.3	−33.4	−25.1	−19.9
	Average	*26.8*	*22.2*	*−1.3*	*−15.0*	*−19.0*	*−35.3*	*−35.3*	*−19.6*	*−25.5*
Product development	Manufacturing	34.6	30.8	3.8	−15.4	−30.8	−11.6	−34.6	−19.3	−19.3
	Wholesale–retail	−7.7	3.9	0.0	−3.9	−30.8	−23.1	−42.4	−23.0	−34.7
	Business services	−10.0	−5.0	−40.0	−20.0	−30.0	−15.0	−40.0	−15.0	10.0
	Average	*7.0*	*11.1*	*−9.8*	*−12.5*	*−30.6*	*−16.7*	*−38.9*	*−19.4*	*−16.7*
Market development	Manufacturing	−6.7	−13.3	−0.1	−13.3	−13.3	−33.3	−33.4	−26.6	−20.0
	Wholesale–retail	58.4	0.0	−8.3	−50.0	−41.6	−58.4	−58.3	−50.0	−33.3
	Business services	61.6	53.9	38.4	7.7	15.4	−38.5	−53.9	−61.5	−53.8
	Average	*35.0*	*12.5*	*10.0*	*−17.5*	*−12.5*	*−42.5*	*−47.5*	*−45.0*	*−35.0*
Diversify	Manufacturing	36.8	58.0	−10.6	−5.3	−10.6	−5.2	0.0	−5.2	−5.2
	Wholesale–retail	29.4	29.5	23.4	−23.6	−5.9	−41.2	−35.2	−23.4	−23.6
	Business services	43.8	37.5	12.4	12.5	18.8	−18.7	−18.8	−25.0	−12.5
	Average	*36.5*	*42.3*	*7.7*	*−5.7*	*0.1*	*−21.2*	*−17.3*	*−17.4*	*−13.4*
	Overall	*24.8*	*21.6*	*0*	*−13.0*	*−15.3*	*−29.3*	*−34.5*	*−22.6*	*−22.6*

*Values are given in "net agree" score.

product development category seem less concerned about confidentiality and fraud than business service firms in other strategic intent categories.

As technology costs being excessive, the "jury is still out". Although there are concerns about technology costs in the business services market development and the wholesale/retail diversify categories this is countered by low scores in the wholesale/retail market penetration and the business services product development categories. Concerns about credit card clearance do not seem to be an issue except in the business services diversify and market development categories – the only two categories to record a positive net, agree score.

A skill shortage measure gets a strong negative score across the board. Skill shortages are more evident in firms that wish to develop new products for existing markets or develop new markets and new products, suggesting that skills may be more of an issue where the objective is to develop new products. Manufacturers in the diversify category are more likely to experience skills shortages than all other classes of firm, followed by manufacturers in the product development category.

Management unwillingness achieves a high negative net agree score. However, the diversify manufacturers are radically different as it is the only sector to reveal any significant negativity among managers. Both the "not relevant" and "no benefits" measures have negative scores across the board, but negativity is less pronounced in manufacturing diversification.

■ Discussion and conclusions

Three research questions are posed in this chapter. The first focuses on whether strategic intent drives e-business adoption and whether it is a function of market position or product innovation. This research shows that those SMEs remaining in their existing markets are the least likely to invest, primarily due to the Internet not being seen as necessary for growth and less interest in winning new customers. The main finding here is that it is product innovation rather than market penetration that drives e-business. This counters current thinking that market penetration is the more critical.

The second research question is whether industry sector is a determining factor in e-business adoption. Only around half the SMEs in all sectors believe e-business is either very important or essential. There is some sectoral difference when firms rate the importance of the Internet for growth. Over 35% of business service firms see the Internet as very important. This compares with just over 20% for manufacturing and wholesale/retail. More research is required to confirm whether there is industry differentiation and the nature of that differentiation.

The final research question asks whether enablers and inhibitors of e-business adoption vary by strategic intent or industry. There is little differentiation between sectors or strategic intent perspectives with customer demand, increasing market share, avoiding loss of market share and improving online services to customers seen as vital to most firms. These findings confirm existing research. This suggests that SMEs believe their market niches are their strengths and where they should continue to compete. The main difference is in the wholesale/retail sector where being able to dispatch goods more quickly is seen as the main driver. This may indicate that this is a more highly competitive market and that firms need to be efficient to survive. Other efficiency factors are viewed as less important. The key difference in strategic intent is that those firms in the product development group perceive the need to improve online services to customers as of lesser importance than reducing operating costs.

Turning to inhibitors, concerns about confidentiality, fraud and the high cost of e-business are the main deterrents across all sectors and strategic intent groups. This concurs with the literature. However, in contrast to other research, most SMEs here do not believe that limited workforce IT skills nor management unwillingness are issues, except in more innovative firms looking to develop new products in new markets. This may be due to firm age and existing skills bases. SMEs also believe, to a lesser degree, that e-business is both relevant and may offer some benefit.

Thus, it appears that the pressure to adopt is driven by external factors rather than internal ones. This may partially explain the cautious approach of SMEs to Internet adoption given their resource constraints; they may be waiting for signs from the market that the investment is required.

18 E-business influencers

■ Introduction

The two previous chapters demonstrate that e-business in small- and medium-sized enterprises is not as advanced as the hype would have one believe. Many firms are still exploring the potential of the Internet for market intelligence. While web sites are also often found, these are mainly brochureware. The adoption of e-business has been shown to be opportunistic, yet little time is spent by firms in exploring the strategic potential. Though there appear to be firms in some industries that recognize the value, the picture is mixed. It is not clear that strategic intent is driving e-business to any great extent.

However, much time and money is being expended by governments, globally, in encouraging SMEs to invest in Internet technologies for e-business. The logic behind such policies is to maintain economic growth, recognizing that SMEs play a pivotal role in business. SMEs can only compete effectively if they are using the same Internet technologies as their larger competitors.

It is not clear if the efforts of government are influencing the adoption of Internet technologies by SMEs for e-business. As shown in Chapter 2, the SME owner is instrumental in decisions to adopt information systems, although IS consultants and suppliers provide the expertise that is lacking internally. This chapter investigates whether Internet technology adoption is any different, particularly due to government intervention. Information system adoption is also influenced by customer pressure; this is also true of Internet technology adoption as shown in Chapter 16.

A case study approach is used to understand the role of government, the owner, customers, and IS consultants and other agents in influencing decisions to develop e-business solutions. All 50 of the case study firms discussed here have decided to use Internet technologies to a greater or lesser degree. These cases were studied over a 3-year period and all were visited at least twice to discuss the influencing factors on their Internet adoption plans. One of the key issues for this research is understanding the relationships between and within organizations and people that influence the decision process. Actor network theory (ANT) provides a useful means to consider relationships as it not only considers the relationship itself, but the strength of that relationship.

Five patterns of Internet adoption strategy are identified with different influencing factors and level of influence. Exemplar case studies are presented to elaborate understanding of the relationships.

Conclusions suggest that, as with other ICT decisions, the owner is key. However, there is evidence that local project support and suppliers are more instrumental in adoption strategies than direct government intervention.

Potential influences on Internet adoption

As discussed in Chapter 16, Internet technologies have the capacity to radically alter firms' approaches to business. This change may be as simple as using e-mail for communication or as complex as disintermediation altering the supply chain relationship. Changing the marketplace and relationships is a complex activity. While the Internet has radically changed communication and research capabilities and has enabled the development of "pureplays", for many established firms, there has been little change in the way they do business. Customer pressure has already been identified as one major influence for Internet technology adoption (Chapter 16). Indeed powerful customers with preferred suppliers give them no choice but to develop e-business tools (Wagner *et al.*, 2003). The wider competitive environment may also influence decisions to adopt, as may the many government initiatives that are on offer.

Competitive environment

The influence of the competitive environment should not be underestimated. The relationships identified by Porter in his five forces model are as apt for the Internet age as they were for the machine age. The Internet is a tool to enhance strategy rather than define it. Firms need to build effective business strategies that enable the strengths of the Internet to work for them in establishing competitive advantage. Indeed, the successful firms will be those in traditional markets that identify innovative ways to deploy Internet technologies. "Pureplays" will be successful if they focus on business strategies that make them distinctive (Porter, 2001). Figure 18.1 identifies the changes in the competitive environment due to Internet technologies.

The five competitive forces still provide a useful structural model by which to understand how the economic value of a product or service is distributed between the different players in the market. The model is still valid even if channels, competitors, suppliers or substitutes change (Porter, 2001).

The use of Internet technologies impacts on industries in a variety of ways. It provides access to new customers through new delivery channels. For example, many high street stores have online shops. Industry efficiency can also be improved by increasing market accessibility relative to traditional substitutes.

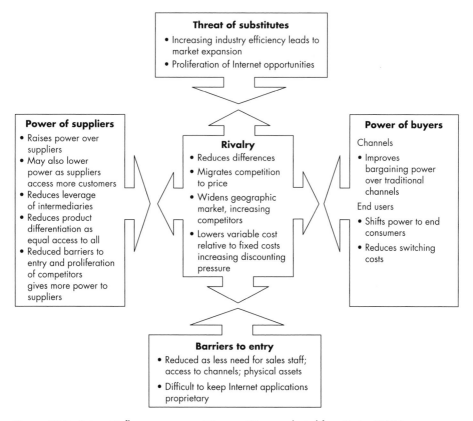

Figure 18.1: Internet influences on competitiveness. (*Source*: adapted from Porter, 2001.)

However, the ubiquity of Internet technologies means that competitiveness is heightened for many firms. Competitor intelligence is more easily available, which increases the bargaining power of suppliers. New substitutes are created through the different delivery mechanisms generated by the Internet. Customer power is likely to rise as switching costs are low using Internet technologies. As with other technologies, Internet-based systems cannot provide sustainable competitive advantage. Indeed, the openness of such technologies means that systems are more accessible. While increasing geographic reach opens up new markets it also puts more firms in competition with each other. Cost structures are changed by the Internet towards increasing fixed costs rather than variable costs (Porter, 2001). Firms are likely to gain the greatest benefits from use of the Internet, if they recognize its potential as a complementor to traditional activities. For example, in the US, customers can order on-line and collect from a local store outlet, which many prefer to waiting for a postal delivery. Benefits can only be achieved through strategic positioning. Before moving to the use of Internet technologies firms need to focus on the economic value to be gained. They need to consider how they will be differentiated from competitors. Firms need to ensure strategic fit between business activities in the supply chain (Porter, 2001). Chapters 7 and 8 demonstrated the value of the five forces model in the SMEs context. The lessons presented here on its value when considering the strategic value of Internet technologies may be as valid. Thus, it is reasonable to suppose that customers, suppliers and competitors are likely to influence adoption.

Influence of government policies on SME Internet adoption

Governments in the European Union and south-east Asia have active intervention policies to encourage SMEs to adopt the Internet. The UK government has developed policy guidelines and web sites that provide information about the opportunities from the Internet. Government business advisors encourage SMEs to take their first steps to Internet use. There are a large number of projects in UK regions run by consortia of local authorities, higher education institutions and business support organizations. For example, there are at least 13 in the Manchester region of the UK (Evans, 2002). The European Union provides funds for projects that support advice and training for SMEs (Lunati, 2000). The Danish government has put in place strategies to ensure diffusion of knowledge and adoption through the economy (Zhu et al., 2003). In Singapore, there are a number of government initiatives to promote e-business in SMEs (Kendall et al., 2001). Malaysia's Vision 2020 provides the strategic framework for the proposed changes to the economy that are expected to be enabled by the use of Internet technologies. A key project for Malaysia is the Multimedia Super Corridor (http://www.mdc.com.my) that provides services and support for firms that are investing in new technologies. Similarly in Korea, government policy has been directed at supporting SMEs (Nugent and Yhee, 2002). In Western Australia, both state and local government have promoted the development of regional e-market places to increase e-business adoption (Standing et al., 2002). However, there is little evidence that these policies are successful in changing attitudes amongst SMEs. In Singapore, it is the existing knowledge of the owner and the relative advantage from e-business that drives adoption (Kendall et al., 2001). While in Korea advice from commercial sources is valued more highly than that of government support (Nugent and Yhee, 2002).

As shown in Chapters 16 and 17, SMEs' decisions to adopt the Internet are dependent upon the relative advantage and indirect benefits they might obtain. Government pull is not likely to be a factor, indeed it is likely to be rejected. The SMEs themselves are often the driver of change with the owner being the predominant force. The external pressure, when it comes, is likely to be from customers.

The potential influencing factors are thus customers, suppliers, competitors, government, Internet adoption projects as well as the owner. Figure 18.2 summarizes the potential different market and institutional influences on Internet adoption.

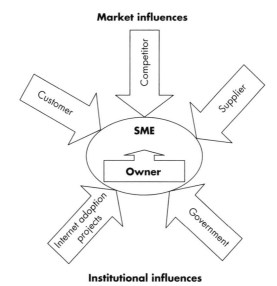

Figure 18.2: Market and institutional influences on SME Internet adoption.

This chapter looks to identify whether, and in what way, the different players influence Internet adoption and e-business strategies in SMEs. As a result of the integrated nature of the market, it is possible that there will be multiple influencers with different degrees of influence. To attempt to understand the relationships it is useful to use a research approach that specifically focuses on this. Actor network theory provides such an approach.

▪ Research approach

Actor network theory provides a means of exploring the patterns of interaction within and between organizations (Conway, 1997). Network analysis focuses on the configuration, nature and content of the set of internal and/or external organizational relationships. The underlying belief is that strategic investment in new technologies requires interactions between number of players. Network analysis enables exploration of the different relationships required for the successful development of innovative technologies (Jones *et al.*, 1997). The network literature identifies the key elements of the network to be the actors, links and flows. Thus, network analysis provides a useful means of modelling case data to explore influencers and relationships.

This chapter uses a framework developed by Beckinsale and Jones (1999) to explore relationships within and between players involved in introducing e-business. Figure 18.3 presents the ANT framework.

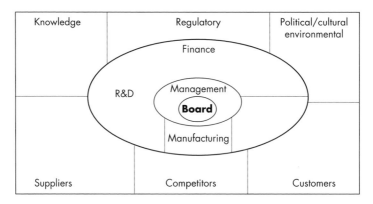

Figure 18.3: ANT framework. (*Source:* adapted from Beckinsale and Jones, 1999.)

The framework considers influencers within and external to the firm. It enables models to be developed that show the relationships between influencers within the firm. For example, within SMEs the owner is likely to be central to any investment decisions (Jones *et al.*, 1997). However, changes in business process may affect or be influenced by the operations manager (see Case study 4.1 Light Assembly Co.). The framework recognizes the role of competitive advantage in the introduction of new technologies, and hence the need to consider the roles of suppliers, customers and competitors in influencing investment decisions. Additionally, external organizations are thought to be increasingly supportive in assisting SMEs in the development of the innovative use of technologies. These external organizations include government schemes, public sector projects as well as collaborative research and development (Beckinsale and Jones, 1999).

Central to the framework is the examination of the sets of relationships involved in any innovation. Relationship variables fall into six categories:

1 Relationship type (operationalized, social and moral) (Kanter, 1972).

2 Formalization (extent of formal recognition).

3 Intensity (strength and frequency of interaction and flow of transaction content over time).

4 Reciprocity (balance and flow over time of transaction content unilateral or bilateral).

5 Multiplexity (the degree to which two actors are linked by multiple role relations (Conway, 1997; Tichy, 1979)).

6 Relationship originator.

Table 18.1: Case firm size

Type of firm	Number of employees	Number of case firms
Micro	0–9	29
Small	10–99	18
Medium	100–249	3

Table 18.2: Industry groups of case firms

Industry sectors	Number of case firms
Automotive	5
Business services	9
IT services	22
Retail	4
Manufacturing	5
Engineering	5

Data collection

Fifty SME cases are used to explore the key influencers on the decision to adopt Internet technologies. It was important for this research to monitor the process over time to determine the development of influencing relationships.

Interviews were held with owners and senior managers in the SMEs to identify their reasons for deciding to undertake Internet adoption. The interviews considered the strategy of the business and the influencing factors in the decision process. Network analysis models are developed for each of the cases. These models show the relationships and the strengths of the relationships. The findings were confirmed with the SMEs. The size of firms and industry groups are shown in Tables 18.1 and 18.2 for completeness.

The sample is convenient, as these are all firms that were known to a local Internet intervention project. These firms might be thought to be enthusiastic adopters of Internet technologies, but as the later analysis shows, this is not always the case as strategic direction appears to be the main driver. Additionally, as indicated in earlier chapters, there is little evidence that industry sector is material in IS adoption.

■ Case analysis

The 50 cases demonstrate five patterns (Table 18.3) that identify the influences that led to their decisions to adopt the Internet. The patterns are determined from an analysis of the networks developed from the interview data. These five patterns indicate different network influences

Table 18.3: Influence patterns of Internet adoption

Network	Market influences		Institutional influences				Firm influences
	Supplier	Customer	Competitor	Knowledge	Regulatory	Government	Owner
Expert (18 firms)		Customer partnership to use Internet technologies to provide new service		Local Internet adoption project used as a means for acquiring subsidized access to Internet			CEO leads e-business development. Strong IS expertise within firm to support Internet technology development
Industry support (4 firms)		Customers asked for Internet technology requirements. But not central to development		Use of consultants to develop market intelligence on Internet technology development. Local Internet adoption project advice used to assist	High influence and support from industry regulator		CEO leads e-business development. IT director manages project development
Customer led (11 firms)		Customers pushing for e-business. Closely guiding SME		Local Internet adoption project used as a means for acquiring subsidized access to Internet			CEO leads. IT director manages project development
ICT Support (10 firms)	IS support firm provides knowledge about opportunities from Internet technologies	Customers beginning to want to use e-mail communication		Local Internet project contacted as part of awareness raising			CEO led
Novice (7 firms)				Local Internet project and other agencies contacted as part of awareness raising			CEO led

on adoption of Internet technologies in the case SMEs. Exemplar cases are presented next to highlight the different approaches taken to Internet adoption. These relationships are examined in the light of the person driving development, this is either the CEO, in smaller SMEs, or the IT director in larger SMEs with an IT department.

The first three relationships suggest that the firms have all developed IT internally to some degree. The decision to adopt the Internet is based on a business requirement to develop and grow the business. There are three models of relationship development here. The first is the expert network, which is primarily evidenced by the IT firms. The second is the industry support network, where SMEs are working in partnership with industry organizations. The third group is the customer-led network, where customer pressure is seen to be instrumental in the decision to invest in Internet technologies. The last two relationships are primarily found in organizations with either limited ICT use or with an internal focus. The fourth network is the ICT support network, where firms have developed internal support systems and are investigating whether there are opportunities to be more customer-focused. The final network, the novice network, is primarily those firms that have little knowledge or experience of the value of ICT to their business.

Expert network

Expert networks are usually firms that are providing an IS-based product or service. Therefore, IS expertise is high within the firm. The customers' requirements are the key determining factor. All work is carried out collaboratively with customers. The CEO is instrumental in the development and promotion of the relationship. There are no other significant influences on the firm.

Case study 18.1

Online education started in 1998 with funding from a university enterprise scheme. It is owned by the CEO. The objectives of the firm are to provide online education services ranging from authoring, consultancy, technology and Internet development services. The firm employs six highly-skilled Internet development staff. All have strong understanding of the technology and how it may be used and designed. All were hired on the basis of this knowledge. The development of the firm's web site is based on customer requirements through consultation sessions with clients. The main customers are universities and colleges. An issue for the firm is that 40% of their business is with one customer. The SME is depending on the Internet for delivery and interaction with customers. For them, fast access to the Internet is vital, the main reason for the firm's involvement with a government support project, CW2000, was to gain access to ADSL at a relatively low price.

The owner of the firm is instrumental in decisions regarding Internet adoption issues. The relationships are between the owner and external players. The customer is the key actor in the relationship. The design of the online learning and delivery of product is determined by the customer requirements. This appears to be the case with many of the IT-sector-based firms. CW2000 is seen in the context of this case as a supplier. The information available to the firm from CW2000 through the Project Director has been influential in supporting the firm and in providing information about the ADSL service.

Industry support network

The industry support network has the most external influencers on adoption of Internet technologies for e-business. The innovative changes being proposed here will lead to major changes in the industry, hence the regulatory bodies are intimately involved in the process. Given that the focus is on e-business, knowledge of how the industry works is vital. Customers are involved primarily for advice on best practice. Managing a major project development of this nature requires organization within the firm. While the CEO is instrumental in setting up these projects, they will be driven by the IT director who has the relevant expertise.

Case study 18.2

Hair products was started in the 1930s as a wholesale trader to supply barbers and ladies hair salons. This is still the major part of the business. The firm employs 80 people and has a turnover of £7.5 million. It has markets throughout the world and sells through a variety of outlets including mail order and trade centres. The biggest growth area for the firm is in the beauty side of the business due to the increasing exploitation by salons of treatments and therapies. It supplies 65% of the beauty salon and hotel sector with beauty products. The firm is working closely with the industry regulatory body to develop e-commerce services for beauty products to sell directly to the public. The site also aims to develop the industry. One approach to this is to provide a salon finder service on the web site as well as links to different product suppliers. As a larger SME, hair products has an IT department with an IT director and three IT staff members. Both the CEO and the IT director believe the *technology can drive the business* and *aid growth and turnover*. While the owner is central to the decision to work with the industry body, the IT department is leading on the web site development. The firm's contact with CW2000 was to find out more about web development opportunities. The firm values the impartial advice that they are offered.

The owner is again critical to the decision to progress Internet development. However, in this case the IT Director is instrumental in co-ordinating IT and Internet development within the organization. There are more external links than in the other cases due to the development of the e-Commerce web site with the Beauty Industry Guild. An interesting link is with the firm in the knowledge segment of the map. This firm is currently assisting in providing information on competitors and their web development plus examining existing web sites. It was through this external knowledge link that hair products heard about CW2000.

Customer-led network

It is not surprising to find customer-led networks as the literature indicates that customer pressure is often a driver to adoption of Internet technologies. Customers indicate to SMEs that they have to adopt e-business to remain preferred suppliers. Customers requirements determine e-business project development. The firm has to increase IS development staff either through contractors or employing more itself. Again, the CEO is at the centre of the decision to change while the development is driven by the IT director. There are no other significant external influences.

Case study 18.3

Agricultural Engineering was established in 1969 to supply the agricultural industry with machine, press work and castings for relevant machines. The firm employs 150 people. It is planning to expand and employ a further 20 people in the near future. The chairman is the owner. There is a CEO and four additional directors who oversee works, technical, commercial and general operations. The firm's main customer accounts for 35% of the £8 million sales. The firm also has a strategy of growth through acquisition. Information system has not been a major element of the business. However, training in the use of IT has been considered important being led by the CEO. A recent takeover, however, brought a number of IS staff with it and there is now a formal IS department in the firm. The acquisition has changed the nature of the business providing an entry into the telecommunications market.

The firm is in close discussions with customers on the development of customer-focused web processes. Much of this is happening via e-mail. As a manufacturer and supplier to automotive firms it had seen change in customers' use of the Internet. Customers such as Massey Ferguson and Saab Scania are driving Internet adoption and the move to limited integration with back-office systems. These customers are pushing to move away from paper communication and utilize e-mail and web sites to communicate job status and assist Kan Ban manufacturing processes in real time. Customers are now demanding e-mail contact with the firm as well as providing information of order progress through the web site. The firm sees the use of the Internet becoming more important as the telecommunication business grows. Internal departments are linked through an Intranet. While the CEO is central to strategic decisions, the IS department is working closely with customers to identify requirements. The firm became involved with CW2000 when ADSL provision was identified as important for speed of information transfer. The information about the possibility of having ADSL was identified by the consultant who was working closely with the firm.

These three networks all demonstrate the value of external relationships to the development of web-based business and ultimately commerce. The expert network and industry network are working in partnership with customers and industry groups to develop business value. Customer pressure is the driver for the customer-led network.

The final two networks, *ICT support* and *novice*, are representative of firms for which IS is a support tool and where customers show little interest in exploiting the relationship electronically.

ICT support network

The main focus of the IS support network is internal integration through local area networks. Communication within the firm is the main driver. There is limited use of external e-mail with suppliers and customers. The CEO is central to all decision making and is at the information gathering stage. There is no pressure to adopt Internet technologies to enable the success of the business value proposition.

Case study 18.4

Construction Co. was founded in 1974 to provide general construction solutions for the building industry. The firm has diversified into commercial and speculative developments and barn conversions. The CEO is the owner. The firm has 22 employees and a turnover of £3.5 million. The owner has no "burning desire" to grow the business. There are no great customer pressures with local customers contributing 80% of sales. Construction Co. has a well-developed internal network used for business support. This network was set up by the CEO, with an electrician to help install the cabling. Staff use internal e-mail regularly. *"The Intranet provides fast and efficient communication in house"*, the CEO said. The technology allows sales assistants to access each other's client databases and examines previous customer contracts to assist in developing quotations.

The IS and the network is now supported by a local IT supplier. The IT supplier has a relationship with CW2000 and informed Construction Co. of the potential to be had from an investment in ADSL to contact customers by e-mail. The firm was less sure about other opportunities from the use of the Internet such as web services. Seminars from CW2000 have proved useful in improving understanding, although the firm is still unsure about the value of a web site. The IT supplier relationship is a major reason for many firms hearing about and getting involved in CW2000.

However, there is little evidence of exploitation with customers. The e-mail communication is limited to one customer and is not expected to increase in the near future. The e-mail and the use of ADSL has been most beneficial in sharing drawings with architects and design engineers.

Novice network

Firms in the novice network category are only just starting to consider the value of Internet technologies to the firm. They are not sure of the value of IS and are exploring opportunities. The CEO is the only person involved in the discovery process. There are no other significant influencers.

Case study 18.5

Machine Components was started in 1977 by the owner. The firm supplies machine components to automotive and manufacturing firms. Turnover is about £0.3 million. There are currently seven employees, six skilled engineers and one administrator. The firm produces computerized machines, motor racing and moulding components. These are all bespoke. The industry is declining and this is putting pressure on the firm. It decided to raise capital through the sale of a building and invest in new machinery to boost business. Gaining ISO 9000 accreditation has also helped here.

The firm has four computers. Two are used for programming machines for production, these are networked. The other two standalone PCs are used for accounting and other administrative activities. The firm uses e-mail with one customer, most preferring the use of Fax. It is not sure whether a web site would provide many benefits as they do not have a clear product to sell, rather they provide a service. However, they find it useful to be able to order online. The firm heard about CW2000 through an advisor at a local government investment agency. The agency provided funds for web site development, but they did not have the skills to progress the design of the web site. CW2000 provided the knowledge and skills required.

This case shows that the drive for Internet development comes directly from the CEO. Information and communication technologies are limited and are directed by the CEO. He is the focal point for all web-based relationship transactions due to the lack of skills in-house. These relationships are common across micro-firms in the engineering and manufacturing sectors. Firms like Machine Components, with no knowledge of IS are reliant on external advice if they can find it.

■ Discussion

Novice network SMEs are unsure of the benefits from Internet adoption. They are encouraged to participate in such projects because they exist rather than for the business benefits that might accrue. Information and communication technologies support network SMEs have recognized the benefits of investing in internal IS systems and see the Internet as a means of marketing and presenting a more innovative image. However, the benefits are not thought through strategically. Industry support SMEs are looking for longer-term benefits through changing the way they are perceived in the market place. However, IS is seen as a means to an end, hence benefits are more likely to be indirect. Both the expert- and customer-led networks perceive direct benefits in the long term from their decision to invest in Internet technologies. However, there are different reasons in each case. Internet technologies are almost the *raison d'etre* for the expert network SMEs. They see direct benefits as an outcome of their business strategy. The customer-led network sees the Internet as a means of locking in its existing customers and gaining new ones as part of their business strategy, thus turning a necessity into a virtue.

Institutional influences on adoption are focused around local Internet adoption projects. SMEs use these to a greater or lesser degree depending upon the stage of knowledge and experience with Internet technology adoption. Where these projects provide subsidized access to Internet technologies firms take the opportunity to reduce costs (expert and customer-led networks). Where firms are developing understanding about the potential then the local intervention project is used for advice (industry support, IS support and novice networks). Clearly governments have not influenced SMEs directly in their decisions on Internet investment. None of the SMEs know of central government schemes to support e-business adoption in SMEs. None of them use the UK Online facilities. This supports previous findings in Singapore (Kendall *et al.*, 2001) and Korea (Nugent and Yhee, 2002). However, e-business is more prevalent among European SMEs in countries where the government has an e-business strategy (Zhu *et al.*, 2003). SMEs tend to build local support networks, hence the preferred involvement with local rather than national knowledge providers.

Strikingly, with market influences, competitors do not feature at all in e-business decisions. This contrasts with Kowtha and Choon (2001) where competitiveness was found to partially influence web site development decisions. Suppliers also feature minimally, indeed there is no evidence for supply chain requirements for e-business. The only supplier evidence is through an IS vendor who provides support. As has been found in other studies, customers are highly influential in the adoption decisions of firms. The different emphases in each case depend upon the level of e-business within the industry.

Within the firm, the CEO is the key driver of e-business opportunities. This is not surprising given the strategic focus of SMEs. The experience and knowledge of IT directors in some SMEs is used to manage and direct e-business projects. Knowledge from local IS suppliers or support agencies providing consultancy services is instrumental in identifying resources. Thus, it is likely to be local intermediaries that influence SMEs choice in developing Internet technologies. External expertise is found to be highly effective for SMEs where there is strong organizational readiness for IS adoption. It is also dependent upon the good relationship between the IS consultant and the SME owner (Thong *et al.*, 1997). The lack of information about opportunity, availability and sources of new technologies can inhibit development (Sharma *et al.*, 2004). This leads to an amended model of influencing factors (Figure 18.4).

From a strategic perspective neither the customer-led nor novice networks have planned their strategic growth in any coherent way (Figure 18.5). The business value of the Internet is not clear to firms who are situated in novice networks, in particular. However, the other three networks, IS support, industry support and expert, all consider the Internet an important part of their future development. The ICT support network is using the technology to provide internal efficiency while seeing little business benefit. The contingent model of Internet adoption developed in Chapter 16 is used here to position the different networks.

The customer-led network is being pushed by customers, but the lack of strategic direction may inhibit the potential business opportunity. However, both the expert and industry support networks see the Internet as integral to their growth and development. The relationships viewed in the analysis appear to support strongly the supplier/customer push theory to Internet adoption and development. However, where trading

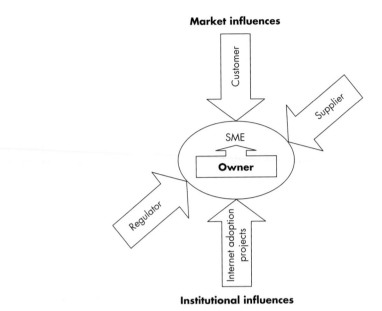

Figure 18.4: Amended e-Business influences model.

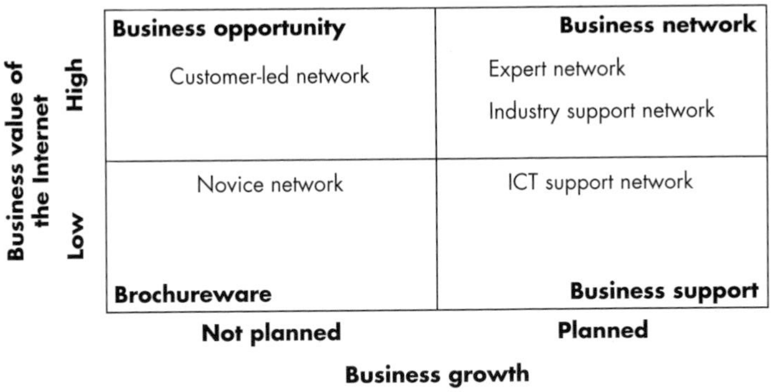

Figure 18.5: Strategic growth opportunities from the SME networks.

partners are themselves not pursuing e-business it is unlikely that SMEs will take a lead (Zhu *et al.*, 2003).

Few of the firms have a formal corporate or Internet strategy. SMEs appear to be investigating the technology and looking for emergent strategies. However, the owner is critical in the decision-making process, even when there is an internal IT department. Mehrtens *et al.* (2002) propose three factors that influence Internet adoption amongst SMEs: perceived benefit, organizational readiness and external pressure. There is evidence here for the latter two factors. However, perceived benefit is a less important factor except in the case of the industry network.

◼ Conclusions

This chapter has identified a number of different e-business adoption patterns for SMEs. These confirm previous research that the customer is instrumental in the decision process. There is little evidence that either suppliers or competition plays a role in the adoption decisions. The focus is on the strategic direction of the firm, which in many cases is emergent. Where there is a planned strategy, SMEs work closely with either customers (expert network) or collaborators (industry network). However, there is still little evidence that e-business is seen as critical to gaining competitive advantage. As Porter (2001) argues that Internet technologies need to be assessed to determine whether and in what way they support the business objectives. Clearly, for many SMEs, this is not obvious. SME owners are aware of the need to use resources wisely, and as e-business is not a business requirement, it has relatively low priority.

Local intervention projects are particularly useful for SMEs, which find access to impartial advice invaluable. The local nature of the advice is the projects are also aware of local service providers, with whom SMEs prefer to work, as shown in Chapter 6. However, the lack of awareness of government information sources suggests that government policy might be better directed at developing local intervention projects and providing information and support to IT suppliers and consultants that will help them support SMEs more effectively. This can take a number of forms from practical support such as grants that can be accessed through the local suppliers to developing networks between suppliers and government agencies to assist Internet adoption.

19 Managing IS: the future

■ Introduction

This book shows that managing information system in small- and medium-sized enterprises is not something that can be left to chance. SMEs can gain as much by developing their information systems strategy conjointly with their business strategy as large firms. However, it is clear that the heterogeneity of SMEs must be acknowledged in the development of appropriate strategies for the development of management IS. This final chapter reviews the issues developed throughout this book.

■ SMEs – a vibrant community

SMEs have been shown to be an exciting and vibrant part of the economy. Their contribution is essential to most countries as they employ the majority of workers. The changes brought about by large corporations focusing on their core competences has helped the rise of SMEs as entrepreneurs identify new areas in the market required to support such actions. This has increased the number of specialist firms in all industries.

Noticeably, the SME sector is an unforgiving one, with 20% of all SMEs failing within their first 3 years. However, failure is not only due to poor business ideas, it is more to do with a lack of understanding of the management issues that have to be addressed in order to be successful. Success can mean many things from providing sufficient income for family members to developing an entrepreneurial empire. To achieve success requires active management.

Management means different things at different times in the life of an SME as they move from the web-based structures which centre on the owner, to more matrix or hierarchy-based structures required of larger organizations as power is delegated to managers. As management structures become more formalized, SMEs require better knowledge and information to manage the growing web. Information systems are an integral part of the management development process.

◼ IS and SMEs

Management IS in SMEs are likely to be relatively simple in the initiation stages of a firm. The use of spreadsheets to manage accounts abounds, although as firms grow they usually adopt a simple accounting package. As SMEs grow the need to manage customers more effectively is apparent and databases begin to be used. Many SMEs install local area networks and use e-mail to contact customers. There is evidence that internal e-mail is being used in larger SMEs to improve communication between branches. However, as seen in the later chapters, there is little evidence that e-business is being undertaken by many SMEs. SMEs are generally pushed to adopt IS by need or by customers – as seen for those that supply major manufacturers.

SMEs tend to be followers in adopting management IS except for a few innovative owners. There is little evidence of the flexibility for which the sector is known in its adoption of IS. Business process redesign is not often evident as a strategic response, neither is there a clear focus on competitive advantage, both of which require firms to be agile in their use of IS. The main response to IS adoption is as a corrective manoeuvre to mitigate threats.

The above is often due to the cautiousness of SME owners, because they want to ensure that they are getting value for money, as resources are usually tight. There is also nervousness about whether the purchased system will satisfy business requirements. As most IS development is outsourced, there is also concern that adequate support is in place to ensure the system keeps working. SMEs are often in a difficult position with IS investment as many large IS firms fee levels are beyond the resources of many of them. Systems are not always designed for the SME, but may be cut down versions of those designed for larger firms, as in the case of some ERP systems. This may lead some SMEs to work with very small IS suppliers, with the risks that they might fail or not be available for support. However, IS adoption is more likely to be successful if SMEs plan in advance and have a strategy for that adoption.

◼ IS strategy – the way forward?

Planning the management IS required to fulfil the current business strategy has long been known to be vital for large corporations. It is also beneficial to growing SMEs. Systems requirements become more complex as the firm grows. While the CEO is critical to the growing SME, better market intelligence and knowledge of the competitive position of the firm is also essential. Firms require ongoing capital investment to grow. To convince investors, financial information about the state of the firm is crucial. Knowledge of sales and costs as well as assets and liabilities are vital. Business success is also in achieving business goals and the critical success factors that underpin them. Information provides the basis for this knowledge.

Information systems strategy provides the means of analysing the management information requirements that are required for effective management. The analysis of success factors to achieve the business strategy provides a useful starting point for the definition of management IS. Information systems strategy is a dynamic activity that needs to be carried out as business strategy is reviewed to ensure that IS are providing effective support for the firm. The issue for many SMEs is that the business strategy is often implicit and emergent. While the SME owner has a clear idea, it is not always communicated through the firm. Additionally, goals are often seen in purely financial terms, whereas SMEs can usefully focus more on customers, innovation and organization. These aspects of the business, all contribute to the financial success of the firm, and business processes need to be reviewed to ensure consistency with business goals. Hence, an organizational approach to ISS that focuses on the relationship between strategic, tactical and operational information requirements is useful for SMEs. The approach also reviews the organizational enablers and inhibitors of information flow in the firm, as there may be no need for additional IS, rather better use of existing systems will provide the required results.

By undertaking ISS, SME owners can plan the systems they require in advance of the need for them and to ensure that they have identified clearly the systems requirements. This ensures that resources will be directed appropriately. As SMEs grow, their systems needs become more complex the strategic focus of IS may need to change.

Strategic perspective on IS in growing firms

There appear to be four strategic responses to IS investment in IS, as identified in the focus-dominance model developed in Chapter 9. This model provides a means of considering strategic management IS needs. The first strategic response is efficiency, found in start-up firms and some life style firms that are not looking for growth. These firms use simple management IS and see no reason to invest further. The co-ordination response is found in growing firms where there is a need to manage the increasing numbers of customers. Adoption is reactive and is usually cost-focused. Firms invest in local area networks and customer databases. There is no review of business processes or of skills and roles within the firm. Some firms are content to manage growth in this way with the current business strategy focusing on market development. Both of these responses are cost-focused, with IS seen as a necessary evil rather than having potential to change the firm.

The collaboration response is primarily found in manufacturing firms, but also those firms that are dependent upon a small number of customers. The development and maintenance of that relationship is critical to these firms hence they need to invest in IS for effective management. The response is likely to be reactive to customers' requirements, but there is recognition of the value of IS. These firms are likely to invest in collaborative systems that enable information exchange such as EDI and Extranets. MRP and ERP systems are also found. The final strategic response is that of repositioning, diversification is the driver here as firms look to develop markets and products, often identifying an innovative new product or means of delivery. Firms here are excited by the opportunities from IS and are experimenters in e-business and knowledge management. These firms show that IS investment is recognized as a value-adding response.

While the research in Chapter 9 identified a number of systems that are found in the various responses, it is clear that as new technologies are available to SMEs, investment is considered. Thus, it is now common for SMEs to have e-mail and web sites, although many will be simply brochureware. Intranets are being developed and Extranets are beginning to replace EDI. The adoption response of new technologies is slower than for large firms for reasons discussed, but gradually SMEs are investing in them. The decision to invest is a combination of identifying value to the business, customer demand and improving communication. Thus, the systems within the focus-dominance model evolve over time, but the premise on which adoption is undertaken is likely to remain the same. For example, Figure 19.1 shows a revised focus-dominance model that takes account of the state of use of Internet technologies in many SMEs.

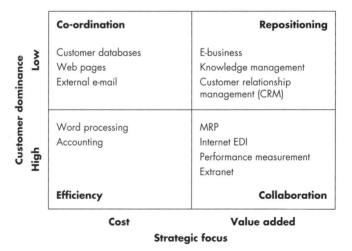

Figure 19.1: Revised focus-dominance model.

Business transformation

The essential issue identified in the focus-dominance model is an underlying dynamic in IS adoption as firms grow. More management IS are required as firms move towards formal management structures that require greater exchange of information to be effective. Most SMEs move from the efficiency to co-ordination scenario, still perceiving IS as a cost. For these firms there is no change from their initial strategic intent of market penetration. These firms are those that are comfortable with steady growth to a limited level, supporting the argument that stages of growth models only have limited validity. These firms follow an evolutionary path with IS with internal integration through the use of a local area network or Intranet. However, there is little thought given to changing business processes to focus on core competencies. Information system is used only to support existing processes. Yet as IS use grows, firms start to recognize that some structural changes may be necessary to improve internal communication.

The other main growth path is towards collaboration, where although customer push is evident, SMEs acknowledge the value-adding potential of IS in their future business development. For these firms product development in collaboration with major customers is critical. The relationship demands that SMEs are able to use IS to enable that collaboration. Business network redesign is central to the strategic use of IS, however, industry demands mean that many firms move directly to this use from simple use of stand-alone systems. Information system adoption is a strategic response, but while management processes may change to aid communication, there is no change in organizational structure or changed roles and skills of staff to achieve strategic alignment. This limits the ability of the firm to use information strategically.

Experience of the use of management IS does persuade some firms to become more innovative in their use of IS and reposition themselves in the market. These firms are following a diversification strategy and are usually run by highly entrepreneurial owners. Hence, once the internal integration benefits of IS have been achieved and the firm is running smoothly, new challenges are sought. Information system is often seen as an opportunity for radical change and essentially new business is spun off that recognizes the network opportunities provided particularly by Internet technologies. As changes are embedded, the need to refocus business processes is undertaken. Again, IS adoption is a strategic response but these firms recognize the need for different structures, processes and skills to achieve full strategic alignment.

Thus, SMEs can benefit from strategic IS, but there is a need to consider its strategic impact upon the firm. Viewing IS as a cost limits the benefits that can be achieved. It may also inhibit future learning and may be one reason why earlier research has found that management IS has not been of benefit to SMEs.

■ Managing knowledge

Knowledge is the use to which strategic information is put to gain strategic value. In today's economy knowledge is the key to competitive advantage. Co-opetition, where firms both compete and collaborate to provide products and services, depends upon exchange of knowledge that supports the development of the relationship. The two forms of knowledge, explicit and tacit, are useful in managing the relationship. For SMEs managing relationships has depended on building informal networks. However, there is a greater need to share formal, explicit knowledge particularly to develop customer relationships. The synergistic use of knowledge means that both firms benefit from the relationship. An additional benefit of co-opetition is for SMEs to be able to leverage business value for themselves from the knowledge exchange. However, only a few SMEs are exploiting the opportunities such knowledge gives them. These tend to be firms looking for new markets who learn from their experiences with existing customers. SMEs in the collaboration scenario are particularly weak at exploiting knowledge opportunities, which is not surprising given their response to invest in externally facing systems before integrating internal ones.

Managing knowledge may require firms to reflect upon their business strategy and their core competencies. The resource-based view of strategy provides a useful means for knowledge-based firms, in particular, to recognize their core competencies. This form of analysis enables firms to recognize the unique qualities that they have and can exploit for competitive advantage. For SMEs the benefits are being able to focus on the core knowledge that they require and hence determine the IS required to deliver the information underpinning it.

To take advantage of knowledge requires more than the introduction of IS. As indicated, realigning the firm by considering the relationships between core competencies through business process design is essential. SMEs can achieve greater value from IS if they review business processes: firms that do undertake radical review of processes tend to be already looking for change. All SMEs can benefit. However, there needs to be commitment from the owner and staff and a clear strategic direction focused upon growth. There is a need to recognize the added value from IS and for firms to put in sufficient investment to ensure success. The support of customers is also invaluable in achieving change.

Managing knowledge is now a critical part of interaction between firms. Internet technologies have made managing relationships easier. However, SMEs are cautious in their adoption of Internet technologies, although again the most adventurous are beginning to exploit their potential.

Are SMEs excited by the Internet?

E-business offer opportunities to radically alter supply chain relationships. However, as Porter recognizes, the benefits can only be achieved if part of a strategic refocusing of the firm to achieve business value from the technologies. The key to adoption in the SME sector is whether business value can be identified and whether growth is planned or emergent. Most SMEs have not yet seen the value of Internet technologies. This is often because IS is not planned strategically or there is little competitive advantage to be gained. SMEs respond to customer pressure as with other IS investments and in some cases the perceived benefit that may be gained from presenting a modern image to the market. Customer demand, gaining market share and not losing customers are the prime reasons for adopting Internet technologies. The owner again is instrumental in the decision process. There is concern among SMEs about confidentiality and fraud. The main support for Internet technologies comes from those firms that are product innovators. These firms value the Internet as a means of identifying suppliers as well as having recognized its potential to develop web-based products. In contrast to other research, market development is not seen as a driver of adoption. This is probably due to the limited development across the whole supply chain where it appears that only some major customers demand the use of e-business.

Limited resources also limit e-business development. Governments have recognized this phenomenon and have instituted intervention projects to assist SMEs to adopt Internet technologies to get their first foot on the e-business path. However, the SMEs that have benefited from such schemes are usually those that are already aware of the potential. The local intervention agencies have been somewhat successful in providing support for SMEs, but there is little awareness of central government support. SMEs have not made progress in either transacting business on the Internet or in transforming themselves to manage using integrated systems. They are still exploring the possibilities and need to be convinced that the investment is worthwhile. However, as the market changes SMEs need to be in a position to take advantage of it.

Lessons for SMEs and researchers

There are several lessons in this book for SMEs in the pursuit of management IS. First, the owner is central to all decision-making. Second, customer pressure, over and above any other competitive force, is a driver for change. Hence, SMEs need to be aware of customers' future requirements for knowledge and information sharing. Third, the greatest benefits from management IS are found when it is adopted as part of a value-adding strategy, rather than viewed as a cost. A cost-focused strategy tends to limit opportunity and means that SMEs are more likely to develop operational systems rather than those that support the business strategy. Fourth, ISS should be undertaken as part of business strategy development, particularly in growing firms to measure success and to ensure strategic alignment. Fifth, there is potential for leverage for the firm if it uses knowledge from partners and collaborators more effectively. Finally, SMEs can usefully review the business value to them of investing in e-business as part of their overall business and IS strategies.

For researchers, this book has drawn together the developing research in IS use in SMEs. It has demonstrated where "large firm" theory works in the SME context and where it fails. The book also demonstrates how rich the SME context is as a research domain and how rewarding it is to work in. SMEs need to use IS better. Hopefully, the theoretical and practical insights this text offers will assist managers and researchers to enable this to happen.

References

Abdullah, H. and Chatwin, C. (1994). Distributed C3 environment for SMEs. *Integrated Manufacturing Systems*, 5(3): 20–28.

Agarwal, R. (1998). Small firm survival and technological activity. *Small Business Economics*, 11: 215–224.

Alter, S. (1992). *Information Systems: A Management Perspective*. Addison Wesley, Mass, USA.

Analoui and Karami (2003). *Strategic Management in Small and Medium Enterprises*. Thomson Learning, London, UK.

Andreu, R. and Ciborra, C. (1996). Organisational learning and core capabilities development: the role of IT. *Journal of Strategic Information Systems*, 5(2): 111–127.

Angehrn, A. (1997). Designing mature Internet business strategies: the ICDT model. *European Management Journal*, 15(4): 361–369.

Angell, I.O. and Smithson, S. (1991). Evaluation, monitoring and control. In *Information Systems Management: Opportunities and Risks*. MacMillan Press, Basingstoke, UK.

Ansoff, I. (1965). *Corporate Strategy*. McGraw Hill Inc. New York.

Avison, D., Powell, P., Keen, J., Klein, J.H. and Ward, S. (1995). Addressing the need for flexibility in information systems. *Journal of Management Systems*, 7(2): 43–60.

Avison, D., Eardley, W. and Powell, P. (1998). Suggestions for capturing corporate vision in strategic information systems. *Omega, International Journal of Management Science*, 26(4): 441–459.

Ayres, R.V. (1991). *Computer Integrated Manufacturing, Vol. 1. Revolution in Progress*. International Institute for Applied Systems Analysis, Laxenburg, Austria; Chapman and Hall, London.

Baker, W. (1990). Market networks and corporate behaviour. *American Journal of Sociology*, 3: 589–625.

Ballantine, J.A., Galliers, R.D. and Stray, S. (1995a). The use and importance of financial appraisal techniques in the IS/IT investment decision-making process. *Project Appraisal*, 10(4): 233–241.

Ballantine, J.A., Galliers, R.D. and Powell, P. (1995b). Daring to be different, capital appraisal and technology investments. In Doukidis, G., Galliers, R., Jelassi, T., Krcmar, H. and Land, F. (Eds). *Proceedings of the Third European Conference on Information Systems*, 1: 87–98.

Ballantine, J., Bonner, M., Levy, M., Martin, A., Munro, I. and Powell, P. (1996). The 3-D model of information systems success: the search for the dependent variable continues. *Information Resource Management Journal*, 9(4): 5–14.

Barrett, J.L. (1994). Process visualisation: getting the vision right is the key. *Information Systems Management*, 11(2): 14–23.

Barth, H. (2003). Fit among competitive strategy, administrative mechanisms and performance: a comparative study of small firms in mature and new industries. *Journal of Small Business Management*, 41(2): 133–147.

Beckinsale, M.J. and Jones, O. (1999). Strategic innovation networks: managing high technology in mature small firms. In Oakey, R. and During, W. (Eds). *High Technology Small Firms in the 1990s*, Vol. VI. Elsevier Science Ltd.

Benjamin, R., Rockart, J., Scott Morton, M. and Wyman, J. (1984). Information technology: a strategic opportunity. *Sloan Management Review*, Spring 25(3): 3–10.

Berry, A., Rodriguez, E. and Sandee, H. (2002). Firm and group dynamics in the small and medium enterprise sector in Indonesia. *Small Business Economics*, 18: 141–161.

Bianchi, C. (2002). Introducing SD modelling into planning and control systems to manage SMEs' growth: a learning-oriented perspective. *Systems Dynamics Review*, 18(3): 315–338.

Bianchi, C. and Bivona, E. (2002). Opportunities and pitfalls related to e-commerce strategies in small-medium firms: a systems dynamics approach. *Systems Dynamics Review*, 18(3): 403–429.

Binks, M.R. and Ennew, C.T. (1996). Growing firms and the credit constraint. *Small Business Economics*, 8(1): 17–25.

Birnberg, J. (1998). Control in inter-firm co-operative relationships. *Journal of Management Studies*, 35(4): 421–428.

Blackler, F. and Brown, C. (1988). Theory and practice in evaluation: the case of the new information technologies. In Bjorn-Anderson, N. and Davis, B.B. (Eds). *Information Systems Assessment: Issues and Challenges*, pp. 351–374, North-Holland, Amsterdam.

Blili, S. and Raymond, L. (1993). Information technology: threats and opportunities for small and medium-sized enterprises. *International Journal of Information Management*, **13**: 439–448.

Bonder, S. (1976). Versatility: an objective for military planning. *Military Operations Research Symposium*. Fort Bliss, Texas.

Bonk, E.T. (1996). 'The information revolution and its impact on SME strategy', The Asian Pacific economic co-operative forum as a model. *Journal of Small Business Management*, **34**(1): 71–77.

Boynton, A. and Zmud, R. (1984). An assessment of critical success factors. *Sloan Management Review*, **25**(4): 17–27.

Brady, A. and Voss, B. (1995). Small is as small does. *Journal of Business Strategy*, **16**(2): 44–52.

Brandenburger, A. and Nalebuff, B. (1996). *Co-opetition*. Doubleday, New York.

Burn, J.M. (1996). IS innovation and organisational alignment – a Professional Juggling Act. *Journal of Information Technology*, **11**(1): 3–12.

Burn, J.M. (1997). A Professional Balancing Act: walking the tightrope of strategic alignment. In Sauer C., Yetton P. and Associates (Eds). *Steps to the Future*. Jossey-Bass Publishers, San Francisco.

Burns, P. (2001). *Entrepreneurship and Small Business*. Palgrave, Hampshire, UK.

Burns, P. and Harrison, J. (1996). Growth. In Burns, P. and Dewhurst, J. (Eds). *Small Business and Entrepreneurship*, 2nd edition. Macmillan, UK.

Caldeira, M. and Ward, J. (2002). Understanding the successful adoption and use of IS? IT in SMEs: an explanation from Portuguese manufacturing industries. *Information Systems Journal*, **12**: 121–152.

Caldeira, M. and Ward, J. (2003). Using resource-based theory to interpret the successful adoption and use of information systems and technology in manufacturing small and medium-sized enterprises. *European Journal of Information Systems*, **12**: 127–141.

Caldwell, B. (1994). Wall street's sharp curve. *Informationweek*, **496**(10): 94–101.

Carr, D. and Johansson, H. (1995). *Best Practices in Re-engineering: What Works and What Doesn't in the Re-engineering Process*. McGraw Hill, NY, USA.

Carrie, A.S., Macintosh, R., Scott, A. and Peoples, G.A. (1994). Linking strategy to production management structures and systems. *International Journal of Production Economics*, **34**: 293–304.

Carrier, C. (1995). Intrapreneurship in large firms and SMEs: a comparative study. *International Small Business Journal*, April–June, 1994: 54–61.

Champy, J.A. (1994). *Re-engineering Management: The Mandate for New Leadership*. Harper Business, London, UK.

Champy, J.A. and Hammer, M. (1994). *Re-engineering the Corporation*. Harper Collins, London, UK.

Chan, Y., Huff, S., Barclay, D. and Copeland, D. (1997). Business strategic orientation, information systems strategic orientation and strategic alignment. *Information Systems Research*, **8**(2): 125–150.

Chang, L. and Powell, P. (1998). Toward a framework for business process re-engineering in SMEs. In Avison, D. (Ed.). *Information Systems Journal*, **8**(3): 199–216.

Chang, L.-J. (2000). Exploring the Links Between Business Process Re-engineering and Small and Medium-sized Enterprises, unpublished Ph.D. thesis, University of Warwick.

Chapman, P., James-Moore, M., Szczygiel, M. and Thompson, D. (2000). Building Internet capabilities in SMEs. *Logistics Information Management*, **13**(6): 353–360.

Chaston, I., Badger, B. and Sadler-Smith, E. (2001). Organizational learning: an empirical assessment of process in small UK manufacturing firms. *Journal of Small Business Management*, **39**(2): 139–151.

Chatfield, A. and Yetton, P. (2000). Strategic payoff from EDI as a function of EDI embeddedness. *Journal of Management Information Systems*, **16**(4): 195–224.

Checkland, P.B. (1981). *Systems Thinking, Systems Practice*. John Wiley & Sons, Chichester, UK.

Checkland, P. and Holwell, S. (1998). *Information, Systems: Making Sense of the Field*. John Wiley & Sons, Chichester, UK.

Checkland, P. and Scholes, J. (1990). *Soft Systems Methodology in Action*. John Wiley & Sons, Chichester, UK.

Childe, S.J., Maull, R.S. and Bennett, J. (1994). Frameworks for understanding business process re-engineering. *International Journal of Operations Production Management*, **14**(12): 22–34.

Churchill, N.C. and Lewis, V.L. (1983). The five stages of small business growth. *Harvard Business Review*, **61**(3): 30–51.

Ciborra, C. (1997). Improvising in the shapeless organisation of the future. In Sauer C., Yetton, P. and Associates (Eds). *Steps to the Future*. Jossey-Bass, San Francisco.

Clayton, T. (1996). 'Long-term planning a must'. *New Zealand Manufacturer*, **15**.

Cohen, D. (1998). Towards a knowledge context. *California Management Review*, **40**(3): 22–39.

Conway, S. (1997). *Focal Innovation Action-Sets: A Methodological Approach for Mapping Innovation Networks*, Research Paper Series Aston University.

Costello, G. and Tuchen, J. (1998). A comparative study of business to consumer electronic commerce within the Australian insurance sector. *Journal of Information Technology*, **13**: 153–167.

Coulson-Thomas, C. (1992). *Transforming the Company: Bridging the Gap Between Management Myth and Corporate Reality*. Kogan Page, London, UK.

Cragg, P. and King, M. (1992a). *Growth in Small Firm Computing, Research Report Series*. Department of Management Systems, University of Waikato, ISSN 1170–733X.

Cragg, P. and King, M. (1992b). IS sophistication and financial performance of small engineering firms. *European Journal of Information Systems*, **6**(1): 410–426.

Cragg, P. and King, M. (1993). Small-firm computing: motivators and inhibitors. *MIS Quarterly*, March; pp. 47–60.

Cragg, P. and Zinatelli, N. (1995). Evolution of IS in small firms. *Information and Management*, **29**: 1–8.

Cragg, P.B. and Finlay, P.N. (1991). IT: running fast and standing still? *Information and Management*, **21**: 193–200.

Craig, J. and Yetton, P. (1992). Business process redesign: a critique of process innovation. *Australian Journal of Management*, **17**(2): 285–306.

Craig, J. and Yetton, P. (1997). The real event of re-engineering. In Sauer, C., Yetton, P. and Associates (Eds). *Steps to the Future*. Jossey-Bass, San Francisco.

Croteau, A.-M. and Bergeron, F. (2001). An information technology trilogy: business strategy, technological deployment and organizational performance. *Journal of Strategic Information Systems*, **10**: 77–90.

Currie, W. (2000). *The Global Information Society*. John Wiley & Sons, Chichester, UK.

Dandridge, T. and Levenburg, N. (2000). Hi-Tech potential: an exploratory study of very small firms' usage of the Internet. *International Small Business Journal*, **18**(2): 81–121.

Daniel, E. and Grimshaw, D. (2002). An exploratory comparison of electronic commerce adoption in large and small enterprises. *Journal of Information Technology*, **17**: 133–147.

Davenport, T.H. (1993). Need radical innovation and continuous improvement? Integrate process re-engineering and TQM. *Planning Review*, **21**(3): 6–12.

Davenport, T.H. and Short, J.E. (1990). The new industrial engineering: information technology and business redesign. *Sloan Management Review*, **31**: 4–16.

Davidow, W. and Malone, M. (1992). The Virtual Corporation, Harper Business, New York.

Dawes, G.M. (1987). Information systems assessment: post implementation practice. *Journal of Applied Systems Analysis*, **14**: 53–62.

Dickson, G.W. and Nechis, M. (1984). Key information systems issues for the 1980's. *MIS Quarterly*, **8**(3): 135–149.

Dodge, H.R. and Robins, J.E. (1992). An empirical investigation of the organisational life cycle model for small business development and survival. *Journal of Small Business Management*, **30**(1): 27–37.

Doukidis, G., Lybereas, P. and Galliers, R. (1996). Information systems planning in small businesses. *Journal of Systems Software*, **33**(2): 189–201.

Doyle, J.R. (1991). Problems with strategic information systems frameworks. *European Journal of Information Systems*, **1**(4): 273–280.

Drucker, P. (1989). *The New Realities*. Mandarin Paperbacks, London, UK.

Dunning, J. (1988). *Explaining International Production*. Unwin Hyman, London.

Dyer, J.H. (1996). Specialized supplier networks as a source of competitive advantage: evidence from the auto industry. *Strategic Management Journal*, **17**(4): 271–291.

Dyer, J. and Singh, H. (1998). The relational view: co-operative strategy and sources of interorganizational competitive advantage. *Academy of Management Review*, **23**(4): 660–679.

Eardley, A., Avison, D. and Powell, P. (1997). Strategic information systems: an analysis of development techniques which seek to incorporate strategic flexibility. *Journal of Organizational Computing*, **7**(1): 57–77.

Earl, M.J. (1989). *Management Strategies for Information Technology*. Prentice Hall International (UK), London, UK.

Earl, M.J. (1996a). An organisational approach to IS strategy-making. In Earl, M.J. (Ed.). *Information Management*. Oxford University Press, Oxford.

Earl, M.J. (1996b). Knowledge strategies: propositions from two contrasting industries. In Earl, M.J. (Ed.). *Information management*. Oxford University Press, UK; pp. 35–62.

Eisenhardt, K. (1989). Building theories from case study research. *Academy of Management Review*, **14**: 532–550.

Eppink, D.J. (1978). Planning for strategic flexibility. *Long Range Planning*, **11**.

Evans, R. (2002). E-commerce, competitiveness and local and regional governance in Greater Manchester and Merseyside: a preliminary assessment. *Urban Studies*, **39**(5–6): 947–975.

Evans, J.S. (1991). Strategic flexibility for high technology manoeuvres: a conceptual framework. *Journal of Management Studies*, **28**(1): 69–89.

Evans, P. and Wurster, T. (2000). *Blown to Bits*. Harvard Business School Press, Boston, Mass, USA.

Farbey, B., Land, F. and Targett, D. (1992). Evaluating investments in IT. *Journal of Information Technology*, **7**: 109–122.

Farbey, B., Land, F. and Targett, D. (1993). *How to Assess IT Investment: A Study of Methods and Practice*. Butterworth Heinemann, Oxford, UK.

Feeny, D. (2000). E-opportunity: the strategic marketing perspective. In Willcocks, L., Sauer, C. and Associates (Eds). *Moving to E-Business*. Random House, London, UK.

Feeny, D. and Ives, B. (1990). In search of sustainability: reaping long term advantage from investments in IT. *Journal of Management Information Systems*, **7**(1): 27–26.

Feindt, S., Jeffcoate, J. and Chappell, C. (2002). Identifying success factors for rapid growth in SME e-commerce. *Small Business Economics*, **19**: 51–62.

Ferrell, J. (1996). Help for the other SMEs. *Manufacturing Engineering*, **117**(2): 20.

Fink, D. (1998). Guidelines for the successful adoption of information technology in small and medium enterprises. *International Journal of Information Management*, **18**(4): 243–253.

Flynn, D.J. (1992). *Information System Requirements: Determination and Analysis*. McGraw-Hill, Maidenhead.

Foong, S.-Y. (1999). Effect of end user personal and systems attributes on computer based information systems success in Malaysian SMEs. *Journal of Small Business Management*, **37**(3): 81–87.

Fuller, T. (1996). Fulfilling IT needs in small businesses: a recursive learning model. *International Small Business Journal*, **14**(4): 25–44.

Galliers, R.D. (1987). Information systems planning in the UK and Australia – a comparison of current practice. *Oxford Surveys in Information Technology*. Oxford University Press, UK; **4**: 223–235.

Galliers, R.D. (1991). Strategic information systems planning: myths, reality and guidelines for successful implementation. *European Journal of Information Systems*, **1**(1): 55–64.

Galliers, R.D. (1993). Towards a flexible information systems architecture: integrating business strategies, information systems strategies and business process redesign. *Journal of Information Systems*, **3**: 199–213.

Galliers, R.D. (1997). Against obliteration: reducing risk in business process change. In Sauer, C., Yetton, P. and Associates (Eds). *Steps to the Future*. Jossey-Bass, San Francisco.

Galliers, R.D. and Sutherland, A.R. (1991). Information systems management: the stages of growth model revisited. *Journal of Information Systems*, **1**: 1.

Galliers, R.D. and Swan, J.A. (1997). Against structured approaches: information requirements analysis as a socially mediated process. *Proceedings: 30th Hawaii International Conference on Systems Sciences*, Los Alamitos, CA: IEEE Computer Society Press, California, USA. 3 January; pp. 179–187.

Galliers, R.D., Pattison, E. and Reponen, T. (1994). Strategic information-systems planning workshops – lessons from 3 cases. *International Journal of Information Management*, **14**(1): 51–66.

Genus, A. and Dickson, K. (1995). *Technological Analysis and Strategic Management*, **7**(3): 283–285.

Ginzberg, M.J. and Zmud, R.W. (1988). Evolving criteria for information systems assessment. In Bjorn-Anderson, N. and Davis, G.B. (Eds). *Information Systems Assessment: Issues and Challenges*, pp. 41–52, North-Holland, Amsterdam.

Goldberg, A., Cohen, G. and Fiegenbaum, A. (2003). Reputation building: small business strategies for successful venture development. *Journal of Small Business Management*, **41**(2): 168–186.

Golden, W. and Powell, P. (1996). The effects of inter-organisational systems on flexibility. In Krcmar, H., Dias Coehlo, J. and Jelassi, T. (Eds). *Proceedings of the 4th European Conference on Information Systems*, Lisbon. July; pp. 1133–1140.

Goss, D. (1991). Small Business and Society, Routledge, London, UK.

Grandon, E. and Pearson, J. (2004). E-commerce adoption: perceptions of manager/owners of small and medium sized firms in Chile. *Communications of the Association for Information Systems*, **13**: 81–102.

Grover, V., Jeong, S.R., Kettinger, W. and Teng, J.T.C. (1995). The implementation of business process re-engineering. *Journal of Management Information Systems*, **12**(1): 109–144.

Grover, V., Teng, J. and Fielder, K. (1993). Information Technology enabled business process redesign, *Omega*, **21**(4): 433–447.

Guha, S., Kettinger, W.J. and Teng, J.T.C. (1993). Business process reengineering: building a comprehensive methodology. *Information Systems Management*, **10**(3): 13–22.

Gupta, M. and Cawthorn, G. (1996). Managerial implications of flexible manufacturing for SMEs. *Elsevier Advanced technology, Technovation*, **16**(2): 77–83.

Hadjimanoulis, A. (2000). A resource-based view of innovativeness in small firms. *Technology Analysis and Strategic Management*, **12**(2): 263–281.

Hagel, J. (1993). Keeping BPR on track. *McKinsey Quarterly*, **1**: 59–72.

Hagmann, C. and McCahon, C. (1993). Strategic information systems and competitiveness. *Information and Management*, **25**: 183–192.

Haksever, C. (1996). Total Quality Management in the small business environment. *Business Horizons*, **39**(2): 33–40.

Hale, A.J. and Cragg, P.B. (1996). Business process re-engineering in the small firm: a case study. *INFOR*, **34**(1): 15–27.

Hammer, M. (1990). Re-engineering work: don't automate, obliterate. *Harvard Business Review*, **68**(4): 104–122.

Hammer, M. (1996). *Beyond Reengineering: How the Process-Centred Organisation is Changing Our Work and Our Lives*. Harper Business, London, UK.

Hammer, M. (2004). Deep change: how operational innovation can transform your company, *Harvard Business Review*, **82**(4): 84–93.

Hansen, N., Gillespie, K. and Gencturk, E. (1994). SMEs and export involvement: market responsiveness, technology and alliances. *Journal of Global Marketing*, **7**(4): 7–27.

Harrington, J. (1991). *Business Process Improvement: the Breakthrough Strategy for Total Quality, Productivity and Competitiveness,* McGraw Hill, New York.

Hashmi, M. and Cuddy, J. (1990). Strategic initiatives for introducing CIM technologies in Irish SMEs. In Faria L. (Ed.). *Computer Integrated Manufacturing – Proceedings of the 6th CIM Europe Annual Conference,* 15–17, May 1990, Lisbon, Portugal. Van Puymbroeck, Springer-Verlag. pp. 93–104.

Hay, M. and Kamshad, K. (1994). Small firm growth: intentions, implementation and impediments. *Business Strategy Review,* 5(3): 49–68.

Heidegger, M. (1977). *The Question Concerning Technology and Other Essays.* Harper Colophon, London, UK.

Henderson, J. and Venkatraman, N. (1993). Strategic alignment: leveraging information technology for transforming organizations. *IBM Systems Journal,* 32(1): 4–16.

Heskett, J., Jones, T., Loveman, G., Sasser, W. and Schlesinger, L. (1994). Putting the service-profit chain to work. *Harvard Business Review,* 72(2): 164–174.

Heygate, R. (1993). Immoderate redesign. *McKinsey Quarterly,* 1: 73–87.

Hill, J. and McGowan, P. (1999). Small business and enterprise development: questions about research methodology. *International Journal of Entrepreneurial Behaviour and Research,* 5(1): 5–18.

Hirschfield, R.J. (1994). *Type A Behaviour, Self-efficacy, and Performance in Small Business Firms.* unpublished DBA thesis, Nova South-eastern University, Fort Lauderdale, Florida, USA.

Hirschheim, R. and Smithson, S. (1988). A critical analysis of information systems evaluation. In Bjorn-Anderson, N. and Davis, G.B. (Eds). *Information Systems Assessment: Issues and Challenges,* pp. 17–37, North-Holland, Amsterdam.

Hochstrasser, B. (1992). Justifying IT investments. *Advanced Information Systems, The New Technologies in Today's Business Environment, Proceedings,* pp. 17–28.

Holland, W.E. and Kumar, S. (1995). Getting past the obstacles to successful re-engineering. *Business Horizons,* 38(3): 79–86.

Holt, D. (1987). *Network Support Systems: How communities can encourage entrepreneurship.* In Churchill, N. (ed.), The Frontiers of Entrepreneurship Research, Babson College.

Hsaio, R. and Ormerod, R. (1998). A new perspective on the dynamics of IT-enabled strategic change. *Information Systems Journal,* 8(1): 21–52.

Hussin, H., King, M. and Cragg, P. (2002). IT alignment in small firms. *European Journal of Information Systems*, **11**(2): 108–127.

Igbaria, M., Zinatelli, N. and Cavaye, A. (1998). Analysis of information technology success in small firms in New Zealand. *International Journal of Information Management*, **18**(2): 103–119.

Janson, R. (1993). Technology – tomorrows determinate. *Ohio Journal of Science*, **93**(4): 78–82.

Janz, B., Wetherbe, J., Davis, G. and Noe, R. (1997). Re-engineering the systems development process: the link between autonomous teams and business process outcomes. *Journal of Management Information Systems*, Summer, **14**(1): 41–68.

Jarvenpaa, S.L. and Ives, B. (1991). Executive involvement and participation in the management of information technology. *MIS Quarterly*, **15**(2): 205–277.

Jeffcoate, J., Chappell, C. and Feindt, S. (2004). Assessing the impact of e-commerce on SMEs in value chains: a qualitative approach. In Al-Qirim (Ed.). *Electronic Commerce in Small to Medium-Sized Enterprises: Frameworks, Issues and Implications*. Idea Group, London, UK.

Jennings, D.F. (1996). Re-engineering: a fast track to nowhere? *Baylor Business Review*, **14**(2): 6.

Johansson, H., *et al.* (1993). *Business Process Re-engineering: Breakpoint Strategies for Market Dominance*. John Wiley & Sons, Chichester, UK.

Jones, O., Cardoso, C. and Beckinsale, M. (1997). Manture SMEs and technological innovation: entrepreneurial networks in the United Kingdom and Portugal. *International Journal of Innovation Management*, **1**(3): 201–227.

Julien, P. and Raymond, L. (1994). Factors of new technology adoption in the retail sector. *Entrepreneurship – Theory and Practice*, Summer.

Julien, P., Joyal, A. and Dehaies, L. (1994). SMEs and international competition: free trade agreement or globalization. *Journal of Small Business Management*, **7**: 52–64.

Kanter, R.M. (1972). *Commitment and Community*. Cambridge University Press, Massachusetts.

Kanter, R.M. (1994). Collaborative advantage: the art of alliances. *Harvard Business Review*, July–August; pp. 96–108.

Kaplan, R. and Murdock, L. (1991). Core process redesign. *McKinsey Quarterly*, Summer: 27–43.

Kaplan, R. and Norton, D. (1996). Using the balanced scorecard as a strategic management system. *Harvard Business Review*, January–February; pp. 75–84.

Keasey, K. and Watson, R. (1993). *Small firm management, ownership, finance and performance*. Blackwell, Oxford.

Keindl, B. (2000). Competitive dynamics and new business models for SMEs in the virtual marketplace. *Journal of Developmental Entrepreneurship*, 5(1): 73–85.

Kendall, J., Tung, L., Chua, K., Ng, D. and Tan, S. (2001). Receptivity of Singapore's SMEs to electronic commerce adoption. *Journal of Strategic Information Systems*, 10: 223–242.

Knight, G. (2000). Entrepreneurship and marketing strategy: the SME under globalization. *Journal of International Marketing*, 8(2): 12–32.

King, W.R. (1987). Strategic planning for management information. *MIS Quarterly*, 2(1): 27–37.

King, M., Cragg, P. and Hussin, H. (2000). IT alignment and organisational performance in small firms. In Hansen, R.H., Bichler, M. and Mahrer, H. (Eds). *Proceedings of the 8th European Conference on Information Systems*. Vienna University of Economics and Business Administration, Vienna, Austria. pp. 151–157.

Kinni, T. (1995). Process Improvement, Part 2: Re-engineering and the quest for breakthrough results. *Industry Week*, 244(4): 45–50.

Klein, H. and Myers, M. (1999). A set of principles for conducting and evaluating interpretive field studies in information systems. *MIS Quarterly*, 23(1): 67–94.

Klein, L.R. and Quelch, J.A. (1997). Business-to-business market making on the Internet. *International Marketing Review*, 14(5): 345–361.

Knorr, R. (1991). Business process redesign: key to competitiveness. *Journal of Business Strategy*, November/December; 48–51.

Kowtha, N. and Choon, T. (2001). Determinants of website development: a study of electronic commerce in Singapore. *Information and Management*, 39: 227–242.

Lawson, R., Alcock, C., Cooper, J. and Burgess, L. (2003). Factors affecting adoption of electronic commerce technologies by SMEs: an Australian study. *Journal of Small Business and Enterprise Development*, 10(3): 265–276.

Lederer, A.L. and Mendelow, A.L. (1986). Issues in information systems planning. *Information and Management*, 10(5): 245–254.

Lee, C. and Chen, S. (1992). The overall environment and the development of Taiwan's small and medium enterprises. *Chung-Hua Institution for Economic Research*, Taiwan.

Lee, C. and Ho, H. (1992). The Financial Management of Taiwan's Small and Medium Enterprises, *Chung-Hua Institution for Economic Research*, Taiwan.

Lefebvre, E. and Lefebvre, L. (1992). Firm innovation and CEO characteristics in small manufacturing firms. *Journal of Engineering and Technology Management*, **9**: 3–4, 243–272.

Lefebvre, L. and Lefebvre, E. (1993). Competitive positioning and innovative efforts in SMEs. *Small Business Economics*, **5**: 297–305.

Lesjak, D. and Lynn, M. (2000). Small slovene firms and (strategic) information technology usage. In Hansen, R.H., Bichler, M. and Mahrer, H. (Eds). *Proceedings of the 8th European Conference on Information Systems*. Vienna University of Economics and Business Administration, Vienna, Austria. pp. 63–70.

Levene, R.J. and Braganza, A. (1996). Controlling the work scope in organisational transformation: a programme management approach. *International Journal of Project Management*, **14**(6): 331–339.

Lewis, M.A. and Gregory, M.J. (1996). *Developing and Applying a Process Approach to Competence Analysis in Sanchez et al., Dynamics of Competence-Based Competition*. Elsevier Science Ltd., Kidlington, Oxford.

Liebeskind, J. (1996). Knowledge strategy and the theory of the firm. *Strategic Management Journal*, **17**: 93–107.

Liedholm, C. (2002). Small firm dynamics: evidence from Africa and Latin America. *Small Business Economics*, **18**: 227–242.

Loebbecke, C. and Van Fenema, P. (1998). Towards a theory of inter-organizational knowledge sharing during co-opetition. In Baets, W. (Ed.). *Proceedings of Sixth European Conference on IS*, Aix-en-Provence, Euro-Arab Management School.

Lucas, H.C. and Olson, M. (1994). The impact of information technology on organizational flexibility. *Journal of Organizational Computing*, **4**(2): 155–176.

Lunati, M. (2000). *SMEs and Electronic Commerce: An Overview*, OECD, Directorate for Science, Technology and Industry Committee, DST/IND/PME, **11**.

Lybaert, N. (1998). The information use in a SME: its importance and some elements of influence. *Small Business Economics*, **10**: 171–191.

Lybereas, P., Myonopolous, N., Doukidis, G. and Galliers, R.D. (1993). *ISP and Entrepreneurial Culture in Medium-sized Enterprises*, ICIS.

Lynch, I. (2000). *Smaller firms unimpressed by ASPs* [Online]. http://www.
thechannel.vnunet.com/News/1109773; June 25, 2002.

Macdonald, K. (2000). *IS Strategy.* University of Bath; Personal correspondence
(1991). In Scott Morton, M. (Ed.). *Corporation of the 1990s.* OUP.

Mahesh, G. and Garret, C. (1996). Managerial implications of flexible
manufacturing for small/medium-sized enterprises. *Technovation*, 16(2): 77–83.

Mambula, C. (2003). Perceptions of SME growth constraints in Nigeria. *Journal
of Small Business Management*, 40(1): 58–65.

Manganelli, R.L. and Raspa, S.P. (1995). Why re-engineering has failed.
Management Review, pp. 39–44.

Martin, C.J. (1989). Information management in the smaller business: the
role of the top Manager. *International Journal of Information Management*,
9: 187–197.

Maynard, R. (1996). Striking the right match. *Nation's Business*, 84(5): 18–20.

McFarlan, F.W. and McKenney, J.L. (1983). The Information Archipelago –
governing the new world. *Harvard Business Review*, July/August; 61(4): 91–99.

McKiernan, P. and Morris, C. (1994). Strategic planning and financial performance
in UK SMEs: does formality matter? *British Journal of Management*, S31–S41.

Mehrtens, J., Cragg, P. and Mills, A. (2001). A model of Internet adoption by
SMEs. *Information and Management*, 39: 165–176.

Meredith, J.R. and Hill, M.M. (1987). Justifying new manufacturing systems: a
managerial approach. *Sloan Management Review*, Summer: 49–60.

Meyer, J. (1993). What is your computer hiding – for those who know where to
look, the information is still there. *ABA Journal*, 79: 89.

Miller, D. and Shamsie, J. (1996). The resource-based view of the firm in two
environments: the Hollywood film studios from 1936 to 1965. *Academy of
Management Journal*, 39(3): 519–543.

Mingers, J. (1997). Combining research methods in information systems: multi-
paradigm methodology. *Proceedings 5th European Conference on Information
Systems*, Cork Publishing, Cork. June; pp. 760–776.

Mingers, J. (2001). Combining is research methods: towards a pluralist
methodology. *Information Systems Research*, 12(3): 240–259.

Mintzberg, H. (1983). *Structure in Fives: Designing Effective Organisations.*
Prentice Hall International Inc, Englewood Cliffs, New Jersey.

Mintzberg, H. (1991). *Crafting Strategy*. In Mintzberg, H. and Quinn, J. (Eds). The Strategy Process: Concepts, Contexts and Cases, 2nd edition. Prentice Hall International Inc, Englewood Cliffs NJ, USA, pp. 105–114.

Mitchell, J. (1973). *Network Norms and Institutions*. In Boissevain and Mitchell (Eds). Network Analysis: Studies in Human Interaction, Mouton, Den Haag.

Nalebuff, B. and Brandenburger, A. (1996). *Co-opetition*. Harper Collins Business, UK.

Nandhakumar, J. and Jones, M. (1997). Too close for comfort? Distance and engagement in interpretive information systems research. *Information Systems Journal*, 7: 109–131.

Nash, T. and Rock, M. (1996). Small firms the big picture. *Director*, **49**(9): 48–92.

Naylor, J.B. and Williams, J. (1994). The successful use of IT in SMEs on Merseyside. *European Journal of Information Systems*, **3**(1): 48–56.

Niederman, F., Branchaeu, J.C. and Wetherbe, J.C. (1991). Information systems management issues for the 1990's. *MIS Quarterly*, pp. 475–499.

Niven, D. (1993). When times get tough, what happens to TQM. *Harvard Business Review*, **71**(3): 20.

Nolan, R.L. (1979). Managing the crisis in data processing. *Harvard Business Review*, **57**(2): 115–126.

Nonaka, I. and Takeuchi, H. (1999). A theory of the firm's knowledge-creation dynamics. In Chandler, A., Hagstrom, P. and Solvell, O. (Eds). *The Dynamic Firm*. Oxford University Press, New York, USA.

Nugent, J. and Yhee, S.-J. (2002). Small and medium enterprises in Korea: achievements, constraints and policy issues. *Small Business Economics*, **18**: 85–119.

O'Callaghan, R., Kaufmann, P. and Konsynski, B. (1992). Adoption correlates and share effects of electronic data interchange systems in marketing channels. *Journal of Marketing*, **56**: 45–56.

Ormerod, R. (1998). Putting soft or methods to work: information systems strategy development at Palabora. *Omega, International Journal of Management Science*, **26**(1): 75–98.

Osborn, C. (1998). Systems of sustainable organisations. *Journal of Management Studies*, **35**(4): 482–509.

Palvia, P. and Palvia, S. (1999). An examination of the IT satisfaction of small business users. *Information and Management*, **35**: 127–137.

Parker, M.M., Trainor, H.E. and Benson, R.J. (1989). *Information Strategy and Economics*. Prentice-Hall, US.

Parsons, G.L. (1985). Strategic information technology. In Somogyi, E.K. and Galliers, R.D. (Eds). *Towards Strategic Information Systems*. Abacus Press, Cambridge, Massachusetts. pp. 182–199.

Perry, C. (1986). Growth strategies for small firms: principles and case studies. *International Small Business Journal*, 5(2): 17–25.

Poon, S. (2000). Business environment and Internet commerce benefits: a small business perspective. *European Journal of Information Systems*, 9: 72–81.

Poon, S. and Swatman, P. (1999). An exploratory study of small business Internet commerce issues. *Information and Management*, 35: 9–18.

Poon, S. and Swatman, P. (2000). Internet-based small business communication: seven Australian cases. In Schmid, B. and Selz, D. (Eds). *EM – Electronic Commerce in Asia, EM – Electronic Markets*. 7,2, 05/97, www.electronicmarkets.org/netacademy/publications.nsf/all_pk/89

Porter, M. (1998). Clusters and the new economics of competition. *Harvard Business Review*, November–December; 77–90.

Porter, M.E. (1980). *Competitive Strategy*. The Free Press, New York, USA.

Porter, M.E. (2001). Strategy and the Internet. *Harvard Business Review*, March; 63–78.

Porter, M.E. and Millar, V.E. (1985). How information gives you competitive advantage. *Harvard Business Review*, 63(4): 140–160.

Powell, P. (1992). IT evaluation is it different? *Journal of the Operations Research Society*, 43(1): 29–42.

Prahalad, C.K. and Hamel, G. (1990). The core competencies of the corporation. *Harvard Business Review*, May–June.

Premkumar, G. and King, W. (1991). Assessing strategic information systems planning. *Long Range Planning*, 24(5): 41–58.

Premkumar, G. and Roberts, M. (1999). Adoption of new information technologies in rural small businesses. *Omega, International Journal of Management Science*, 27(4): 467–484.

Proudlock, M., Phelps, B. and Gamble, P. (1998). IS decision-making: a study in information-intensive firms. *Journal of Information Technology*, 13(1): 44–66.

Quayle, M. (2002). E-commerce: the challenge for UK SMEs in the twenty-first century. *International Journal of Operations and Production Management*, 22(10): 1148–1161.

Quayle, M. and Christiansen, J. (2004). Business issues in the 21st century: an empirical study of e-commerce adoption in UK and Denmark SMEs. In Al-Qirim (Ed.). *Electronic Commerce in Small to Medium-Sized Enterprises: Frameworks, Issues and Implications*. Idea Group, London, UK.

Rackoff, N., Wiseman, C. and Ullrich, W. (1985). Information systems for competitive advantage: implementation of a planning process. *MIS Quarterly*, **9**(4): 285–294.

Ramsey, E., Ibbotson, P., Bell, J. and Gray, B. (2003). E-opportunities of Service Sector SMEs: an Irish cross-border study, *Journal of Small Business Enterprise Development*, **10**(3): 250-264.

Rangone, A. (1999). A resource-based approach to strategy analysis in small-medium sized enterprises. *Small Business Economics*, **12**: 233–248.

Reid, G. (1999). *Information Systems Development in the Small Firm*, CRIEFF Discussion Paper Series No. 0002. ISSN 1364-453-X, University of St Andrews, Scotland.

Reid, G. and Jacobsen, C. (1988). *The Small Entrepreneurial Firm*. Aberdeen University Press, UK.

Reid, G. and Smith, J. (1999). *Information Systems Development in the Small Firm: Tests of Contingency, Agency and Markets and Hierarchies approaches*. University of St Andrews, Centre for Research into Industry, Enterprise, Finance and the Firm Discussion Paper 9905.

Reid, G. and Smith, J. (2000). What makes a new business start-up successful. *Small Business Economics*, **14**: 165–182.

Rhodes, E. and Carter, R. (2000). SME entrepreneurialism. *Proceedings of ICSB World Conference*, June, Brisbane.

Ribbler, J. (1996). Delivering solutions for the knowledge economy. *On-line*, **20**(5): 12–19.

Riemenschneider, C., Harrison, D. and Mykytyn, P. (2003). Understanding IT adoption decisions in small business: integrating current theories. *Information and Management*, **40**: 269–285.

Robertson, S. and Powell, P. (1997). In search of flexibility: the mercator case. In: Murphy, C., Galliers, R., O'Callaghan, R. and Loebbecke, C. (Eds). *Proceedings of the 5th European Conference on Information Systems*, Cork.

Rockart, J. (1988). The line takes the leadership – is management in a wired society. *Sloan Management Review*, **29**(4): 57–64.

Rockart, J.F. and Short, J.E. (1989). IT in the 1990s: managing organisational interdependence. *Sloan Management Review*, **30**: 7–17.

Roper, S. (1999). Modelling small business growth and profitability. *Small Business Economics*, **13**: 235–252.

Rosenfeld, S.A. (1996). Does co-operation enhance competitiveness? Assessing the impact of inter-firm collaboration. *Research Policy*, **25**(2): 247–263.

Rosenhead, J., Best, G. and Parston, G. (1986). Robustness in practice. *Journal of the Operational Research Society*, **37**(5): 463–478.

Rothwell, R. and Beesley, M. (1989). The importance of technology transfer. In Barber, J., Metcalfe, J.S. and Porteous, M. (Eds). *Barriers to Growth in Small Firms*. Routledge, UK.

Ryan, J. and Hepworth, M. (1998). The building of a European Information Society and its impact on small and medium enterprises growth. In Oakey, R. and During, W. (Eds). *New Technology Based Firms in the 1990s*. Paul Chapman, London.

Sadowski, B., Maitland, C. and van Dongen, J. (2002). Strategic use of the Internet by small and medium-sized companies: an exploratory study. *Information Economics and Policy*, **14**: 75–93.

Sanchez, R., Heene, A. and Thomas, H. (1996). Towards the theory and practice of competence-based competition. In Sanchez, *et al.* (Eds). *Dynamics of Competence-Based Competition*. Elsevier Science Ltd, Kidlington, Oxford.

Santarelli, E. and D'Altri, S. (2003). The diffusion of e-commerce among SMEs: theoretical implications and empirical evidence. *Small Business Economics*, **21**: 272–283.

Sauer, C. (2000). Managing the infrastructure challenge. In Willcocks, L., Sauer, C. and Associates (Eds). *Moving to E-Business*. Random House, London, UK.

Sauer, C. and Burn, J. (1997). The pathology of strategic alignment. In Sauer, C., Yetton P. and Associates (Eds). *Steps to the Future*. Jossey-Bass, San Francisco.

Sauer, C. and Yetton, P. (1997). The paths ahead. In Sauer, C., Yetton, P. and Associates (Eds). *Steps to the Future*. Jossey-Bass, San Francisco.

Savioz, P. and Blum, M. (2002). Strategic forecast tool for SMEs: how the opportunity landscape interacts with business strategy to anticipate technological trends. *Technovation*, **22**: 91–100.

SBS (2003). www.sbs.gov.uk/statistics/smedefs.php

Schumpeter, J. (1962). *Capitalism, Socialism and Democracy*. Harper and Row, New York.

Scott, M. and Bruce, R. (1987). 5 Stages of growth in SMEs. *Long Range Planning*, **20**(3): 45, 45–52.

Scott Morton, M. (1991). The Corporation of the 1990s. *Information Technology and Organisational Transformation*. Oxford University Press, Oxford.

Sellers, G. (1997). Tools for Managing your Business Process, CMA Magazine, September; pp. 25–27.

Sharma, S., Wichramasinghe, N. and Gupta, J. (2004). *What should SMEs do to succeed in today's knowledge-based economy*. In Al Qirim, N. (Ed.). Electronic Commerce in Small to Medium-Sized Enterprises: Frameworks, Issues and Implications, Idea Group Publishing, London, UK.

Sia, S.K. and Neo, B.S. (1996). The impacts of business process re-engineering on organisational controls. *International Journal of Project Management*, **14**(6): 341–348.

Sillence, J., Macdonald, S., Lefang, B. and Frost, B. (1998). E-mail adoption, diffusion, use and impact within small firms: a survey of UK companies. *International Journal of Information Management*, **18**(4): 231–242.

Silverman, D. (1998). Qualitative research: meanings or practices? *Information Systems Journal*, **8**(3): 3–20.

Sinclair, S.W. (1986). The three domains of information systems planning. *Journal of Information Systems Management*, Spring: 8–16.

Sisaye, D. and Bondnar, G.H. (1996). Re-engineering as a process innovation approach to internal auditing. *Internal Auditing*, **11**(3): 16–25.

Skrovan, S.J. (1995). Re-engineering for revenue: developing closer relationships. *Chain Store Age Executive with Shopping Centre Age*, **71**(8): 8A(2).

Smith, J. (1998). Strategies for start-ups. *Long Range Planning*, **31**(6): 857–872.

Spender, J. (1996). Making knowledge the basis of a dynamic theory of the firm. *Strategic Management Journal*, **17**: 45–62.

Standing, C., Sims, I., Stockdale, R., *et al.* (2003). Can e-marketplaces bridge the digital divide? Working Conference on Information Systems Perspectives and Challenges in the Context of Globalization, June 15–17, 2003, Organizational Information Systems in the Context of Globalization, pp. 339–353.

Stanworth, M. and Curran, J. (1973). *Management Motivation in the Smaller Business*. Gower Press, Epping, UK.

Stevenson, R. (1993). *Strategic Business Process Engineering: A systems thinking approach using ITHINK*. In Spurr, K., Layzell, P., Jennison, L. and Richards, N.

(Eds). Software Assistance for Business Re-engineering, John Wiley and Sons Ltd, Chichester, UK.

Stewart, T.A. (1993). Welcome to the revolution. *Fortune*, **128**: 15.

Stoddard, D., Jarvenpaa, S. and Littlejohn, M. (1996). The reality of business reengineering: Pacific Bell's centrex provisioning process. *California Management Review*, **38**(3): 57–78.

Storey, D. (1994). *Understanding the Small Business Sector*. Routledge, London, UK.

Storey, D. and Sykes, N. (1996). Uncertainty, innovation and management. In Burns, P. and Dewhurst, J. (Eds). *Small Business and Entrepreneurship*, 2nd edition. Macmillan, UK.

Storey, D.J. and Cressy, R. (1995). *Small Business Risk: A Firm and Bank Perspective*. Working Paper, SME Centre, Warwick Business School, University of Warwick, UK.

Sveiby, K. and Lloyd, D. (1987). *Managing Know How*. Bloomsbury Publishing, London.

Swan, J.A. and Galliers, R.D. (1996). Networking: the future of information systems. *Data Base*, **27**(4): 92–98.

Symons, V. and Walsham, G. (1988). The evaluation of information systems: a critique. *Journal of Applied Systems Analysis*, **15**: 119–132.

Synnott, W.R. (1987). *The Information Weapon – Winning Customers & Markets with Technology*. John Wiley & Sons Inc, New York.

Talwar, R. (1993). Business re-engineering – a strategy-driven approach. *Long Range Planning*, **26**(6): 22–40.

Tam, K.Y. (1992). Capital budgeting in information systems development. *Information and Management*, **23**: 345–357.

Teng, J.T.C., Grover, V. and Fiedler, K.D. (1994). Re-designing business processes using information technology. *Long Range Planning*, **27**(1): 95–106.

Teo, T. and Pian, Y. (2003). A contingency perspective on Internet adoption and competitive advantage. *European Journal of Information Systems*, **12**: 78–92.

Tersine, R., Harvey, M. and Buckley, M. (1997). Shifting organisational paradigms: transitional management. *European Management Journal*, **15**(1): 45–57.

Thong, J. (2001). Resource constraints and information systems implementation in Singaporean small businesses. *Omega*, pp. 143–156.

Thong, J., Yap, C.-S. and Raman, K. (1997). Environments for information systems implementation in small businesses. *Journal of Organizational Computing and Electronic Commerce*, **7**(4): 253–278.

Tichy, N.M. (1979). Social network analysis for organisations. *Academy of Management Review*, **4**: 4.

Tinnila, M. (1995). Strategic perspective to business process redesign. *Management Decision*, **33**(3): 25–34.

Tofler, A. (1987). Bracing the organisation for the Third Wave Society. *Nolan, Norton & Co. Symposium, Global transformations: Redesigning Business with Information Technology, Stage by Stage*, **7**(1): 15–17.

Tse, T. and Soufani, K. (2003). Business strategies for small firms in the new economy. *Journal of Small Business and Enterprise Development*, **10**(3): 306–319.

Tushman, M., Newman, W. and Romanelli, E. (1986). Convergence and upheaval: managing the unsteady pace of organisational evolution. *California Management Review*, **29**(1): 29–44.

Van Akkeren, J. and Cavaye, A. (2000). Factors affecting entry-level Internet technology adoption by small firms in Australia. *Journal of Systems and Information Technology*, **3**(2): 33–47.

Van Den Ven, A. (1986). Central problems in the management of innovation. *Management Science*, pp. 590–607.

Venkatraman, N. (1990). Performance implications of strategic coalignment – a methodological perspective. *Journal of Management Studies*, **27**(1): 19–41.

Venkatraman, N. (1991). IT induced business configuration. In Scott Mouton, M. (Ed.). *The Corporation of the 1990s: Information Technology and Organisational Transformation*. Oxford University Press, New York.

Venkatraman, N. (1994). IT-induced business transformation: from automation to business scope redefinition. *Sloan Management Review*, Winter: 73–87.

Volberda, H. (1996). Towards the flexible form: how to remain vital in hypercompetitive environments. *Organizational Science*, **7**(4): 359–374.

Wagner, B., Fillis, I. and Johansson, U. (2003). E-business and e-supply strategy in small and medium-sized businesses (SMEs). *Supply Chain Management*, **8**(3–4): 343–354.

Wainewright, P. (2002). Weekly Review: ASPs Have Been Where Web Services Are [Online]. http://www.aspnews.com/analysis/analyst_cols/article/0,2350, 4431_1582921,00.html; 05.03.2003

Walsham, G. (1993). *Interpreting Information Systems in Organisations*. John Wiley & Sons Ltd, Chichester, UK.

Ward, J.M. (1988). Information systems & technology application portfolio management – an assessment of matrix based analyses. *Journal of Information Technology*, 3(3): 169–177.

Ward, J., Griffiths, P. and Whitmore, P. (1990). Strategic Information Systems Planning, J. Wiley and Sons, Chichester, UK.

Ward, J. and Griffiths, P. (1996). *Strategic Information Systems Planning*, 2nd edition. John Wiley & Sons, Chichester, UK.

Ward, J. and Peppard, J. (2002). *Strategic Planning for Information Systems*, 3rd edition. John Wiley and Sons, Chichester, UK.

Warren, L. and Hutchinson, W. (2000). Success factors for high-technology SMEs: a case study from Australia. *Journal of Small Business Management*, 38(3): 86–91.

Wastell, D., White, P. and Kawalek, P. (1994). A methodology for business process redesign: experiences and issues. *Journal of Strategic Information Systems*, 3(1): 23–40.

Waterman, R.H., Peters, T.J. and Phillips, J.R. (1991). Structure is not organisation. In Mintzberg, H. and Quinn, J. (Eds). *The Strategy Process*, 2nd edition. Prentice Hall, New Jersey, USA; pp. 309–314.

Webster, J. (1995). Networks of collaboration or conflict? Electronic data interchange and power in the supply chain. *Journal of Strategic Information Systems*, 4(1): 31–42.

Willcocks, L. (1992). Evaluating information technology investments; research findings and reappraisal. *Journal of Information Systems*, 2: 243–268.

Willcocks (2003). Evaluating the outcomes of information systems plans: managing information technology evaluation – techniques and processes. In Galliers, R.D. and Leidner, D.E. (Eds). *Strategic Information Management – Challenges and Strategies in Managing Information Systems*, 3rd edition. Butterworth Heinemann, Oxford, UK.

Willcocks, L. and Sauer, C. (2000). Moving to e-business: an introduction. In Willcocks, L., Sauer, C. and Associates (Eds). *Moving to E-Business*. Random House, London, UK.

Wind, J. and West, A. (1991). Reinventing the Corporation. *Chief Executive*, pp. 72–75.

Witherill, J.W. and Kolak, J. (1996). Is corporate re-engineering hurting your employees? *Professional Safety*, **41**(5): 28–32.

Woods, L. (1996). Steering safely through a crisis. *Nation's Business*, **84**(9): 33–35.

Wu, H. and Chou, T. (1992). Obstacles and reactions of Taiwan's small & medium enterprises. Chung-Hua Institution for Economic Research, www.mdc.com.my

Yap, C., Soh, C. and Raman, K. (1992). Information system success factors in small business. *Omega*, **20**(5–6): 597–609.

Yetton, P. (1997). False prophecies, successful practice, and future directions in IT management. In Sauer, C., Yetton, P. and Associates (Eds). *Steps to the Future*. Jossey-Bass, San Francisco.

Yetton, P. and Sauer, C. (1997). The paths ahead. In Sauer, C., Yetton, P. and Associates (Eds). *Steps to the Future*. Jossey-Bass, San Francisco.

Yetton, P., Johnston, K. and Craig, J. (1994). Computer-aided architects: a case study of IT and strategic change. *Sloan Management Review*, Summer: 57–66.

Yin, R. (1994). Case Study Research. *Design and Methods*, 2nd edition. Sage, California.

Zairi, M. and Sinclair, D. (1995). Business process re-engineering and process management. *Management Decision*, **33**(3): 3–16.

Zhu, K., Kramer, K. and Xu, S. (2003). Electronic business adoption by European firms: a cross-country assessment of the facilitators and inhibitors. *European Journal of Information Systems*, **12**: 251–268.

Index

3D model of IS success 120–21, 134

Accounting systems 30, 47, 164
Activity based costing system 95
Advanced manufacturing technologies
    (AMT) framework 99
Alignment *see* Strategic alignment
Alliances 239
AMT *see* Advanced manufacturing
    technologies
Ansoff's strategic intent matrix 180,
    191, 340

Balanced business scorecard 115, 126,
    134, 141–2, 151–2
Benefits from IS investment 172
Business processes
    increasing complexity of 30
Business process re-engineering 52, 210,
    293–314
    framework for SMEs 296–8
    nature of 294–6
    towards a learning organization
        309–11
Business process review 214
Business strategy frameworks 97, 100
Business systems 2, 33
Business themes 273, 279–80, 283–4,
    290
Business transformation through IS
    201–15, 377
    internal integration 202, 205, 211
    localized exploitation 201–2, 205, 209
Business network redesign 203, 207,
    210–11, 306, 309, 377
Business process improvement 209
Business process redesign 53, 202, 207,
    213, 294–5
Business scope redefinition 201, 203,
    208, 210, 212, 227
    integration with IS 244

Market and product development
    174
    survival 196
Business value 212

CAD *see* computer aided design
CEO *see* Chief Executive Officer
Characteristics of small firms 19
Chief Executive Officer (CEO) 21, 369
Churchill and Lewis five-stage model of
    growth *see* SMEs stages of growth
    models
Clusters – industry 127, 180, 197
Collaborative advantage 65, 91
Collaborative working 238
Competence building 269, 283, 286, 288
Competence leveraging 269, 273, 280,
    283, 287–8
Competition 1, 269
Competitive advantage 6, 27, 52–3, 91,
    237, 265
    importance of 121
    insights 112
    IT-based 48
    structuralist debate 160
Competitive environment 21
Competitive pressures 30, 46, 201
Competitiveness 1, 38, 43–4, 126–7,
    219, 269
    alignment of technology with business
        strategy 39
Competitors 30, 240
Complementors 240, 357
Computer Aided Design (CAD) 64, 94,
    152, 207, 227
Co-opetition 237, 239–41, 244–5, 293, 378
    synergy and leverage 241–5, 246,
        252–3, 256, 258, 260, 261
    towards a theory of knowledge
        exchange 240–2
Core capabilities 266–71

Core competences 134, 203, 208, 212,
    265–7, 269–70
  analysis 280
  definition 276
  in knowledge-based firms 288
  modeling 275
  Prahalad and Hamel hierarchical
    model 270, 275, 287
Cost reduction strategy 95
Critical success factors 37, 84, 114, 134
CRM – see Customer relationship
    management
Customer databases 162, 185
Customer pressure 21, 47, 212
Customer relationship management
    (CRM) 39
Customer resource lifecycle 99
Customer satisfaction 37, 126
Customers 1–2, 21, 161, 246
  cost reduction demands 228
  driving force for IS 244
  influence on information systems 63–5
  influences of major 78
  informal relationships 99
  relationship building 67, 212

Data 1, 36
Dynamic business context 6, 218

E-business 39, 208, 212, 317–38, 369, 379
  adoption ladder 317
  and SMEs 319–21
  defining 317–19
  drivers and inhibitors 342–3, 327,
    348–53
  importance 347
  importance of strategic commitment
    338
  influencing factors 320–1, 338,
    341–2, 358
  competitive environment 356–7
  government initiatives 358, 369
  influencers 355–6
  segmentation strategy 327–8, 368–9
    brochureware 327–31
    business network 336–7
    business opportunity 331–3
    business support 333–6
E-commerce 48, 318

EDI see electronic data interchange
Electronic Data Interchange (EDI) 64,
    94, 103–4, 149, 161, 177,
    207, 227
E-mail 39, 48, 206, 317, 325–6
Enterprise resource planning systems
    (ERP) 39, 46
Entrepreneur 24–5
Entrepreneurial firms 19
ERP – see Enterprise resource planning
    systems
Evaluation of IS and IT 69–85
  approaches 70–4, 80
  organizational approach 81–2
  practice 71–3
  SME issues 73–9
  technostructure 81
Existing IS
  importance and effectiveness of 102
Extranets 39, 67, 163

Firm
  background to SMEs 27
  failure 23, 373
  fast growth 26
Five Forces Model 91, 100–2, 116, 139,
    153, 266
Flexibility and innovation in SMEs 22,
    54, 374
Flexibility manoeuvres 52–3, 67, 374
Flexibility through IS 27, 51–68, 120,
    175, 293
  issues 51–4
  planning for 55–6
  SMEs 54–5, 65–6
Flexible manufacturing 54
Focus-dominance model 159, 161–5,
    184–95, 198, 201, 211–3, 222,
    239–44
  collaboration 163, 168–9, 172–3, 239,
    226–8
  co-ordination 163, 168, 170, 172, 225–6
  customer dominance 163, 243
  efficiency 162–3, 167, 171, 224
  repositioning 163, 169, 173, 228–9
  strategic focus 163, 226
    cost focused 49, 230
    value added 49, 231
  strategic intent 339–41

strategic responses to IS investment
        161–3, 170–5, 185–8, 194–5, 226,
        231–2, 252–3, 256, 259, 375–6

Game theory 241
Game-theoretic model 237, 245, 252–3
Generic strategies 95, 140–1
Globalization 1, 293
Growing the business 26, 28–31
Growth 186–7, 189, 198
    access to finance makes easier 26
    formal management structures 20,
        26, 31
Growth firms 24

Heath Springs Case Study 137–55
Hierarchical structures 31
Hollow factory concept 65
Hypercompetition 51

ICT, *see* information and communications
        technology
Independence 21
Individuals – roles and skills 210
Informal network relations 190, 195, 197
Information 1–2, 36
    architecture 43
    basis of information systems strategy
        111
    and communication technology plans
        206
    exchange 67, 244, 262
Information intensity matrix 91, 96,
        134, 153, 268
    management issues 151
    needs of managers 147–8, 280
    primary management resource 1
    strategic resource 3, 35, 106, 204, 208,
        212, 214
    strategic role 2, 210
    use of to manage day-to-day
        operations 244
    value and use of 35
    society 35
Information and communications
        technology (ICT) plans 206, 322,
        325, 327, 332, 346, 363, 366, 370
Information systems (IS) 2–3, 33–7,
        161, 237

adoption 46–7, 190, 229
    business growth 179–81
    structural issues 189–95
    alignment 6
    benefits 174, 214
    competitive advantage from 39, 265–6
    as a competitive weapon 127
    core systems 39
    cost-focused strategies 230
    efficiency and effectiveness 2, 150,
        186, 196
    exploit the potential 210
    to improve communication 30
    innovation 217
    investment 2, 49, 57, 186, 207
    manage internal communications 225
    management information 61
    non-strategic 169
    simple 30
    strategic use 230–1
    suppliers 198
    supporting management decisions 2,
        47, 374
Information systems planning (ISP)
        76, 179
Information systems in SMEs 374
    bespoke software commissioned 46
    contact with vendors and consultants
        45
    decision support systems 47
    external consultants, use of 22
    external IS resources – lack of trust 173
    external software provider 107
    formal systems 30, 38
    department – lack of 45
    development 63
    investment
        in operational management
            systems 2, 3
        increases survival rates 161
        lack of 57
        response to crisis 24
    limited in-house IT skills 62, 74,78
    limited investment in IT 55
    no link to business strategy 225
    operational focus to IS 125
    standalone systems 61
    weakness in planning and control of
        IS 77

Information systems strategy (ISS) 6,
        35, 43, 89, 111, 169, 177,
        266–7, 375
    approaches 110–11
    multi-paradigm approach 111–13
    nature of 89–90
    organizational approach 6, 89,
        109–15, 117, 121, 134
    recommendations 120–1
    in SMEs 43–44, 109–10, 114–22
    theory 87
Information technology (IT) 37, 237
    adoption 56, 219
    key to flexibility in SMEs 56
Innovation 2, 19, 26–7, 56
Integrated systems 61
Internet 2, 37, 196, 207, 231, 346, 379
    benefits 48, 318
    growth and competitiveness in SMEs
        322–37
Internet adoption 4, 211–2, 320, 368
    relationships
        customer support network 365–6
        expert network 363–4
        ICT support network 366–7
        industry support network 363–5
        novice network 367–8
Inter-organizational systems 187
    planning 107
Intranets 206
IS – see information systems
IS competencies
    weaknesses in 217
IS/IT opportunities – production,
        management support and
        customer relations 94, 161
IS/IT suppliers 190, 195
ISP – see information systems planning
ISS – see information systems strategy

Just-in-time manufacturing 64

Knowledge 1–2, 24, 33, 36, 237–8,
        242, 247
    exchange 247, 252, 258
    management 197, 239, 378
        in SMEs
        the role of information systems
            242–6

systems 36–9, 189
    networks 238
    sharing 237–9, 252–3, 261, 266
        ambiguous attitude 256, 261
        explicit 246, 248–61
    transfer 246–7
Knowledge-based firms 27, 267–8, 286
    resources 265–6
    small businesses 267–8

LAN, see Local Area Network
Learning environment 67
Learning process 27
Lifestyle advantages 23
Lifestyle firms 24
Limited companies 27
Local Area Network (LAN) 163, 170,
        175, 206

Macro-economic uncertainties 26
Management information 93
Management IS 24, 26, 186
    efficiency, emphasis on 38, 77
    expanding customer base 30
    importance of 37–43
    limited 172
    negative impact on performance 47
    in SMEs 160
        benefits 48
        introduction 47–8
    team 27, 30
    training 33
Managerial skills 28, 33, 214
Managing knowledge
    role of IS 242
Managing uncertainty and risk 26
Market 21, 24
    niche 27, 30, 346
    opportunity 25
    position 30, 121
    uncertainty 21
Materials requirements planning (MRP)
        39, 61, 94, 99, 103, 147–9, 152,
        162, 164
Maturity 30
McFarlan-McKenney strategic grid see
        Strategic Grid
Measure business success – little
        support 126

Misalignment 229
MIT'90s model 217–9, 229, 231–3
Monitoring systems 24
MRP – *see* Materials requirements
        planning

Nature, role and value of information
        systems 36
Network growth 212
Network relations 208
Nolan's stages of growth model
        105–6, 150

Open book management 64
Operational improvement 185
Operational management 94
Organization of IS in SMEs 62
Organizational culture 119, 131–3
Organizational dynamics 6
Organizational flexibility 91
Organizational inhibitors and
        enablers 119
Organizational knowledge 26
Organizational structure 29, 31
    change 201
Organizing and Managing SMEs 31
Ormerod's implementation analysis
        model 135, 152–3
Outsourcing 2, 46, 204
Owner 4, 21, 31–3, 127–31, 173, 196, 226
    ability to manage uncertainty and
        risk 26
    delegate activities to professional
        managers 32
    enthusiasm 179
    IS experience 198
    knowledge 2
    limited IS knowledge 110, 160
    owner–manager 25, 296
    personality 22
    role in introducing IS 44
    strategic objectives 159
Ownership 26

Partnership 25
Perceived benefits 46
Perfect competition 21
Performance measurement 258
    system 149

Performance measures 115
Personal influences 22
PESTEL analysis 115–6, 134
Plan to manage business growth 44
Positioning frameworks 102, 107
Preferred supplier 107
Product innovation 27
Production forecasting 64
Production technologies 22
Professional managers 32
Project-based approach 31
Pureplays 2, 356

Quality 27
    conditions 62
    of product 26
    products and processes 93
        evidence of 64
    standard – BS5750, 65

Relationship management 258
Relationships with customers 35
Research approaches
    action research 277
    actor network theory 359–61
    case studies 4–7, 22
    critical pluralism 113
    exploratory 4, 67
    multi-dimension research
        situations 113
    study of social phenomena 6
Research paradigms 112
Resource poverty 22
Resource-based analysis 134, 270
Resource-based view of strategy 27,
        268, 378
Resource-based view of the firm
        265–7
Resources
    Limited financial 133–4
Risk 23
Risk of failure 161
Role of management IS 35

Sales and Marketing information 147
Scarcity of capital resources 26
Schumpeter – creative destruction 213
Seven-S model 73, 133, 150, 153,
        164, 191

Short-term decision-making 26
Short-term management 29
SISP *see* Strategic Information Systems
        Planning
SMEs
    approaches to business growth 3,
        23, 27
    benefit
        cost saving 238
    benefits from IS investment 172
    birth, death and growth 22–8
    business intelligence 24
    business strategy 74, 83, 111, 114,
        185, 196
    capital resources 80
    day-to-day survival 26
    definition 19–20
    drivers of growth 19
    dynamic sector 22
    employee size 20
    failure factors
        customer and market
            requirements 23
    focus on operational planning 27
    growing the business 28–31
    growth 179
    heterogeneous 19
    high firm failure rates 69
    improving efficiency 73
    independence 19
    influences 20–2
    investment
        issues in SMEs 83–5
    knowledge generation 238
    lack of strategic planning 55
    limited capital 2
    limited flexibility in 66
    limited management information 97
    limited management skills 23
    limited resources 22, 239
    limited resources
        capital 76, 83
        financial 45, 76, 173, 184
    limited strategic planning 27
    limited view of planning 110
    location of firm 28
    long-term business strategy 24
    loss of strategic direction 26
    management

    development process 373
        information systems an integral part
            373
        devolution 26
        experience 25
    non-bureaucratic organizations 238
    operate in niche markets 126
    operational efficiency 238
    operational focus 2
    organizational flexibility 297
    organizational structure
        organic 57, 111, 239
        spiders web 31
    organizing and managing 31–3
    resource constraint 160, 175
    size 19
        and knowledge of management
            team 32
    small management team 31
    staff 33
    strategic benefits 160
    strategic context 172–3, 177
    strategies
        incremental change 296
    structure 19
    survival 68, 73, 297–8
    technical infrastructure 63
    transformation paths 209–12, 233
    under-capitalization 23, 26
    understanding business drivers 3
    unstructured organizations 31
    value of knowledge 246
    vibrant and growing sector 19
    Stages of Growth Models 2, 29–31,
        44, 177–8, 180
Soft systems analysis 247
    housing consultancy 277–9
Soft systems methodology 113, 117–9,
        134, 144–7, 153, 270, 272, 277,
        287, 289
Sole traders 27–8
Sourcing IT 35, 45–6
Spreadsheets 30, 36, 184
Stages of development 29
    of management information 38
Stages of Growth in SMEs
    response to crisis 29
Strategic alignment 6, 35, 41, 43, 120,
        180, 217–34

business strategy 41, 217
dynamics 170, 177
Flower and Samios Case 219
issues 217–8
opportunities 218–22
paths in SMEs 222–9
stagnation 217
Strategic coherence 232
Strategic context of IS investment 159
Strategic drivers 179
Strategic fit 217
Strategic focus
cost 231, 243–4
Strategic grid 102–4, 119, 134, 149, 153
Strategic information systems
frameworks 91–106, 112
Earl's Framework of Frameworks
91–3, 106–8, 112
awareness frameworks 94–7, 107
opportunity frameworks 97–102,
107
positioning frameworks 102–6, 107
Strategic Information Systems Planning
(SISP) 266, 282, 288
housing consultancy case study
272–86
Strategic initiatives 21
Strategic Intent 191–5, 197, 339, 345
Strategic IS dynamics 177
Strategic management 3
information 94
tools 24
Strategic objectives 24
Strategic opportunities from IS 115
Strategic planning 6, 29–30
Strategic response – development of new
competences 231
Strategic role of information 37
Strategic synergy 232

Strategic vision 91
Strategies 3
Strategy 26–7, 95, 211
development 196
Structural issues 189
Structured methods 63
Study of social phenomena 6
Sub-contracting 190, 195
Success 30
Suppliers 1
Supply chain networks 67
Support systems 39
Survival 23, 27, 29
SWOT analysis 115, 117, 134
Systems flexibility – limited 187, 212
Systems implications in managing SMEs
33
Systems support 46

Taxonomy of systems 39
Technology fitting frameworks 97–9
Trundlers 23

Value chain 67, 98–9, 101, 108–9,
143–4, 153, 266
analysis 117, 267, 287
firm 91, 144
Industry 91, 203, 237
limitations 287–8
Value for money 2
Value realization 217
Value-adding processes 117
Venkatraman, N. 201, 208, 210, 212

Walsham's social context/social
process/content model 112
Web sites 48, 206, 320, 325–6
Word processing systems 39, 47, 164, 184
World Wide Web 37, 317